**PSYCHOLOGY:
A NEW
PERSPECTIVE**

PSYCHOLOGY:

A New Perspective

Dalmas A. Taylor
The University of Maryland

Sidney A. Manning
Federal City College

Winthrop Publishers, Inc.
Cambridge, Massachusetts

Library of Congress Cataloging in Publication Data

Taylor, Dalmas Arnold.
   Psychology, a new perspective.

   Includes bibliographies and index.
   1. Psychology. I. Manning, Sidney Alpern, joint author. II. Title. [DNLM: 1. Psychology. BF121 T239p]
BF121.T345   150   74-23579
ISBN 0-87626-698-7 pbk.

Cover photo by Shirley Ward

Copyright © *1975 by Winthrop Publishers, Inc.*
  17 Dunster Street, Cambridge, Massachusetts 02138

All rights reserved. No part of this book may be reproduced in any form or by any means without permission in writing from the publisher. Printed in the United States of America.
10 9 8 7 6 5 4 3 2 1

To our former students
who have inspired this approach
to presenting psychology
through their many challenging
questions and insights

Contents

Preface   xii

Division A
Getting Started   1

Unit 1
Why Psychology?   3
    Psychology and the psychologist

Unit 2
The Confusion of Tongues   9
    Concepts and methods psychologists use

Unit 3
Questions   16
    Issues in psychology

Summary   20
Glossary   21
References   23
Suggested Readings   23

Division B
What's Out There?   25

Unit 4
The Human Camera   27
    Visual perception

Unit 5
Tuning In   41
    Auditory perception

Unit 6
Change That Is Not Change   47
  Discrepancies between physical stimulus and percept

Unit 7
Senses — There Are More Than Five   58
  Taste, smell, skin and body senses

Summary   67

Glossary   70

References   72

Suggested Readings   73

Division C
Gaining Information and Knowledge   75

Unit 8
Why Do We Try?   77
  Motivation

Unit 9
What Do We Get?   82
  Reinforcement

Unit 10
A Learning Principle: Classical Conditioning   86

Unit 11
Another Learning Principle: Operant Conditioning   91

Unit 12
Human Learning: Input/Output   97
  Expectancy and set

Unit 13
In Search of Language   102
  Language and verbal learning

Summary   111

Glossary   114

References   116

Suggested Readings   116

Division D
Who's Capable?   119

Unit 14
Capability: Given or Acquired?   121
Intelligence

Unit 15
The Numbers Game   125
Intelligence testing

Unit 16
The Extremes: The Deficient and the Superior   133
Retarded and gifted individuals

Unit 17
Nothing is Ever Black or White   139
Racial differences in IQ scores

Summary   143

Glossary   144

References   145

Suggested Readings   147

Division E
Don't Bother Me, I Can't Cope   149

Unit 18
Who's Who: The Labeling of Normal and Abnormal   151

Unit 19
Neurotics: Builders of Dream Houses   159

Unit 20
Psychotics: Occupants of Dream Houses   165

Unit 21
The Mind-Body Trap   174
Psychophysiological and brain disorders

Unit 22
Personality Disorders: Violations of the Code   *179*

Summary   *186*

Glossary   *189*

References   *191*

Suggested Readings   *193*

Division F
How Do We Cope?   *195*

Unit 23
The Number is the Meaning   *197*
  Personality assessment

Unit 24
Meaning Explained   *203*
  Personality theory

Unit 25
Change: Communication with the Psyche and the Soma   *211*
  Therapeutic techniques

Summary   *219*

Glossary   *221*

References   *223*

Suggested Readings   *224*

Division G
To Be Or Not To Be . . . Affected By Others   *227*

Unit 26
Obey!   *229*
  Authoritarianism and obedience

Unit 27
Follow the Leader: Conformity and Social Influence   *236*

Unit 28
Forces that Compel: Social Power   *241*

Unit 29
Folkways and Stateways: Prejudice and Racism   *244*

Unit 30
Contagious Behaviors   253
Summary   260
Glossary   262
References   265
Suggested Readings   267

Division H

Environment: Outside and Inside   269

Unit 31
The "Behavioral Sink"   271
   Population theories

Unit 32
It's All in Your Head   277
   The brain; the peripheral nervous system; the endocrine system

Unit 33
Brain Control and Genetic Engineering   284

Unit 34
The Brave New World: Medicine for our Leaders   289
   Technology and biochemical control

Unit 35
We Are What We Eat   296
   Diet and nutrition

Summary   302
Glossary   304
References   306
Suggested Readings   308

Division I

Feelings   311

Unit 36
Why Do I Feel This Way?   313
   Emotion

x   Contents

Unit 37
Excitement   *319*
   Stress and arousal

Unit 38
Fear and Anxiety   *324*

Unit 39
Love   *329*

Summary   *334*

Glossary   *337*

References   *338*

Suggested Readings   *339*

Division J
Expansion or Escape?   *341*

Unit 40
Falling Apart To Come Together   *343*
   Isolation and alienation

Unit 41
Right and Wrong   *351*
   Moral development

Unit 42
Encounter! The Elusive Search   *361*
   Intensive Group Experiences

Unit 43
The Trip to Nowhere?   *368*
   Marijuana and LSD

Summary   *374*

Glossary   *377*

References   *379*

Suggested Readings   *381*

Acknowledgments   *383*

Name Index   *387*

Subject Index   *393*

Preface

This is a text for introductory undergraduate psychology courses, and we hope it is like no other introductory psychology text on the market. The impetus for this text comes in part from the complaints of hundreds of students taking their first psychology course. These students were "turned off" by psychology for two basic reasons: (a) a discrepancy between their expectations and the actual material covered, and (b) the zealousness with which we convinced them (and ourselves) that psychology is an experimental science. The latter often necessitated the hard-nosed behavioristic approach.

It has been our observation in recent years that some of our colleagues have been having success by approaching the introductory course from the perspective of issues and topics and imposing theoretical and empirical discipline upon discussion. This approach has the advantage of permitting students to be optimally involved by discussing something that concerns or interests them while still receiving full exposure to classic, substantive material in psychology. The task of the instructor, then, is to develop and explain these events within the context of formal psychology. Anyone who has had to respond to students' concerns about "civil disobedience," "black power," and the "credibility gap" will readily appreciate the distinction being made here.

Psychologists have been aware of this distinction for some time. Anderson (1970) in an *American Psychologist* article notes:

It is true that the planning of a course in general psychology in the 1940s did not have to take account of the discrepancy between the wishes and expectations of the professor, which tended often to be traditional, and the interests of students, which envisioned more orientation toward personal social application.

The point is further made in citing a 10-year follow-up study by Kriedt (1949), in which a trend was found among students to be "more tolerant of, and more willing to help people, and less interested in mechanical and methodical work and in solitary activity." Anderson concludes, citing from his own data, that since World War II "emphasis seems to have shifted rather strongly, to more concern with personality, adjustment, motivation, emotion, social, and the more humanistic or person-centered areas."

Introductory texts are beginning to reflect this shifting emphasis. It is our intention not that this text be humanistic but that it relate, through psychology, to the contemporary concerns and issues with which students today are involved.

We take the position that psychology, and education, have failed to relate to the student. Perhaps we are just beginning to be confident enough about our methods, our theories, and our findings to relate them to students' interests.

This text is an effort at formalizing the technique discussed above. We have presented the materials in divisions; each division is further divided into units. The units are intended to make the students more aware of conceptualization and application within the broader division. This arrangement will also permit the instructor to make assignments in a more flexible manner than provided by the organization of traditional textbooks.

Within this context we apply the traditional focus on theory and empirical findings where appropriate. Accordingly, concepts such as conditioning, motivation, and reinforcement are fully covered. Hence, the perspective we are attempting to bring to the introductory student is an emphasis on problems of immediate interest from real life rather than an indoctrination into rules and language from artificial, simulated, and experimental situations. Each unit begins with an example or the presentation of a well-defined issue. Having developed this issue, we then introduce appropriate discussions from themes and research in psychology. The advantage of this approach, we feel, is that we can put a stop to students' developing a negative attitude toward all of psychology because of the traditional and often dogmatic approach to the "science of behavior." Instead, students should be able to gain a better perspective on problems and concerns of vital personal importance and simultaneously appreciate the empirical and theoretical efforts underlying the development of these issues in psychology.

Some students develop negative attitudes toward psychology as a result of their concern with the ethical conduct of psychologists in the pursuit of research activities, especially with research involving human subjects. Although psychologists, in response to the increasing criticism and attack regarding ethical issues, have recently set about the task of revising their ethical code, controversy still exists around these policies. It is important for the beginning student of psychology to realize that ethical guidelines, no matter how stringent, will always to some extent be dependent upon the integrity of the researcher. As will be seen in this text, with diligent care and well-thought-out research designs, most problems can be studied without violating the rights and integrity of human subjects, and a good deal of research has been conducted without any violation of the rights of individuals.

Of necessity, we have included some materials and language that may seem too technical or detailed for the introductory undergraduate student. Often in condensing and reporting scientific material, it is necessary to include statistical language or symbols to indicate how the validity of the assertion was achieved. A glossary of statistical and conceptual definitions has been included at the end of each division to minimize this problem. For students who want to extend their exposure to given topical areas, we have included some suggested readings at the end of each division.

It is difficult in an undertaking of this nature to acknowledge all those who have contributed to its successful completion. So it is appropriate that we apologize at the beginning for those whom we may overlook. Initially, we would like to express our extreme appreciation to Stan Evans, former editor at Winthrop Publishers, for having the confidence in this project to offer us a contract, and to Paul O'Connell for sustaining that commitment after Stan's departure. Barbara Sonnenschein, David Robinson, Bill Sernett, and the Winthrop production staff merit our sincere thanks.

Many typists have labored over manuscript preparation — JoAnn Hunter, Irma Nicholson, Pat Talley, and Eunice Burton. Without their invaluable assistance, we could not have completed this book. Finally, we hope the photography on the cover and beginning each division enhances the themes we have tried to present. We are grateful to the students and faculty at Annandale High School in Annandale, Virginia, who made these photographs possible.

Our spouses and families deserve special recognition for their patience and support throughout the many struggles involved in bringing this book to fruition. Thanks to Faye, Monique, Carla, and Courtney Taylor; and Jan, Pamela, and Sean Manning.

D. A. T.
S. A. M.

PSYCHOLOGY:
A NEW
PERSPECTIVE

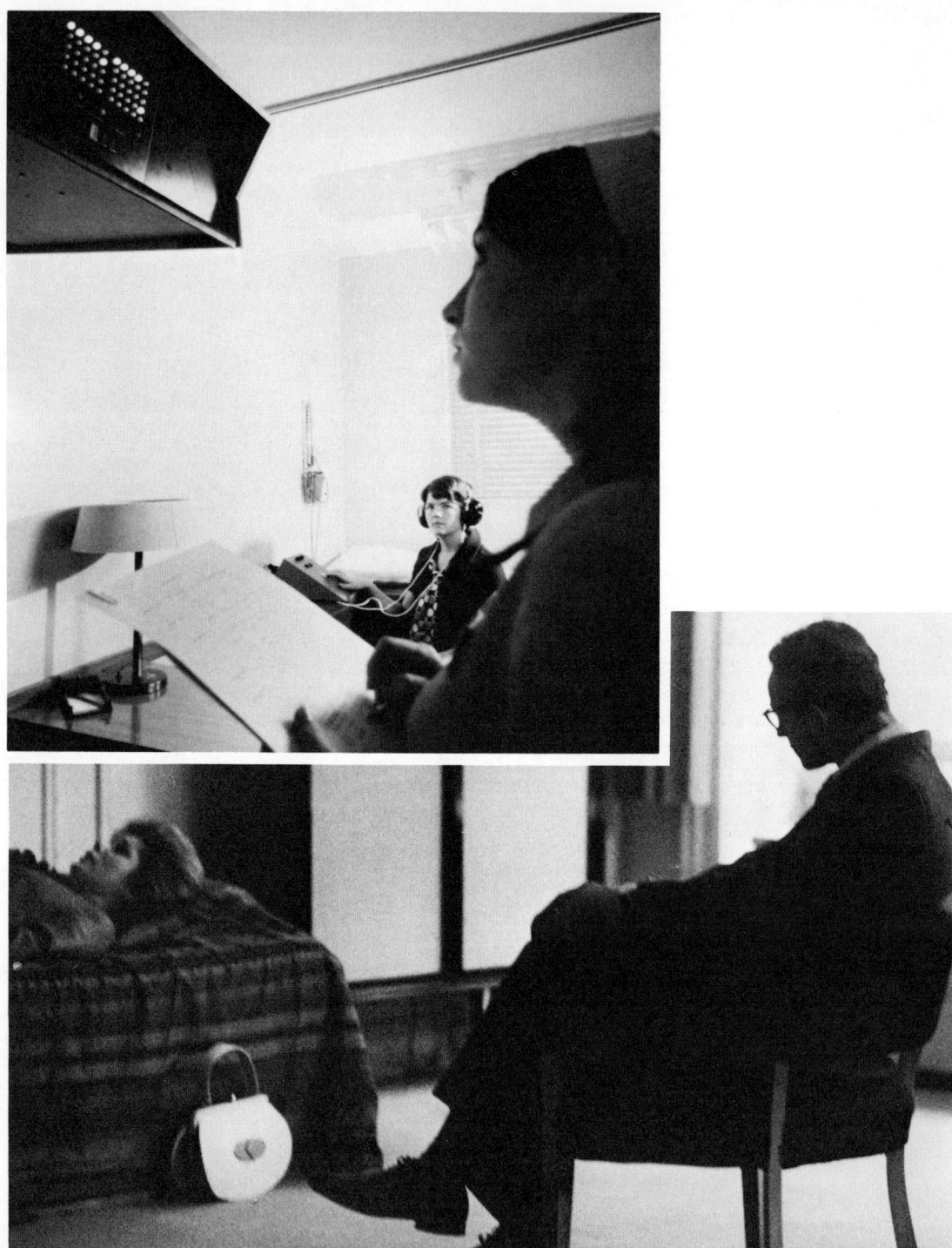

Top: Photo by Phil Harrington *(Look)*. Courtesy of IBM Corp.
Bottom: Lee Lockwood from Black Star

A

Getting Started

Unit 1
Why Psychology?

Have you ever asked yourself: "Why should I take a course in psychology?" Or, "What can I expect to get from a course in psychology?" It has been our experience that students enter introductory psychology courses knowing little of what to expect. Most have heard of Sigmund Freud or something about personality. When questioned about the definition of psychology, most say that psychology is the study of the mind. Further, there is the belief that understanding one's mind and the minds of others will lead to more effective relations and a happier life. Some students are merely seeking the gratification associated with intellectual achievement, while others are simply fulfilling a requirement for graduation. Psychology is a young but growing discipline and therefore perhaps is a long way from fully satisfying all of the varying reasons for which students elect an introductory psychology course. However, its promise lies in its commitment to submit questions about people and behavior to empirical test. No single idea or theorist dominates the field; all thinking and ideas can be evaluated in a standardized framework. This approach will become obvious to the reader when we consider the divisions in this text.

Definition of Psychology

Technically, psychology means the study of the mind (psyche), but American psychologists have never been comfortable with this definition. Psychologists have preferred instead definitions that embrace overt behavioral events — verbalizations, muscular responses, and the like. Hence, most psychologists have defined psychology as *the scientific study of behavior*. Included in this definition are internal mental processes such as thinking and feeling which are inferred from external, overt behavioral events. It is from this perspective that most introductory texts and introductory psychology courses present information to the new student. Our focus here will also be on behavior. Additionally, we have tried to make the treatment of each topic meaningful to your current concerns, as well as interesting and provocative.

Psychologists by no means have a monopoly on the study of behavior. Behavior is a complex phenomenon and is studied by anthropologists, sociologists, historians, and psychiatrists. To a limited extent, biologists, physicists, and chemists occasionally study behavior. Each of these professionals works in a discipline that is independent of the others, but there is a great deal of overlap among them. Sociologists and anthropologists, for example, specialize in the study of groups, but then so do some psychologists. Biologists, on the other hand, have learned much about physiological factors that influence behavior. A good deal of this knowledge has been quite useful to psychologists, particularly the physiological psychologists. The relationship of psychology to, on one hand, sociology and other behavioral and social sciences and, on the other hand, biology and other natural sciences makes it a kind of meeting ground for those interested in the study of behavior.

Some of you will look to this text for solutions to problems or for information useful in improving your personalities. Others will seek information on or answers to major problems faced by humanity: war, crime, poverty, racism, etc. It would be intellectually arrogant and dishonest to promise you pat formulas to solve these problems. However, in their focus on behavior, psychologists have generated information and constructed theories that can facilitate your understanding of many of the problems we are confronted with today. It is our hope that the level of understanding achieved from psychology will eventually point to clear possibilities for solutions to many of our pressing problems. For the sake of not promising too much, however, we caution you that an introductory text and course must necessarily be somewhat of a survey of the discipline. Therefore, some depth of treatment is compromised by the necessity for breadth.

Unlike application in the physical sciences, in order for behavioral changes to occur the individuals instrumental in advocating change must undergo change themselves. This has been a very difficult thing for humans to do. Our accomplishments in the missile race, for example, have been remarkable. In twelve short years, we entered the race from behind, passed the Russians, and by 1969 had twice landed men on the moon for the first time in the history of the world. Yet for hundreds of years we have tried to solve our racial problems, and solutions are still wanting. It seems that the major difficulty in this latter area, as with most social problems, is that individuals who advocate improvement and change are rarely willing to submit themselves to any of the uncomfortableness or sacrifice often necessary to accomplish change. It is our hope that today's generation will come to understand and surmount this difficulty.

PSYCHOLOGISTS AND PSYCHIATRISTS

In approaching the definition of psychology, we automatically get involved with just what it is that a psychologist does. Before discussing that, however, it might be useful to clear up one source of confusion for many lay people and students: what is the difference between a psychologist and a psychiatrist? As can be seen in Box 1-1, the basic difference between a psychologist and a psychiatrist is the kind of training that each receives.

> **BOX 1-1   EDUCATIONAL DIFFERENCES AND SIMILARITIES BETWEEN THE PSYCHOLOGIST AND THE PSYCHIATRIST**
>
> | Psychologist | Psychiatrist |
> |---|---|
> | *Undergraduate* (Liberal Arts) | *Undergraduate* (Liberal Arts) |
> | Major: Psychology and/or other behavioral or social science | Major: Chemistry, biology, or other natural science |
> | Years: 4 | Years: 4 |
> | Degree: B.A./B.S. | Degree: B.A./B.S. |
> | *Graduate* (Academic) | *Graduate* (Professional) |
> | Major: Psychology | Major: Medicine |
> | Years: 4 | Years: 4 |
> | Degree: Ph.D. | Degree: M.D. |
> | (Optional M.A./M.S. after 2 years) | |
> | *Postgraduate* | *Postgraduate* |
> | Internship (clinicians only) — 1 year | Internship (rotating medical services) — 1 year |
> | | Residency (psychiatry) — 3 years |

Psychologists receive their basic undergraduate training in the behavioral sciences, most often majoring in psychology. After four more years of graduate work, each receives a Ph.D. which requires, in part, the completion of a dissertation based upon an original research project. During these four years of graduate training, each student elects a specialization which usually coincides with his or her career choice. Some of the specialty areas from which students may choose are: experimental and physiological, clinical and counseling, industrial, social and personality, and developmental (more will be said about these later). Only when a student elects a clinical specialization is an internship, usually in a mental hospital, required. During the last years of graduate training and internship, clinical students are taught psychological diagnosis, psychotherapy including psychoanalytic techniques, and other interview procedures. Clinical research is also a part of their training for a Ph.D.

The psychiatrist, on the other hand, pursues a natural science major as an undergraduate and receives medical training leading to an M.D. after four years of professional school. During medical school the primary focus is on medical diagnosis and treatment with some psychology included. Following a one-year internship, the physician may then elect to pursue a residency in psychiatry. During this time he or she is trained in the various forms of psychotherapy and learns to apply skills and the knowledge of drugs, electroshock, and other medical procedures to the treatment of the mentally ill. A psychoanalyst is a psychologist or psychiatrist who subscribes to Sigmund Freud's theory of personality and treatment. While there are many differences between a psychologist and a psychiatrist, in this last instance there is a great deal of similarity or overlap in professional application. The prime distinction here is that only psychiatrists, because of their medical training, may prescribe and administer drugs.

As indicated above, students not electing to pursue clinical training complete their last graduate years in one or more of a number of other specialty areas. In these cases no internship is required. The one exception is the student interested in counseling psychology, who does an internship in either a hospital or another mental health or community facility. Persons who come to see a counseling psychologist are usually not as severely disturbed as those seeking the help of a clinical psychologist or psychiatrist. The counseling psychologist primarily helps clients with vocational and academic problems. Some counseling psychologists engage in the practice of psychotherapy.

SUBFIELDS IN PSYCHOLOGY

As mentioned above, comparing psychologists to psychiatrists is only one way of indicating what a psychologist is or what a psychologist does. To describe what a psychologist does requires a little more effort than merely contrasting and comparing psychologists with psychiatrists. This is primarily because there are a number of subfields in psychology and the activities of these subfields are varied.

Table 1-1 provides a breakdown of the numbers and percentages of psychologists in the various subfields of psychology. Of approximately thirty-five

TABLE 1-1 Number and percentage of psychologists trained and working in various subfields of psychology

Area or Subfield	Number	% of Total
Clinical	8400	30.7
School and educational	3366	12.3
Experimental and physiological	3098	11.3
Counseling	2751	10.0
Industrial/organizational and engineering	2134	7.8
Social	1629	5.9
Developmental	1605	5.9
Quantitative	1505	5.5
Personality	1068	3.9
Community	671	2.5
Other	1144	4.9
Total	27371	

Based on data from a December 1972 survey by the American Psychological Association.

thousand members of the American Psychological Association, 27,371 responded to the questionnaire used to gather these data. As can be seen in Table 1-1, clinical psychologists constitute the largest subfield (30.7 percent), and counseling psychologists are fosrth in rank (10 percent).

To some extent, the content of the divisions in this text corresponds to the primary endeavors of the subfields listed in Table 1-1. Psychology, like other disciplines, is concerned with knowing — and by knowing we are better able to explain, hredict, and control. These functions are accomplished, as in other sciences, through a division of labor. Some of the subfields are concerned solely with the development and formulation of information. Hence, through controlled observation of behavior, explanation is achieved through the development and refinement of theories. These theories presumably aid in the understanding of known facts and facilitate making connections and discovering previously unknown relationships. A second group of these subfields is characterized by the quest for understanding for purposes of treating behavior disorders and by the application of information to problems in governmental, industrial, and educational institutions.

A large number of psychologists consider themselves experimental or physiological researchers (11.3 percent). The major activities engaged in by these psychologists are pure (or basic) research and the development of theories. Perception (covered in Division B of this book), learning (Division C), intelligence (Division D), emotion (Division I), motivation (Division J), and the biological basis of behavior (Division H) are the typical conceptual areas pursued by experimental psychologists. Social behaviors (Division G) are studied by social psychologists, who also use experimental procedures. Most of the psychologists listed in Table 1-1 use controlled experimentation as the preferred method of establishing cause-and-effect relationships among the behaviors they study. Exceptions to this are psychologists who are primarily interested in the application of their knowledge to social or individual problems. Personality and therapy (Division F) and the study of behavior pathology (Division E) are applied areas that chiefly involve clinical psychologists, counseling psychologists, and, to a more limited extent, personality and community psychologists. These descriptions and relationships are by no means exhaustive; however, they should oive the student a better appreciation for who psychologists are and what psychologists do.

Ethics

Increasingly, psychologists have come under criticism and attack regarding ethical conduct in the pursuit of research activities. This criticism has come from psychologists themselves and from others. The abuses cited range from misuse of research results and exploitation of minority groups and women to violation of subjects' rights as persons. A good deal of this criticism is naturally aimed at research on humans, especially children, who are deceived, manipulated, and, according to some, "devalued."

In response to these criticisms, psychologists have recently set about revising their ethical codes. Key features of the proposed revisions include:

1. The privacy of all experimental subjects is to be protected by securing "informed consent." This guideline obviously calls for all human participation in research to be on a volunteer basis and requires that experimenters do not coerce subjects into participating.
2. Experimenters may not expose subjects to anything that causes lasting harm, such as the induction of hazardous drugs or other agents.
3. Subjects are not to be exposed to any manipulations or treatments that will change their lives in any way.
4. Researchers are encouraged to debrief fully and honestly so that subjects leave the experimental situation no more distressed than when they arrived.

This last point has long been a standard practice in social-psychological research. Milgram's experiment (discussed in Division G) led subjects to believe that they were administering painful electric shocks to another individual. A good deal of effort was subsequently employed to assure the subjects that the shock apparatus was a fake and that no harm was done to the other person. Nonetheless, this particular experiment, probably more than any other study in psychology, has been criticized as a violation of experimenter ethics.

The guidelines of ethical practice for psychologists seem to be ample regarding prohibitions against the induction of physical pain. However, there seems to be a basis for "reasonable" men and women to disagree as to what constitutes psychological pain. The position of one of the strong critics of the revised guidelines is reflected in one of her principles: "Scientific ends, however laudable these may be, do not by themselves justify the use of means that in ordinary transactions would be regarded as reprehensible" (Baumrind, 1971, p. 890).

Ethical guidelines, no matter how stringent, will always depend for their effectiveness on the integrity of the researcher. Nonetheless, strong guidelines seem warranted, though they do impose restrictions on the scientist's use of human subjects. With diligent care and well-thought-out research designs, most problems can be studied without violating the rights and integrity of human subjects. The social psychologist and others working with humans are most affected by these restrictions, but, as will be seen in the divisions in this text, a good deal of research is possible without any violation of ethical codes.

Unit 2
The Confusion of Tongues

In reading this text, you will undoubtedly discover words and concepts with which you are not familiar. We have tried to minimize this problem by avoiding traditional psychological language when an appropriate alternative appeared to simplify matters without loss of meaning. In many instances this was not possible. To help in these instances, a glossary is provided at the end of each division. Nonetheless, some discussion of the verbal framework within which psychologists operate should prove to be immensely helpful.

Perhaps the two most common words used by psychologists are *stimulus* and *response*. The importance of these two words relates to our discussion of behavior in Unit 1. As we indicated, psychologists have largely restricted themselves to the study of observable behavior or processes that can be inferred from observable behavior. One way of conceptualizing this is in the schema in Figure 2-1.

As indicated in this diagram, observable behaviors are *stimulus situations* (a) and *response patterns* (d). By stimuli (plural of stimulus) the psychologist means those events in the environment of the organism (O) that he experiences via his sensory apparatus (e.g., eyes, ears). The world of stimuli is essentially chemical and physical. That is, stimuli are characterized as vibration, radiation, chemical processes, pressure, or some combination of these. These *stimulus situations* (a) act on the organism's *sense receptors* (b)

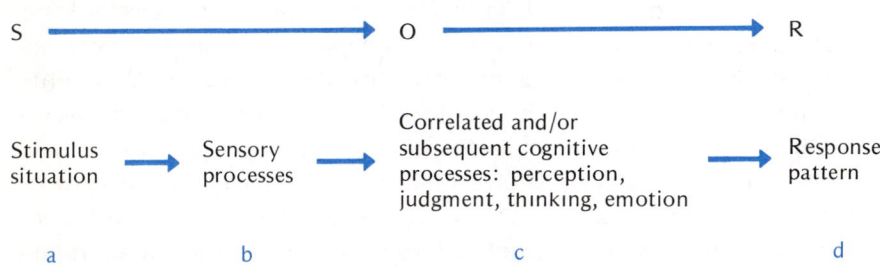

FIGURE 2-1   The subject matter of psychology: observable and related processes

and, in turn, are transmitted via sensory pathways to the central nervous system where *cognitive events* (c) determine the nature of the *response patterns* (d). Response patterns are behavioral events or acts performed by individuals. These events cover a wide range of activities engaged in by both lower animals and humans. Some examples of behavior are eye blinking, muscle twitching, salivation, running, jumping, reading, and driving an automobile. Obviously, this is only a small sample of the many behaviors that psychologists study. The important thing to remember here is that for the psychologist a behavioral event is an observable event.

Scientific Language and Rules

In order for psychologists to communicate their ideas and findings with precision to each other and to other scientists, they must have a common language. The everyday language of the layman is not adequate because some of its vocabulary lacks precision and operational clarity. Operational clarity is achieved by giving precise definitions to observable events that represent concepts. The necessity for precision and clarity is not unique to the scientific community. Effective communication is necessary in most areas of life. However, the problem is of paramount importance to any scientific endeavor because, as stated above, the scientist's major thrust is to achieve understanding and develop explanations (ultimately in the form of theories). When this is the goal, language cannot be vague as is often the case in nontechnical areas; the precision and logical consistency of language facilitate the discovery of causal explanations. Most nontechnical communication (i.e., common sense) is characterized by informality and rarely, if ever, is concerned with scientific explanations of cause and effect.

The observations and findings of scientists are always checked for their validity by experimental methods. Validation is often missing in, for example, conventional wisdom which is usually communicated through proverbs. Consider the possible contradictions in the following two pairs of proverbs:

Birds of a feather flock together
and
Opposites attract

Absence makes the heart grow fonder
and
Out of sight, out of mind

In nontechnical situations, individuals tend not to question these differences and simply use each proverb whenever it seems appropriate without regard for any inconsistency or confusion.

Figure 2-2 shows the procedures employed by psychologists that aid in establishing standardized terminology, controlled investigation, and logical explanations of the behavioral events being studied. These three procedures respectively are (a) *operational definition:* definition in terms of observable events, (b) *experimental manipulation:* methodological procedures that relate variables, and (c) *causal explanation of relationships:* establishing factual rela-

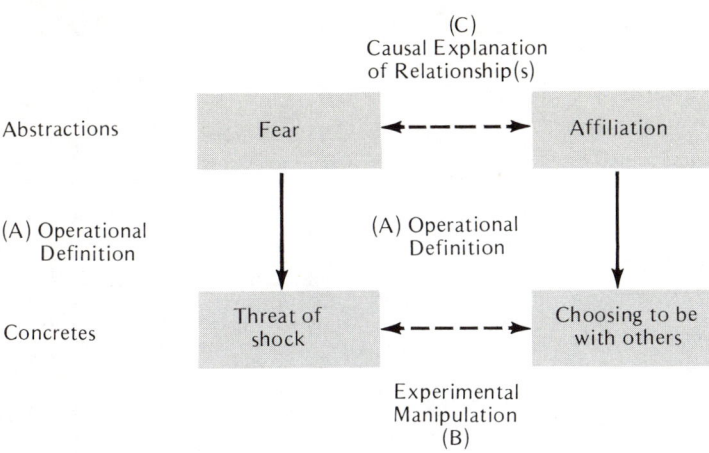

FIGURE 2-2   Processes psychologists employ in standardizing language

tionships between concepts. Let's take these in turn and relate them to our model in Figure 2-2.

OPERATIONAL DEFINITION

In order to study any behavior, one has to define the concepts or behaviors in question. In some instances this process is fairly straightforward, but in others the problems are rampant. If you wanted to study speed in turtles there would be no problem. You would simply get a stopwatch and time the movement of turtles from one location to another. On the other hand, if you wanted to study intimacy you might encounter as much difficulty as you would in trying to explain the color red to a blind man. The same level of difficulty might be encountered in attempting to define love.

These difficulties by no means indicate that we cannot study these behaviors. Scientists have come to agree on definitions of such concepts in terms of the techniques used to study these behaviors. In Figure 2-2, for example, if you wanted to study the relationship between fear and affiliation you would first have to define *fear* and *affiliation* operationally. In this case, the operations used to assess these behaviors (i.e., threat and preference to be with others, respectively) form the basis for "operational definitions." This procedure forces us to move from the vague level of abstractions to concrete behaviors that lend themselves to observation and measurement. Additionally, this procedure discourages the posing of questions that can't be answered scientifically.

EXPERIMENTAL MANIPULATION

Once concepts have been defined, the psychologist must engage in a systematic effort to discover the nature of the relationship between the behaviors being

The Confusion of Tongues

studied. In order to accomplish this, the psychologist usually creates an artificial situation in which two or more events are simulated. Then, by varying one (the independent variable) and observing the nature of change in the other (the dependent variable), inferences about causality can be made. For example, by varying the level of threat of shock (Figure 2-2) we can observe the number of expressed preferences to be with others. If there is a greater tendency to choose to be with others when the threat of shock is high, it may be concluded that high fear produces more affiliation than low fear.

The major effort of psychologists is directed at understanding behavior. The most widespread way of accomplishing this is by means of experimental manipulation. Through experimental manipulation, psychologists are able to discover systematically what variables are related to behavior. An additional advantage to this carefully spelled-out approach is that it provides ample opportunity to validate the process by which relationships are discovered.

CAUSAL EXPLANATION OF RELATIONSHIPS

The statement above, characterizing the relationship between fear and affiliation, exemplifies the final step in the experimental process. That is, the assertion that increases in fear produce corresponding responses in affiliative behaviors can be made with confidence since it is the direct result of experimentation. Only when we have manipulated fear and observed subsequent behaviors (e.g., affiliation) are we able to formulate the nature of the

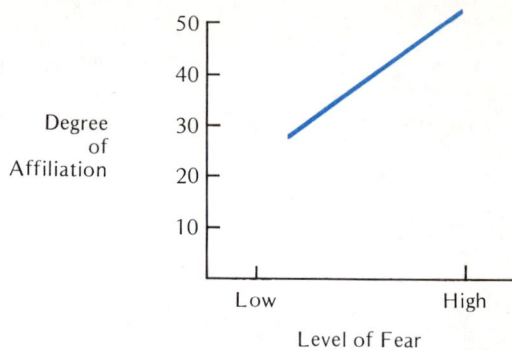

FIGURE 2-3 The relationship between fear and affiliation

relationship between these two variables (see Figure 2-3).

The student, however, should be aware of the differences between experimental manipulation and manipulation by advertising agencies and the media. Advertising often very clearly links pleasures and other forms of positive incentives with the product being sold. And very often the news media report two events that are related in such a way that the reader or listener will assume that one causes the other. In both instances, the manipulation results from the deliberate, or not so deliberate, practice of packaging things in such a way that the true nature of the relationship is distorted. The distortion, very often, would disappear if only more information were given. The psychologist's adherence to the scientific approach in investigating behavior and communicating discovered relationships overcomes the distortions that frequently occur in advertising and news reporting. Without a carefully controlled procedure for observing and reporting behavior, informal observations (like rumors) will be increasingly modified and distorted with successive reports of the observed events. Strict rules of language, rigorous methodological frameworks, and logically precise conclusions will result in far better communication of behavioral events, and in turn will produce a greater amount of understanding than is accomplished by more casual and informal means like newspaper headlines and commercial ads.

Correlational research. Experimental research, as mentioned above, is usually the preferred method of psychologists in their efforts to understand behavior. However, depending on the problem being studied and the goals of the experimenter, another type of research might be preferable. Correlational research consists of observing the relationship between two or more variables. It attempts to determine if, when one variable is high, another variable is also high (a positive correlation), is low (a negative correlation), or varies independently (no correlation). A correlational study is an efficient way of collecting a large amount of data about relationships and interrelationships of variables in a relatively short time. The major weakness of correlational studies is that they leave the cause-and-effect relationship ambiguous. Although in many cases we can be fairly certain of the direction of causation, a correlation between two variables does not indicate which variable affects the other. Another serious ambiguity in all correlational studies is the possibility that neither variable is affecting the other. Any number of unspecified factors may be affecting one or both of the variables being observed. For example, if you were to observe that a car horn sounded each time the lights went out in the room, you would not be likely to argue that one caused the other. We generally refer to such instances as being coincident.

Laboratory vs. field research. Both experimental and correlational research can be done in either the laboratory or the field, and each setting has advantages and disadvantages. Research in the field tends to deal with real people or animals in real situations, as opposed to experimental subjects in relatively unreal situations in the laboratory. Thus, field research tends to minimize suspicion among subjects toward experimenters and the consequents of this suspicion: susceptibility to bias and lack of spontaneity. Field research can also collect data from a wider variety of subjects than are attracted to the experimental laboratory and thus adds to the generality of the findings. Another advantage of work in the field is that it enables the observation of extremely powerful variables and situations that could not be studied in the laboratory. On the other hand, the major disadvantages of field research stem from the lack of the experimenter's control over the situation. Many random events and conditions enter into a field study and often obscure the effects of the variables in which we are interested. In particular, it is difficult to find pure manipulations of the independent variable and pure measures of the dependent variable in the field. If the manipulation is not pure, the interpretation of the effect is ambiguous.

The major advantage of laboratory research is the control over the situation that it provides, minimizing extraneous factors and eliminating random variations in procedure. Therefore, the laboratory is the ideal place in which to set up a situation that is designed to study a specific problem. The basic disadvantages of laboratory work center around two aspects of the situation. First, the subject's knowledge that he is being studied may create effects on his behavior which could produce bias in the results or obscure relationships and effects that actually exist. Second, limitations on the kinds of manipulations that can be performed mean that laboratory research usually deals with relatively nonextreme levels of variables, making it difficult to find the effect of a variable even when the effect exists. A relatively minor disadvantage is that laboratory work tends to deal with a restricted population of subjects and thus limits the generality of the findings. However, this problem can be eliminated if sufficient ingenuity and effort are exercised to attract a wide range of subjects to experimental laboratories.

The point of this discussion has not been to convince the student that only scientists can ask and answer questions. To the contrary, most disciplines (e.g., religion, history, philosophy) are continuously and intimately involved in formulating questions and answers regarding behavior, the nature of the universe, the origin of life, the existence of God, and so on. However, the student should have an appreciation for the way in which psychologists approach these questions, and should keep these procedures in mind when encountering the various discussions of behavior in later divisions in this text.

INDEPENDENT AND DEPENDENT VARIABLES

The variable that the psychologist investigates and manipulates (systematically varies) is referred to as the *independent variable*. It is the stimulus in the conceptualization described earlier in this unit. Earlier we defined stimuli as environmental and other events experienced by an organism. In experimentation, the psychologist manipulates or varies these events in order to assess their impact on other behaviors. Varying the level of fear (operationally, varying the level of threat), for example, is an instance of an independent variable. The psychologist in that case was interested in how fear affects affiliative behaviors. The independent variable in this case is said to be a causal variable. The behavior or response of interest was the subject's choice to be alone or with others (affiliation). In psychology this behavior is called the *dependent variable*. All of the behaviors to be studied in this text, which are behaviors that psychologists are interested in, are dependent variables. The dependent variable is the response variable in the conceptualization discussed earlier and is denoted by the letter R. The dependent variable, then, is the effect that is produced by the experimenter's manipulation.

Measuring Behavior (The Use of Numbers)

A psychologist observing behavior usually must have some way of recording the event. Most behaviors can be measured or assigned numbers on an *a priori* or predefined basis. For example, physiological behavior can be measured directly by using instruments, learning can be measured by counting scores on a test, and attitudes can be measured by scores on a paper-and-pencil questionnaire or scale. On the other hand, some behaviors can be measured simply by counting the frequency of their occurrence. In all cases, when the observations are translated into numbers they become data. The importance of this process is twofold: (1) data on the same behavioral events can be collected by others to check for their reliability, and (2) statistical-mathematical operations can be performed on data, permitting one to summarize behavioral events and determine their statistical confidence (i.e., how representative these data are of a larger universe of behaviors).

Measurement is a crucial aspect of any science, for it determines the way in which observations must be recorded. The outcome of this process is a standardized way of characterizing the events being observed. For the psychologist this is extremely important because measurement of behavior is at a far more primitive stage than is measurement in the physical sciences. Nonetheless, psychologists have developed adequate techniques for measuring the behaviors in which they are interested. All the conclusions about behavior presented in this text grew out of the measurement process just discussed.

As will become obvious to the reader, all psychologists do not necessarily agree with the conclusions regarding a given set of events. However, improved measuring techniques and replication (duplication) of findings tend to reduce these differences. To this end, the reader should be alerted that the findings of psychology are not considered proved facts but tentative or provisional conclusions. And as data become more and more reliable they are integrated into a larger framework.

Unit 3
Questions

Psychology as a formal discipline is not quite a hundred years old. Yet most of the questions and issues posed by psychologists in their effort to understand behavior are no different than those raised by Greek philosophers in the days of Plato and Aristotle.

The strongest impetus to methods of observation, measurement, and deriving conclusions, however, came from the astronomers Copernicus, Kepler, and Galileo, each of whom defied authority in arguing for his conclusions regarding the solar system. The importance of the contributions made by these men is in the use of the processes of observation, measurement, and deduction in arriving at information. Additional significant influences upon the discovery and development of psychology as a separate discipline came from the French philosopher, mathematician, and physiologist Descartes, who formulated many of the questions regarding the brain and behavior into the mind-body concept which argued for a universe composed of two substances — material and mental.

Finally, the term *motivation*, which forms an important part of psychology today, is derived from the eighteenth-century theory of hedonism which asserts that human behavior is motivated by the desire to gain pleasure and avoid pain. As will be seen in Division C (Gaining Information and Knowledge), a modern-day version of hedonism (reinforcement) is a fundamental concept in learning theory.

Again, the questions about behavior and the world around us are not new, and answers to many of them remain incomplete. In some instances, the questions have grown more complex as a result of discovered information. And most significantly, observation has increasingly become the standardized method of inquiry. As this has occurred psychologists and other scientists have developed better instruments and become more sophisticated in formulating both questions and answers.

As indicated above, philosophers theorized about and formulated answers to the questions repeatedly raised by man about himself in relation to the universe. However, as more and more information about the nervous system became known, developments from physics, chemistry, and biology were applied to the study of man's behavior. These merging disciplines (philosophy and science) intersected in the disciplines of physiology and psychophysiology. During this time tremendous efforts were made to determine the localization of function in the brain. This effort began in the context of *phrenology*, which held that the various mental functions could be analyzed by studying the shape of the skull, and was extended to a search for body location of mental functions such as sensation, intellect, and emotion. It was also during this era that the electrophysiology and chemistry of nerve impulses became known. Finally, the sense physiologists provided us with new information and with new theories regarding vision, hearing, touch, taste, and smell.

Given this historical development, it was only natural that early efforts in modern psychology depended heavily on contributions from biology. This thrust focused on the relationship between an organism's internal systems and its behavior. The two systems which were predominant in these activities were the nervous system and endocrine system (see Division H). Hence, modern psychology at the turn of the century was almost totally behavioristic in that it tended to exclude (with some exceptions) considerations of most mental events. This was conceptualized as S-R (stimulus-response) psychology and enhanced the rigor of the experimental approach. On the other hand, the rigor might be viewed as having spread to influencing the development of more objective referents of mental events. Consequently, psychology has developed to a point of being more secure with the study of both physical and mental behaviors.

A Buzzing Mass of Confusion?

The first sensation which an infant gets is for him the Universe. And the Universe which he later comes to know is nothing but an amplification and an implication of that first simple germ which, by accretion on the one hand and intrassesception on the other, has grown so big and complex and articulate that its first estate is varememberable (James, 1890, p. 8).

These words were written by William James, the founder of the first experimental psychology laboratory in America at Harvard University. James was attempting to describe a newborn infant's first perception of the world. Since perception involves a meaningful organization of raw stimuli, it is unlikely that the first sensory experience of the world could be intelligible. However, in time developmental experiences aid in bringing increasing clarity and meaning to one's universe. In developing the divisions in this text we have tried to follow a comparable format.

As indicated earlier, people have for years sought to bring meaning and understanding to their environment and their behavior. The points of entry for such experiences are the sensory modalities (eyes, ears, etc.). Information from the outside world is transmitted via these avenues to the central nervous system (which includes the brain), where it is processed and translated into behaviors. This is essentially a learning experience and is comparable to the process described in the passage from James. We have attempted to follow this sequence in the developmental plan of this book.

Thus, the first division of this text deals

with perception. Essentially, we consider basic questions about the anatomy and physiology of the modalities involved in organizing our worlds. The next divisions (Divisions C and D) are concerned with problems of learning and issues in intelligence, respectively. In both these instances, and frequently throughout the book, the issues are discussed in the context of current issues and problems. In Division E we consider the problems of adjustment.

Problems of adjustment are rampant in our culture. Some of the most prominent problems find expression in social movements. For example, the *women's liberation movement* is an organized effort to break through the numerous socially imposed norms which most women have internalized that restrict their behaviors into certain sex-typed roles. With a long history of being regarded as inferior to the male, the female is only recently beginning to assert her ability to equal or surpass the male in many important pursuits. The psychologist's interest in this area is focused around the following questions: Who are the feminists, and what are their demands? What is the motivational base for the movement, and what will be some consequences of the movement? How will the family as a social unit, culturally defined sex roles, and a woman's self-concept be affected? An example of the psychologist's role in explaining the women's liberation movement is derived from Sherif's (1970) statement that a social movement always arises from a motivational base that is related to social problems. In an effort to understand the motivational base for the feminist movement, Goldberg (1968) found that women express more confidence in men than in women. Female college students were asked to rate literary passages on several criteria. While in actuality all passages were written by the same person, some of the passages given to each subject were said to be written by males, others by females. The female subjects gave higher ratings to passages attributed to male authors. This outcome tends to support the notion that women have come to assume their own inferiority as factual (a self-fulfilling prophecy).

Equally conspicuous as a social problem with implications for adjustment is homosexuality. *Gay liberation* is an organized movement on the part of homosexuals to remove the stigmas attached to them and to allow them to assert their homosexuality openly rather than live a sheltered life in the fear of being rejected and degraded by society. Male homosexuality has received considerable attention by researchers. The psychologist's interest in this area concerns getting some of the facts straight about homosexuality, including an accurate estimate of the number of individuals who have had homosexual experiences; theorizing about the causes of homosexual object choice; studying the differences among homosexual types; examining homosexual personality and background, etc.

In an attempt to test the notion that homosexuals who are not seeking psychiatric help are no different in personality than heterosexuals who are not seeking help, Hooker (1957) matched 30 men who were homosexual but not seeking psychiatric help with 30 heterosexuals in regard to their age, I.Q., and educational attainment. Each subject was administered a set of personality tests, which were then evaluated by experienced clinical psychologists who did not know the respondent's sexual object choice. These experts were not able to pick out homosexual subjects reliably, nor did the homosexual subjects receive worse ratings on general adjustment. In both groups, a wide range of personality types, character structures, and interests existed.

Division F concentrates on the issues of personality and individual differences among human beings. The final two units in that division address the issue of therapy. Several forms of therapy are discussed, including the controversial technique of psychosurgery.

In Division G the focus of the discussion shifts to problems experienced as a result of influences from others. This division explores problems such as obedience, conformity, attitudes, and helping behaviors. Many groups and clubs are present on any college campus, ranging from bicycling and tennis clubs to organizations such as student government associations and women's liberation groups. Why do some students join these groups while others are content with simply attending their classes and returning home? What personality characteristics will lead certain individuals to join one group or another? Within a group, who are the active members and who are the persons who always conform to the norms established by these active members? The psychologist's interest in groups would include an attempt to answer these questions. In Division G we explore some of these issues as they relate to questions raised by involvement in contemporary society. Of special significance in this division is a concern with group membership requirements that compel individuals to engage in behaviors that are potentially harmful or destructive to others.

The biological and chemical bases of behavior form a part of the content of Division H. The division focuses principally on behavior control and ecology. The growing concern for creating and maintaining a healthy environment has led many college students, as well as individuals of all age groups, to utilize the bicycle as a means of transportation in place of the air-polluting, exhaust-emitting automobile. In addition to its function of "cleaning up the environment," bicycling can be useful as a personal health measure, obviously providing much more exercise for an individual than does sitting in an automobile. The psychologist's concern in this growing trend has been in attempting to explain what factors have led to the increasing interest in ecology, why some individuals are more involved in the movement than others, the psychological effects that the environment has on the individual and subgroups, and what the possible consequences of the trend are.

Division I discusses issues related to feelings and emotion. Various theories of emotion are considered. Additionally, the psychoanalytic view of anxiety and the physiological basis of fear are developed. This division is concluded with an introduction to theories of liking and love.

Finally, in Division J we cover a number of problems and issues confronted by young adults. Even after organizing one's world there are still problems of alienation and morality. For example, the issues concerning the legalization of marijuana are of great significance for college students today. Although in many sections of this country the laws pertaining to marijuana use and possession are becoming more lenient, many students are still reluctant to use marijuana because they are afraid of being detected and punished. The psychologist's concern in this area would be to examine the psychological effects of smoking marijuana and to present empirical evidence indicating the presence or absence of negative or positive psychological effects and consequences. Only through data derived from controlled scientific studies will the arguments on this issue cease to be based on faulty generalizations and absolute standards. Psychological findings relevant to this issue are discussed in Division J, and two units in this division give some attention to strategies designed, to some extent, to cope with the problems discussed here. Included in the discussion is a treatment of encounter and sensitivity groups.

SUMMARY

Psychology is defined by most psychologists as the scientific study of behavior. Behavior is a complex phenomenon and is studied in many fields besides psychology. Although psychologists have no monopoly on the study of behavior, psychology's relationship to the behavioral and social sciences and to the natural sciences makes it a kind of meeting ground for those interested in the study of behavior. In their focus on behavior, psychologists have generated information and constructed theories that facilitate the understanding of many of the problems we are confronted with today.

One source of confusion for many people is in determining the difference between a psychologist and a psychiatrist. The major difference between the two professions is in the kind of training each receives. In professional application, the prime distinction is that only psychiatrists, because of their medical training, may prescribe drugs. Describing what a psychologist does is somewhat difficult because there are many subfields in psychology, each involving different activities. In general, psychology is concerned with knowing — for by knowing we are better able to explain, predict, and control. Psychologists gather information in many content areas (e.g., learning, personality, child development) and use many different techniques (e.g., theory development, experiments).

Increasingly, psychologists have come under criticism and attack regarding their ethical conduct in the pursuit of research activities, especially in their research on humans. In response to these criticisms psychologists have recently set about the task of revising their ethical codes. Nonetheless, controversy still exists, for ethical guidelines, no matter how stringent, will always to some extent depend on the integrity of the researcher.

In order for psychologists to communicate their ideas and findings with precision to each other and to other scientists they must have a common language. The language cannot be vague as is often the case in nontechnical areas, for the precision and logical consistency of language facilitate the discovery of causal explanation. The procedures employed by psychologists that aid in establishing standardized terminology, controlled investigation, and logical explanations of the behavioral events being studied are, respectively, (a) operational definition: definition of concepts in terms of concrete behaviors that lend themselves to observation and measurement; (b) experimental manipulation: methodological procedures that allow a systematic discovery of what variables are related to behavior; and (c) causal explanation of relationships: establishment of factual relationships between concepts as the direct result of experimentation. Additionally, psychologists conduct field or naturalistic studies which involve observation of ongoing events. The variable that the psychologist investigates and manipulates (systematically varies) in order to assess its impact on behavior is referred to as the *independent variable*. The behavior or response of the subject to that independent variable is referred to as the *dependent variable*. When psychologists observe behavior they usually must have some way of recording the event. When observations are translated into numbers, either on an a priori basis or simply by counting the frequency of their occurrence, they become *data*. The importance of this measurement process is twofold: (1) data on the same behavioral events can be collected by others to check for their reliability, and (2) statistical or mathematical operations can be performed on data which permit one to summarize behavioral events in a standardized way and determine their statistical confidence. As data become more and more reliable they are integrated into a larger framework.

Psychology as a formal discipline is not quite a hundred years old. Yet most of the questions and issues posed by psychologists in their effort to understand behavior are not new, and answers to many of them remain incomplete. Philosophers formulated answers to and theorized about the questions repeatedly raised by man about himself in relation to the universe. As more information about the nervous system became known, developments from physics, chemistry, and biology were applied to the study of man's behavior. Therefore, it was only natural that early efforts in modern psychology depended heavily on contributions from biology. This thrust focused on the relationship between an organism's internal systems and its behavior, excluding considerations of most mental events. This conceptualization enhanced the rigor of the experimental approach, allowing development of more objective referents of mental events. Consequently, psychology has developed to a point at which it is more secure with the study of both physical and mental behaviors.

GLOSSARY

A priori: relating to or derived by reasoning from self-evident propositions; presupposed by experience without examination or analysis

Causal explanation of relationships: establishing factual relationships between concepts

Dependent variable: a behavioral response, or response sequence, observed in an experimental situation in relation to an independent variable

Ethical code: guidelines for psychologists to follow in their pursuit of research activities involving human subjects to ensure against violation of individuals' personal rights or integrity

Experimental manipulation: methodological procedures that relate variables

Experimental method: scientific data collection which involves the manipulation of one or more independent variables, control of other related variables, and observation of one or more dependent variables

Hedonism: eighteenth-century theory which asserts that human behavior is motivated by the desire to gain pleasure and avoid pain

Independent variable: variable which is manipulated (systematically varied) and observed in an experimental setting

Mind-body formulation: idea developed by Descartes which argued for a universe composed of two substances — material and mental

Operational definition: concrete definition of abstract terms so as to ensure the possibility of observation and measurement

Perception: internal processes associated with the elaboration, organization, and combination of events initiated by sensation; organizing and interpreting of information

Phrenology: theory which held that the various mental functions, such as intellect and emotion, can be analyzed by studying the shape of the skull; extended to a search for body location of mental functions

Psychiatrist: a physician who has received advanced training in psychotherapy and who, using these skills and the knowledge of medical procedures, treats the mentally ill in either a hospital, a private clinic, or a private office

Psychologist: a person who pursues a program of graduate training in psychology with heavy emphasis on theory and the use of scientific method to study behavior. After receiving the Ph.D. degree, the individual may join the staff of a university or college to teach and conduct research or may become an applied psychologist.

Psychology: the scientific study of behavior

Reliability: the dependability of a test — the degree to which it can be expected to yield similar scores when measuring the same variable on different occasions

Response: a behavioral event or act performed by an individual as a result of an external or internal stimulus

Stimulus: an event in an individual's environment that is experienced via one's sensory apparatus

Theory: a system of ideas comprising abstract concepts, rules about the interconnections of these concepts, and ways of linking these concepts to observed events

Validity: the degree to which a test measures what it is intended to measure

REFERENCES

Baumrind, D. Principles of ethical conduct in the treatment of subjects: Reaction to the draft report of the committee on ethical standards in psychological research. *American Psychologist,* 1971, *26,* 887–896.

Goldberg, P. Are women prejudiced against women? *Trans-Action,* 1968, *5,* 28–30.

Hooker, E. The adjustment of the male overt homosexual. *Journal of Projective Techniques,* 1957, *21,* 18–31.

James, William. *The principles of psychology.* Vol. II. New York: Henry Holt and Company, 1890.

Sherif, M. On the relevance of social psychology. *American Psychologist,* 1970, *25,* 144–156.

A symposium. New York: Appleton-Century-Crofts, 1969.

Rosenthal, R. A. *Experimenter effects in behavioral research.* New York: Appleton-Century-Crofts, 1966.

Watson, R. I. *The great psychologists: From Aristotle to Freud.* (2nd ed.). Philadelphia: Lippincott, 1968.

SUGGESTED READINGS

American Psychological Association. *A career in psychology.* Washington, D.C.: American Psychological Association, 1970.

Clark, K. E., and Miller, G. A. (Eds.). *Psychology: Behavioral and social science survey.* Englewood Cliffs, N.J.: Prentice-Hall, 1970.

Krantz, D. L. (Ed.). *Schools of psychology:*

Photo by Agnes M. Fromer

B

What's Out There?

Unit 4
The Human Camera

Examine the cover of this book for about thirty seconds. Now concentrate on listing as many pieces of information as you can that you acquired from your visual examination of the cover. Your eyes identified the shapes of the objects and gave you information on which lines were vertical and which were horizontal. You were able to determine the outline of figures and immediately distinguish each figure from the background. Each color was immediately identified and distinguished from all other colors. The shapes of the letters were not only differentiated, they were identified, grouped into words, and "read." You probably can cite many more pieces of information that you acquired by visual examination, and all of it was obtained in an extremely brief period of time.

We constantly use our eyes to gather information, but we seldom think about the almost miraculous efficiency and effectiveness of these two small organs. We become so used to this vast source of information that we seldom, if ever, stop to think about how much we use our eyes. Yet if we do think about it, none of our senses appears more important to us than vision. Information coming to us through the visual sense seems to dominate our lives. To understand what is involved in seeing, we will have to find the answers to three questions:

1. What is the physical energy in the outside world that stimulates our eye and produces vision?
2. How is this energy that strikes the eye translated into neural energy, and how is it transmitted within the organism?
3. How do we translate this neural energy into meaningful sights, e.g., red shoes, blue sky, tall people, small dogs?

The Physical Stimulus

The stimulus that strikes the eye and eventually produces vision is light, part of the electromagnetic spectrum. The light that we can see represents only a very small portion of the entire electromagnetic spectrum (see Figure 4-1). This visible light has three basic components, each corresponding to a different aspect of what we see. These three basic components of light are *wavelength, intensity,* and *complexity.*

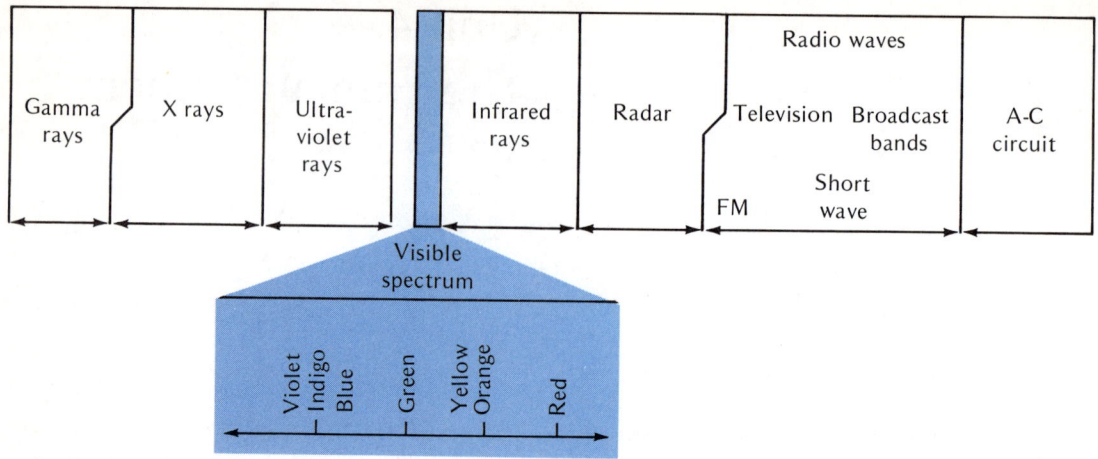

FIGURE 4-1 The electromagnetic spectrum. The *visible spectrum* is the only portion to which the human eye is sensitive.

Wavelength. The wavelength of the physical stimulus is seen as hue or color. As the length of the light wave increases, the perceived color of the stimulus changes from violet through blue and all the colors until it reaches red. Waves shorter than those producing the violet color and longer than those perceived as red do not act on the eye in a way that stimulates visual perception; that is, we can't see them.

Intensity. This aspect of the physical stimulus refers to its strength. When converted into visual terms, it is seen as the brightness of a light. Within the entire visible spectrum, regardless of what the wavelength is, the brightness of any light can vary from the point at which it is just barely visible to a level at which it is painful to view.

Complexity. This characteristic of the physical stimulus refers to the purity of the wavelength. This aspect is perceived as the saturation of a stimulus. A light that is completely pure or perceived as highly saturated is not diluted by grayness or whiteness. When a light is unsaturated or impure, it is made up of not only light waves representing the perceived color, but a relatively large proportion of gray or white as well. Pastel colors are relatively unsaturated, containing a great deal of whiteness relative to the particular color perceived.

Each of these three aspects of the physical stimulus, light, exists outside of the organism. All can be measured and evaluated by physical instruments. When the light strikes the eye, each of these three aspects of light causes different reactions in the visual apparatus, reactions that result in the perception of color, brightness, and saturation.

From Physical Stimulus To Neural Energy

Thus far we have discussed the physical properties of light, the stimulus that is "out there." But how does this physical stimulus get inside? How are the wavelength, intensity, and complexity of the stimulus transformed into neural energy which can be handled by the human organism? The physical stimulus, when it strikes the eye, is focused so that it strikes the light-sensitive cells. These cells function to convert the physical energy into neural energy which can then be transmitted to the brain.

THE EYE-CAMERA ANALOGY

The analogy between the eye and the camera is an old and, in some ways, a useful one (see Figure 4-2). A camera allows light through a lens. This lens can be varied in size depending upon the amount of light available. It focuses the light on the film, which records the image. In projecting the image, the lens inverts the image so that it is recorded upside down. In a somewhat similar manner, light passes through the lens of the eye. This lens also varies in size, inverts the image, and projects it onto the retina (which contains the light-sensitive elements). These elements record the physical energy and translate it into neural energy.

The usefulness of the analogy between the camera and the eye is limited, however, for the complexity of the eye is far greater than that of the camera and the path of light through the eye involves many more structures than are found in a camera (see Figure 4-3).

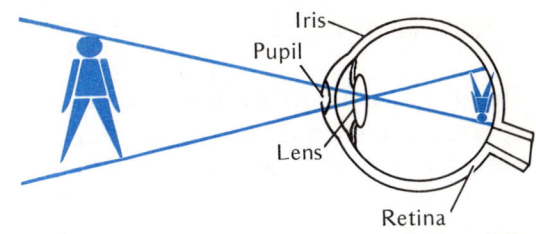

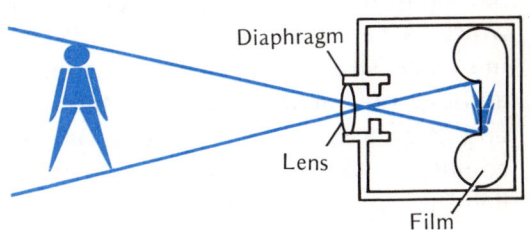

FIGURE 4-2 Both the eye and the camera focus the image by means of an adjustable lens. This lens inverts the image and projects it onto a light-sensitive surface.

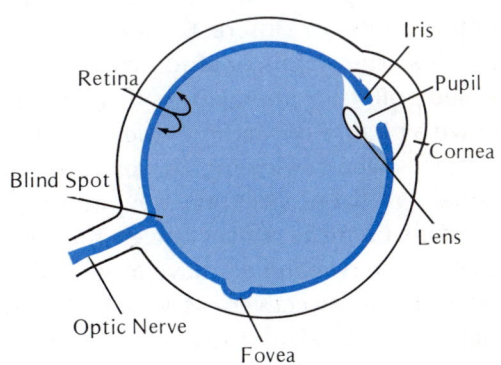

FIGURE 4-3 The human eye

STRUCTURE OF THE EYE

The light first strikes the *cornea,* the curved, transparent layer covering the eye. The curved shape of the eye allows the cornea to pick up many more light waves from a much wider area than would be possible if the surface of the eye were flat. The light which strikes the cornea passes through a small opening in the *iris* which is called the *pupil.* The iris is a muscular structure which can contract and expand, varying the size of the pupil and thus altering the amount of light admitted into the eye. In extremely dim light, the pupil opening is large in order to allow a maximum amount of light to enter the eye. As the brightness of the light increases, the size of the pupil decreases. The job of the pupil is to allow enough light into the eye for adequate stimulation of the receptor cells, but to keep the incoming light at a level low enough so that there is no pain or damage inflicted on the eye.

It has been found that the size of the pupil varies not only as a function of the amount of light, but also as a result of the attractiveness or interest value of the stimulus. The pupils of students who endorsed politically liberal ideas dilate when shown a picture of Martin Luther King but contract when viewing a picture of George Wallace. The reverse pattern is found in political conservatives (Barlow, 1969). Some researchers have argued that it is not the attractiveness which causes dilation, but the intensity of stimulation (Janisse, 1973). It is argued that both highly attractive and highly unattractive stimuli will produce pupil dilation. In any case, it seems clear that our emotions are reflected in our eyes.

After passing through the pupil the light strikes the *lens,* which serves as a focusing structure. The shape of the lens varies in order to permit the most accurate focusing of the light. The shape of the lens is controlled by the *ciliary muscles.* The lens projects the visual image onto the *retina,* focusing it on the most sensitive portion of the retina, an area known as the *fovea.* The periphery or outer portion of the retina is responsive only to the movement of a visual object, not to its form or color. It serves only to pick up movement occurring at the very edge of the visual field, giving us a cue that something is there. In response to this cue, we turn our eyes or head, or both, in order to focus on the object and to identify it.

The retina contains the light-sensitive cells, the *rods* and *cones.* It is these cells which convert the physical energy of the light into neural energy. The neural energy from the rods and cones is transmitted to the brain by way of the optic nerve. The point at which the optic nerve enters the eye is known as the *blind spot.* There are no light receptors located in this area, so that any light striking the area is not perceived.

The fibers which make up the optic nerve do not remain bound together until reaching the brain. Rather, fibers from the nasal (inner) side of each eye cross over and join fibers from the temporal (outer) side of the other eye at a point known as the *optic chiasma* (see Figure 4-4). The two groups of fibers then lead to a number of different areas of the brain,

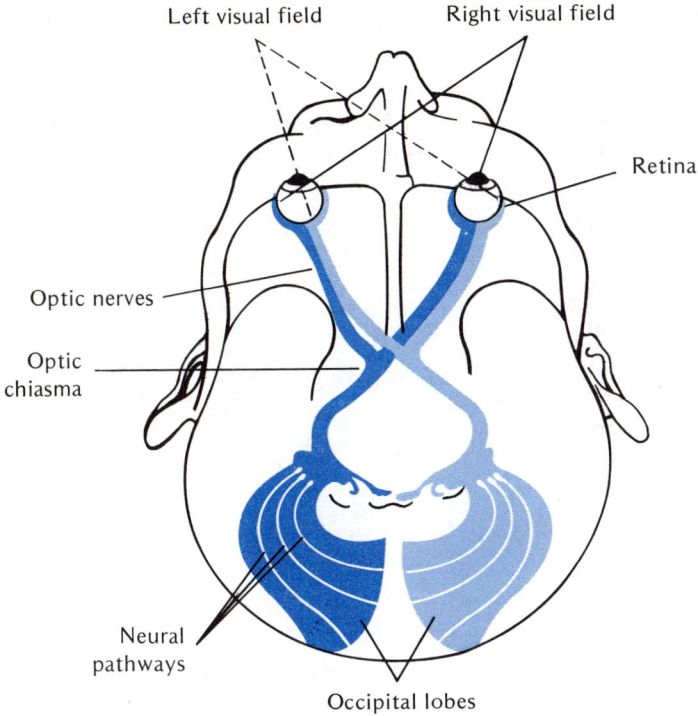

FIGURE 4-4 The pathway of the optic nerve from the eye to the brain. Images from the right visual field of both eyes are carried back to the left portion of the brain. Images from the left visual field of both eyes go to the right side of the brain. The point at which nerve fibers from each eye join and cross is the *optic chiasma*.

areas that control the shape of the lens and the size of the pupil and that record the neural pattern representing the visual image. The last area is known as the *visual projection area* and is located in the cerebral cortex of the brain.

Translation of Neural Energy Into Visual Perception

The neural energy that is elicited in the retina and passed into the brain by the optic nerve is coded in a way that translates it into visual experience. This code is known as the *afferent code*. Understanding of this code is far from complete, although there are hypotheses about how it operates.

Afferent code for hue. The rods in the retina are responsive primarily to light-dark differences, while the cones are the receptor cells for color. There are three different kinds of cones, each responsive to one of three different colors: red, green, and blue. We know that all colors can be produced by various mixtures of wavelengths representing these three colors. The energy recorded in the cones is transmitted through the nervous system, and when the impulses reach the brain, cells there add a further portion of the afferent code for color. Some of these cells, which we shall call Type A, are responsive to all wavelengths, whereas others (Type B) respond only to one particular wavelength, being inhibited in the presence of all others. A combination of the pattern of cones responding and the pattern of brain cells responding makes up the neural representation for color or hue. Each different mixture of wavelengths creates a different response pattern in the cones and in the brain cells.

Afferent code for saturation. The code for saturation is apparently transmitted through the patterning of the same brain cells used for color coding. We noted that some brain cells, Type A, are responsive to all wavelengths, and others, Type B, are inhibited in the presence of all but one wavelength. If saturation is low (the light stimulus is not pure), there is a high level of activity in the Type A cells in comparison to the amount of activity in the Type B cells. If the stimulus is pure or highly saturated, relatively more of the neural activity is concentrated in the Type B cells.

Afferent code for brightness. As noted above, the cones in the retina are the receptors responsible for color, and the rods are responsible for light-dark differences. As the intensity of the light increases, there is a greater response in the rods. This creates greater neural activity, activity which is reflected in those brain cells responsive to all wavelengths, Type A. Therefore, the brighter the incoming stimulus, the higher the level of activity in those cells concerned with brightness. The amount of neural activity is then translated into the perception of brightness.

As stated previously, the understanding of these codes is highly tentative. Scientists are only beginning to investigate fully the brain and central nervous system activity.

Depth Perception

Depth perception is a phenomenon that has long puzzled the layman and the scientist alike. The retina, like a photograph or a painting, is only a two-dimensional surface, capable of relaying information only about the vertical and the horizontal dimensions. But the world is three-dimensional; it has depth. And it is this three-dimensional world that is perceived by people, in spite of the two-dimensional retina. In viewing a picture and in interpreting the retinal pattern, we see three dimensions. How do we do it? Where does the third dimension, depth, come from? The way in which the eyes function provides cues that tell us about the relative distance of different objects. The two-dimensional patterns on the retina are interpreted in a way that adds additional cues.

BINOCULAR CUES

The fact that we have two eyes enables us automatically to pick up information that helps us to judge the depth of a perceived scene. The two eyes are located in different places and thus receive slightly different pictures of the same scene. The brain takes these two pictures and puts them together to form one perception. However, the slight difference between the two images, called *retinal disparity*, serves as a cue to the depth of the objects which are perceived.

Another aspect of binocular vision which may contribute to the perception of depth is *convergence*. The eyes change their position depending on the distance of the viewed object from them. The eyes rotate somewhat toward each other to focus on relatively close objects, and rotate away from each other to view distant objects. The muscles that are responsible for this eye movement may be providing further information on the distance of the object, allowing us to judge the depth.

MONOCULAR CUES

Some cues to depth are not dependent on the functioning of both eyes, but can be fully received and interpreted with only one eye. *Interposition* of objects occurs when one object blocks the view of another. We know that nearer objects can block our view of those which are farther away, so we see a partially concealed object as being farther away than a fully revealed one. We simply place a depth interpretation on the incoming sensory information. The girl in Figure 4-5 is seen as being closer than the window

Photo by Agnes M. Fromer

FIGURE 4-5 Interpositioning of objects serves as a depth cue. Since the window frame is partially blocked from view by the girl, it looks more distant.

The Human Camera

Photo by Agnes M. Fromer

FIGURE 4-6 We perceive depth when we look at this picture because of four different depth cues (see text).

frames because of the cues offered by interposition.

Perspective refers to a series of cues used by artists to create an image of depth. In perceiving objects, we use these same cues to aid us in correctly inferring the depth of the objects. The first of these perspective cues is based on the fact that objects which are farther away appear smaller than do closer objects. The trees in the center of Figure 4-6 appear to be farther away than those on

34   What's Out There?

the far left and right, in part because of their differences in size. Another cue to depth is the *texture gradient*. Distant objects tend to appear less detailed and smoother in texture than closer objects, and this difference can be used as a depth cue. Note that the blades of grass in the lower right corner of the figure have more detail than those on the left side of the picture. This difference in detail creates the illusion of depth. Another such perspective cue is *linear perspective*. We know that two parallel lines seem to come closer and closer together, finally touching at the horizon. We use this information to interpret the distance of objects. The edges of the road in Figure 4-6 appear to be converging. A final cue related to perspective is that of the height of objects in a horizontal plane. Objects which are more distant appear to be higher than objects which are relatively close. This is a third cue which gives us information on the relative distance of the figures in Figure 4-6.

Use of monocular depth cues to create illusions of depth is the basis of much great art. Note how Canaletto has used linear perspective and interposition to create a powerful three-dimensional effect on a flat surface (see Figure 4-7). The Escher lithograph in Figure 4-8 uses monocular depth cues "incorrectly" to create a confusing and illusory effect.

Through experience we learn to interpret the pattern of light and shadow present in a visual image. We learn to use this information to make judgments about

Photo by courtesy of the National Gallery of Art, Washington, D.C.

FIGURE 4-7 Monocular depth cues used in Canaletto's *View in Venice* create a strong feeling of three-dimensionality.

Courtesy of Vorpal Gallery, San Francisco

FIGURE 4-8 In Escher's *Waterfall*, depth cues are used "incorrectly." The towers are the same size and so appear to be equidistant; the structure beneath them indicates that the one on the right is closer. The interpositioning of the waterfall in front of the structure indicates that the tower on the left is closer.

depth. Figure 4-9 illustrates how a change in light and shadow will alter the perception of an object.

A final important cue to depth is that obtained by the movement of the observer. Look at two objects, one of which is near to you and one of which is farther away. Now move your head from side to side. The closer object appears to be moving very quickly, while the object which is farther away appears to be moving much more slowly.

36 *What's Out There?*

Our ability to perceive depth and to respond to it appropriately is, in part, a function of our experiences. One of the interesting experiential factors is the ability to engage in self-propelled movement through the environment. An experiment by Held and Hein (1963) demonstrates the importance of this factor. They designed an apparatus which enables one kitten to move at will, while a second kitten engages in no self-propelled movement (see Figure 4-10). Since the two were linked together, each had the same amount of movement, differing only in whether such movement was self-initiated. The kittens were then tested on a visual cliff apparatus (see Figure 4-11). The active kittens, when placed on the platform, always moved to the "shallow" side. The passive kittens moved to the "deep" side almost as often as to the "shallow" side. Without self-propelled movement, the kittens did not know how to respond appropriately to different depths.

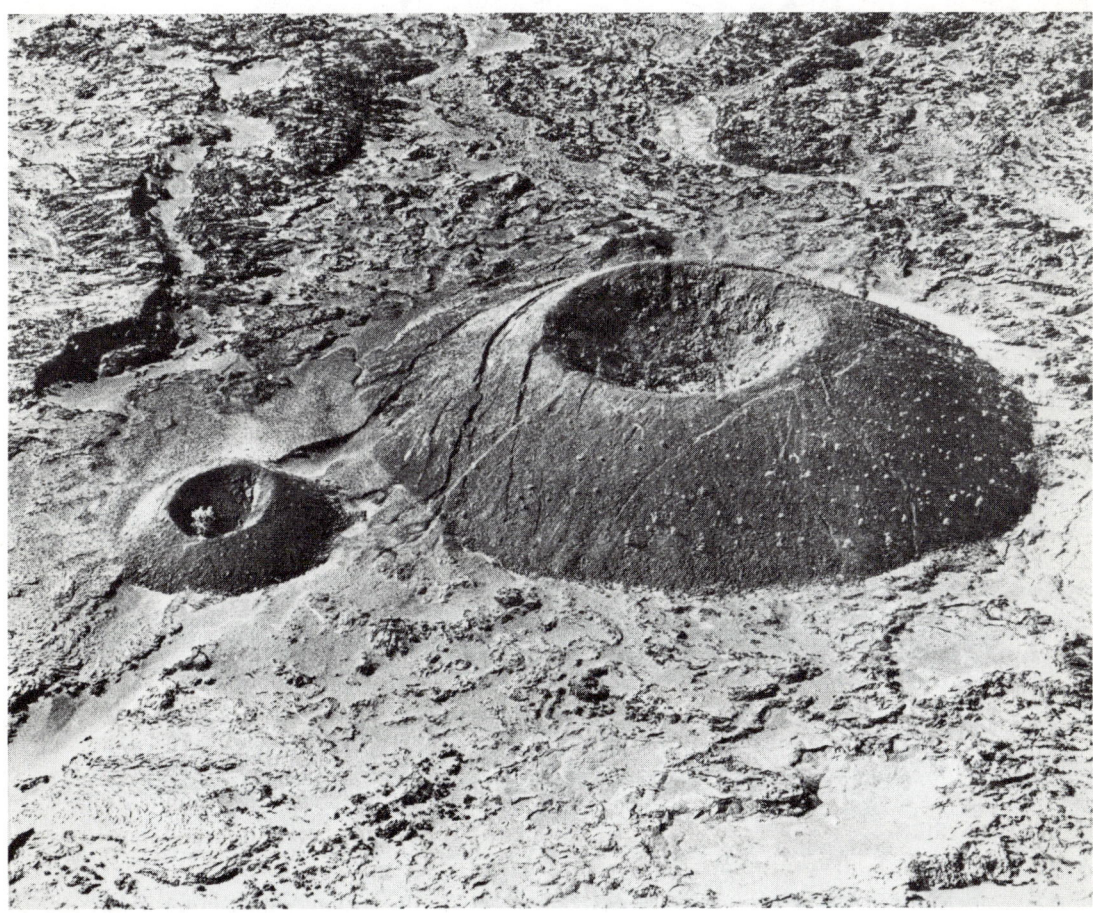

Wide World Photos

FIGURE 4-9 A view of the cinder cones on the island of Hawaii—until you turn it upside down

The Human Camera 37

FIGURE 4-10 The apparatus designed by Hein and Held to produce active and passive movement

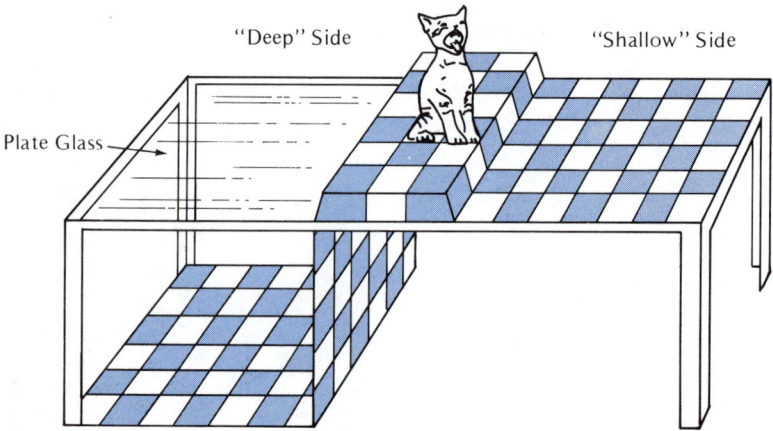

FIGURE 4-11 The visual cliff apparatus used to test depth perception

Psychophysics

As is the case with all of our senses, there is not a perfect correspondence between what is out there in the real world and what we visually perceive to be there. One of the reasons for this discrepancy is the limitation of the sensory system itself. There are some wavelengths that the receptors in our eye simply cannot record. There are changes in stimuli that are too rapid for the speed of transmission of which our nervous system is capable.

38 *What's Out There?*

There are some changes in light that are so slight that our nervous system fails to pick up the difference and records no change.

The study of the relationship between the nature of the physical stimulus and the individual's perception of that stimulus is known as *psychophysics*. Certain regular relationships have been discovered between the physical stimulus and the perception of it. In studying these relationships, three basic questions are of interest:

1. Which stimuli are perceived and which are not?
2. Is a change in the physical stimulus always perceived as a change?
3. As different stimuli are combined, is the perception of each different from its perception in isolation?

Absolute threshold. In examining which stimuli are perceived and which are not, we are studying what is known in psychophysics as the *absolute threshold*. The absolute threshold is the amount of physical energy that is necessary for perception to occur 50 percent of the time. The threshold is defined in terms of percentage of responses because the sense organs vary in their acuity and because of the problems in measurement. For example, when an individual is repeatedly presented with a stimulus close to the absolute threshold, he may perceive it on some trials but not on others. Since we cannot draw a fixed line between stimuli that are always seen and stimuli that are never seen, we rely on probabilities to define the threshold.

We noted earlier (Figure 4-1) that there are portions of the electromagnetic spectrum that cannot be seen by the human eye. Wavelengths that are shorter than those found in the violet range are said to be below the absolute threshold for the human eye. Those wavelengths in the infrared range and longer are above the human's absolute threshold.

Difference threshold. The second element of interest in studying the relationship between the physical stimulus and the perception of that stimulus is the perception of change. A stimulus may change physically, as measured by specific instruments, but we do not always see it as changed. In studying the perception of change we are examining the *difference threshold*. The question which is asked is how large must the change in the physical stimulus be before it is perceived as changed 50 percent of the time by the individual, or what is the magnitude of stimulus change necessary for there to be a *just noticeable difference* (j.n.d.). Anything which is below the difference threshold is a change in a physical stimulus which is not perceived as change — that is, we don't see the difference. In a brightly lit room, one does not notice that striking a match increases the brightness level of that room, although in terms of physical intensity there has been a measurable increase. But a match lighted in a dark room produces a clear perception of increased brightness.

Perception in context. The final question in the study of the relationship between the physical stimulus and the perception of it is how the perception of a particular stimulus changes as a result of changes in

The Human Camera

FIGURE 4-12 An example of simultaneous contrast. The gray circle reflects a constant amount of light, yet it appears to be brighter when surrounded by black than when surrounded by white.

the surrounding elements. Figure 4-12 gives an example of how the perception of a stable stimulus changes as a function of its surroundings. It illustrates *simultaneous contrast,* in which the perception of a stimulus is altered by the context in which it occurs. The gray circle in the center of the figure reflects a constant amount of light (is of equal brightness throughout). But the portion of the circle surrounded by black is seen as brighter than the portion that is surrounded by white.

The human organism also tends to impose structure on his perceptions, structure which goes beyond the simple input of the nervous impulses. That is, he does not see simply what the receptors record, but changes the recording in many different ways. Some of these changes serve to create better organization, some create more stability than actually exists. Some changes are made so that perception fits more fully into the individual's idea of the way the world should be. Some changes are made so that the perception fills the individual's unique needs which result from his own experience. These changes will be discussed more fully in the third unit of this division.

The visual sense, as we noted at the beginning of this unit, records a vast and complex amount of information. Its processing of this information is efficient, although not always a perfect representation of the outside world. But even with its "flaws," the visual system performs a miraculously complex task.

Unit 5
Tuning In

The auditory sense is second in importance only to vision. Sight and hearing may be so important in our information-gathering process in part because they are both distance senses. That is, the sensory organ (eye, ear) does not have to come in direct contact with the source of stimulation for a sensation to occur. The eye doesn't have to touch a light bulb in order to see the light, nor does the ear have to be pressed against the radio to hear the music. Hence, these senses allow quick and efficient gathering of information over a wide area of the environment. All other senses except the sense of smell (olfaction) are contact senses: the sense organ must be in direct physical contact with the source of stimulation in order for a sensation to occur.

Concentrate for a minute on the wide range of sensory information you are receiving at this time. Now, mentally eliminate each sensation that results from a stimulus whose source is not in physical contact with the sense organ. Although the weight and texture of the book in your hand would still be sensed, the color and words would be gone. Although you would still feel the clothes on your body and be aware of your body's position, you would no longer be aware of the color or pattern of your clothes nor hear the noise caused by a shift in the position of your body. A great deal of information is lost by elimination of the distance senses. And if contact with the sense organ were required for sensation, the efficiency of our information-gathering process would be greatly reduced.

In order to understand how the auditory sense operates, we must answer the same three questions which were asked in relation to vision:

1. What is the nature of the physical stimulus (sound)?
2. How is the physical energy transformed into neural energy, and how is it transmitted within the organism?
3. How is this neural energy that is received by the brain translated into the sounds we perceive?

The Physical Stimulus

The physical stimulus in audition is a sound wave. The sound wave is a form of mechanical energy which causes compression and expansion of the molecules

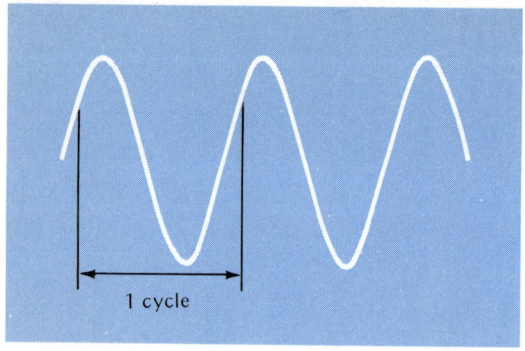

FIGURE 5-1 A sound wave

in the air. If one strikes the string of a guitar, it vibrates. This motion causes changes in the molecules of air which surround the string. As the string moves to the left, it compresses the air through which it passes. As it moves to the right, the molecules to the left expand and those to the right contract. This process creates a sound wave, as pictured in Figure 5-1.

The auditory stimulus, like the visual stimulus, has three components: *frequency, amplitude,* and *complexity.*

Frequency. The frequency of the wave refers to how fast it vibrates. More specifically, frequency is recorded as the number of cycles of a sound wave per second. One cycle is the total vibration of the wave, or one entire movement from compression to expansion and back to the original point of compression. The frequency of vibration of the auditory stimulus is heard as the pitch of the sound — the higher the frequency (the faster the vibration), the higher the pitch of the perceived sound (see Figure 5-2). If one looks at the strings of a guitar or of a piano, one will notice that they vary in their thickness. The heavier or thicker strings vibrate relatively slowly and produce low-pitched sounds. The lighter or thinner strings vibrate much more quickly, producing high-pitched sounds.

Amplitude. This aspect of the physical stimulus for audition refers to the extent of expansion and compression of the molecules. Pictorially it can be seen as the height of the wave, or how far off the baseline the wave extends (see Figure 5-3). The amplitude of the stimulus is heard as the loudness of the sound. The greater the amplitude of the sound wave, the louder the sound.

Complexity. The tones we have talked

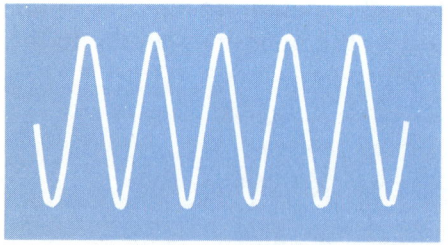 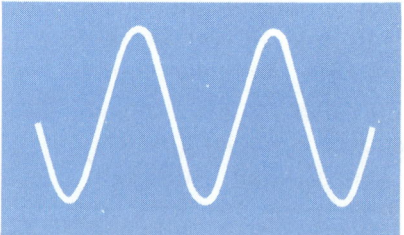

FIGURE 5-2 Two sound waves of different frequency. The sound wave on the left has a higher frequency than the one on the right, and so would be heard as having a higher pitch.

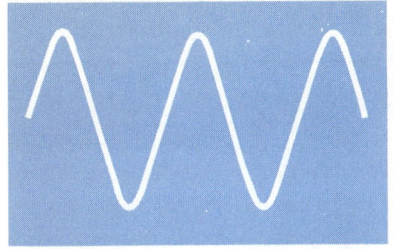 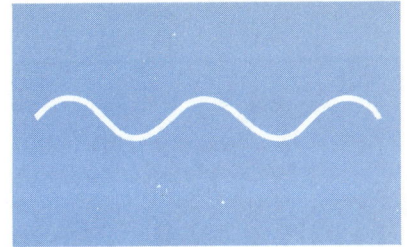

FIGURE 5-3 Two sound waves of different amplitude. The sound wave on the left has a greater amplitude than the one on the right, and so would be heard as louder.

about so far are what are called *pure tones*. That is, the tone is composed of sound waves of a single frequency. In the world outside the laboratory, such tones seldom occur. Rather, the sounds we hear are complex, made up of many different tones. When a particular string of a guitar is struck, it vibrates as a whole at a certain frequency *(fundamental tone)*. But the various parts of the string are vibrating also and creating sound waves of different frequencies. The additional sounds, called *overtones,* have less amplitude than the fundamental tone but have an important effect on what we hear. The perception of complexity is called the *timbre* of the sound.

From Physical Stimulus to Neural Energy

The receptor for sound is the ear, and it is this organ which receives the sound wave and transforms it into neural energy. As the sound waves enter the ear, they pass through the *auditory canal* (see Figure 5-4). At the end of this canal is a sensitive membrane called the *eardrum*. The eardrum is a thin membrane which vibrates as a result of the impact of the sound waves. The eardrum then transmits the sounds to the three small bones in the middle ear, known as the *hammer, anvil, and stirrup* (or, more technically, the *malleus, incus, and stapes*). The last of these bones, the stirrup, is attached to a membrane called the *oval window*. The vibration of the stirrup is transmitted to the oval window, which in turn conducts the sound to the *cochlea*. Located in the cochlea are hair cells which serve as the basic receptor for sound. The movement of the oval window causes changes in the cochlea which are recorded by the hair cells, transforming the physical energy into neural energy. This neural energy is then transmitted by the auditory nerve to various areas of the brain.

Translation of Neural Energy Into Auditory Perception

AFFERENT CODE FOR AUDITION

We noted in the unit on vision that the afferent code is the code that translates the neural energy from the receptors into perception. There is an afferent code for audition as there is for vision, and it translates the neural energy into the perception of a sound.

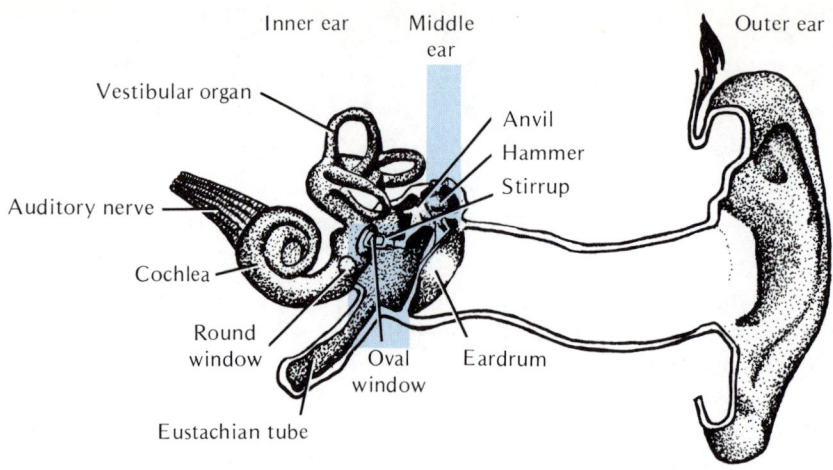

FIGURE 5-4 The human ear

The code for loudness involves the number of nerve impulses which are produced by the incoming stimulus. As the intensity of the stimulus increases, the number of nerve impulses generated by the hair cells in the cochlea is increased, and this is interpreted as increased loudness. The pitch of the sound is coded by the location within the cochlea from which the nervous impulses are transmitted: the hair cells are located along the length of the interior part of the cochlea, and different locations are related to different pitches of the sound waves received.

The exact manner of coding of pitch and of loudness is not fully established, making the above statements partially speculative. In the case of the afferent code for timbre, however, not even a speculative statement can be made. There is little evidence of how the complexity of the stimulus is coded for translation into perception.

LOCALIZATION OF SOUND

Audition, as noted before, is a distance sense. As a result, the sounds are not only recorded and heard, they are localized. That is, when we hear a sound we are generally able to locate its source. If someone calls your name from a distance, you immediately turn in his direction even if he was not visible when he spoke to you. How do we know where the sound comes from? What cues do we use to locate the sound? The primary cue is related to the physical structure of the sense organ — that is, we have two ears located in different places. This difference in location causes the sound waves reaching the ears to differ in three ways:

1. A sound that comes from a source to our right strikes the right ear a fraction of a second before it strikes the left ear. We have the ability to discriminate this small difference in time, enabling

44 *What's Out There?*

us to tell whether the sound came from the right or the left.
2. There is a slight difference in the amplitude of the sounds striking the two ears. If a sound originates at the right side of the head, the amplitude is greater for the stimulus reaching the right ear than for the stimulus reaching the left ear. Perceptually this means that the sound is slightly louder in the right ear than it is in the left ear.
3. The sounds arriving at the two ears are said to be out of phase with one another. As noted, the sound wave arrives at the two ears at different times. This means that while the right ear may be recording the sound wave at one point in its cycle, the left ear is recording the same wave at a different point in its cycle. Thus the brain is receiving two different "pictures" of the same sound in much the same way that it receives two different pictures of the same visual image from the two eyes.

Our accuracy in localizing sound is greatest when the source is directly opposite one of our ears. As the source of the sound moves more toward the front of our head, the back of our head, or directly overhead, the accuracy of our ability to locate the sound decreases.

Psychophysics

In the same way that what we see is not a perfect representation of the physical stimulus for vision, the perception of a sound is not a fully accurate representation of the physical energy produced by the source. Psychophysics studies the same types of relationships between the auditory stimulus and the perception of this stimulus as were discussed in relation to vision.

Absolute threshold. There are absolute thresholds for sound that represent the amount of physical energy which can be perceived 50 percent of the time. There are sounds whose frequency is too low or too high to be perceived. Although human beings cannot hear the sounds of these frequencies, they can be heard by other animals. Bats and dogs can hear sounds at frequencies far above those that we can hear. The dog whistle is based on knowledge of this ability. When we blow it, we hear nothing. The dog, however, does hear it and comes running. Our insensitivity to sounds of very low frequency is perhaps a blessing. If we perceived these sounds we would hear all of the vibrations of our own bodies.

There is also an absolute threshold for the intensity of a sound. If the intensity is too low, the sound is too soft and we do not hear it. As a sound increases in intensity, it reaches a level at which, although we can hear it, it causes pain and damage to the ear. Extensive exposure to extremely loud sounds can cause serious damage, resulting in some loss of hearing. This damage has been found in rock musicians and in individuals who work around jet airplanes.

Difference threshold. Difference thresholds exist for audition as they do for vision. Some changes in the frequency, amplitude, or complexity of a tone are so small that we cannot hear them. We notice no change in the sound, although a change in the physical stimulus can be recorded.

Perception in context. Perception of the auditory stimulus changes as a function of the context in which the perception occurs. The frequency and the amplitude of the sound waves interact to affect the perception of the pitch and the loudness. Tones of low frequency sound louder than high-frequency tones of exactly the same amplitude. Similarly, two tones of equal frequency will be perceived as having different pitch if the tones differ in amplitude.

The auditory sense does not appear as crucial to us in our day-to-day functioning as does vision. This may be partly because we concentrate more on the use of vision than we do on hearing. When one loses the use of his eyes, however, hearing becomes the primary source of information about the world. The blind individual attends to the auditory cues more fully and uses the information he obtains from them much more completely than does the sighted individual. Those who can see frequently use their eyes to check on information that has been obtained from the ears. We hear a car and turn to look for it, hear a crash and look to see what has broken. The blind individual cannot perform the visual double-check. But the effectiveness and mobility which a blind individual can develop attests to the fact that the ears can provide a vast amount of crucial information.

The real importance of audition in our lives is demonstrated, however, in individuals who became deaf. Emotional disturbance occurs more frequently in such people than in those who are blind. This appears to be because loss of hearing cuts off our communication with other people. Although nonverbal communication through facial expression and body movement is important, verbal communication is our main channel for social interaction. Its sudden loss when an individual loses his hearing can have serious emotional effects.

Unit 6
Change That Is Not Change

A radio is playing and we are studying. When the program is suddenly interrupted for a special news bulletin, our attention is drawn to the radio and we realize we have not heard anything on the radio for the past hour.

Five people witness a bank robbery committed by a single man in broad daylight. All have ample time to observe him and have a clear view of him. The police arrive shortly after the robber escapes and get five different descriptions of the man.

We walk into a chemistry lab and are instantly aware that the room reeks with the odor of sulphur. A short time later we are unable to smell anything, although the sulphur is still in use.

Why? Surely the sound waves from the radio are not being diverted away from the ear. The man the eyewitnesses saw was a single individual, not five. And the chemical has not stopped producing the odor.

This unit will be devoted to looking at a wide range of factors which will help to explain the frequent discrepancies between the physical stimulus as it is received and recorded by the receptor (sense organ) and the stimulus as it is perceived by the individual. Some of these factors are related to the physical nature of the receptor mechanism. Some are related to the nature of the individual as a whole — his way of approaching the world, his learning and experiences, his expectations.

Adaptation

One of the basic factors which affects perception is adaptation. When we go into the bright sunlight from a dimly lit house, our eyes hurt and we are unable to see clearly. In time, however, we get used to the bright light so that it no longer bothers us and our vision is clear. When walking into a room in which there is a strong unpleasant odor, we are intensely aware of it. In time, however, we get used to it and we are no longer even aware of the odor. This process of "getting used to" stimuli is the process of adaptation.

More precisely, adaptation refers to a decrease in the sensitivity of a particular sensory receptor in the presence of constant stimulation. The phenomenon of adaptation applies not only to the senses of vision and olfaction, but to other senses as well. In general, the various receptors gradually reduce the input from a source of stimulation that is constant and unchanging. It is as though the receptor or central nervous system decides that no more information can be derived from this constant stimulus, so no more time will be spent on it.

Attention

A more active factor involved in perception is attention. There is a multitude of stimuli acting on our sensory receptors at any moment. We perceive or are aware of only a very few of these stimuli. We focus our attention on certain of the stimuli and block out all others. Shift your attention now from the reading of this book to your feet. In the process of doing that, you have become aware of the pressure stimulation of the shoe on your foot — a source of stimulation which was there before but of which, because your attention was focused elsewhere, you were unaware.

FACTORS DETERMINING ATTENTION

There are a number of factors that determine which of the many stimuli acting on our receptors will gain our attention. Stimuli that are unusual or are particularly intense will attract our attention. When we walk down a busy street we don't see the people who pass us — unless someone comes into our visual field who is dressed in an extreme style or who is unusually tall. We are not aware of the sound or sight of the traffic until one of the drivers suddenly honks his horn.

Our internal needs, our expectancies, and our experiences also determine the focus of our attention. Nothing stands out on a printed page more clearly than one's own name. Training in a particular field of study is a type of experience which focuses attention as well. A psychologist will immediately "tune in" to a radio program which shifts to a discussion of psychological topics, while the biologist will not.

PHYSIOLOGICAL CORRELATES

There is apparently a physiological mechanism which underlies the psychological phenomenon of attention. In an early experiment on this phenomenon, the electrical activity of the cochlear nucleus of a cat was measured (Hernandez-Peon, Scherrer, and Jouvet, 1956). During this recording, the cat's ear was stimulated by a series of clicking sounds. As can be seen from the top portion of Figure 6-1, the sound produced an electrical response, indicating that the cat "heard" the sound. While the sounds continued, a jar containing two mice was placed in front of the cat. The electrical responses from the ear decreased dramatically. As the cat's attention shifted to the mice, he stopped receiving electrical impulses resulting from the sound stimulation.

There is apparently a mechanism in the brain which serves as a "gating mechanism." This mechanism allows reception of stimulation from one sensory channel while blocking out information from other sensory systems. It seems to send a message to all receptors — except those receiving the information upon which attention is focused — not to transmit any incoming information because the brain is busy at the moment. This mechanism is of crucial importance, for it allows the brain to deal in an efficient manner with incoming stimulation and receive only the amount of information which does not overload it, thereby preventing reduction in the effectiveness of its functioning.

Aftereffects

Perception of a stimulus for a period of time can alter the functioning of the receptor after the stimulus is removed. If you stare at a red surface for a period of time, then look at a gray surface, you will see green rather than gray. If you look at a bright light for a brief period of time, when you look away you will see spots of various colors. These phenomena are *aftereffects*. That is, they show the effect of a stimulus on a sense organ after the stimulus is removed. Aftereffects can also be produced in sensory modalities other than vision. Prolonged stimulation of the ear by a loud noise may produce ringing in the ear after the noise has stopped.

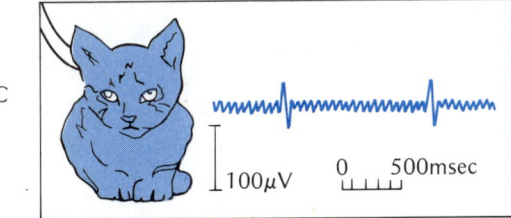

FIGURE 6-1 Recordings of the neural activity in the cochlear nucleus. A shows neural activity in response to two clicks. In B, the cat is looking at two mice in a bottle, and, although the clicks are still being sounded, the activity in the cochlear nucleus is dramatically reduced. In C, the mice have been removed and the neural activity has returned to normal.

Constancy

The world around us is in a constant state of flux. As a result, our sense organs are bombarded with constantly changing energy patterns. Yet we don't perceive the changes, even though the organs have the ability to record them. We tend to impose an order on our perceptions so that they remain relatively stable or constant.

In discussing perception of an object, we can make a distinction between the actual physical object *(distal stimulus)* and the pattern of physical stimulation on the sense organ *(proximal stimulus)*.

Constancy refers to the fact that our perception of an object is usually more a result of the dimensions of the distal stimulus than of the proximal stimulus.

Size constancy. In Figure 6-2, the actual size of the tree (the distal stimulus) is the same for both views. However, the dimensions of the retinal images (the proximal stimulus) are quite different, due to the different viewing distances. Nonetheless, in both instances we would "see" the trees as being of the same height. This is an example of size constancy. It appears that we take the sensory image, correct for the distance of the object, and come up with a fairly accurate perception of actual size. As long as the cues to distance are reasonably clear, we are quite accurate in our perception of the actual size of an object despite dramatic differences in the energy pattern at the receptor.

Brightness constancy. The perception of brightness also illustrates the constancy effect. The perception of brightness refers to how white, gray, or black an object appears. Physically, it is a function of the intensity of the light reflected from an object. Yet a white shirt looks as bright in the sunlight as it does in a dim room — in

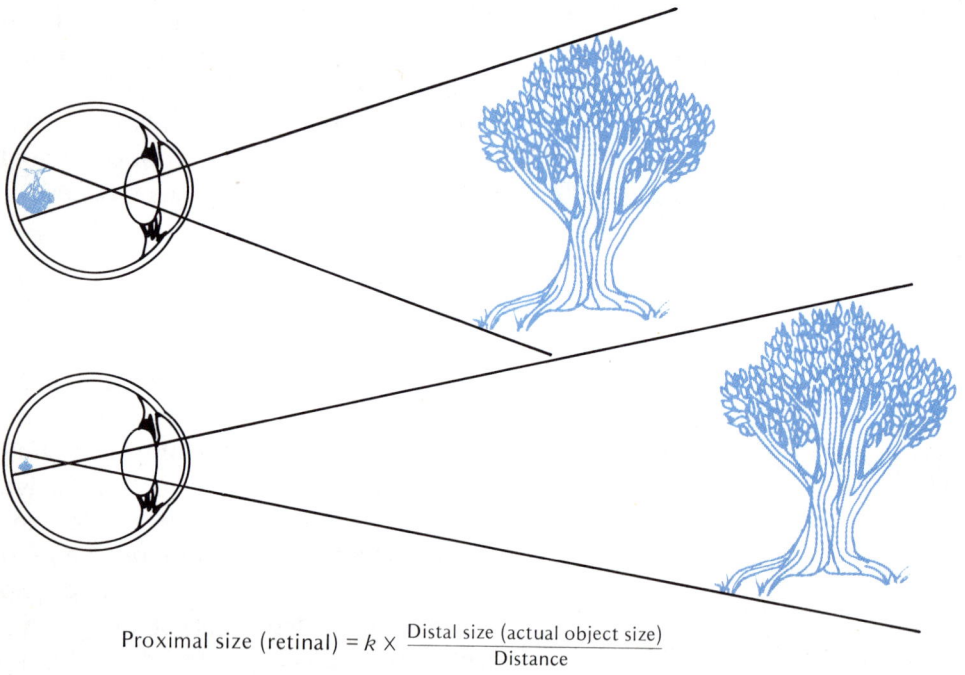

Proximal size (retinal) = $k \times \frac{\text{Distal size (actual object size)}}{\text{Distance}}$

FIGURE 6-2 An example of size constancy. In the formula, k is the distance from the retina to the lens (assumed to be constant). It is evident that although the size of the retinal image (proximal size) changes, the actual size of the object (distal size) is perceived as constant.

spite of vast differences in the amount of light reflected. Here again we make corrections in the incoming sensory information in order to impose some stability on the world.

Shape constancy. Finally, our perception of shape shows constancy. There is rarely an exactly rectangular image projected on the retina when we look at a book or a window, yet we can quickly and accurately identify the shape of these objects. This is true of most of the objects with which we have frequent contact. In spite of the many different shapes that each object forms in its retinal image, we perceive the object as having a stable shape.

Organization

We noted in the section on constancy that various pieces of information about a perceived object are integrated in order to come up with a fairly accurate and stable perception of the object. Another form of integration of the components of the sensation is found in perceptual organization. This area of perception has been extensively examined by the Gestalt psychologists. This school of psychology stresses that perception is not simply the sum of sensory elements stimulated, but that the very process of perception adds something. The basic law of the Gestalt approach is the *law of Prägnanz,* which states that any perception will be as "good" as possible. Goodness of perception refers to the simplest, most consistent, and most stable perception. A number of principles of perception have been derived from this basic law.

Similarity. When a complex pattern of stimuli is presented, we tend to organize it in a way that places the similar objects together. *A* in Figure 6-3 is not seen as having a stable overall pattern. Rather, each dark and light element is seen as relatively isolated. In *B,* however, the organization is immediate and compelling. We see rows of dark and rows of light. Because of the factor of similarity, the dark squares are grouped together and the light squares are grouped together.

Proximity. A second principle of perceptual organization states that objects that are close together or in proximity to one another tend to be grouped together. In *A* of Figure 6-4 we see six separate lines. When we look at *B,* however, we tend to perceive not six separate lines but three pairs of lines. The immediate grouping of elements which takes place when viewing *B* is due to the pattern of proximity.

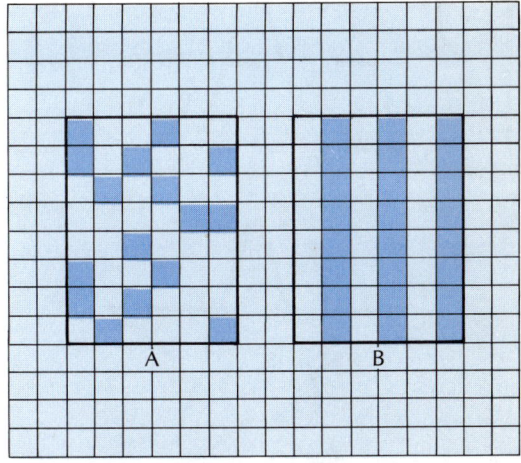

FIGURE 6-3 Perceptual organization according to the principle of similarity

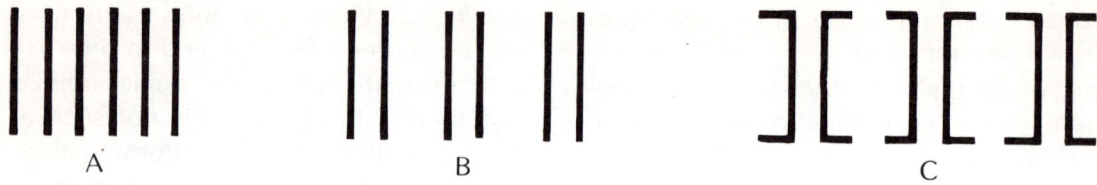

FIGURE 6-4   Perceptual organization according to the principle of proximity

Closure. In order to obtain the best possible organization of a sensation, we tend to close or fill in spaces. We have no trouble reading the word in Figure 6-5 or identifying the shape pictured. The sensation is incomplete — nothing more than a series of short lines. But we fill in spaces, obtain the closure, and are readily able to identify the forms.

Figure-ground. One of the most basic organizational principles involves the division of perception into figure and ground. Generally the shape or color of an object makes it stand out. It is perceived as a figure which is located in front of what appears to be the more distant and continuous ground. The immediacy of this form of perceptual organization is made clear by examination of Figure 6-6. You immediately see the man and the chair as figures, standing out against a continuous background. Sometimes the cues as to which portion is figure and which is ground are not clear, producing what is called a *reversible figure* (Figure 6-7).

Illusions

Most of the factors discussed so far increase the stability, structure, or efficiency of perception. But these very factors, this imposition of interpretation upon the incoming sensory stimulation, can cause error in perception, or what is called *illusion*. The relationship among elements of stimulation can cause us to make inaccurate interpretations of the incoming information.

In Figure 6-8, which of the circles in *A* is larger? Which line in *B* is longer? In both cases they are equal, although we interpret them differently because of the different contexts in which they appear. In *C*

FIGURE 6-5   Perceptual organization according to the principle of closure

Courtesy of Museum of Fine Arts, Boston

FIGURE 6-6 El Greco's *Fray Felix Hortensio Paravicino* provides an example of a clear figure-ground contrast.

FIGURE 6-7 A reversible figure

of Figure 6-8, are the lines straight or curved? All are straight, but once again the context alters the perception so that it is inaccurate. D in this figure illustrates how cues to depth can be used to produce inaccurate perceptions. Because the two vertical lines appear to come together, we interpret them in terms of the linear perspective cue, seeing the top as farther away than the bottom. In addition, we know that the more distant of two objects of equal size appears smaller. The image on the retina of the top horizontal line is the same size as that of the bottom horizontal line. Since the top line is seen as farther away, it "must be" larger. Cues to depth can also create impossible figures (Figure 6-9). This figure is seen as three-pronged at the bottom and U-shaped at the top, but it is not possible to see a single image of this figure.

Experiential Factors

Personal experience and motivational factors also affect perception, giving it a

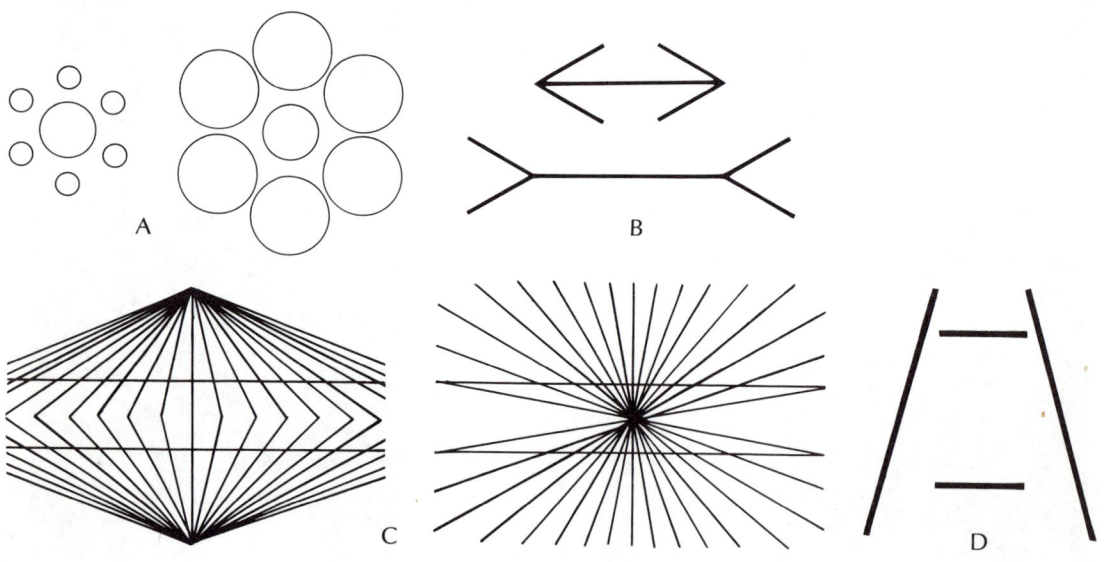

FIGURE 6-8 What do you see? (A) Are the two central circles equal in size? (B) Are the two horizontal lines the same length? (C) Are the horizontal lines parallel? (D) Which horizontal line is longer?

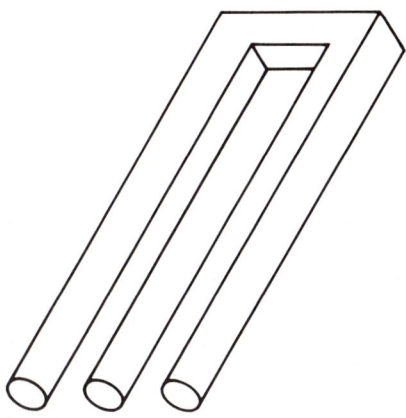

FIGURE 6-9 An impossible figure

quality of uniqueness and individuality. One's expectancy or set can be a powerful determinant of perception. A set is a predisposition to behave or respond in a certain way. It can force us to perceive things that are not there and to fail to perceive things that are there. If we expect to receive a telephone call from someone, the voice on the other end of the line will sound like that of the expected caller. If we expect to have a certain question on an exam, we may misperceive the actual question and give an answer for the question we expected.

A great many experimental studies have been conducted to demonstrate the effect of set or expectancy on perception. In one study (Carmichael, Hogan, and Walter, 1932) subjects were briefly shown a series of ambiguous figures (see Figure 6-10). The name given to each of the figures differed for the two groups of subjects. For half of the subjects, the figures were described according to the terms listed in Word List I of Figure 6-10, while the other subjects were given Word List II to describe the same figures. After briefly viewing the objects, the subjects were asked to draw what they had seen. Comparison of the two sets of reproduced figures indicates that what the subjects "saw" and remembered was affected by what they expected to see on the basis of the verbal label of the object.

INDIVIDUAL MOTIVES

An individual's drives or motives can also affect what he perceives. Often such perceptions serve to fill a need that is very strong at the time of the perception, so that we "see what we want to see." The mirage seen by the parched individual struggling through the desert is an example of a perception which fills a need. In one study, McClelland and Atkinson (1948) tested subjects who had not eaten for from one to sixteen hours. The subjects were shown blurred, ambiguous pictures and asked to identify what they saw. Those who had not eaten for sixteen hours reported seeing food in the pictures much more often than those who had eaten just prior to the experiment.

Social motives as well as physiological needs can have an effect on perception. Individuals vary in their need for achievement. Some have an extremely high need to excel, while others do not. In one study (McClelland and Liberman, 1949) words were flashed briefly before the subjects, and they were required to identify them. Some of the words were related to achievement (e.g., *strive*), and others were not. Subjects who scored high on a test of need achievement identified the achievement-related words more quickly than did subjects with low achievement needs.

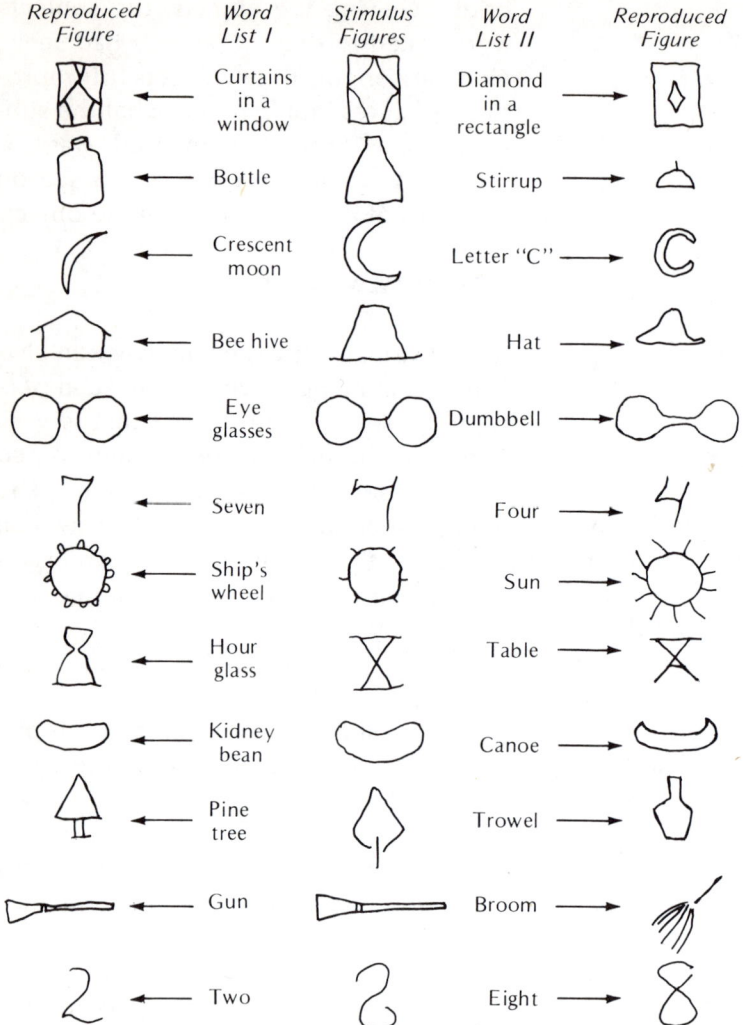

FIGURE 6-10 An illustration of the effects of expectancy on perception. The stimulus figures were presented to subjects and identified according to the descriptions used in either Word List I or Word List II. Note the differences in the figures reproduced by the subjects in the two groups.

Perhaps one of the most crucial factors in perception is the individual's unique experience. How do we know the book is a rectangle? Because we know that a rectangle is a figure in which each pair of opposite parallel sides is equal and the sides are joined by right angles. Knowing this, we need only "look" at the object to see if it is a rectangle. Observations on individuals who gain sight after being

56 What's Out There?

blind from birth, however, indicate that the knowledge of what an object is and looking at it are not enough for visual identification (London, 1960). We need experience, or practice, in looking. Observations on a ten-year-old boy who had suffered from cataracts from birth, preventing all but light-dark vision, support the importance of experience. After the cataracts were removed, the child was unable to name objects that he saw. He could recognize things only by touching them, using the sense with which he had experience. He could not distinguish the number of any set of objects by vision alone, or recognize simple shapes. He was also unable to judge distances. He ran into objects and could only avoid them by using his hands to guide him. Only after extensive experience can such people learn to use the information which they obtain through their eyes.

The culture in which we live has a crucial effect on our experiences and in turn on our perceptions. Turnbull (1961) reports an experience with a member of the Bambuti pygmy tribe of the Congo. The pygmy's name was Kenge, and, like all members of his tribe, he had always lived in the dense forest. The denseness of the forest prevents vision of all but fairly close objects; thus, he had little experience with viewing objects in the distance. Turnbull took Kenge onto a plain where a herd of buffalo was visible a great distance away. Kenge asked what type of insects the buffalo were. When told that they were buffalo, he laughed and asked not to be told such stupid stories. He could not accept the fact that they were buffalo. As they drove closer to the animals, Kenge believed that witchcraft was being performed to make the animals grow larger. He was not being primitive or superstitious — he was trying to explain a perception which was beyond his realm of experience. Similar types of explanation crop up in our culture when people "see" objects flying in the sky: they must be flying saucers sent by some alien power.

Perception, then, is a complex experience, depending on the state of the receptor organ, what is currently taking place in the brain, the structure of the stimulus, and the needs and experiences of the individual. It is little wonder that two people looking at the same person will see different things and that two people listening to the same record will hear different music.

Unit 7
Senses — There Are More Than Five

This unit is devoted to what are commonly called the "minor" senses. They are labeled minor in part because we do not use them as extensively nor pay them as much attention as we do the "major" senses of vision and audition. Their lack of importance may be due also to the fact that vision and audition appear to be better developed in human beings.

But we also live in a society which tends to downgrade the very use of the minor senses. For example, we seem to be moving toward an odorless society because our social norms label a wide range of odors offensive. We have sprays and powders for almost every part of the human body — and have thus largely removed all human odors. We have sprays for our homes as well to remove all possible odor. Taste is also losing its importance. In a society of packaged food ("just add water"), more and more of what we eat tastes the same. Nationwide fast-food chains have caused eating out, too, to acquire a sameness. No matter where you go, McDonald's hamburgers all taste the same. As for the sense of touch, only babies can enjoy it — and not for long. Watch young children and observe the joy they get from touching.

Before too many months have passed, however, restrictions are imposed. Glass can't be touched because it might break. Tables and walls can't be touched because they will show fingerprints. Bugs can't be touched because they might bite. Dirt can't be touched because it will make one dirty. Furniture can't be touched because you get it dirty. And most important, people can't be touched unless they are members of your family. These minor senses may be less well developed than vision and audition because they get so little exercise.

These senses are so minor that many people don't know how many senses there are. The commonly cited number is five: touch, taste, smell, sight, and hearing. In fact there are many more. The sense of touch alone is actually made up of the senses of pressure, pain, cold, and warmth. In this unit we will examine all the remaining senses, for a total of close to a dozen sensory systems.

Taste

To the sense of taste is attributed most of the joys of eating. But in fact the taste sense is not the sole source of enjoyment

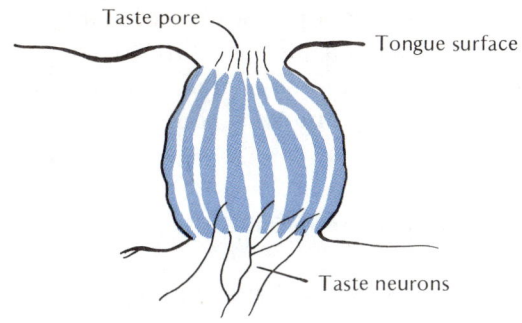

FIGURE 7-1 A taste bud

of food. Texture, temperature, and especially smell make important contributions to this enjoyment. Taste is probably one of our least important senses. It may make life more pleasurable, but it contributes little to gaining crucial information about the world around us.

The primary receptor for taste is the *taste bud*. The normal adult has about ten thousand taste buds, which are scattered over the tip, sides, and back of the tongue, with a few located in the back of the mouth and throat. The taste buds are located in the *papillae* of the tongue, which are the small bumps which you can see scattered over its surface. Within each taste bud is a group of taste receptors. Each of these receptors, called a hair cell, contains a small hair which extends into the space between the papillae (Figure 7-1). When we eat, the food is chewed and mixed with saliva. This process dissolves the chemicals in the food so that they can enter the spaces where the hairs are located. This dissolved food, when it comes in contact with the taste receptor, sets off the reaction which fires a nerve attached to the hair cell and sends the message to the brain.

The receptors respond to four basic kinds of taste: salt, sour, sweet, and bitter. The sensitivity to each of these tastes varies on different parts of the tongue, with maximal sensitivity to each taste located in the portions of the tongue illustrated in Figure 7-2.

Smell

The primary stimulus for smell is a chemical substance which is carried in the air. For a chemical in the air to be smelled, it must be gaseous or volatile. The air containing the gaseous chemical enters the nose and passes into the lungs. Along the way, at the top of the nasal passages, the

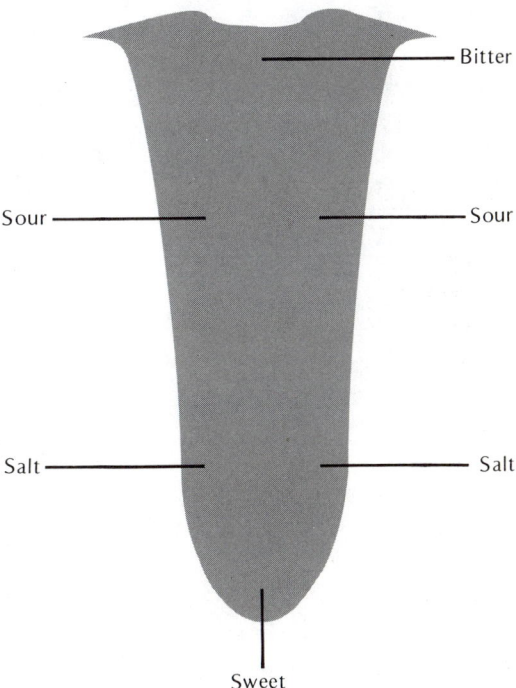

FIGURE 7-2 The location on the tongue of sensitivity to four basic tastes

Senses — There Are More Than Five 59

air passes the location of the receptor for smell — the *olfactory epithelium* (Figure 7-3). This structure contains millions of receptor cells which are responsible for the perception of odor. When breathing normally, we are aware of some odors. However, if we want to smell something carefully and completely, we sniff or breathe in more strongly. This sniffing makes the odor seem more prominent. This is because the olfactory epithelium is not on the direct pathway of the air. The strong intake of air forces the odorous chemical into better contact with the receptors, thus improving our perception of the smell.

STEREOCHEMICAL THEORY

Researchers who have studied smell have attempted to identify basic odors similar to the basic tastes. The attempt so

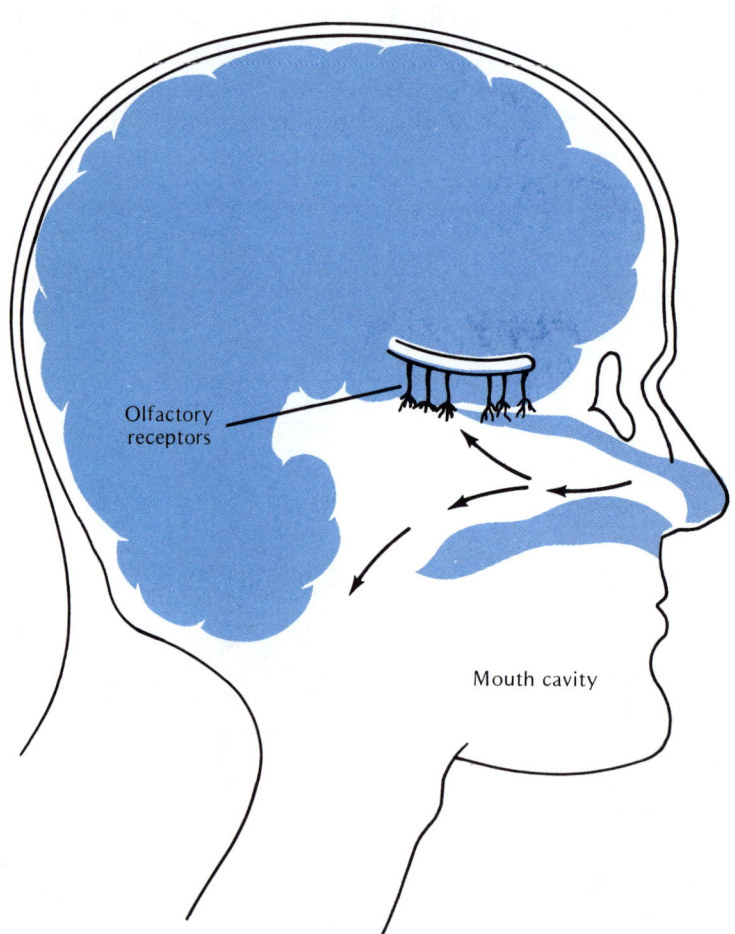

FIGURE 7-3 The location of olfactory receptors

60 *What's Out There?*

far has not been wholly successful. Each theory of how we smell includes a different grouping of basic odors. Although no single theory has gained strong support or widespread acceptance at the present time, one of the most popular is the stereochemical theory (Amoore, Johnston, and Rubin, 1964). This theory is based on the knowledge that the different chemicals we smell have different molecular shapes (Figure 7-4). These shapes correspond to hollow areas of various shapes in the receptor area. The molecule of camphor and other substances with a similar odor are spherical in shape and fit into a bowl-shaped depression in the olfactory epithelium. Chemicals with a musky odor are disc-shaped and fit into a disc-shaped depression in the olfactory epithelium. According to this theory, there are seven basic odors, five of which have distinctive shapes corresponding to hollows in the receptor area: floral, camphorous, musky, minty, and ethereal. The other two basic odors, pungent and putrid, cause sensations of smell as a result of the pattern of electrical charge which they create, rather than their particular shape.

Although this theory can deal with the basic or common component in each of the seven odors, it does not yet handle the great amount of variety within each odor. We can all readily identify the odor of mint, yet we can also clearly distinguish between peppermint and spearmint. Exactly how we do this is still unclear. The answer lies in further research on the interaction between the chemical components of gaseous materials and the physiological responses of the olfactory receptors and the brain.

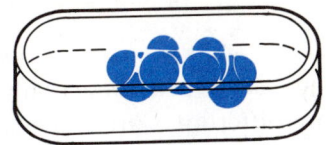
Ethereal

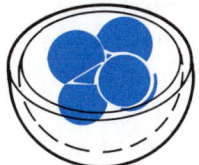
Camphoraceous

Musky

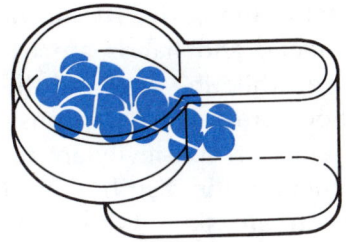
Floral

Minty

FIGURE 7-4 The characteristic shape of the molecules of the five basic odors and the shape of the corresponding depressions in the olfactory epithelium

Skin Senses

What we usually call touch is actually made up of four different skin senses: pressure, pain, cold, and warmth. In an effort to understand the location and functioning of the skin senses, the various areas of the skin have been mapped. That is, stimuli for the four different skin senses have been applied to points all over the body to determine which points are sensitive to which stimuli. It has been found that the skin has more spots that are sensitive to pain than to any other of the skin senses. The next largest number of sensitive spots are those responsive to pressure, followed by those sensitive to cold and those sensitive to warmth.

The sensation of pressure or touch arises from the movement or deformation of the skin. Our sensitivity to touch varies in different parts of the body. The tip of the tongue, fingers, and hands are extremely sensitive, while the heel and the trunk of the body are relatively insensitive. The differences in sensitivity are related to differences in the distribution of pressure spots in the skin. Where the concentration of such spots is heaviest, we find the greatest sensitivity.

PAIN

The sense of pain is probably the most complex of the skin senses. Not only are pain spots distributed all over the skin surface in greater frequency than pressure, warmth, or cold spots, but other sensory receptors report pain as well. An excessively bright light, loud noise, or spicy food will create a sensation of pain.

The basic stimulus for pain is described as any stimulus which is intense. The intensity of the stimulus is related to the extent of the destruction or damage it causes to body tissue, and this may be the more basic cause for the sensation of pain.

Although we spend little time thinking about this sense and do not use its information as frequently as we do information from some of our other senses, such as vision and audition, the pain sense may be the most crucial to our survival. Without the sense of pain, we have few cues to tell us when to protect ourselves from physical danger. If we touch a hot stove, we immediately pull our hand away. The quickness of the pain and of the response to it prevents serious burns. If we had no sense of pain, we would not know that we were in danger until the smell of burning flesh alerted us — and by that time, the burn would be far more serious. The pain of a sprained ankle prevents us from walking on it, thus allowing for healing and preventing more serious injury. Without this pain there is nothing to tell us not to continue walking and thereby produce even more damage. Pain serves as a cue: it notifies us that something is not right and that we should take the necessary steps to prevent the situation from becoming more serious.

Pain is clearly open to subjective interpretations, so that one type of injury may be experienced as agonizing by one individual but barely noticeable by another. Certain individuals from the Middle East can lie on a bed of nails with what appears to be little discomfort, whereas most of us could not endure such pain. In natural childbirth, many women go through the labor and delivery

BOX 7-1 ACUPUNCTURE AS ANESTHETIC

Within the past several years, the use of acupuncture as a medical technique has attracted the interest of Western scientists. Many of them have put aside their biases and have attempted to understand why it works. One of the uses of acupuncture that seems to be most successful is its use as an anesthetic. There is documentation of cases in which patients have undergone operations without pain, with acupuncture used as the only anesthetic. When the technique is used in this way, the acupuncturist inserts needles into specific points in the body. These needles are then rotated or electrically stimulated during the course of the operation.

There is evidence that this procedure eliminates pain. But how? One of the foremost psychological theories of pain offers a possible explanation for the phenomenon. According to the gate control theory of pain, two of the sources of neural input in the sensation of pain are small and large neurons from the receptors (Melzack and Wall, 1965). The small fibers are responsive to strong pain and continue to respond for long periods of time after stimulation. The large fibers are responsive mainly to low-intensity pain stimuli and respond for only a brief time after stimulation. Within the spinal pathway is a "gate" which can open or close, allowing transmission of pain messages or blocking such messages. The gate tends to open on firing of the small fibers but closes when the large fibers fire. Theoretically, then, if the large fibers are continuously stimulated with a mild pain stimulus, the fibers will continue to fire and the gate will be closed. This will prevent the transmission of nerve impulses from the small fibers to the brain, and thus prevent the perception of pain.

In one study it was found that application of a very mild electrical shock relieved or eliminated chronic pain in some patients. The same phenomenon may be occurring in acupuncture. The needles may provide mild pain stimulation, activating the large fibers and closing the gate. Thus the information from the small fibers, which are activated by the stimulation from the operative procedures, is prevented from reaching the brain. The patient feels no pain.

with little pain. Yet other women scream in agony. Some of us can hardly see a dentist's drill without feeling sharp pain, while others sit in a calm and relaxed manner throughout the process of tooth drilling without anesthesia.

Melzack and Scott (1957) have demonstrated that early experience may be a powerful determinant of the perception of pain. They found that dogs raised in isolation failed to respond to stimuli usually perceived as painful in the same way that nonisolated dogs responded. The dogs raised in isolation did not attempt to get away when their noses were touched with a lighted match. They also showed

Senses — There Are More Than Five

little if any evidence of discomfort when pricked with a pin. Pain, it seems, has its origins as much in psychological as in physical factors. The perception of pain appears to increase, often dramatically, as a result of the fear and anxiety connected with it.

COLD AND WARMTH

The ability to detect temperature depends on two separate but interacting senses: perception of cold and perception of warmth. The body has fewer cold spots than either pain or pressure spots, and even fewer warm spots. These spots do not respond to stimuli of specific temperatures as being cold or warm, but respond rather to changes in skin temperature. A stimulus that is at least 1° or 2° C lower in temperature than the current skin temperature stimulates the cold receptors and produces the perception of cold. A stimulus that is at least 1° to 2° C warmer than the skin temperature stimulates warm receptors and produces the perception of warmth. One can demonstrate how the receptors respond to change rather than to absolute temperature by filling three cups with water of different temperatures: warm, tepid, and cool. If you first place your hand in the warm water, then into the tepid, the latter feels cool. However, if you place your hand in the cool water first, the tepid water feels warm.

It has been noted that if one of the cold spots is stimulated with a fairly hot stimulus (110° F or more), there is a strong sensation of cold produced. This phenomenon is called *paradoxical cold* and is necessary for the perception of hot

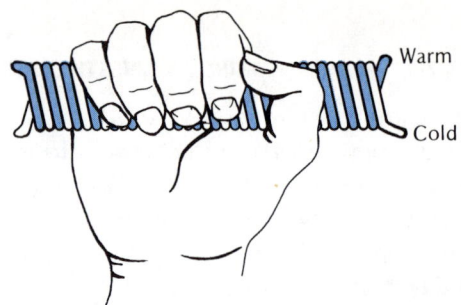

FIGURE 7-5 If only cold water or only warm water is in the grid, one gets the sensation of cold or of warmth, respectively. If both cold and warm water are run through the grid simultaneously, there is a painfully hot sensation.

stimuli. If the skin is warmed slightly, the receptors for warmth respond and we feel warmth. If the skin is cooled, the cold receptors respond and we feel cold. If the stimulus is hot (over 110°F), both receptor systems respond and produce the perception of heat, which is different from the perception of warmth. When only a cold receptor is stimulated by a hot stimulus, we perceive or feel cold — an error in perception. The need for firing of both warm and cold receptors at the same time to produce the perception of heat can cause another type of error in perception. If you touch something warm and something cool at the same time, you will quickly withdraw your hand as though burnt (Figure 7-5). The dual stimulation of the two sets of receptors produces what is called *paradoxical heat*.

Kinesthesis

The kinesthetic sense is the sense in charge of telling us "where we are at."

More specifically, it gives information on the position of the parts of our body. This sense consists of receptors in three different places:

1. Receptors in the muscles, which are stimulated whenever the muscle is stretched
2. Receptors in the tendons connecting the muscle to the bone, which are stimulated whenever the muscle contracts
3. Receptors in the joints, which are stimulated each time there is any movement in the position of the joints

The kinesthetic sense serves to give us immediate feedback on the position of all parts of the body. Because of this sense, we can walk without watching our legs and scratch our back without watching our fingers. Needless to say, our efficiency is greatly increased by the ability to move our limbs and body with automatic feedback on the motion.

Vestibular Sense

This sensory system is responsible for keeping track of the position and movement of the head. The receptor for this sense is located, together with the cochlea, in the inner ear. Because of its location, it was believed that the vestibular structure was a part of the hearing apparatus. Pierre Flourens, studying the functioning of the parts of the inner ear in the 1820s, sectioned parts of the vestibular apparatus in pigeons. He found that, although their hearing remained normal, they could no longer walk straight, could not fly, and did not hold their heads normally. It was this work which led to the discovery of the function of the vestibular sense.

The vestibular receptor comprises two subsystems. The first (Figure 7-6) is made up of three *semicircular canals:* posterior, superior, and lateral. At the base of each canal is an enlargement called the *ampulla*. Each of the semicircular canals is in a different plane so that each can

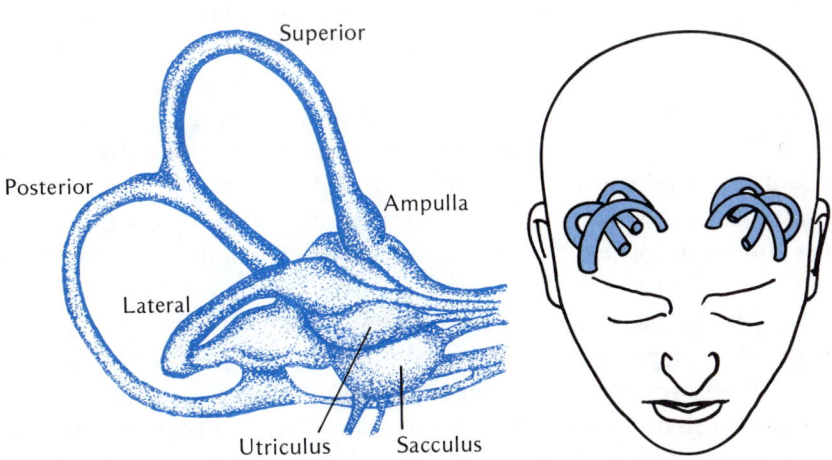

FIGURE 7-6 The vestibular system and its location in the head

respond to a different plane of movement: up-down, back-forth, and side-to-side. The canals are filled with a liquid which moves whenever the head rotates. The movement of the fluid stimulates the hairlike receptors in the ampulla, which send the message on the nature of movement to the brain. The receptors in the ampulla do not respond to continuous movement. Rather they respond to changes in rotation, either acceleration or deceleration.

The second part of the vestibular system contains the two vestibular sacs — the *utriculus* and the *sacculus*. These structures are filled with a fluid which contains tiny crystals called *otoliths*. The receptors are located along the walls of the utriculus and the sacculus. When the head is tilted or moved, the crystals come in contact with the receptors, causing sensation. This part of the vestibular sense is responsible for reporting the position of the head. Sensation arises from this system even without rotation, unlike the semicircular canals. This portion of the vestibular sense tells us if our head is upright or tilted.

Extrasensory Perception

Despite claims to the contrary, ESP is not an idea well liked by most psychologists. They are biased against the study of this phenomenon. The reasons for this bias are easy to discover. Psychology has for the past one hundred years struggled to gain acceptance as a true science. Psychology is like the nouveau riche family attempting to be acknowledged and accepted by the old, established families — physics, chemistry, and biology. In this struggle, psychology shies away from association with disreputable individuals. ESP, with its connotations of mysticism rather than science, definitely falls into the disreputable category as far as most psychologists are concerned.

Extrasensory perception includes three basic phenomena:

1. *Telepathy* involves the communication or transfer of thoughts from one person to another.
2. *Clairvoyance* involves the perception of objects or events that are not influencing the known sense organs; e.g., "seeing" someone in another room or "reading" a letter in a sealed envelope.
3. *Precognition* is awareness of an event before it occurs.

Much of the research on ESP has involved the use of cards. The typical pack consists of 25 cards of five different types, each type containing a different symbol. In experiments on telepathy, one individual views the cards one at a time and thinks of the pictured symbol while another individual acting as a receiver attempts to write the name of the symbol on each card viewed and thought of by the sender. In clairvoyance experiments, the individual tries to guess the order of the cards, which may be face down in front of him or sealed in an envelope. In precognition experiments, the subject attempts to predict which card the experimenter will display. Although the results of some of this research offers evidence for the existence of ESP, at least in the case of some individuals, the gathering and analysis of the data do not meet rigorous scientific requirements. There can be little doubt that the existence of ESP has not been clearly demonstrated.

There is more to the issue of ESP, however, than whether it has been scientifically demonstrated. There is also the issue of the attitude of psychologists toward the phenomenon. Dember and Jenkins (1970, p. 301) state that "ESP is not a viable scientific concept." Edwards (1968, p. 116) takes an even stronger position, stating that "time need not be spent upon a will-o'-the-wisp quality of a very small percentage of the population of normal individuals, a quality that, furthermore, does not mesh with any information we have about perception. As a very small, elusive, and hard-to-believe phenomenon, it is perhaps justifiably ignored."

These statements reflect not only the lack of convincing evidence for ESP but a strong and definite bias against even the study of the phenomenon. The proponents of ESP have little more than the belief in ESP to support them. But many great scientific discoveries have been made by individuals who had only a belief that they were right and who persisted in pursuing that belief. Because we do not know of any form of energy or stimulus that can be transmitted to account for ESP does not mean that such energy does not exist. Because we do not know of any receptor structure for receiving this type of information does not mean that there are no such receptors.

Psychologists need not all believe in or study ESP. But the field should create an atmosphere that encourages discovery of any kind, an atmosphere that cannot exist when the field is populated by closed minds. No one has yet demonstrated that ESP exists. But no one has yet demonstrated that it does not.

SUMMARY

We constantly use our eyes to gather information, but we seldom think about the almost miraculous efficiency of these two small organs. To understand what is involved in seeing we must examine the physical energy which stimulates the eye, how this energy is translated into neural energy, and how neural energy is translated into meaningful sights.

The physical stimulus for vision is light, part of the electromagnetic spectrum. There are three physical components of light, each of which corresponds to one aspect of what we see. *Wavelength* is the quality perceived as *color* or *hue*. *Intensity* is the strength of the stimulus which corresponds to the psychological component of *brightness*. *Complexity* is the purity of the stimulus, which is perceived as *saturation*.

The light strikes the *cornea* of the eye and passes through an opening in the *iris* called the *pupil*. The *lens* focuses the light and projects it onto the *retina* where light-sensitive cells *(rods* and *cones)* convert it into neural energy which is transmitted to the brain via the *optic nerve*. The translation of neural energy into visual experience is accomplished by an *afferent code.*

Depth perception is a puzzling phenomenon. The retina can transmit only two-dimensional information, yet we perceive three dimensions. Several factors serve as cues to the third dimension. *Retinal disparity,* a slight difference in views received by each eye, and *convergence,* change in eye position as a function of an object's distance, are binocular cues to depth. *Interposition* (one object blocking another from view), *perspective, light-shadow patterns,* and observer movement are monocular cues to depth.

There is no perfect correspondence between the physical stimulus and what we perceive. The study of the relationship between the physical stimulus and the perception is known as *psychophysics.* Psychophysics studies the *absolute threshold* — the point above or below which the physical stimulus is not perceived — and the *difference threshold* — the amount of change necessary in the physical stimulus for it to be perceived as changed (the *just noticeable difference,* j.n.d.).

Second only to vision in terms of importance in information gathering is the auditory sense. The physical stimulus in audition is a *sound wave,* a form of mechanical energy which causes compression and expansion of air molecules. The auditory stimulus has three physical components and three corresponding psychological components: (1) *frequency* — speed of vibration of the wave, which is heard as *pitch;* (2) *amplitude* — extent of expansion and compression of air molecules, perceived as *loudness;* and (3) *complexity* — purity of the wave, which is heard as *timbre.*

Sound waves enter the ear and then pass through the auditory canal and are transmitted along by a series of structures (eardrum, hammer, anvil, stirrup, oval window) to the *cochlea.* The cochlea contains *hair cells* which transform the physical energy into neural energy which is then transmitted to the brain via the auditory nerve.

As is true for vision, the perception of sound is not a fully accurate representation of the physical stimulus. The psychophysical relationships of absolute thresholds and difference thresholds are also applied to auditory stimuli.

Many factors help explain the frequent discrepancies between the physical stimulus and the perception of it.

1. *Adaptation* refers to a decrease in the sensitivity of a receptor in the presence of continued stimulation.
2. *Attention* serves to restrict the amount of incoming sensory information. Attention rests, at least in part, on a physiological mechanism in the brain known as the "gating mechanism." This mechanism allows reception of stimulation from one sense while blocking input from other senses, thus preventing an overload of information in the brain which could reduce its efficiency.
3. *Aftereffects* result from the fact that perception of a stimulus for a period of time can alter the receptor's functioning after the stimulus is removed.

4. *Constancy effects* refer to our tendency to perceive things as they exist in the world rather than in terms of energy patterns at the receptor.
5. *Perceptual organization* deals with a group of organizational factors set forth by Gestalt psychology which states that any perception will be as "good" (simple, consistent, and stable) as possible (law of Prägnanz). From this basic law have been derived the principles of *similarity*, *proximity*, *closure*, and *figure-ground organization*.
6. *Illusions* are those perceptual interpretations which are erroneous in nature, producing large perceptual inaccuracies.
7. *Experiential factors* tend to give our perception a quality of uniqueness and individuality. Our perceptions may be affected by what we expect to perceive, by our physiological and social needs, and by our personal and cultural experiences.

Perception, then, is a complex experience, depending on the state of the receptor, current activity in the brain, the structure of the stimulus, and the needs and experiences of the individual.

The commonly cited number of senses is five. However, there is a total of close to a dozen sensory systems. *Taste* is probably one of our least important senses, serving primarily to make life more enjoyable rather than to supply crucial information about the world. The primary receptor for taste is the *taste bud*, which contains a group of receptors called *hair cells*. The receptors respond to four basic tastes: salt, sour, sweet, and bitter.

The primary stimulus for *smell* is a gaseous or volatile chemical in the air. The receptor is the *olfactory epithelium*, which contains millions of receptor cells. There is no single explanation of how this sense operates. The *stereochemical theory* is one of the most popular theories. It states that specific odors are a function of (1) the relationship between the molecular shape of the gaseous chemical and the corresponding shape of the receptor area, and (2) the electrical charge created by the chemical.

The skin senses encompass four different sensory systems: *pressure*, *pain*, *cold*, and *warmth*. Sensitive spots for each of these systems are distributed throughout the body. The sensation of pressure arises from the movement or deformation of the skin. The basic stimulus for pain is described as any intense stimulus which causes tissue destruction or damage. Pain is open to much subjective interpretation, possibly having as large a psychological as a physical component. The ability to detect temperature is made up of two separate but interacting senses — cold and warmth. The stimulus for each of these senses is not any absolute temperature, but rather any change in skin temperature.

The *kinesthetic sense* serves to give us immediate feedback on the position of all parts of our body. The *vestibular sense* is responsible for keeping track of the position and movement of the head. The receptor for this sense is located in the inner ear.

What's Out There?

Extrasensory perception includes three basic phenomena: *telepathy, clairvoyance,* and *precognition.* Although results of research offer some evidence for the existence of ESP in at least some individuals, the gathering and analysis of the data often fail to meet rigorous scientific requirements. The existence of ESP has not been clearly proved or disproved.

GLOSSARY

Absolute threshold: the amount of physical energy of a stimulus that is necessary for that stimulus to be perceived 50 percent of the time

Adaptation: a decrease in responsiveness of a sensory receptor in the presence of constant stimulation

Afferent code: the code which translates neural energy resulting from sensory stimulation into perceptual experience

Aftereffect: a temporary change in the operation of a receptor after removal of a stimulus that has been present for a period of time

Ampulla: the enlargement at the base of each of the semicircular canals in the vestibular system which contains the receptors that respond to changes in speed of rotation of the head

Anvil (incus): one of the small bones in the middle ear that transmits sound waves

Blind spot: the point in the retina at which the optic nerve enters the eye. No visual receptors are present in this spot, and any visual image striking this area is not seen.

Ciliary muscles: the muscles that control the shape of the lens in the eye

Clairvoyance: perception of an object or event that is not stimulating the known sensory receptors

Cochlea: the portion of the ear that contains basic receptors for sound

Cones: light-sensitive cells in the retina that respond to color differences

Constancy: the tendency to perceive physical objects in a stable manner, one which closely conforms to their actual physical characteristics (e.g., size, shape) despite differences in the pattern of energy received at the receptor

Convergence: the binocular depth cue based on the fact that the eyes maintain a different position when viewing distant objects than when viewing objects that are close. The muscles that control the change in position may provide a cue as to the distance of the object.

Cornea: the curved, transparent outer layer of the eye

Difference threshold: the smallest amount of change in the physical energy of a stimulus that will be perceived as a change — a just noticeable difference (j.n.d.)

Distal stimulus: a stimulus as it physically exists in the world

Eardrum: the membrane at the end of the auditory canal that vibrates when struck by sound waves

Fovea: the portion of the retina that has the highest concentration of light-receptor cells and is the most sensitive to visual stimulation

Gating mechanism: the mechanism that

allows reception of stimulation from the sensory channel on which attention is focused, simultaneously blocking sensory input from other channels

Gestalt psychology: the school which stresses the organization of perception by the individual. The basic tenet is that what we perceive is more than what is represented by the pattern of energy at the receptor.

Hammer (malleus): one of the small bones in the middle ear through which sound waves are transmitted

Incus: see *Anvil*

Interposition: the monocular depth cue based on the fact that an object partially blocked from view by another object is seen as more distant

Iris: the muscular structure in the eye that can contract and expand, thus varying the size of the pupil which is at its center

Just noticeable difference (j.n.d.): see *Difference threshold*

Law of Prägnanz: Gestalt law stating that any perception will be as "good" (i.e., simple, consistent, stable) as possible

Lens: the structure in the eye that varies in shape to obtain the most accurate focus on the visual image

Malleus: see *Hammer*

Olfactory epithelium: the site of receptors for smell, located at the top of the nasal passages

Optic chiasma: the point at which the nerve fibers from the nasal (inner) half of each eye cross over and join fibers from the temporal (outer) half of the other eye

Otoliths: crystals found in the fluid within the utriculus and sacculus in the inner ear which, when the head is moved, come in contact with the receptors to produce the sensation of movement

Oval window: the membrane at the opening of the inner ear to which the stirrup is attached and to which the stirrup conducts the sound waves. The oval window in turn conducts the sound waves to the cochlea.

Papillae: small bumps on the surface of the tongue in which taste buds are located

Paradoxical cold: the sensation of cold produced when a cold receptor is stimulated with a fairly hot stimulus (110° F or more)

Paradoxical heat: the sensation of extreme heat produced if a warm stimulus and a cold stimulus are applied to the skin at the same time

Precognition: knowledge of a future event

Proximal stimulus: the pattern of energy at the receptor site

Psychophysics: the study of the relationship between the nature of the physical stimulus and the perception of that stimulus

Pupil: the small opening in the iris of the eye through which light is admitted

Pure tone: a tone composed of sound waves of a single frequency

Retina: the area at the back of the eye that contains the light-sensitive receptor cells

Retinal disparity: the binocular depth cue based on the fact that the two eyes obtain slightly different views of the same scene

Rods: light-sensitive cells in the retina which record light-dark differences

Sacculus: one of the two vestibular sacs in the inner ear which contain the receptors responsible for sensing movement of the head

Stapes: see *Stirrup*

Stereochemical theory: theory of smell which states that the odor of a chemical is a function of its molecular shape and electrical charge

Stirrup (stapes): one of the small bones in the middle ear through which sound waves are transmitted

Telepathy: communication or transfer of thoughts from one person to another

Utriculus: one of the two vestibular sacs in the inner ear which contain the receptors responsible for sensing movement of the head

REFERENCES

Amoore, J. E., Johnston, J. W., Jr., and Rubin, M. The stereochemical theory of odor. *Scientific American*, 210(2), 1964, pp. 42–49.

Barlow, J. D. Pupillary size as an index of preference in political candidates. *Perceptual and Motor Skills*, 1969, 28, 587–590.

Carmichael, L., Hogan, H. P., and Walter, A. A. An experimental study of the effect of language on the reproduction of visually perceived form. *Journal of Experimental Psychology*, 1932, 15, 73–86.

Chapanis, A., Garner, W. R., and Morgan, C. T. *Applied experimental psychology*. New York: Wiley, 1949.

Dember, W. N., and Jenkins, J. J. *General psychology: Modeling behavior and experience*. Englewood Cliffs, N.J.: Prentice-Hall, 1970.

Edwards, D. C. *General psychology*. (2nd ed.). New York: Macmillan, 1968.

Held, R., and Hein, A. Movement produced stimulation in the development of visually guided behavior. *Journal of Comparative and Physiological Psychology*, 1963, 56, 872–876.

Hernandez-Peon, R., Scherrer, H., and Jouvet, M. Modification of electric activity in cochlear nucleus during "attention" in unanesthetized cats. *Science*, 1956, 123, 331–332.

Janisse, M. P. Pupil size and affect: A critical review of the literature since 1960. *Canadian Psychologist*, 1973, 14, 311–329.

London, I. D. A Russian report on the postoperative newly seeing. *American Journal of Psychology*, 1960, 73, 478–482.

McClelland, D. C., and Atkinson, J. W. The projective expression of needs: I. The effect of different intensities of the hungar drive on perception. *Journal of Psychology*, 1948, 25, 205–222.

McClelland, D. C., and Liberman, A. M. The effect of need for achievement in recognition of need-related words. *Journal of Personality*, 1949, 18, 236–251.

Melzack, R., and Scott, T. H. The effects of early experience on the response to pain. *Journal of Comparative and*

Physiological Psychology, 1957, *50*, 155–161.

Melzack, R., and Wall, P. D. Pain mechanisms: A new theory. *Science*, 1965, *150*, 971–979.

Morgan, C. T., and King, R. A. *Introduction to psychology*. (4th ed.). New York: McGraw-Hill, 1969.

Mueller, C. G. *Sensory psychology*. Englewood Cliffs, N.J.: Prentice-Hall, 1965.

Turnbull, C. M. Some observations regarding the experiences and behavior of the Bambuti Pygmies. *American Journal of Psychology*, 1961, *74*, 304–308.

SUGGESTED READINGS

Forgus, R. H. *Perception: The basic process in cognitive development*. New York: McGraw-Hill, 1966.

Graham, C. H. *Vision and visual perception*. New York: Wiley, 1965.

Hansel, C. E. M. *ESP: A scientific evaluation*. New York: Scribner's, 1966.

Mueller, C. G. *Sensory psychology*. Englewood Cliffs, N.J.: Prentice-Hall, 1965.

Neisser, U. *Cognitive psychology*. New York: Appleton-Century-Crofts, 1967.

Stevens, S. S., and Warshofsky, F. *Sound and hearing*. New York: Time-Life Books, 1965.

Photo by Lucien Samaha

C

Gaining Information and Knowledge

Unit 8
Why Do We Try?

One youngster, who had never read it before, was fascinated by *Time* magazine. For four weeks he copied articles and parts of articles daily from the same well-worn copy. His teacher was delighted. Not only had he written more in that month than he may have written before in a lifetime, but his conversation was full of the things he was reading.

Fader and Shaevitz, 1966, p. 30.

Why did the student in the above example suddenly start to write? Why didn't he do it before? The answers lie in part in the concept of motivation. Motivation may be best understood as the "why" of behavior. It is the force that impels behavior. We know that people do many and varied things. But why? Why do some people take up skydiving? Why do some people hijack airplanes? Why do some people read only fiction while others read only nonfiction? Why do some students "learn" while others don't? Motivation answers these questions by stating that there are certain needs which are filled by performing these activities. The needs which function in all people can be seen as divided into two general classes: inborn and learned.

Inborn Needs

These are basic needs which are related to the survival of the organism or of the species. Such things as hunger and thirst and the need for elimination, sleep, sexual activity, and the avoidance of pain fall into this category. There are certain changes which take place in the body and cause an individual to seek out something which will satisfy the need. When we ask why John is eating dinner, the most obvious answer is that he is hungry. To state it in somewhat more psychological terms, he eats because he has a need for food. This need is created by a deficiency in his body which is noted by certain parts of the brain. These structures then send out a signal which results in his eating. Other inborn needs function in generally the same way. This signaling function, or the creation of the need, is necessary for the survival of the individual and the species. If we don't eat, we will die. If we don't engage in sexual activity, the species will soon be gone. So the body has the mechanisms necessary to motivate the individual or to create needs.

There are other needs that research indicates may well be inborn. These are called the *stimulus needs*. In order to function well, we need a certain quantity and variety of stimulation. If we do not have enough stimulation, or if the stimulation is not varied enough, we tend to suffer psychologically. This can make us ineffective in dealing with our environment. At the extreme is the case of total sensory deprivation, in which the individual has almost no access to any sort of stimulation (see Figure 8-1). Under such conditions, intellectual functioning may be impaired and the individual may experience unusual visual sensations or other dramatic symptoms. The solitary confinement of a prisoner can approach this type of total deprivation. The prisoner is away from the sounds of other inmates, has nothing to see but four blank walls, and has little taste stimulation if fed only bread and water.

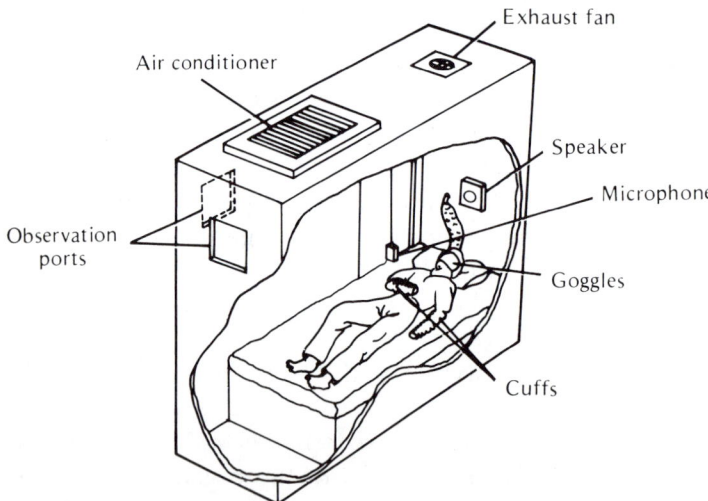

FIGURE 8-1 A sensory deprivation chamber. The subject lies on a cot. Cardboard cuffs are placed over his hands and forearms, and his eyes are covered with translucent goggles. The constant noise of an exhaust fan is the only sound audible.

Curiosity and the search for novelty are needs which are particularly expressive of our general need for variety of stimulation (see Figure 8-2). People seem to find new things rewarding. That is, they will do something just because it is different, just because they wish to know about it. Evidence has been gathered on many species, including human beings, indicating that they will learn a new task just to experience something different.

The stimulus needs may well be important for survival, as are the biological needs discussed. Knowledge about one's environment may be necessary for survival. The baby animal which explores its surroundings under the protective eye of its mother will be far more able to deal with its environment when left alone. In addition, such knowledge may increase our efficiency in performing a wide range of behaviors.

Learned Needs

There are certain needs that have been learned in the process of development. We shall see later, when we discuss learning, how this occurs. But it is important to note that these needs are a product of

Courtesy of H. F. Harlow

FIGURE 8-2 These monkeys are busily working on locks which open nothing. There is no external reward given for their work. They seem to do it simply because they enjoy it, providing some evidence for the existence of stimulus needs.

each individual's unique history and will therefore differ considerably from person to person. Examples of such needs are the need for social approval, the need to affiliate, the need to dominate, and the desire for prestige and economic success.

MOTIVATION AND EDUCATION

That these needs are learned and that they therefore differ from person to person is a crucial factor often overlooked in the educational system, and one that may be used to understand why some people don't read and write. If we are going to do something or learn something we must have a reason. This reason is motivation. The schools often assume that social approval, in the form of the teacher's praise or good grades, is motivating to everyone and will therefore lead them to learn. This factor obviously didn't motivate the student described at the start of this unit, or he would have written much more prior to his discovery of *Time* magazine. Such factors as social approval or teacher acceptance are not motivating for some people. They simply don't care if the teacher smiles at them or if they get good grades. There is therefore no reason for them to learn.

Other kinds of motivation that are implicitly used by the educational system are future economic success and prestige. Along this line, Postman and Weingartner (1969, p. 47) state that

one of the main differences between the "advantaged" student and the "disadvantaged" is that the former has an economic stake in giving his attention to the curriculum, whereas the latter does not. In other words, the only relevance of the curriculum for the "advantaged" student is that, if he does what he is told, there will be a tangible payoff.

Some students simply don't see future economic status as rewarding. Perhaps it is because such things are not valuable to them. Perhaps it is because they feel that their racial, religious, or sexual identity will prevent them from achieving these goals anyway. The main point is that for students to learn anything, they must be motivated. For any educational system to work, it must work within the framework of motives that are meaningful for its students. Otherwise, as Postman and Weingartner (1969) have stated, the teacher will "teach," but the students will not "learn."

Any of these factors may have been operating to prevent the *Time* magazine reader discussed from reading and writing. A type of motivational system which may have been instituted in his case is discussed by Postman and Weingartner. In their book *Teaching as a Subversive Activity,* they discuss the importance of the concept of relevance. Relevance, at its most basic level, refers to what students are interested in, what they think is important. Postman and Weingartner imply this approach in advocating a new education which allows students to pursue and question those things which are of interest to them. It is suggested that underlying this approach is the curiosity drive. It is important for all species to learn about their environment, because without such knowledge they cannot know what is dangerous, what is edible, what is safe. This curiosity drive is, then, one which could be used to develop student learning. The reward would be finding out something of interest, rather than getting a smile, a grade, or a prestigious job. It has the advantage of being relatively noncompetitive, so that students can spend more time listening to one another rather than trying to beat one another out in number of smiles, grade, or job level.

Such an approach stresses the uniqueness and individuality of the student. Different students will be interested in different things. But if curiosity is encouraged by allowing a student to seek out information of interest, information that is relevant, this response of seeking out new information may generalize to many types of knowledge. The student discussed at the beginning of the unit was not motivated prior to reading *Time* magazine. Perhaps it was because what he had been required to read and write about filled no need in him. He may not have been interested in reading about Dick and Jane and their dog Spot. He may have been unable to see any good reason for writing about what he did on his summer vacation. But apparently news of the current world interested him, filled a need in him — so he read and wrote.

People can and will learn. But in order for them to do it, ways must be found of challenging and interesting them. There must be some relationship between the material to be learned and the individual's needs. For the teacher, then, the question becomes: How can I find and present material that will fill the needs of the students so that they will try — and will learn?

Unit 9
What Do We Get?

"I don't know why Michael keeps throwing tantrums. It's been going on for months and nothing seems to stop them. Whenever he is frustrated or doesn't get his way, he begins to scream and kick and cry. The only thing that stops him is picking him up."

The mother speaking above is not unusual. The world is full of children who persist in doing the "wrong" thing in spite of their parents' attempts to get them to do the "right" thing. In order to understand why the wrong behavior persists, we must try to find out not only why the individual does it (motivation), but what he gets for doing it (reinforcement). In more psychological terms, we must determine what follows the behavior, or what the consequence of the act is. Michael is getting something for his tantrums: his mother picks him up. If what we get for performing a behavior is valuable, we are more likely to behave the same way again. Michael likes to be picked up, so he continues to have tantrums. If what we get for performing a behavior is not liked, we should be less likely to continue to behave in that way.

Defined technically, a reinforcer is a stimulus that affects the frequency of a response, either increasing it or decreasing it. The concept of reinforcement is closely tied to the concept of motivation. If we are motivated to get something or to stay away from something, that "thing" is the reinforcer.

Types of Reinforcement

A *positive reinforcer* (or reward) is a stimulus that increases the frequency of a response. It is something for which you have a need and therefore something you will perform some act in order to get (see Figure 9-1). If offered five dollars to clean your room every day, it is likely that you will clean your room more often. If kindness to another person leads to returned kindness, you will be kind more often.

A *negative reinforcer* is a stimulus that is unpleasant to the individual. It functions

Courtesy of Seagram Distillers Company

FIGURE 9-1 Advertisers' attempts to sell products are often based on the implication that if you behave in a certain way (i.e., use their products), you will obtain certain positive reinforcers.

What Do We Get? 83

to increase the frequency of the response which leads to its removal. Let us say that isolation is a negative or unpleasant state for Michael. He does not like to be alone. If isolation always occurs as soon as the tantrum starts and if he is allowed back into the company of his family when he stops, the isolation serves as a negative reinforcer. Performing the "right" behavior (nontantrum behavior) removes the negative state of isolation, and thus the nontantrum behavior is more likely to occur again.

The concept of a negative reinforcer should be distinguished from that of *punishment*. The function of a negative reinforcer is to increase the frequency of a particular response. When the response occurs, the negative reinforcer or unpleasant state is removed. The response that removed it is more likely to occur again. A punishment, on the other hand, does not serve to increase the frequency of a specific response. Rather, it suppresses or eliminates a specific response with no direct effect on the production of the desired response. These differences are made clear in Table 9-1.

If Michael is spanked (punished) for throwing tantrums, he will probably stop them. But even if he does, we don't know what he will do instead. He may start simply telling his mother he is angry and discussing it with her (the desired response), or he may start throwing things around the house when angry (another undesirable response). The punishment told him what he should not do but gave him no information on what he should do. The punishment stops when the "wrong" response stops. The negative reinforcer stops when the "right" response occurs. For this reason, punishment is generally seen as a less effective modifier of behavior than either negative reinforcement or positive reinforcement. It can be used effectively, however, if during the suppression of the unwanted response the correct response is elicited and positively reinforced. If Michael is spanked for his tantrum, the behavior may stop temporarily. He may, however, do the same thing the next time he is angry, or come up with an even more unacceptable behavior. If, however, his mother talks to him about his anger and positively reinforces more acceptable responses to it, it is more likely that the next time he is angry he will respond with the acceptable behavior rather than with a tantrum.

TABLE 9-1 Effects of reinforcement

Type of reinforcement	Value	Effect
Positive reinforcement	Pleasant	Increases frequency of behavior
Negative reinforcement	Unpleasant	Increases frequency of behavior
Punishment	Unpleasant	Decreases frequency of behavior

What Constitutes Reinforcement?

We know that positive reinforcers involve pleasant states for an individual and that negative reinforcers and punishments involve unpleasant states. But how do we know what is pleasant or unpleasant for a given individual? How do we know if the consequences of an individual's behavior are liked or disliked by him?

The answer can be found in part in the concept of motivation. We noted in the last unit that we have certain biological needs. Anything that satisfies or fills these needs is a reinforcer. When the biological need of hunger is present, food serves as a positive reinforcer. We have a biological need to avoid pain. Therefore, when pain is applied it can serve as a negative reinforcer or a punishment. Any response that stops the pain will be more likely to occur again.

But simply saying that a reinforcer is related to a biological need does not tell us how it will operate. Food given to a hungry person will usually serve as a positive reinforcer. Food given to one who has just eaten too much will probably be viewed as unpleasant. So in order to decide how a reinforcer is going to operate, we must know the level of the need in the person at a given time.

The problem of determining which reinforcers will operate in which ways is further complicated by the learned needs. We know what the biological needs of a person are because they are the same for all people. We only have to determine how strong they are at a particular time to determine if something will be reinforcing. In the case of a learned need, however, we first have to determine if that need is present in the individual. An offer of job advancement for good work will not be a positive reinforcer for a person with low achievement needs. Isolating a child from his classroom peers is not a punishment for the child with low affiliation needs.

A final factor that complicates the problem of choosing an appropriate reinforcer is that at any one time many needs are operating in the individual. It is the strongest need that determines how the reinforcement operates. Many a parent has spanked his child repeatedly for tantrums, only to find that the child continues to have them. Surely the spanking is negative, since it involves inflicting pain. But the child may have other needs that are stronger than the need to avoid pain. He may have a strong need for attention. This, combined with a situation in which the parent generally gives the child little attention, makes the attention value of the spanking more positive than the negative value of the pain.

The concept of reinforcement is essential to the understanding of behavior. It is also important in any attempts to change behavior. Many psychologists say that if a behavior persists, it must be producing a positive reinforcer. So when we try to understand why someone continues to do something, we must locate the reward that the person is receiving. When we wish to develop a behavior in someone, we must find a positive reinforcer we can give for that behavior. And we must make sure that it fills the individual's unique needs and is reinforcing to *that* individual.

Unit 10
A Learning Principle: Classical Conditioning

Little Albert wasn't afraid of white rats. He enjoyed playing with them. One day while Albert was playing with a white rat, a very loud noise was suddenly sounded, scaring Albert. From that moment on he was afraid of the white rat and wouldn't play with it. He was also afraid of a furpiece belonging to his mother, of pieces of white cotton, and of men with white beards.

Watson and Raynor, 1920.

What happened to Little Albert is not uncommon, although his particular experience was part of an experiment. His behavior was trained through a process known as classical conditioning (see Figure 10-1). Albert was exposed to a stimulus (a sudden loud noise) that caused an automatic response (fear). When the noise was heard, Albert was playing with the white rat. The sequence of events was as follows: rat–noise–fear. The noise and the rat became associated. Due to this association, the response to the noise was also associated with the rat, causing the sight of the rat to lead to fear.

The Classical Conditioning Process

In more general terms, we start with two stimuli. One stimulus elicits a response automatically, without training. This stimulus is called the *unconditioned stimulus* (US; in this case, the sudden loud noise). The behavior that occurs in response to the US is called the *unconditioned response* (UR; fear). The other stimulus used in classical conditioning is called the *conditioned stimulus* (CS; rat). This stimulus is neutral in the

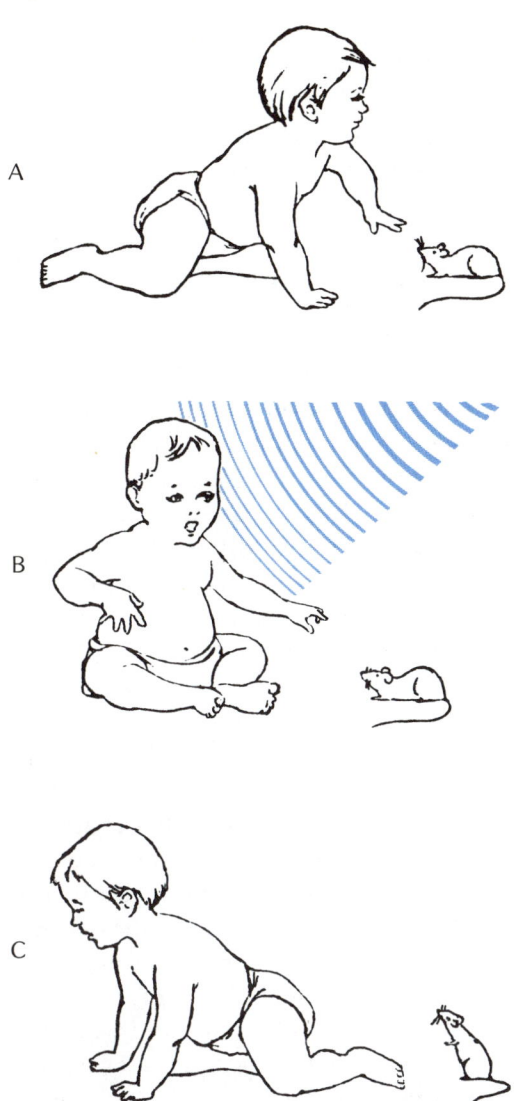

FIGURE 10-1 Before conditioning, Albert reaches for the rat (A). Then a loud noise is presented, causing fear (B). After this conditioning experience, the baby is afraid of the rat (C).

the US produces the learning in which the CS comes to elicit the response which is similar to the UR. It is called the *conditioned response* (CR; fear). Table 10-1 illustrates what is occuring during the process of conditioning.

The unconditioned stimulus serves as the reinforcer in this type of learning. Reinforcement was defined in the last unit as a stimulus that affects the frequency of the response. In the example of Albert, the noise (US) is the reinforcer for it affects the frequency of the response (fear). Without the noise, no fear response to the rat would develop.

Extinction

Two other aspects of classical conditioning are important for full understanding of this type of learning and its relevance to human behavior. We need to be concerned not only with how the learning occurs, but with how it is eliminated. *Extinction* is the process by which a response is eliminated. If one wishes to stop the performance of the behavior, one removes the reinforcer. If the CS is repeatedly presented alone (i.e., without the reinforcer or US), the individual will eventually stop giving the CR. In our example, if Albert is exposed to the white rat often enough without hearing the loud noise, eventually he should stop feeling fear of the rat. He will, in effect, say to himself that really there isn't anything about the rat that he should fear, so he will stop being afraid when he sees it. This decrease in the fear response is caused by the removal of the reinforcer (US).

sense that it elicits no response that would interfere with or prevent the occurrence of the UR. Pairing of the CS with

A Learning Principle: Classical Conditioning

TABLE 10-1 The process of classical conditioning

Stage	Responses elicited	Example
Before conditioning	CS ⟶ no competing response US ⟶ UR	White rat ⟶ play Loud noise ⟶ fear
During conditioning	CS ↓ US ⟶ UR	White rat ↓ Loud noise ⟶ fear
After conditioning	CS ⟶ CR	White rat ⟶ fear

It should be noted that extinction does not necessarily occur quickly or easily. The more learning trials that have preceded it, the more difficult extinction is to achieve. For extinction to occur, the individual must have many trials with no reinforcer present and these trials must occur close together (massed trials). If the individual is given a brief rest after the massed extinction trials, he will show an increase in the response when the CS is again presented. This increase following a rest period is called *spontaneous recovery*. Since the requirement of many trials grouped together occurs infrequently in daily life, an individual who learns a conditioned response in childhood may perform it throughout his life with no further reinforcement.

Variations on the Process

Classical conditioning was originally discovered by Pavlov (1927), who noted that if a bell (CS) were sounded just before placing meat powder (US) in the mouth of a dog and eliciting salivation (UR), the dog would in time salivate to the sound of the bell alone (CR). As we have noted, the US is defined as a stimulus that at the start of the learning produces a response (UR) consistently and automatically. Once the dog is conditioned to salivate to the bell, Pavlov found, the bell can be used as a US to train salivation to another stimulus. We can, for example, present a light, then the bell, and the animal will salivate (without any meat powder present). Over repeated trials, the animal will learn to salivate to the light. In the same way the white rat could be used to train Albert to fear another stimulus. This process is called *higher-order conditioning*. Theoretically, it allows for long chains of learned responses to be developed with responses to stimuli far removed from those that were linked to the original reinforcing stimulus. Albert's fear can "spread" to a wide range of stimuli associated with the rat, even though the sudden loud noise is not presented again.

Classical conditioning was first studied primarily in reference to simple reflexive responses, such as salivation or eyeblink. The importance of classical conditioning to human behavior becomes much clearer by examination of the *conditioned emotional response*. An infant is born with a few emotional responses which are elicited by a few specific stimuli. The infant cries when hungry or when exposed to a sudden loud noise. At a slightly older age, the child responds to a face or to tickling with a smile. These are US-UR pairs, and the same responses can be conditioned to a wide variety of stimuli by the simple conditioning procedure described above. Through this process, a new stimulus (CS) can acquire the emotional response, either pleasant or unpleasant, that corresponds to the US (noise, tickling) with which it was paired. This is what happened to Albert. The UR of fear was produced automatically by the US of noise. Association of the noise with the white rat (CS) produced learning so that the emotional response elicited by the noise is now elicited by the rat as well.

Some stimuli that may evoke emotional responses are shown in Figure 10-2.

There is another process which increases the power and range of the conditioning phenomenon. It is known as *stimulus generalization*. Pavlov's dog salivated not only to the specific bell used in training but to other bells as well. Albert after conditioning was afraid not only of white rats, but of other white furry objects which were similar to the rat (see Figure 10-3). The CR will be given not only to the particular CS that occurred in the learning situation, but to other stimuli which are similar to it. Through this process of stimulus generalization, the emotional tone conditioned to one particular object will also be elicited in the presence of other, similar objects.

Applications to Human Behavior

Let us look at a few examples of the process of conditioning in order to understand more fully how these processes can affect our emotional responses to the world. Suppose that every night when Daddy comes home from work, Johnny is sitting in the living room. When Daddy walks in and Johnny sees him, the door Daddy has just come through slams shut, startling the child and making him cry. To simplify the situation, let us say that this greeting is about all the attention Daddy gives the baby. What would one expect the child's basic emotional response to his father to be? Would this have any effect on the child's emotional response to other men similar to his father? What about his later classroom behavior if his teacher were male?

FIGURE 10-2 These symbols not only have particular meanings for us, but they evoke emotional responses which may have been acquired through classical conditioning.

A Learning Principle: Classical Conditioning

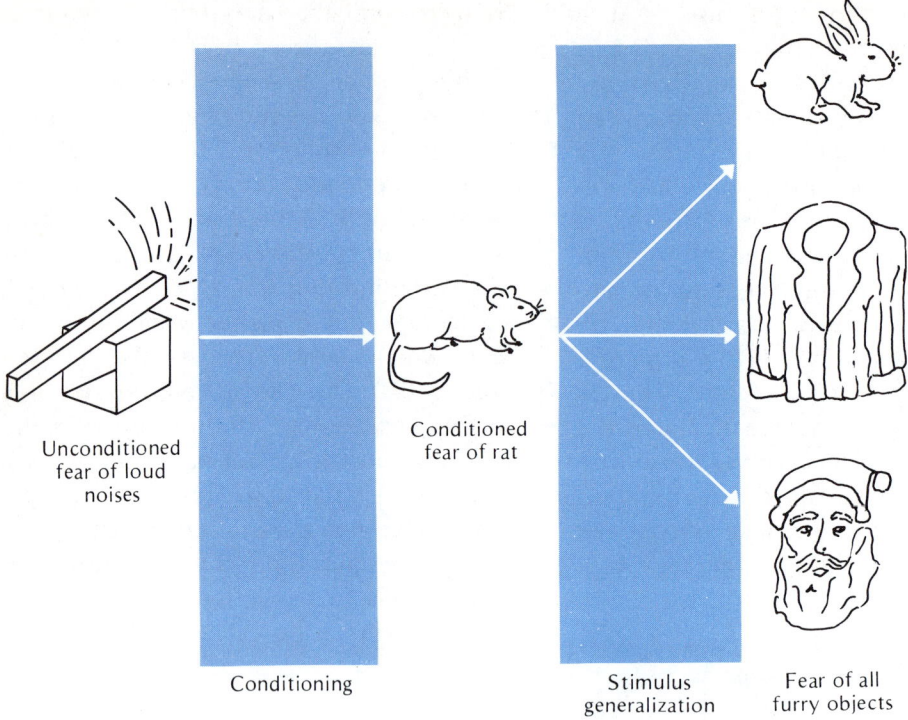

FIGURE 10-3 The conditioning of Little Albert. Albert had an unconditioned fear of loud noises. Through conditioning, this fear was attached to the rat. The process of stimulus generalization produced fear of other furry objects.

To take another example: pain leads to a negative emotional response. Not only does spanking serve as a punishment, it serves as a US leading to a UR (negative emotional response). During cleanliness training, the child is spanked for dirtying himself. Although the spanking may be limited to dirtying himself with his feces, it may also include playing outside in the dirt — the blacker the dirt, the worse the offense. Even if not spanked for anything but defecation, the child will very likely generalize the negative emotional response to other dirt. Dirt is generally dark or black. Does this have any implications for his emotional response to the color black? to black people? How would one expect a white teacher who had undergone severe cleanliness training to respond to his or her black students?

The process of classical conditioning has widespread and important effects on the development of human behavior. The way we see other people, the way we respond to certain objects, the way we feel about certain events may all be colored by an emotional response from early conditioning.

Unit 11
Another Learning Principle: Operant Conditioning

A group of third-grade public school students were removed from their regular classes and put into a special class. They were "behavior problems": they wouldn't stay at their desks, were frequently loud and disruptive in class, and had not mastered basic reading and arithmetic skills. In their new class they were given points for good work: One point for each addition problem solved correctly. Five bonus points for a whole assignment correctly completed. The points were not meaningless tokens. Nor were they added up to give the student a grade. They were "money" which could be used to buy food, school supplies, and "time off." Ten points would buy a candy bar, 25 points would buy a felt-tip pen (any color), 100 points would buy an hour out of class in the student lounge.

The description of the class above is not real. It was not taken from an actual situation. But there are schools that are using techniques very similar to those described in order to change student behavior. These students are taking part in behavior modification programs which attempt to change behavior through *operant conditioning* techniques.

The Operant Conditioning Process

In the operant learning situation, any behavior which an animal or person is capable of performing can be trained. In the above example, the responses being trained were "appropriate classroom behaviors" or, more specifically, correct answers to arithmetic problems.

These responses were taught through a process called *shaping,* which uses the method of *successive approximations*. This is a gradual training process in which one does not wait for the total response to occur before reward is given. Rather, reward is given each time a response occurs that is closer to the desired behavior than was the preceding response. In the above example, points were not

Copyright 1955 by United Features Syndicate, Inc.

withheld until the first arithmetic problem was completed. In the early stages of training, the students may have been given points for just sitting at their desks — a response that brings them closer to the desired response of correctly solving an arithmetic problem. Then, once the response of sitting at their desks for a reasonable period of time was learned, they may have been given points for opening their math books, for looking at them, and so forth. Once each step (e.g., sitting at the desk) in the approximation of the final response is learned, no more reinforcement is given for it. Now, reinforcement is obtained only for the next closer response (opening the book). Through this gradual process, the behavior of the individual is shaped to the desired response.

Extinction

The process of extinction applies to operant learning as well as to classical conditioning. Extinction, as defined in the preceding unit, involves withholding reinforcement, resulting in the elimination of the response. If students stop receiving points for correct answers, they will eventually stop giving them. Extinction, as we noted in the discussion of classical conditioning, does not occur immediately but takes place over a period of time. Nonetheless, this would seem to create important problems when we are teaching behavior that we want the individual to retain. The teacher obviously can't follow the students all of their lives, giving them points for each arithmetic problem correctly solved. Yet we want the students to continue to solve such problems after they leave the classroom.

There are two solutions to this difficulty. We can ensure the continuation of the response by substituting another reward for the points, a reward that will always be available to the individual. Such rewards as "pride in one's work" can be used as a substitute for points. This is a reward that the student can internalize, and thus the behavior will be automatically maintained.

Schedules of Reinforcement

There is a second factor which can slow down or prevent extinction of a desired response. This is the *schedule of reinforcement* under which the response has been learned. In the above example, each student received a point every time he or she correctly solved a problem. This pattern of reinforcement is called a *continuous reinforcement schedule*, and it produces relatively fast learning. The

92   *Gaining Information and Knowledge*

relationship between the response (solving problems) and the reinforcer (points) is clear: the two always occur together. It is therefore relatively easy for students to figure out what they are supposed to do to get the points, even if the system is not explained to them. The continuous reinforcement schedule, however, also produces fairly quick extinction. If the reinforcement is stopped, the students quickly see that they're getting nothing for their work, so they stop.

There is a second type of schedule, and this type provides reinforcement for only some of the correct responses. It is called a *partial reinforcement schedule*. Under this schedule the learner may receive a reinforcement for one out of every five responses, or receive a reinforcement every ten minutes (assuming a response occurs at any time following the interval), or receive a reinforcement "every now and then." Under partial reinforcement schedules it may take the learner longer to acquire the response, but extinction is slower (see Figure 11-1). When the reinforcer is removed in extinction, it may take a while before the absence of the reinforcer begins to affect the individual's behavior. The individual has made many

Copyright Paolo Koch; courtesy of Rapho Guillumette Pictures

FIGURE 11-1 The persistence of slot machine players gives a clear example of the power of a partial reinforcement schedule to produce behavior highly resistant to extinction.

responses during training without receiving reinforcement, so the extinction situation doesn't seem so different. The subject is used to performing a fairly large number of responses for a single reinforcement. A partial reinforcement schedule can then offer a solution to our problems with students. We can train them initially on a continuous reinforcement schedule to obtain fairly quick learning. Then we can give them points less and less often for correct responses, gradually shifting them to a partial reinforcement schedule. This, combined with a shift to a different type of reinforcer, will enable the students to continue to perform the desired response even after they have left the classroom.

Variations on the Process

The process of *stimulus generalization* can further broaden and extend the effects of operant learning. As we discussed in the unit on classical conditioning, in stimulus generalization the response learned to one stimulus is given to other, similar stimuli. If we view the response in a general rather than a specific manner (the response is giving correct answers rather than adding correctly), the training we have accomplished might generalize in a way which is beneficial to the students. They have, in relation to arithmetic, learned to give responses (the correct answers) to stimuli (the teacher's problems) in order to obtain a reinforcer (points). If generalization takes place, they may give correct responses to similar stimuli such as other problems presented by the teacher or math problems they find outside the classroom.

Discrimination learning. The process in discrimination learning involves a reversal of the stimulus generalization process. The individual learns to give a response to a particular stimulus but to withhold the same response from similar stimuli. This is done by positively reinforcing a response to one stimulus and not reinforcing, or extinguishing, the response to other stimuli. The child when he first learns to say "Mommy" is reinforced with smiles and hugs from his mother. Due to generalization, however, he uses the word to refer to many similar stimulus objects: all women who appear to him to be similar to his mother. The process of discrimination learning corrects this "error" by reinforcing him only when he says "Mommy" to his mother. The process of discrimination learning is really the process by which we learn differences among objects and persons.

Students in the classroom also undergo discrimination learning. They may at first generalize the addition responses they have learned by giving the sum of any two numbers in an arithmetic problem. In time, they learn to discriminate among multiplication problems, subtraction problems, and addition problems, giving different responses.

Operant learning with negative reinforcers. So far we have talked mainly about behaviors that were positively reinforced. When the individual is faced with a negative reinforcer, he tries to respond in a way that will eliminate it. As was noted in the unit on reinforcement, any behavior that eliminates a negative reinforcer will be more likely to occur again. There are two basic types of operant learning that occur in the presence of negative reinforcers. The first type is *escape learning*. When a negative reinforcer is applied and a response is then given which stops the negative reinforcer, this response tends to be learned. The individual learns the response that allows escape from the unpleasant condition. When a baby touches a hot stove, a negative reinforcer is applied — the child is burned. The response of pulling the hand back is the escape response. The child then goes a step further and learns not to touch the stove at all, thus avoiding the pain (negative reinforcer) (see Figure 11-2). This is *avoidance learning*. Avoidance learning differs from escape learning in that in the former, the negative reinforcer is not received. The response is given before the negative reinforcer occurs, thus preventing or avoiding it.

For the student in the classroom, boredom is often a powerful negative reinforcer. The student may begin to daydream, a response which allows escape from the classroom and its boredom. In time an avoidance response may be developed: the student may simply stop attending school and thus avoid the boredom altogether.

Both escape and avoidance learning involve learning through the use of negative reinforcers. They differ in that in escape learning the negative reinforcer is always received and the response follows it. In avoidance learning, the response is given before the negative reinforcer and prevents its occurrence.

Applications to Human Behavior

Operant learning principles can be broadly applied to human behavior in order to produce change. The relatively simple situations of teaching a child to eat, to pick up his toys, and to use the toilet all involve operant learning principles in that reward is given for performing the desired response. These principles

FIGURE 11-2 The child touches the hot stove, receives a burn (negative reinforcer), and gives the escape response of removing her hand. In the future, she will avoid the negative reinforcer entirely simply by not touching the hot stove.

can also be applied in the classroom, as we have noted above.

Operant training is used also as a form of therapy for abnormal behavior. When one is "abnormal," according to the operant theorists, one has learned incorrect responses. To make the person normal, we must extinguish the abnormal responses by withholding the rewards they produce and teach normal behaviors by rewarding such behaviors when they occur.

Operant learning also can be used to train physiological responses. We can teach people to speed up or slow down their heart rates, to dilate or contract their blood vessels, or to change their brain wave patterns by the use of positive reinforcers. To those who hold strictly to an operant theory, we can change almost any behavior through operant learning. Whether or not this is true, it must be acknowledged that such techniques are powerful tools of change.

Unit 12
Human Learning: Input/Output

Teachers in grades one to six were told that their students had all been tested for their academic potential for the coming year using the Harvard Test of Inflected Acquisition. They were told that some students had indicated potential for dramatic improvement in classroom performance (Group A). The tests for other students indicated that they would continue to perform at the same level as they had the previous year (Group B). It was found that Group A students did show substantial improvement in their classroom performance and on intelligence tests. Students in Group B, however, did not improve academically.

Rosenthal and Jacobson, 1968.

The above example is a common one in the school setting. General ability tests are given and students' performance is compared with their test scores. Often such test scores are predictive of class performance. The example cited above, however, is different in one way. The tests given to the students were standard intelligence tests, not "inflected acquisition" tests. The test scores were not used to assign students to groups. Rather, students were randomly assigned to Group A or Group B. The only differences between the groups were the differences the teachers *thought* were there. Nonetheless, the students in the two groups showed a difference over time in both classroom performance and general intelligence scores. The teachers' expectations and perceptions of the students had a very real effect on how the students actually performed (see Figure 12-1).

In the discussion in Division B, we noted that we do not simply record incoming stimuli as does a tape recorder or a television camera. Rather, we evaluate them in the very process of perceiving. This evaluation process is probably most marked in our perception of other people. Teachers, being people, evaluate

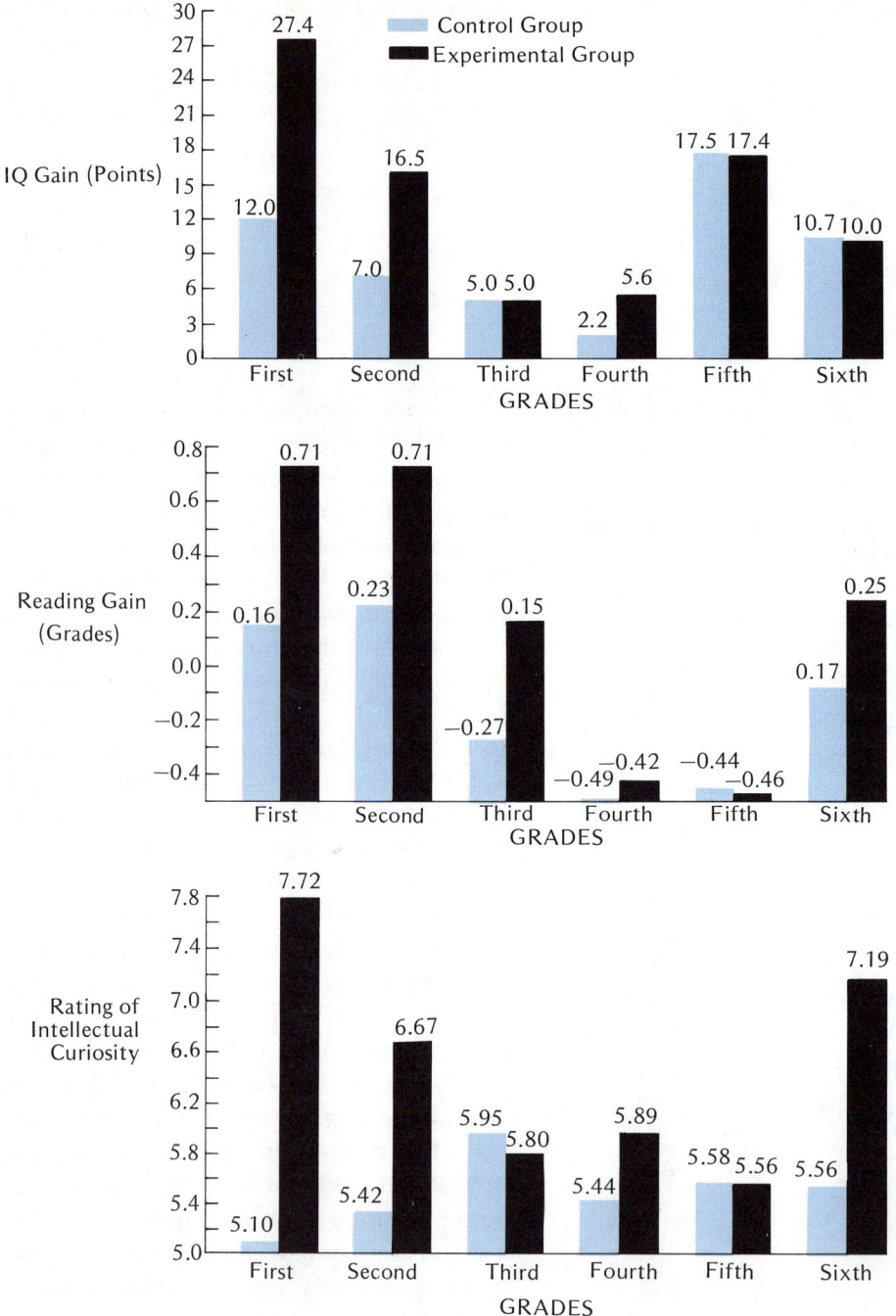

FIGURE 12-1 Group A (experimental group) showed gains over Group B (control group) in total IQ, reading grades, and intellectual curiosity.

their students on the basis of their perceptions of them. They see them as good or bad, capable or incapable, cooperative or disruptive. Students, at least to some extent, are probably all aware that these perceptions have an influence on their grades. They suspect, sometimes with good cause, that they did poorly on an essay or exam because the teacher didn't like them. The Rosenthal and Jacobson (1968) work, however, points out that the teachers' evaluations can have a more indirect, and possibly more damaging, effect on students' performance. These researchers note that the evaluation of individuals leads to expectations about how they will behave. If students are "good," they are expected to do well on a test, with the reverse being true for "bad" students. These perceptions and expectations have an influence on the actual performance of the students.

The perceptions of the teacher are not the only ones that create problems in the learning process. The perceptual approach of the student can also create difficulties. We noted in Division B that what we perceive is not given in the sense that we see exactly what is "out there." Perception is a unique experience for each individual since it is determined by one's own past experiences, by one's needs, by one's attitudes, and by one's values. The uniqueness of perception is relevant to the educational system in that each question heard by a student is perceived by that student in a unique way, and each answer given is a result of individual perceptions. What this means is that students may very well give the "wrong" answer to a question because they interpreted it differently than did the teacher who asked it. This does not make too much difference in the area of relatively factual information, as when a teacher asks how many states there are in the Union or who is president. These questions may or may not be important for the student to be able to answer, but we can all agree that there is probably one right response.

The real difficulties arise in questions that require interpretive answers, such as supplying the meaning of a particular poem. Much of our educational system rests on the interpretation of information rather than on the giving of factual responses. And it is here that teachers often impose their own perceptions on their students. Postman and Weingartner (1969) argue that learning should be a process of expanding perception rather than a process of figuring out how someone else perceives things. Schrank (1972) takes this proposition one step further by suggesting various exercises for the development of our senses, noting that we see and hear a great deal but that we observe and listen to very little.

In general, then, the student who is forced into an educational system which demands similar perceptions rather than extensive use of one's unique perceptual abilities is condemned to failure.

As was discussed in Division B, perception is a function of the physical stimulus, the operation of the sensory apparatus, and psychological characteristics of the perceiver. This unit has so far dealt with the psychological characteristics of the perceiver and their effects on learning. The operation of the sensory apparatus can also have an effect on learning. There are many sensory problems which pro-

Photo by Agnes M. Fromer

duce inadequate sensory functioning. This inadequacy, in turn, can interfere with learning. It is fairly well known that visual or auditory deficiencies can produce behavior that makes a child seem "stupid" when in fact the problem is merely that the student cannot see or hear what is going on in the classroom. This problem is fairly well recognized, as demonstrated by the widespread use of standardized hearing and vision tests for schoolchildren. There are, however, more subtle sensory difficulties which may have as profound an effect on learning as do simple hearing and visual deficiencies.

In the aphasias, for example, the individual has difficulty in understanding language. In one type of aphasia, the individual has difficulty understanding the meaning of spoken words and has trouble finding the right words to use when speaking. In such instances the child would probably be classified as retarded when in fact the difficulty lies in certain areas of the brain and is due to physiological malfunctioning.

In another type of perceptual disorder, the individual perceives words as reversed. Instead of seeing the word TAR, he sees it as RAT. When the child reads such reversals aloud, the teacher is likely to conclude that the child doesn't know how to read. In fact the student can read very accurately what he or she sees — but that perception is distorted.

The major importance of discussing these physiological problems in perception is to note that many educational difficulties which are attributed to slow learning, retardation, improper motivation, or similar causes may be instead problems of not seeing or "improper" hearing. It would probably be a wise rule never to classify children as poor learners until we are sure that they are functioning well at a physical level.

Learning is not simply a matter of motivation, reinforcement, and the proper learning procedure. In order to understand the learning process fully, we must understand the perceptions of the teacher and the learner.

Unit 13
In Search of Language

A human being is a verbal animal, one which relies heavily on verbal behavior to communicate knowledge, feelings, desires, and hopes. Most of what one learns as a student is verbal — new words and new ways of putting them together. Babies spend much of their time learning new physical skills, but most of the learning of adults is verbal. For all of this verbal learning to occur, one must first learn a verbal language.

The Structure of Language

The most basic unit of language is the *phoneme*. Each language has a certain limited number of phonemes upon which the entire language is built. The English language has forty-five of these basic sounds. Everything we say in the English language represents a combination of these forty-five sounds.

Phonemes do not have any meaning by themselves. However, they are combined to form *morphemes* which do have meaning. Many morphemes are words, such as *book* (a combination of three phonemes) or *sun*. Other morphemes do not form words by themselves but still have meaning. The suffix *-ed* is a morpheme because it conveys meaning. Prefixes such as *pre-* and *post-* are also morphemes. The morphemes are combined with other morphemes to form words. From the forty-five phonemes of the English language we are able to form well over half a million words.

But knowing the words is not enough for one to be able to communicate in a language. One must also learn *grammar*, the rules of combination that allow us to put words together in a meaningful way. For many students, learning grammar becomes a hateful, if necessary, task during elementary school. Yet without the learning of these rules, communication would be impossible. Grammar tells us not only how to combine words meaningfully but how different combinations of words can convey different meanings. The following three sentences clearly demonstrate the importance of grammatical rules:

1. John chased the dog up the stairs.
2. The dog chased John up the stairs.
3. The dog John stairs up chased.

Sentences 1 and 2 immediately convey quite different meanings because of our knowledge of grammar. Sentence 3 conveys no meaning because it fails to follow grammatical rules.

Learning of Language

Because language is such an important tool in our way of life, the learning of it by a child is a crucial process. The basic sound-making ability necessary for spoken language is inborn. Babies spontaneously "babble," making all the basic sounds (phonemes) necessary for spoken language. In fact, children make sounds that are not a part of their native languages. As an early step in language learning, phonemes not part of the child's native language are eliminated, while those that will be needed to form morphemes and words are retained. Through practice, the child gradually learns to combine these phonemes into morphemes and words. By approximately age two the child has learned some basic rules of grammar and can form simple three- and four-word sentences. Although the child may make errors in the use of some grammatical rules, these are frequently "good" errors. That is, the child who says, "I comed home today" has made an error, but it is "good" in the sense that the error demonstrates knowledge of the grammatical rule for forming the past tense. Only the knowledge of exceptions to the rule is lacking.

THEORIES OF LANGUAGE LEARNING

Two of the theories which are commonly used to explain language learning are the operant learning theory and the observational learning theory. The operant theory states that language is learned in the same way as any other operant behavior: through the application of reinforcements. That is, the child is rewarded for using the phonemes of the language and for forming words and grammatical sentences. Other, unwanted verbal behaviors are extinguished by being ignored or removed through punishment. The observation theory states that the verbal learning of a child is based primarily on imitation. Children listen to their parents and copy their verbal behavior, thus developing their own linguistic ability.

NONHUMAN LANGUAGES

Attempts to teach other animals a language indicate that the operation of both of these processes is important in language learning. Attempts to teach a spoken language to chimpanzees had been unsuccessful. But success was obtained when the Gardners (Gardner and Gardner, 1969) began to teach their chimpanzee, Washoe, to speak with gestures. Since chimpanzees naturally show more use of the hands than verbalization, Washoe was taught sign language. The language-learning technique used was a combination of operant and observational methods. Washoe was able to learn the 34 signs shown in Table 13-1 in twenty-two months. She also learned to combine them into two- and three-word sentences. She had mastered 85 signs by the age of four and almost 160 by the age of five.

Premack (1971) used standard operant procedure to teach the chimpanzee Sarah a "written" language. The language was

TABLE 13-1 Signs used reliably by chimpanzee Washoe within twenty-two months of the beginning of training. The signs are listed in the order of their original appearance in her repertoire.

Sign	Description	Context
Come-gimme	Beckoning motion, with wrist or knuckles as pivot.	Sign made to persons or animals, also for objects out of reach. Often combined: "come tickle," "gimme sweet," etc.
More	Fingertips are brought together, usually overhead. (Correct ASL form: tips of the tapered hand touch repeatedly.)	When asking for continuation or repetition of activities such as swinging or tickling, for second helpings of food, etc. Also used to ask for repetition of some performance, such as a somersault.
Up	Arm extends upward, and index finger may also point up.	Wants a lift to reach objects such as grapes on vine, or leaves; or wants to be placed on someone's shoulders; or wants to leave potty-chair.
Sweet	Index or index and second fingers touch tip of wagging tongue. (Correct ASL form: index and second fingers extended side by side.)	For dessert; used spontaneously at end of meal. Also, when asking for candy.
Open	Flat hands are placed side by side, palms down, then drawn apart while rotated to palms up.	At door of house, room, car, refrigerator, or cupboard; on containers such as jars; and on faucets.
Tickle	The index finger of one hand is drawn across the back of the other hand. (Related to ASL "touch.")	For tickling or for chasing games.
Go	Opposite of "come-gimme."	While walking hand-in-hand or riding on someone's shoulders. Washoe usually indicates the direction desired.
Out	Curved hand grasps tapered hand; then tapered hand is withdrawn upward.	When passing through doorways; until recently, used for both "in" and "out." Also, when asking to be taken outdoors.
Hurry	Open hand is shaken at the wrist. (Correct ASL form: index and second fingers extended side by side.)	Often follows signs such as "come-gimme," "out," "open," and "go," particularly if there is a delay before Washoe is obeyed. Also, used while watching her meal being prepared.

TABLE 13-1 (continued)

Sign	Description	Context
Hear-listen	Index finger touches ear.	For loud or strange sounds: bells, car horns, sonic booms, etc. Also, for asking someone to hold a watch to her ear.
Toothbrush	Index finger is used as brush, to rub front teeth.	When Washoe has finished her meal, or at other times when shown a toothbrush.
Drink	Thumb is extended from fisted hand and touches mouth.	For water, formula, soda pop, etc. For soda pop, often combined with "sweet."
Hurt	Extended index fingers are jabbed toward each other. Can be used to indicate location of pain.	To indicate cuts and bruises on herself or on others. Can be elicited by red stains on a person's skin or by tears in clothing.
Sorry	Fisted hand clasps and unclasps at shoulder. (Correct ASL form: fisted hand is rubbed over heart with circular motion.)	After biting someone, or when someone has been hurt in another way (not necessarily by Washoe). When told to apologize for mischief.
Funny	Tip of index finger presses nose, and Washoe snorts. (Correct ASL form: index and second fingers used; no snort.)	When soliciting interaction play, and during games. Occasionally, when being pursued after mischief.
Please	Open hand is drawn across chest. (Correct ASL form: fingertips used, and circular motion.)	When asking for objects and activities. Frequently combined; "Please go," "Out, please," "Please drink."
Food-eat	Several fingers of one hand are placed in mouth. (Correct ASL form: fingertips of tapered hand touch mouth repeatedly.)	During meals and preparation of meals.
Flower	Tip of index finger touches one or both nostrils. (Correct ASL form: tips of tapered hand touch first one nostril, then the other.)	For flowers.
Cover-blanket	Draws one hand toward self over the back of the other.	At bedtime or naptime, and, on cold days, when Washoe wants to be taken out.
Dog	Repeated slapping on thigh.	For dogs and for barking.
You	Index finger points at a person's chest.	Indicates successive turns in games. Also used in response to questions such as "Who tickle?" "Who brush?"

TABLE 13-1 (continued)

Sign	Description	Context
Napkin-bib	Fingertips wipe the mouth region.	For bib, for washcloth, and for Kleenex.
In	Opposite of "out."	Wants to go indoors, or wants someone to join her indoors.
Brush	The fisted hand rubs the back of the open hand several times. (Adapted from ASL "polish.")	For hairbrush, and when asking for brushing.
Hat	Palm pats top of head.	For hats and caps.
I-me	Index finger points at, or touches, chest.	Indicates Washoe's turn, when she and a companion share food, drink, etc. Also used in phrases, such as "I drink," and in reply to questions such as "Who tickle? (Washoe: "you"); "Who I tickle?" (Washoe: "Me.")
Shoes	The fisted hands are held side by side and strike down on shoes or floor. (Correct ASL form: the sides of the fisted hands strike against each other.)	For shoes and boots.
Smell	Palm is held before nose and moved slightly upward several times.	For scented objects: tobacco, perfume, sage, etc.
Pants	Palms of the flat hands are drawn up against the body toward waist.	For diapers, rubber pants, trousers.
Clothes	Fingertips brush down the chest.	For Washoe's jacket, nightgown, and shirts; also for our clothing.
Cat	Thumb and index finger grasp cheek hair near side of mouth and are drawn outward (representing cat's whiskers).	For cats.
Key	Palm of one hand is repeatedly touched with the index finger of the other. (Correct ASL form: crooked index finger is rotated against palm.)	Used for keys and locks and to ask us to unlock a door.
Baby	One forearm is placed in the crook of the other, as if cradling a baby.	For dolls, including animal dolls such as a toy horse and duck.
Clean	The open palm of one hand is passed over the open palm of the other.	Used when Washoe is washing, or being washed, or when a companion is washing hands or some other object. Also used for "soap."

(Gardner and Gardner, 1969, pp. 668–9.)

made up of a set of plastic symbols, each standing for a different word. Sarah was taught to use this language by being rewarded for choosing correct symbols during training, with no reward or punishment given for incorrect answers. After two years of training, Sarah could use 130 words, could form sentences, and could correctly use grammatical forms such as pluralization, negation, the conditional, and quantifiers.

The scientific community is justifiably skeptical about the idea of talking chimps. All reported attempts to teach them a verbal language have been failures. But little by little the all-important evidence is accumulating which supports the possibility of chimpanzees learning language (Fleming, 1974). Evidence of Washoe's early linguistic development was viewed as interesting but not scientifically important until she could: (1) demonstrate an extensive system of names for objects in her environment; (2) sign about objects not physically present; (3) use signs for concepts as well as for objects, agents, and actions; (4) invent semantically appropriate combinations; and (5) use proper order when it is semantically necessary.

All of these criteria have been met by at least one chimp; most of them have been demonstrated in several chimps. But as the type of data demanded as evidence of language becomes more complex, it is increasingly difficult to decide which criteria are reasonable; we have no definition of language that allows us to recognize it outside the context of vocal human communication.

This presents an unusual situation — how can we recognize a language that is not exactly like human language so that we can compare them? Although there is currently no answer to this question, the possibility of one is becoming stronger.

Words and Concepts

Our language is a symbolic one. Words are not objects; they simply stand for or refer to specific objects. Most words, in addition, do not refer to a single object but to groups of objects. When we use the word *car*, we may be referring to any one of a large class of objects that have certain characteristics in common, e.g., four wheels, an engine, a steering wheel. Words are thus concepts — symbols that refer to the common properties of objects or events. When we use the word *square* we are referring to any four-sided figure that has sides of equal length with each corner forming a ninety-degree angle. This object may be large, small, red, blue, or spotted. But the concept *square* refers to a certain set of properties that will be held in common by all objects which are squares, in spite of other differences they may have.

The child's learning of language is accompanied by concept learning. Even before learning the word *ball*, for example, the child may demonstrate some understanding of the concept by throwing all round objects that are available. Experience with the world enables the child to go from broadly generalized concepts to narrower and more refined concepts. The first time the child tries to bounce an apple, he or she comes to realize that the concept of ball must be revised: a ball cannot be defined by its roundness alone.

Through a gradual process of discrimination learning, the child refines concepts and is able to make fewer errors in classifying objects.

VERBAL LEARNING

Learning of verbal language is crucial in our society, for most of our later learning is based on language. As noted previously, much of our learning in high school and college is the learning of new words — verbal learning.

Because of the importance of verbal learning, psychologists have long been interested in the process and in the factors which can facilitate this process. One of the most important factors in facilitating verbal learning is the factor of meaningfulness. *Meaningfulness* refers to the number of associations which an individual can make to the items being learned. The greater the number of associations, the more meaningful the material and the easier it is to learn. A list of words such as *cat, chair, football* would be easier to learn than a list containing words such as *icon, traduce,* and *eon.* The factor of meaningfulness underlies and makes valid student requests for relevance in education. Relevance in learning situations often involves relating academic material to the experiences of the student. This process should increase the meaningfulness of the material by adding associations to the words used, thus making the material easier to learn.

Memory

Learned material is stored in memory. Once it is learned, we do not always have it in our conscious minds, yet it is stored in memory and can usually be called forth when we need it. Psychologists have discovered two forms of memory. Although not all psychologists agree that they are totally different processes, most believe that they are.

Short-term memory. Short-term memory refers to the storage of information for relatively short periods of time. We have access to information in short-term memory for a brief period (probably less than 60 seconds), and then it is "gone." The most common example of this can be found in our memory for phone numbers. One can look up a number and store it long enough to dial. Within a minute, however, one cannot remember the number. Short-term memory allows us to hold information in memory that we need only briefly, thus preventing long-term memory from being cluttered up with unnecessary information.

Long-term memory. Long-term memory involves the storage of information for days, weeks, months, or years. Rehearsal of information apparently transfers it from the temporary storage of short-term memory to long-term memory, where it can be held and recalled after long periods of time.

DIFFERENCES BETWEEN SHORT-TERM MEMORY AND LONG-TERM MEMORY

Short-term storage contains relatively few memories. Long-term storage, on the other hand, contains so many different items that they are impossible to count. The number of items which can be held in short-term memory is, according to Miller (1956), "the magical number seven, plus or minus two." For example, if you read the numbers 6222369 once, you can easily repeat them without looking back. But to perform the same task with the numbers 3016222369 is far more difficult and will usually involve errors. The capacity of short-term memory can be increased, however, by the process of "chunking" material, or forming it into groups or clusters. In this way, each chunk forms one unit and one can remember 7 ± 2 units. The numbers used above, when chunked as 301-622-2369, are far easier to remember. In the same way, memory for the letters THEHOUSEISSOLD is unlikely after one reading, but once chunked into the words THE HOUSE IS SOLD, they become easy to recall.

FORGETTING

Most students are as concerned with the problem of forgetting as with the problem of learning. All have been faced with the experience of feeling certain that learning has been accomplished, yet being unable to remember the material on an exam. There are a number of theories of forgetting that attempt to explain why forgetting occurs.

Decay theory. According to this theory, the memory is recorded in terms of a neural pattern or trace. When a memory is stored but is not used, the memory trace fades and in time disappears.

Interference theory. This theory holds that our memory of certain things is interfered with by other learning experiences stored in memory. If we have learned the French word for *book* and later have learned the Spanish word for *book*, we may not be able to recall the French word because of the interference of the Spanish.

Repression theory. According to Freudian theory, we forget because we want to. This is known as motivated forgetting. That is, if a memory is painful or embarrassing, we are motivated to push it out of our conscious mind, or forget it. Although there is evidence that this type of forgetting occurs, it probably doesn't account for all forgetting.

Failure in retrieval. According to this approach, forgetting is caused by the inability to retrieve or pull out the memory. If the appropriate cue is present, the memory can be produced. Without the appropriate cue, we are unable to remember. An analogy to a computer best illustrates the process. A computer has a vast store of information which can be called forth only if requested in the proper way. The computer, let us assume, can calculate the equation $(45 + 36)/14 =$. However, if the question is not asked properly the computer will give an incorrect answer or will not answer at all. It has not forgotten — it has failed to retrieve the information because the appropriate cue was not present.

HOW TO REMEMBER

Probably the best advice one can give on how to remember is to learn the information well in the first place. Once you have studied until you think the material is

BOX 13-1 THE MIND OF A MNEMONIST

Have you ever wished you could learn information quickly and easily, after only one reading? Or dreamed of not forgetting a single thing you had learned? Astounding memory abilities are possible, but they occur only rarely. The case of S. is such an example (Luria, 1968). This man could easily remember lists of seventy words or numbers after only one reading. He could recite them from memory in any order — and could remember all the items and correctly recall them fifteen years later. How did he do it?

It was accomplished in part through some unique, and perhaps inborn, ability to make use of mnemonic devices. One of the most interesting aspects of his ability was *synesthesia*. Synesthesia is a process in which an experience in a single sensory modality (such as vision) is perceived as having components of other sensory modalities. A sound heard by S., for example, had not only an auditory component but visual, gustatory, and tactile components as well. A 50-cycle, 100 db. tone produced a visual sensation of a brown strip against a dark background with red, tonguelike edges, a taste of sweet-and-sour borscht, and a feeling that gripped his tongue. The complexity of his perception is shown in a comment made to one of his colleagues (Luria, 1968, p. 24): "What a crumbly, yellow voice you have." Numbers too had their own images. A 2 was seen as rectangular, as whitish in color, and as a high-spirited woman. This extra information which was attached to each incoming bit of information served as an aid in later recall.

When S. was given a long list of items to learn and remember, the images associated with each item were "distributed" along a road or street that he knew. To recall the items, he then simply had to "walk" along the street and name each item as he "saw" it. This approach did cause occasional omissions in his recall because of bad placement of the "objects," as illus-

---

learned, study some more. This is known as *overlearning,* and it can have a dramatic effect on retention. If one can learn a list of words and give the first error-free recitation of them after ten trials, an additional ten trials of practice (100 percent overlearning) will almost double the amount retained for up to a month (Krueger, 1929).

Another aid to memory is the use of *mnemonic devices* or strategies (see Box 13-1). These are methods of coding or organizing material to be learned. One of the most successful mnemonic devices involves the use of techniques to increase the meaningfulness of the items to be learned. If one has a list of ten words to learn, it is far easier to do so if they can be incorporated into a sentence. Mnemonic devices are used by memory-improvement courses. In trying to improve one's memory for names, one

trated in the following (Luria, 1968, p. 36):

I put the image of the *pencil* near a fence . . . the one down the street, you know. But what happened was that the image fused with that of the fence, and I walked right on past without noticing it. The same thing happened with the word *egg*. I had put it up against a white wall and it blended in with the background. How could I possibly spot a white egg up against a white wall?

Lest one begins to dream of the joy this ability would bring, we should look also at its disadvantages. When a list of items was being learned, each item had to be read off one at a time with three to four seconds between each item. When information was given at a faster rate, S. was overwhelmed with a vast confusion of images. Think of the problems he would have in handling a one-hour classroom lecture. His mnemonic ability also severely slowed his reading speed, for the images involved in each portion of a sentence had to be fully worked out before he could go on to the next part of the sentence. If the interpretation of the first part didn't fit with the second, he had to start all over again, as illustrated in the following passage (Luria, 1968, p. 112):

I was read this phrase: "N. was leaning up against a tree . . ." I saw a slim young man dressed in a dark blue suit (N., you know, is so elegant). He was standing near a big linden tree with grass and woods all around. . . . But then the sentence went on: "and was peering into a shop window." Now how do you like that! It means the scene isn't set in the woods, or in a garden, but he's standing on the street. And I have to start the whole sentence over from the beginning.

Thus, such astounding memory abilities may appear to be a beautiful dream. But they could well serve as such an impediment to our usual way of gathering information that they would take on nightmarish qualities.

commonly picks a distinctive characteristic of the person and associates it with the name. Thus, the next time the person is met, observation of that characteristic should evoke the memory of the name.

Students who wish their study efforts to be as productive as possible should try to use mnemonic strategies to organize the material to be learned. Then, to ensure successful retention, they should, unfortunately, study some more.

SUMMARY

Motivation is the force which impels behavior. The needs which function in all people can be divided into two general classes: *inborn* and *learned*. Inborn needs are related to the survival of the organism or of the species, and include hunger, thirst, and the needs for elimination, sleep, sexual activity, and the avoidance of pain. There are other needs, called *stimulus needs,* which research indicates may be inborn also. In order to function well psychologically and to effectively deal with our environment, we need a certain quantity and variety of stimulation. Curiosity and the search for novelty fall into the category of stimulus needs.

Learned needs are those which have been acquired in the process of development, such as the need for approval, the need to affiliate, and the need to dominate. These needs, because they are learned, may differ extensively from person to person. This is a crucial factor in education, for without motivation adequate learning will not occur. For any educational system to work, it must function within the framework of motives that are meaningful to its students.

To understand why a behavior persists, we must know not only why the individual does it (motivation) but also what is gained by doing it (reinforcement). A reinforcer is a stimulus which affects the frequency of a response, increasing or decreasing it. A *positive reinforcer* (reward) is a stimulus that increases the frequency of a response. A *negative reinforcer* is an unpleasant stimulus which increases the frequency of the response that leads to its removal. A *punishment* is an unpleasant stimulus that suppresses or eliminates the response which it follows. It has no direct effect on the production of a desired response. Punishment is generally seen as less effective in modifying behavior than either negative or positive reinforcement.

It is often difficult to determine which reinforcers will operate in which way for a given individual. The effect of a particular reinforcing stimulus is dependent on the strength at that time of the need the stimulus fills, on whether or not a need is present (in the case of learned needs), and on which need is the strongest at the time. Thus, when we wish to develop a behavior in another person, we must find a reinforcer that will fill the individual's unique and current needs.

Classical conditioning is a learning process which has important effects on human behavior. We start with two stimuli: the *unconditioned stimulus* (US) and the *conditioned stimulus* (CS). The US elicits a response automatically, without training. The response which occurs automatically to the US is called the *unconditioned response* (UR). The second stimulus, the CS, is neutral in the sense that it elicits no response that would interfere with or prevent the occurrence of the UR. Pairing of the CS with the US produces learning in which the CS comes to elicit a *conditioned response* (CR) which is similar to the UR. The US serves as the reinforcer in this type of learning. If one wishes to stop the performance of the behaviors, one removes the reinforcer. This process is called *extinction*. If the individual is given a brief rest after a group of extinction trials, an increase in the response to the CS will occur. This increase following a rest period is called *spontaneous recovery*.

The general importance of classical conditioning becomes clearer by examination of two processes: conditioned emotional response and stimulus generalization. In the *conditioned emo-*

tional response, the US produces an emotional response (UR) which becomes attached to a previously neutral CS through conditioning. *Stimulus generalization* refers to the fact that a CR will be given not only to the particular CS used in training, but to other, similar stimuli. Through this process, the emotional tone conditioned to one particular object will also be felt in the presence of other, similar objects.

A second type of learning is *operant learning*. Any behavior the person is capable of performing can be operantly trained. The training technique is called *shaping* by the method or *successive approximations*. This is a gradual process in which each response of a series of responses that more and more closely approximates the final desired behavior is rewarded, until the total response is given. After training, withholding the reinforcer will produce *extinction* (elimination of the response). Two methods can be used to slow down or prevent extinction after the individual leaves the training situation. One method is to use a reward that is generally available to the subject. Another method relates to the schedule of reinforcement used in training. A *continuous reinforcement schedule,* in which all correct responses are reinforced, produces relatively fast learning but also fairly quick extinction. Under a *partial reinforcement schedule,* which provides reinforcement for only some of the correct responses, learning is somewhat slower but extinction is also slower. Use of partial reinforcement schedules and widely available reinforcers will permit continued performance of the response even after the individual has left the training situation.

Stimulus generalization can broaden the effect of operant training since the response learned to one stimulus will be given to other, similar stimuli. *Discrimination learning* involves a reversal of stimulus generalization. The individual learns to give a response only to a specific stimulus, not to similar stimuli. This is accomplished by reinforcing only responses given to the specific stimulus.

There are two basic types of operant learning that occur in the presence of negative reinforcers: escape learning and avoidance learning. In *escape learning,* the response learned allows the individual to end the unpleasant condition (negative reinforcer). *Avoidance learning* involves giving the response before the negative reinforcer occurs, so that the negative reinforcer is not received at all.

Perception can create many problems in learning. A teacher's perception of students can have an effect on their performance, increasing or decreasing it. The students' unique perceptual styles may affect how they interpret lectures, questions, and assignments, thus altering what they learn. Finally, physiological problems in the sensory apparatus can affect learning. Many difficulties in education which are attributed to slow learning, retardation, improper motivation, etc., may be instead problems in the functioning of the sensory apparatus.

Human beings are verbal animals, relying heavily on verbalization to communicate with others. The most basic units of spoken language are *phonemes,* which are the limited number of sounds out of which the entire language is built. They are combined into *morphemes,* which are the smallest language units having meaning. Words, which are single morphemes or combinations of morphemes, are grouped into sentences according to the rules of combination known as *grammar.*

The basic sound-making ability necessary for spoken language is inborn. Babies spontaneously "babble," making all the basic sounds (phonemes) necessary for spoken language. Through learning, the child gradually eliminates sounds not part of the native language and learns to form morphemes, words, and sentences from phonemes. Two theories are commonly used to explain how this learning occurs: (1) *operant theory,* which stresses the use of reinforcement and (2) *observation theory,* which stresses imitation.

Words are not objects; they simply stand for or refer to objects. Most words refer to groups of objects and are therefore called *concepts:* that is, symbols that refer to common properties of objects or events.

Because of the importance of language in our society, psychologists have long been interested in factors which facilitate verbal learning. One of the most important of these is *meaningfulness* — the number of associations made to items being learned.

Once material is learned, it is stored in memory. *Short-term memory* retains small amounts of information (five to nine items) for about sixty seconds. If we wish to retain information for longer periods, we transfer it to *long-term memory,* where it may be stored indefinitely.

Once information has been stored in long-term memory, why do we forget it? There are several theories which attempt to answer this question:

1. *Decay theory* states that forgetting occurs due to the fading of the memory trace.
2. *Interference theory* states that forgetting occurs because of interference by other learning.
3. *Repression theory* states that we forget because we want to, because a memory is unpleasant.
4. *Failure of retrieval* states that when the appropriate cues for recalling the memory are not present, then forgetting occurs.

An aid to better memory is *overlearning.* Organizing or coding material to be learned through the use of *mnemonic devices* also aids memory.

GLOSSARY

Avoidance learning: a learning situation in which giving the correct response prevents or avoids a noxious stimulus

Chunking: grouping or clustering material to increase short-term memory capacity

Classical conditioning: the learning process in which two stimuli are associated, resulting in the transfer of the response given automatically to one of the stimuli to the other, previously neutral stimulus

Concept: a symbol which refers to common properties of a group of objects or events

Conditioned response: the response the individual learns to give to the conditioned stimulus in classical conditioning

Conditioned stimulus: the stimulus which is neutral at the start of classical conditioning and which through association with the unconditioned stimulus comes to elicit the conditioned response

Continuous reinforcement schedule: pattern of reinforcement in operant conditioning in which every correct response given by the individual is reinforced

Decay theory: theory stating that forgetting occurs due to fading of the memory trace

Discrimination learning: the process whereby the individual is trained to give a response to a particular stimulus but to withhold the response to other, similar stimuli

Escape learning: a learning situation in which the subject, by giving the correct response after receiving a noxious stimulus, escapes from the stimulus

Extinction: the procedure of withholding the reinforcer for a given response in order to decrease the frequency of that response

Grammar: language rules of combination

Higher-order conditioning: a form of classical conditioning based on prior learning; after conditioning is well established, the conditioned stimulus is used as an unconditioned stimulus and is paired with a new neutral stimulus

Interference theory: theory stating that forgetting occurs because of the interference caused by other learning

Learning: any relatively permanent change in behavior which results from the individual's experience or practice

Mnemonic devices: methods of organizing or coding material to be learned that aid in retention and later recall

Morpheme: the smallest unit of language which has meaning

Motivation: any force that impels behavior

Negative reinforcer: a noxious stimulus; its occurrence increases the frequency of the response that leads to its removal

Operant conditioning: a method of altering the frequency of responses by the appropriate application of reinforcers

Partial reinforcement schedule: a pattern of reinforcement in which only some of the correct responses are reinforced

Phoneme: any of the basic units of sound from which all words of a language are constructed

Positive reinforcer: a pleasant stimulus; its occurrence will increase the frequency of the response with which it is associated

Punishment: an unpleasant stimulus; its occurrence will tend to decrease the frequency of the response which it follows

Reinforcement: any stimulus which, when it occurs, has an effect on the frequency of a response

Repression theory: theory stating that forgetting is motivated; we forget because an experience is unpleasant or painful

Shaping: the procedure of selectively reinforcing those responses which are progressively more similar to the one desired; training method for operant responses

Spontaneous recovery: an increase in the performance of an extinguished response after a rest period

Stimulus generalization: the process by which the response learned to one stimulus is also elicited by other, similar stimuli

Trace: a neural pattern representing a memory

Unconditioned response: the response which occurs automatically to the unconditioned stimulus in classical conditioning

Unconditioned stimulus: the stimulus in classical conditioning which automatically evokes the unconditioned response

REFERENCES

Fader, D. N., and Shaevitz, M. H. *Hooked on books*. New York: Berkley Publishing Corp., 1966.

Fleming, J. D. Field report: The state of the apes. *Psychology Today*, 1974, *2*(2), 31–48.

Gardner, R. A., and Gardner, B. T. Teaching sign language to a chimpanzee. *Science*, 1969, *165*, 664–672.

Heron, W. Cognitive and physiological effects of perceptual isolation. In P. Solomon, et al. (Eds.), *Sensory deprivation*. Cambridge, Mass.: Harvard University Press, 1961.

Kagan, J., and Havemann, E. *Psychology: An introduction*. New York: Harcourt Brace Jovanovich, 1972.

Krueger, W. C. F. The effect of overlearning on retention. *Journal of Experimental Psychology*, 1929, *12*, 71–78.

Luria, A. R. *The mind of a mnemonist*. New York: Basic Books, 1968.

Miller, G. A. The magical number seven, plus or minus two: Some limits on our capacity for processing information. *Psychological Review*, 1956, *63*, 81–97.

Pavlov, I. P. *Conditioned reflexes* (G. V. Anrep. trans.). London: Oxford University Press, 1927.

Postman, N., and Weingartner, C. *Teaching as a subversive activity*. New York: Delacorte Press, 1969.

Premack, D. Language in chimpanzee? *Science*, 1971, *172*, 808–822.

Rosenthal, R., and Jacobson, L. *Pygmalion in the classroom*. New York: Holt, Rinehart and Winston, 1968.

Schrank, H. *Teaching human beings*. Boston: Beacon Press, 1972.

Watson, J. B., and Rayner, R. Conditioned emotional reactions. *Journal of Experimental Psychology*, 1920, *3*, 1–14.

SUGGESTED READINGS

Atkinson, J. W. *An introduction to motivation*. Princeton, N.J.: Van Nostrand Reinhold, 1964.

Birney, R. C., Burdick, H., and Teevan, R.

G. *Fear of failure.* New York: Van Nostrand Reinhold, 1969.

Glaser, R. (Ed.) *The nature of reinforcement.* Columbus, Ohio: Merrill, 1971.

Logan, F. A. *Fundamentals of learning and motivation.* Dubuque, Iowa: Brown, 1970.

Pavlov, I. P. *Conditioned reflexes.* New York: Oxford University Press, 1927.

Skinner, B. F. *The behavior of organisms.* New York: Appleton-Century-Crofts, 1938.

Photo by Linda Russell

D

Who's Capable?

Unit 14
Capability: Given or Acquired?

A revolutionary war soldier, given the name of Kallikak by the researcher who studied him, was the father of two separate families — one legitimate and one illegitimate. Before marrying, he had an affair with a tavern maid who was said to be mentally defective. They had one son. Four hundred and eighty of the descendants of this union were located. One hundred and forty-three were feebleminded, thirty-three were judged to be sexually immoral, and twenty-four were alcoholics. An analysis of the offspring of Kallikak's marriage to a woman reputed to be of better mental ability, as well as of higher social class, indicated that of the five hundred descendants of this union, only a few were considered socially undesirable or mentally defective.

Goddard, 1912.

This "study," along with others like it, led to the theory that low intelligence, as well as immorality, was inherited. Today our manner of studying the hereditary basis of intelligence is somewhat more sophisticated, but the question still remains: Does the intelligence level of the parents limit the intellectual development of the child? Before we can tackle this issue, it is first necessary to define the term *intelligence*.

What Is Intelligence?

Many psychologists throughout the history of IQ testing have defined intelligence as that which an intelligence test measures. Although this is a clear statement of how the concept is measured (operational definition), it doesn't really help us to understand the concept itself. The problem is to discover if there is a definition which exists independently of the test and which may be applied both within and across cultures. That is, what is this thing we are trying to measure when we develop a test of intelligence?

There are probably as many definitions of intelligence as there are people who have worked with the concept. We will look briefly at two of the definitions to see if they are useful in understanding the hereditary basis of intelligence.

According to Binet (Binet and Simon, 1916, p. 43), "to judge well, to comprehend well, to reason well . . . are the essential activities of intelligence." Although at first glance this seems reasonable, it does present some difficulties. The question is: to judge and comprehend what? It seems unreasonable to require good judgment and comprehension of everything. And in fact intelligence tests, as we shall see when we examine them, test only a sample of an individual's judging, comprehending, and reasoning.

Wechsler (1958, p. 7) offers a definition of intelligence that is somewhat broader: "the aggregate or global capacity of the individual to act purposefully, to think rationally, and to deal effectively with his environment."

This definition is important because it is general enough to apply cross-culturally. However, the specific behaviors which indicate purposeful action, rational thinking, and effective dealing with the environment vary from culture to culture. The capacity to read well is important to success in the American culture. Such a skill will not, however, significantly help those in the relatively isolated Eskimo culture to deal effectively with their environment. There the ability to hunt and fish skillfully is far more important and would therefore reflect intelligence in that particular culture.

The effect of social values is clear in the case of the Kallikaks cited at the beginning of this unit. The "bad" side of the family engaged in behaviors that were socially unacceptable. Such behaviors may have represented effective dealing with the environment in which these people found themselves as a result of their social class. But society does not examine the effectiveness of the behavior within a particular social environment. Rather, it defines what behaviors are to be called intelligent and expects them to apply equally across situations.

Our particular society values learning and its consequents (money and prestige), and so those behaviors which enable attainment of these values are defined as intelligent. Pursuit of other values through purposeful, rational, and effective behaviors is simply not "defined" as intelligent behavior. The main point here is that the definition of intelligence has a strong social basis. All societies would probably include learning of something as a factor in intelligence. But what it is that is to be learned is socially restricted. This society does not place high value on the attainment of interpersonal skills, on learning how to be sensitive, or on learning to care. Such things are simply not within this society's definition of the skills it wants learned, so learning them is not considered to be a sign of intelligent behavior.

Hereditary And Environmental Effects On Intelligence

The nature-nurture controversy is one which has taken as its subject matter almost every kind of human behavior. Intelligence has been no exception. In its general form this controversy attempts to answer the question, "Is a particular behavior determined by hereditary factors or by environmental experience?" Several approaches have been taken in an attempt to identify the determinants of intelligence.

PARENT AND NATURAL CHILD STUDIES

This approach involves the study of the relationship between the IQ scores of the parents and the IQ scores of their natural children. Since parents and children share the same genetic components, the relationship between their IQ scores should give an estimate of the contribution of heredity to intelligence. The technique used has been simply to measure the IQ of the parents and of the children, evaluating the relationship between these scores by means of a statistical technique known as a correlation. Correlations can vary from .00 to 1.00. A zero correlation would indicate that there is no relationship between the IQ of the parent and the child. A correlation of 1.00 would indicate a perfect relationship. Negative correlations (minimum of -1.00) are also possible. This would indicate an inverse relationship; i.e., the higher the IQ of the parents, the lower the IQ of the children.

Studies of this kind have generally found a correlation of about .50, which indicates that there is a fairly strong relationship between the IQ scores of parents and their natural children. The problem with such studies in determining hereditary components is that there is no way to isolate how much of this effect is due to genetic components. Not only do parents and children share the same genetic material; they usually share the same environment. Highly intelligent parents give their children not only a specific genetic endowment, but also an environment which may or may not tend to encourage intellectual development. Parents of low intelligence may not provide the environmental circumstances that allow their children to maximize their intellectual potential.

ADOPTED CHILDREN STUDIES

In an attempt to solve the problems found in the natural child studies, research on adopted children has been conducted. Two types of relationships have been studied. By examining the correlation between a child and his or her natural parents from whom the child has been separated, one can look at the isolated effects of heredity. Correlations between the IQ of the same child and that of the adoptive parents, with whom the child lived but shared no genetic endowment, would allow examination of the isolated effects of environment. If the two correlations were compared, one could tell whether heredity or environment made a greater contribution to the child's intelligence.

The results of these studies has not, however, provided any clear-cut answer. Rather, different studies have given different results. Some research showed the contribution of hereditary factors to the child's intelligence to be as high as 80 percent. Other studies showed that the hereditary component was far less. These latter studies indicate that an improved environment can have a substantial effect on the intelligence of the child, raising IQ to a higher level than would be predicted from the IQ level of the natural parents.

There are several reasons studies of adopted children don't reveal more consistent results. First of all, the time at which a child is taken from the natural parents is important. If the child stays with them for a number of years, the environment of the natural parents will have a strong effect on intellectual development — an effect that may persist even after the child moves to a new home. A second important factor deals with whether the environment provided by many orphanages causes retardation of intellectual development. Finally, due to the practice of adoption agencies of placing children in homes similar to their natural homes, the adoptive environment is often similar to what the natural parents would have provided. These confounding factors make it difficult to separate clearly environmental from hereditary effects in studies of adopted children.

TWIN STUDIES

A third group of studies has involved examination of the relationship between the IQ scores of identical twins and the relationship between IQ scores of fraternal twins. Identical twins have identical genetic endowment, while fraternal twins are no more similar in genetic endowment than ordinary siblings. These studies consistently show that there is a higher correlation between the IQ scores of identical twins than between fraternal twins, supporting a hereditary interpretation. It has also been found that the relationship between the IQ scores of fraternal twins is higher than that between ordinary siblings. Since there is no greater genetic similarity within a pair of fraternal twins than within a pair of ordinary siblings, these results would suggest that the environment of fraternal twins must be more similar. Once again the confounding influence of environment enters, preventing clear separation of hereditary and environmental effects.

The only conclusion which one can come to based on the data currently available is that both heredity and environment have an effect and it is no longer realistic to try to prove that intelligence is totally determined by one or the other factor. This conclusion is generally accepted by most behavioral scientists. There is still controversy, however, over efforts to determine the relative importance of environment and of heredity. The hereditarians tend to focus on an 80-percent hereditary influence as suggested by Jensen (1969). In trying to determine the relative hereditary and environmental contributions, we are first going to have to be more certain than we are at present of exactly what it is we are measuring.

Unit 15
The Numbers Game

John Ertl was born in Hungary. During the late fifties, while in Canada, he took a standard intelligence test. His score was 77, placing him at a subnormal intellectual level. Despite this assessment, made while he was a graduate student at the University of Ottawa, he continued his studies and received a Ph.D. in psychology.

You may conclude that you can earn a Ph.D. in psychology with subnormal intelligence; or you may conclude that the test was not a reliable assessment of Dr. Ertl's ability. Cases like Dr. Ertl's occur frequently. His education and career represent accomplishments far above average. But he "fails" on IQ tests. In order to understand how this can happen, it is necessary to examine the tests used to evaluate intelligence. In this unit, three specific intelligence tests will be discussed. They are only a small sample of the IQ tests available, but they are among the most well known. Each has a special area in which it is most useful. The Stanford-Binet was developed for children and is best used for this population. The Wechsler Adult Intelligence Scale was designed for adults. The Goodenough-Harris Drawing Test is an example of a nonlanguage test.

The Stanford-Binet

This test, originally named the Binet-Simon, was developed by Binet in order to evaluate subnormal children in the Paris school system. In 1908 the test was expanded and the concept of mental age was introduced for the first time. Mental age (MA) was defined in terms of the score obtained by an average child at a given age. That is, an MA of 7 indicated that the child performed at the same level as an average seven-year-old as defined by Binet's sample.

In 1916 Terman did extensive revisions of the test. Since at that time Terman was at Stanford University, the 1916 and subsequent revisions have been called the Stanford-Binet. The test was divided into subtests representing the average performance of different age groups. For example, the subtest for three-year-olds included such tasks as pointing to parts of the body and naming familiar objects. The subtest for nine-year-olds included constructing sentences from three words and making rhymes. Some objects used in the test are shown in Figure 15-1. Specific, detailed instructions were also developed and were to be used by all administrators.

Photo by Sheila A. Farr. Copyright © 1974 by Houghton Mifflin Co.

FIGURE 15-1 A child works with objects used for intelligence testing in the Stanford-Binet.

126 *Who's Capable?*

The items on the test were standardized on approximately fourteen hundred children and adults, including average, defective, and superior subjects. However, the standardization sample represented native-born white urban individuals only. This created an automatic bias against other subcultural groups. White urban individuals learn different things than black urban individuals or white rural individuals do. So a test that measures things that the white urban child learns will by definition fail to measure what other subcultures have learned. This factor increases the probability of producing lower scores for individuals from other subcultural groups.

The 1916 test introduced the ratio intelligence quotient (IQ) for the first time. This score was obtained by dividing the subject's mental age by the chronological age (CA): IQ = MA/CA × 100. The score of the test is arranged so that the average score is 100: the average seven-year-old, for example, will have an IQ of 7/7 × 100, or 100.

It should be remembered that the MA is only a test score. It represents the number of questions answered correctly by individuals as compared with others in their age group. If different questions were asked, the subject might receive a different MA. Since the mental age is only a score, it can be used only in a descriptive sense. In other words, it can tell what the individual knows but cannot explain the individual. IQ scores can go up or down depending on certain external conditions such as the sex or race of the tester; this is further evidence that the score is not a perfect reflection of how much the individual knows.

The most recent revision of the Stanford-Binet was made in 1960. Few major changes were introduced into the form of the test itself. The revision involved primarily an updating of the items. The content of the test varies at different age levels, with verbal skills being stressed more with increasing age. The subtests for lower levels include eye-hand coordination, perceptual discrimination, and ability to follow instructions. The older age group tests include vocabulary, analogies, and proverb interpretation.

TEST EVALUATION

One of the methods for evaluating a test is to measure what is called *validity*. We say a test is valid if it measures what it is supposed to measure. If I ask you what 46 × 24 equals, I can claim that this "test" is a valid measure of arithmetic. However, if the same question is said to measure knowledge of history, you would question its validity. Much of the validity research on the Stanford-Binet involves correlation between IQ and various measures of academic achievement, i.e., determining whether those who score high on the Stanford-Binet also do well in academic pursuits. These correlations for the most part fall between .40 and .70. Since it stresses verbal skills, the Stanford-Binet correlates most highly with those academic subjects that are predominately verbal in nature.

Another method for evaluating a test is to measure its *reliability*. This is a measure of the consistency of a test — whether it provides the same results for the same individual when tested more than one time. Although the same score is not found or expected for an individual when the two testings are separated by many years, tests given close together in time should give similar results. The reliability of the Stanford-Binet has been found to be quite high.

CULTURAL BIAS

The Stanford-Binet has often been criticized for its largely verbal content. Such content discriminates against those who are not a part of the mainstream, white, middle-class culture. The test is not culture-free and should not be used for a comparative evaluation of the intelligence of other cultures or subcultures. It can be used only as an indication of the potential success of an individual in the current educational system, and as such it is a useful tool.

The Wechsler Adult Intelligence Scale

Although the Stanford-Binet has items that were developed for adult use, its original structure as a test for children does not make it highly valid for testing of adults. It does not accurately measure changes and differences in adult intelligence. The Wechsler Adult Intelligence Scale (WAIS) was developed specifically for adults and more accurately reflects their intellectual abilities.

The test was first developed in 1939 as the Wechsler-Bellevue Intelligence Scale. The WAIS is a recent revision of this test. Like the Stanford-Binet, it is divided into subtests. These subtests are not, however, grouped according to age levels, but rather are arranged in order of increasing difficulty. The WAIS gives a Verbal IQ and a Performance IQ, as well as a Full Scale IQ representing a combination of the verbal and performance measures. There are six verbal subtests and five performance subtests (see Box 15-1). The performance scales include Picture Arrangement, Picture Completion, Block Design, and Digit Symbol.

TEST EVALUATION

Few validity data have been gathered on this test. The author of the test argues for its content validity, which means that the test material is consistent with his definition of intelligence and that previous similar tests have served as useful tools. The WAIS has been correlated with other IQ tests, with most correlations being above .50. Correlations with the Stanford-Binet are generally between .60 and .90, indicating that one's score on the Stanford-Binet will be similar to the score obtained on the WAIS. There are some specific areas in which the two give different results. Older subjects and less intelligent subjects tend to score higher on the WAIS than on the Stanford-Binet. The WAIS, like the Stanford-Binet, gives IQ scores which change over time. Intellectual ability appears to grow rapidly and to peak between the ages of twenty-five and thirty, followed by a gradual decline in later years.

CULTURAL BIAS

The same problems of cultural bias exist on the WAIS as are found on the

BOX 15-1   VERBAL SUBTESTS FROM THE WECHSLER ADULT
INTELLIGENCE SCALE (Wechsler, 1944).

Subtest	Illustrative Items
1. General information	Who is the president of the United States? Who wrote Hamlet? What is ethnology?
2. General comprehension	What is the thing to do if you find an envelope in the street that is sealed and addressed and has a new stamp? Why are shoes made of leather? Why are people who are born deaf usually unable to talk?
3. Arithmetical reasoning	How much is four dollars and five dollars? How many hours will it take a man to walk twenty-four miles at the rate of three miles an hour? Eight men can finish a job in six days. How many men will be needed to finish it in a half day?
4. Digit span — repeat either forward or backward	5,8,2 4,2,7,3,1 2,7,5,8,6,2,5,8,4
5. Similarities — in what ways are these things alike?	Orange-banana Air-water Fly-tree
6. Vocabulary	Apple Microscope Traduce

Stanford-Binet. Let us look more closely at the illustrative items in Box 15-1. The items in the digit span portion appear fairly general and in fact yield little differences among ethnic or social groups. Given that the individual knows numbers, such a task should be relatively free of cultural bias. But let us look at the general information items. These clearly reflect the bias of this society. The student who does not know the president may well know who is head of the Black Panthers or leader of the California grape workers' strike. Surely it can be argued that the latter two items of information are in many cases more important for dealing effectively with a specific environment. Knowledge of who wrote *Hamlet* indicates breadth of knowledge, but is it any more relevant to purposeful thinking

Copyright Los Angeles Times. Reprinted with permission.

than knowing the name of the author of *Soul on Ice*? And in the case of both *Hamlet* and *Soul on Ice*, isn't knowledge and personal understanding of the content more important than being able to give the author's name?

The point is that IQ tests deal to a great extent with items someone considers important, and answers do indicate broad knowledge. But the bias inherent in the tests must make one wary of applying the term *intelligence*. A ghetto youth or a migrant worker might have stored a vast amount of useful and relevant knowledge about his environment, but it probably doesn't include the definition of *traduce*.

Goodenough-Harris Drawing Test

The Stanford-Binet and the WAIS have been criticized because they stress language skills and are therefore culturally dependent. Many attempts have been made to develop a nonverbal and relatively culture-free test. The Goodenough-Harris Drawing Test is one example (Harris, 1963). The test was originally developed in 1926 as the Goodenough Draw-A-Man Test. The subject's task was merely to draw a picture of a man. In the 1963 revision, there are two alternate forms allowing the subjects to be tested on drawings of either men or women. The drawings are scored on over 70 items, including body parts pictured, clothing details, proportion, and perspective. Subjects are evaluated on their drawings in terms of the details they are aware of in other people in comparison with other children their age. Typical drawings are shown in Figure 15-2.

The test, however, is not totally culture free, as has been shown by many studies. Dennis (1942) administered the test to Hopi Indian children. He found that the boys scored higher on the test, which would seem to indicate that they were more intelligent than the girls. This sex difference was due, however, not to differential intelligence of boys and girls but to the fact that within this particular culture the graphic arts are almost entirely a male activity. The boys had had more practice with drawing and so could do it better.

To develop a truly culture-free test had been conceded to be an impossible task. Goodenough and Harris (1950, p. 399), after reviewing results of cross-cultural studies, concluded that

the search for a culture free test, whether of intelligence, artistic ability, personal-social characteristics or any other measurable trait is illusory, and the naive assumption that the

130 Who's Capable?

mere freedom from verbal requirements renders a test equally suitable for all groups is no longer tenable.

Neural Efficiency Analyzer

The development of a new type of test, however, holds promise of eliminating some of the more cultural factors. It should be noted that this test is in a very early stage of development and that therefore most information on it is of a tentative nature. The technique uses a machine called a neural efficiency analyzer. The subject places on his or her head a helmet containing electrodes which record brain waves. These waves are fed into a computer for analysis. Once the helmet is on, the individual views lights which are flashed at random intervals. The "score" involves the time it takes the brain to respond to these lights. The faster the response, the more "intelligent" the subject. This test, which was developed by Dr. John Ertl, is viewed as a test not of general intelligence but of a component of intelligence. More specifically, it measures the speed of information transmission in the brain, which, it is hypothesized, is related to basic learning capacity. The test is culturally unbiased to the extent that it does not rely on specifics of what an individual has learned but rather on the speed of transmission of information. In addition, it has the advantage of being quick to administer (less than five minutes) and being usable on many individuals previously out of the range of conventional IQ tests (young children, illiterates, and the physically handicapped). Although it correlates highly with conventional intelligence tests, indicating that it is in some ways

FIGURE 15-2 Children's drawings of a man illustrate differences in relevant details. *(A)* is by a boy aged 5 years, 1 month; *(B)* is by a girl aged 8 years, 2 months; *(C)* is by a boy aged 9 years, 6 months; and *(D)* is by a boy aged 12 years, 9 months.

related to learning ability, there have been instances in which it has "discovered" that a child who had been classified as subnormal was in fact not intellectually inferior.

The evaluation of this test is not unanimously positive. The data in support of the approach have been mixed and many psychologists feel that it is too early to tell how useful the test will be. Nevertheless, the neural efficiency analyzer represents a totally new concept in intelligence testing. Hopefully, this apparatus or future developments will enable evaluation of intelligence that reflects more accurately what an individual's capability really is.

What of importance can we glean from this review of intelligence testing? Has the approach any value? Some authors have suggested doing away entirely with the concept of intelligence and the testing of it and dealing with individuals, not scores. Although this suggestion is not without value, neither is the concept of intelligence. Traditional IQ scores do predict academic success in most cases. If we were to change our concept of what academic success should be, then the tests would also have to be changed.

But, as noted earlier, the tests are not "bad" per se — it is the uses to which they have been put that are often totally unjustifiable and inexcusable. John Ertl was lucky. The test score of 77 was not used to prevent him from continuing his education. Others have not been so lucky. The tests can be used as guides to aid students and teachers in full development of the students' potentials. They should never be used, as they frequently are, to classify or define individuals as though they were static objects. Intelligence test scores are not fixed and unchangeable any more than people are. If one understands the meaning of IQ tests and scores, they can be useful, though limited, tools. If they are misunderstood, they become dangerous weapons wielded against individuals.

Unit 16
The Extremes: The Deficient and the Superior

All geniuses are pale and skinny.

All retardates look funny.

Very bright people are all a little crazy.

Retardates should be locked up — they are dangerous to other people.

These and other stereotypes about intellectually deficient and superior individuals are common. As is true with any group of people who are different, those who fall into the intellectually extreme categories are the subject of many myths. This unit will examine the intellectual extremes in an attempt to put such stereotypes in their proper perspective.

Intellectually Deficient Individuals

CAUSES OF RETARDATION

The causes of retardation are many. The American Association of Mental Deficiency gives eight categories of mental retardation and six supplementary groupings to evaluate causation. Two general categories of causation are sometimes used.

Familial retardation. In these cases there is no known disease, injury, or organic defect that has caused the retardation. Approximately 75 percent of all retarded people are classified as familial. They score in the retarded range on IQ tests, but no organic or physiological defect can be found which could be the cause of their retardation.

Physiologically defective retardation. In this type of retardation, the deficiency is attributed to some organic or physiological malfunction. There are a number of retardation syndromes that fall into this category.

Down's syndrome, or mongolism, is a syndrome that combines retardation with certain specific physical characteristics such as a small, round head, a skin fold over the eye, a fissured tongue, and short, stubby fingers. Some types are associated with the presence of an extra chromosome, so that the retarded individual has forty-seven chromosomes instead of the normal forty-six. This particular form of Down's syndrome also appears to be associated frequently with older mothers.

Cerebral palsy is another condition which may lead to the development of mental retardation, in addition to the motor disorders characterizing the disease.

Phenylketonuria (PKU) is a disorder in which there is a chemical imbalance within the body that can lead to retardation. Fortunately, the onset of the symptoms of this disorder is relatively slow and there is a simple chemical test available to diagnose the disorder in infants. A special diet, if started at an early age, will prevent the onset of the mental retardation.

CLASSIFICATION OF MENTAL RETARDATION

The severity of mental deficiency varies widely. The formal classification of retardates in terms of IQ is done on a five-level scale (Heber, 1959, p. 58) as shown in Table 16-1. At the lowest level in the classification is the *profound* retardate, whose IQ is below 20.* These individuals generally evidence physical disorders, such as blindness or deafness. The profound retardate generally shows no speech development, and motor development is very poor. These individuals are generally considered to be incapable of improvement through training, and they require extensive care for life.

The *severe* retardates are those with IQs from 20 to 35. They have some primitive speech and language skills, and their motor development is more advanced than that of profound retardates. Through training, these individuals are capable of developing certain self-help skills, such as feeding and dressing themselves. They may also develop some simple work skills, although most work must be limited to carefully controlled and supervised environments. Although severe retardates can develop more skills than profound retardates, they still generally need lifelong care and supervision.

The *moderate* retardates, with an IQ range of 36 to 51, show fewer neurophysiological complications and have better speech and language development. In addition, their motor development approaches normal levels. These individuals profit from self-help and work training. Although some lifetime supervision is often necessary,

---

*IQ scores quoted are based on the Stanford-Binet test.

TABLE 16-1 Formal classification system of retardates

Level	IQ Range	Characteristics
Profound	0–19	Physical disabilities Little if any speech Extremely poor motor development Requires lifelong care
Severe	20–35	Primitive speech Can learn simple self-help skills May learn simple work skills, but must be supervised
Moderate	36–51	Adequate speech development Motor development near normal Learns self-help and simple work skills
Mild	52–67	Most basic skills the same as normal, but development slower and does not reach same level of sophistication
Subnormal	68–83	Performance only slightly below average

they may be capable of at least partial self-support.

The *mild* retardates (IQs from 52 to 67) make up 85 percent of all retardates. They develop most of the skills that normal individuals do, but the development is often slower than normal and does not reach as sophisticated a level. The fifth level (IQs of 68 to 83) consists of individuals whose performance is only slightly subnormal.

SOCIAL AND OTHER SKILLS

The classification of a person as retarded and the level of retardation assigned should not be determined solely by the IQ level. Current definitions of retardation focus not only on the intellectual impairment of the individual but also on adaptive behaviors and social skills. The American Association of Mental Deficiency includes the examination of adaptive behavior as part of its formal evaluation of the retardate (Heber, 1959).

The Vineland Social Maturity Scale (Doll, 1953) has been developed to evaluate the social skills of an individual. The test assesses the competence of the individual in terms of personal independence and social responsibility. Table 16-2 gives the different categories of behaviors measured, along with some of the specific behaviors included in each category.

The evaluation of their social competence as a part of classification of mental

TABLE 16-2 General categories and sample behaviors from the Vineland Social Maturity Scale

General Category	Sample Behaviors
Self-help, general	Balances head Asks to go to toilet Tells time to quarter hour
Self-help, eating	Drinks from cup or glass assisted Eats with spoon Cares for self at table
Self-help, dressing	Pulls off socks Washes hands unaided Exercises complete care of dress
Locomotion	Moves about on floor Goes about neighborhood unattended Goes to distant points alone
Occupation	Transfers objects Performs responsible routine chores Performs expert or professional work
Communication	"Crows," laughs Makes telephone calls Communicates by letter
Self-direction	Is trusted with money Buys all own clothing Provides for future
Socialization	Reaches for familiar people Plays difficult games Shares community responsibilities

(Doll, 1953)

retardates is not, however, without problems. Social competence represents a value judgment. It varies from community to community and fluctuates with varying social and economic conditions within the community. In spite of these weaknesses, the addition of social maturity measures to the evaluation of the retarded gives a better total picture of the individual's abilities and potentials.

In general, an individual with a low IQ functions at a retarded level in most skills. There are rare exceptions, however, in the individual known as an "idiot savant." Horwitz, Kestenbaum, Person, and Jarvik (1965) report a case of twenty-four-year-old twins whose IQ scores were in the 60 to 70 range. They had, however, an astounding ability to calculate information related to dates. They could answer such questions as, "On what date of the year 2002 does the first Friday fall?" or, "In what year does April 21st fall on a Sunday?" One of the twins was accurate only within the current century, while the other had an accuracy range of 6000 years.

POTENTIAL

Special training of retardates at certain levels can improve their abilities. In one study, special preschool education of children with IQs from 45 to 80 led to increases in IQ and social abilities that were significantly greater than the gains of comparable children who received no special education. The amount of improvement that can be obtained varies with the child; retardates with organic or biological defects tend to show less improvement (Kirk et al., 1958). More research is needed to determine how to tap the full potential of the retarded child.

The retardate does not, however, remain a child forever. What happens to him when he reaches adulthood? Those individuals with extremely low IQs are generally confined to some sort of institution. Individuals falling in the mildly retarded range have been studied a number of times in an attempt to answer this question. For those subjects not in institutions, it has been found that the marriage rate was close to that of normal individuals, the majority of offspring were in the low normal range of IQ but were not retarded, and approximately 88 percent of the subjects were found to be employed and living in adequate homes. Although these subjects had a somewhat higher-than-average arrest record, the offenses for the most part were minor. In addition, it was discovered that the average IQ of the subjects had risen from 58 when first tested to 81 when retested almost twenty years later. It was concluded that "many children whose test scores and academic performance suggest mental deficiency develop into self-sufficient and desirable citizens as adults" (Charles, 1953, p. 67). Perhaps with more extensive training more of these individuals could become self-sufficient. We have devoted so little time and effort to the training of the retarded that their potential for development is largely unknown. Until the emphasis shifts from "custodial care," which is equivalent to keeping the retarded out of sight, their potential will remain unknown.

Intellectually Superior Individuals

CHARACTERIZATION

At the other extreme of the IQ range are the gifted — usually classified as those with IQs above 135. The first extensive study of these superior individuals was done by Galton (1869). He partially refuted the stereotype of the genius as small, weak, and bespectacled, for he found many of his subjects were physically superior. Galton concluded that the gifted are at one extreme of the physical scale or the other: either physically superior or very weak.

In a more extensive study, and perhaps the most definitive to date, Terman and his colleagues (Terman, 1926; Terman and Oden, 1947, 1959; Burks, Jensen, and Terman, 1930) studied over fifteen hundred subjects with IQs over 135. Most of the subjects were in the IQ range of 135 to 170, although some had IQs as high as 200. The subjects were studied over a thirty-five-year period. Most came from intellectually superior parents. As children they tended to talk early, were physically well developed, tended to be somewhat more mature than their peers, and were seen by their teachers as having positive emotional, moral, and social traits. In school many showed accelerated progress, with over 50 percent of the grades of the males and 75 percent of the grades of the females being A's. These individuals graduated from college with honors three times as often as students in the average college population.

As adults, these gifted subjects tended to maintain their physical and intellectual superiority, working primarily as professionals or semiprofessionals or in the higher business occupations. Terman's work has rather conclusively put an end to the stereotype of the gifted person as an individual inferior in physical characteristics and socioemotional adjustment. This work demonstrates that the intellectually superior individual tends to be superior in most aspects of behavior.

Hollingsworth (1942) studied only individuals with IQ scores above 180. Although her results in general confirm Terman's findings on lower-IQ subjects, she tended to find more maladjustment among her subjects. The general superiority of the gifted individual may peak in the 135 to 170 IQ range, with higher IQ levels showing less ease of adjustment.

CORRELATED FACTORS

In a survey of high-intelligence males, McCurdy (1957) examined the background factors that such individuals have in common. The primary factors found to characterize the childhood of these subjects were a great deal of attention from parents and other adults, intensive education and love in the early years, and a relatively isolated life in terms of peer associations. This is not to say that such practices will lead to a high level of intelligence, but that such childhood experiences may encourage highly intelligent individuals to develop their potential.

People at the intellectual extremes are different from those in the middle intellectual ranges in terms of their test scores. They are like others in that they are all different from each other. *All* retardates do not look funny, nor are *all* geniuses skinny. Stereotypes of those in the intellectually extreme groups are no more accurate than stereotypes of any other large and diverse group of people.

Unit 17
Nothing is Ever Black or White

It is often forgotten that the *fact* of racial differences is so immediate and compelling to most people that the burden of proof is on those who claim equality — not the reverse. . . . The evidence for Negro-white equality in intelligence under comparable conditions . . . is not even moderately convincing . . . Negro-white differences are so regular and persistent as strongly to suggest a genetic basis.

Garrett, 1962, p. 260.

I can only conclude that there is no scientifically acceptable evidence for the view that ethnic groups differ in innate abilities.

Klineberg, 1963, p. 203.

Which of the above statements is correct? Are there inborn differences between the races in basic intellectual abilities? Or do the observed differences result from differences in environmental factors? That blacks have obtained lower scores on conventional IQ tests cannot be doubted. Numerous studies clearly demonstrate this fact (see Shuey, 1966, for a complete review). The problem is in the interpretation of these findings. Should they be attributed to an innate inferiority of blacks, or are they due to the environmental differences that exist between blacks and whites in this country?

Hereditary Approach

The view that test score differences are due to racial disparities has been restated recently by Jensen (1969), thus rekindling the controversy. He discusses the general effect of hereditary factors on intelligence, using racial differences as an example. Although admitting that no single line of research is sufficient, he concludes that when all the data are taken into account it is "not an unreasonable hypothesis that genetic factors are strongly implicated in the average Negro-white intelligence differences" (p. 82). He also concludes that the discrepancy found between test scores for blacks and whites "cannot be completely or directly attributed to discrimination or inequalities in education" (p. 82).

Shuey (1966), in an extensive review of the literature, finds what she considers overwhelming evidence that blacks do score lower than whites and concludes that the data "inevitably point to the presence of native differences between Negroes and whites as determined by intelligence tests" (p. 521). This interpretation of the evidence is also supported by other authors.

Environmental Approach

The racial equality found on IQ tests when infants are tested, before the effects of the environment have had much chance to work, is one important argument in favor of the environmentalists' viewpoint. Several researchers have failed to find that white infants are intellectually superior to black infants.

Another important piece of evidence on hereditary equality has been found by Ertl in his work with the neural efficiency analyzer. Although blacks have not yet been compared with whites on this test, Mexican-Indian children have been compared with whites. This particular subculture, like the blacks, usually scores lower on conventional IQ tests than their white counterparts. However, scores on the neural efficiency analyzer show no differences.

Researchers who support the environmental approach do not dispute the fact of lower test scores for blacks but contend that such scores are attributable to environmental differences. There are several areas of investigation that can clarify the issue (see Figure 17-1).

Socioeconomic factors. Among the factors that could contribute to the test score differences is the generally lower socioeconomic status of blacks. There are several studies which have been cited by hereditarians as evidence that socioeconomic status is not an important factor. These studies have attempted to match the races in terms of so-

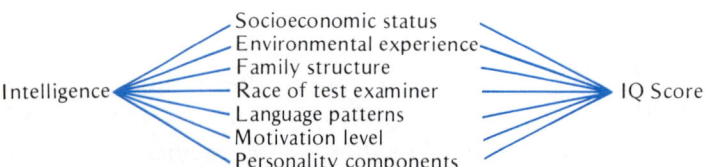

FIGURE 17-1 The basic intelligence of an individual is filtered through all the individual difference factors in its translation into an IQ score. It is clear why it is difficult to compare the IQ scores of two individuals who differ on one or more of the individual difference factors and to determine to what extent a score is caused by hereditary or environmental factors.

cioeconomic status and then compare the IQ scores. This procedure ensures that the scores of any group of black subjects would be compared only to whites of the same socioeconomic status. These studies show that black subjects score lower than whites of the same socioeconomic level.

The results of these studies have, however, been criticized by the environmentalists. The largest problem is that of accurately matching the socioeconomic status of the races, a task far more difficult than it may seem.

In addition, within the same socioeconomic level there are differences in the environmental circumstances of blacks and whites. For example, Deutsch and Brown (1964) found that father absence in the home led to significantly lower IQ scores for both black and white children. Since there are more homes without a father in the black community, this factor may be relevant to an explanation of the overall differences. It should be made clear here, however, that this is a hypothesis, not a conclusion.

Language. The stress on language in most IQ tests has also been cited as a possible cause of the racial differences. The evidence in this area is not clear, for the results on nonlanguage tests have been conflicting. Some studies show that racial differences are not present on nonlanguage tests, while others show differences of up to ten points. It may be, however, that other culturally biasing factors are operating within these tests, as was pointed out in the unit on testing. The importance of language as a discriminatory factor should be kept in mind, for the language patterns of blacks and whites are often quite different.

Motivation. Environmentalists have frequently stated that differences in motivation may cause the racial differences in scores. As we have noted, IQ tests, although related to the potential to learn, actually measure what has already been learned. The white student is motivated to learn the kinds of things these tests measure by, among other things, the knowledge that extensive learning and its correlate, academic success, will lead to occupational and financial rewards. Such a motivator may not apply, as we noted in the division on learning, to black children who believe that their general knowledge and ability will have little, if any, effect on their occupational or financial success. Until there are black children who can feel confident that their future success will reflect their knowledge, the role of motivators probably cannot be adequately assessed.

Special training. Also important to this controversy is the question of whether special training to make up for the alleged environmental differences can raise the IQ scores of blacks. Studies by Klineberg (1935a) and Lee (1951) are relevant to this point, for they have demonstrated that the IQs of southern blacks improve after moving north where conditions are somewhat better. The scores of these subjects also increased with the increased length of stay in the North. Other studies have shown that special or "remedial" training can raise IQ scores of blacks. In most of these studies, the IQ scores of the blacks remained below the white norms even after special education. This failure of blacks to attain white norm levels is another argument used by those who favor the hereditary viewpoint. It may, however, merely be the result of the fact that special training starts too late.

Personality. The basic factor of personality differences between blacks and whites should be evaluated. In two extensive studies of black personality (Kardiner and Ovesey, 1951; Karon, 1958), it was found that black subjects showed low self-esteem and high levels of aggression. None of this is surprising when one examines the social conditions in which blacks have been forced to live, yet the differences may bear some relation to IQ score differences. Some particularly poignant examples of the basic black-white differences are found in Goodman's study of race awareness in children (1952). When shown a picture of two men and asked to describe what he saw, a four-year-old white boy said it was a picture of "a good man — and a black one" (p. 29). A four-year-old black girl stated, "The people that are white, they can go up. The people who are brown, they have to go down" (p. 28). Another four-year-old black girl arrived one morning and proudly announced that she had scrubbed and scrubbed that morning, and she had almost come white (p. 38). Can these black and white children be "equated" in order to compare intelligence?

Black or White?

It is clear that the evidence does not unequivocally support either the hereditary or the environmental viewpoint. As stated above in the general discussion of heredity, both factors probably play a role. But at this time our tools simply aren't sophisticated enough to evaluate the different contributions of each with any accuracy.

The task of identifying and evaluating all potential environmental influences is far from complete. Klineberg (1935b) has listed seven environmental factors which could affect test results: motivation, rapport, culture, social status, economic status, language, and schooling. All of these must be taken into account before we can begin to compare black-white intelligence differences.

Perhaps most important is that all the studies and opinions discussed so far base their conclusions on the conventional intelligence test — a seriously flawed measure in terms of cultural bias. How can we evaluate hereditary influences across races or classes with a test that is designed to measure the learning experience of the white middle-class child? The testing situation, as well as the test itself, may inhibit the performance of black subjects. Forrester and Klaus (1964) have demonstrated that the presence of white examiners may inhibit the performance of blacks, and white examiners primarily have been used to test black subjects.

Wrightsman (1968, p. 20) states that the controversy cannot be resolved, in part, because "the environmental factors influencing the two groups are so different." Until these environmental factors are identified and evaluated, attributing racial differences to hereditary variables will lead, as it has in the past, to Merton's "self-fulfilling prophecy": when people "define situations as real, they are real in their consequences" (1948, p. 193).

SUMMARY

There are many definitions of intelligence but no universally accepted one. Some define intelligence as the IQ test score, while others define it in terms of comprehension, reasoning, purposeful behavior, or rationality. All definitions involve social values and hence contain social bias.

The nature-nurture controversy concerning intelligence attempts to discover whether intelligence is determined by hereditary factors or by environmental experience. Although several approaches have been taken in an attempt to identify the determinants of intelligence, the difficulties of separating hereditary and environmental effects have not been overcome. Most behavioral scientists generally accept the conclusion that both heredity and environment have an effect.

There are many measures of intelligence:

1. The *Stanford-Binet* was developed for children and is best used for this population. The test is made up of a series of subtests representing average performance for different age levels. The intelligence score is obtained from the relationship between the score on various subtests *(mental age)* and the chronological age of the subject. Since the Stanford-Binet stresses verbal skills, it correlates most highly with those academic subjects which are predominantly verbal in nature. The standardization sample and the largely verbal content of the test create a bias in favor of mainstream, white, middle-class, urban individuals. This bias increases the probability of lower scores for individuals from other subcultural groups.

2. The *Wechsler Adult Intelligence Scale (WAIS)* was developed specifically for adults and more accurately reflects their intellectual abilities than the Stanford-Binet. The test is divided into subtests of increasing difficulty. Verbal IQ scores, Performance IQ scores, and total IQ scores can all be obtained from this test. The results are generally similar to those found with the Stanford-Binet.

3. The *Goodenough-Harris Drawing Test* was developed in an attempt to establish a nonverbal and relatively culture-free test. It evaluates intelligence by scoring drawings of people in terms of the amount of detail shown. The test, however, has been shown not to be totally culture free.

4. A new type of test, which is in a very early stage of development, holds promise of eliminating some of the cultural factors. The *neural efficiency analyzer* measures the speed of information transmission in the brain, a measure which is hypothesized to be related to basic intellectual capacity. More research is needed to evaluate adequately this technique.

Intellectual extremes can be examined in an attempt to put common stereotypes in proper perspective. At one extreme are the *intellectually deficient individuals,* usually classified as those with IQs below 84. Mental retardation has many causes, which are generally categorized as either familial or physiological. In *physiologically defective retardation,* the deficiency can be attributed to some organic or physiological malfunction. Most retarded people are classified as *familial;* i.e., as showing no organic or physiological defect as the cause of retardation. The severity of mental deficiency is classified in terms of IQ on a five-level scale: profound, severe, moderate, mild, and subnormal (in increasing order of intellectual ability).

The classification of a person as retarded and the assessment of the level of retardation is not only a function of the IQ score but of the social skills of the individuals as well. The *Vineland Social Maturity Scale* serves to evaluate these social skills and helps to give a better total picture of the individual's abilities and potentials. Although an individual with a low IQ functions at a retarded level in most skills, special training can improve his or her abilities and help the person to develop into a self-sufficient and desirable citizen.

At the other extreme of the IQ range are the *gifted,* usually classified as those with IQs above 135. In the most definitive study of these individuals to date, Terman rather conclusively put an end to the stereotype of the gifted as inferior in physical development and socioemotional adjustment. This work demonstrated that the intellectually superior individual tends to be superior in most physical, social, and intellectual aspects of behavior.

Numerous studies have demonstrated that blacks obtain lower scores on conventional IQ tests than do whites. The problem is whether these differences should be attributed to innate inferiority of blacks or to environmental differences that exist between the races. Among the environmental factors that could contribute to the test score differences are the generally lower socioeconomic status of blacks, father absence in the home, inhibition of test performance of black subjects in the presence of white examiners, stress on language in tests, and differences in motivation. One important argument in favor of the environmentalists' viewpoint is the racial equality found on IQ tests of infants, before the effects of the environment have had a chance to work. On the other hand, the failure of blacks to attain white norm levels after special education is an argument used by those favoring the hereditary viewpoint. The evidence does not unequivocally support either the hereditary or the environmental viewpoint. The task of identifying and evaluating all potential environmental influences is far from complete.

GLOSSARY

Cerebral palsy: a condition, characterized by motor disorders, which may also lead to the development of mental retardation

Down's syndrome: a syndrome which combines retardation with certain physical characteristics; associated with genetic defect in some cases; mongolism

Familial retardation: retardation in which no known disease, injury, or organic defect can be located as the causal factor

Intellectually superior: gifted; as individuals are usually classified, applies to those with IQs above 135

Mental age: the score of an individual on an IQ test which reflects the level of his or her mental development in comparison with others the same age

Mental retardation: subaverage intellectual functioning and impairment of social skills

Mongolism: a syndrome which combines retardation with certain physical characteristics; associated with genetic defect in some cases; Down's syndrome

Reliability: measure of the consistency of test scores

Phenylketonuria (PKU): a disorder in which there is a metabolic malfunctioning in the body which, if uncorrected by diet, will cause mental retardation

Physiologically defective retardation: mental retardation for which a specific physiological or organic cause can be found

"Self-fulfilling prophecy" (Merton): when one predicts or expects a behavior from another person, the probability of that behavior occurring is increased

Validity: the extent to which a test measures what it is intended to measure

Vineland Social Maturity Scale: a test developed to evaluate social skills

REFERENCES

Asher, J. John Ertl's neural efficiency analyzer: Bias-free test, or just a "neat gadget"? *American Psychological Association Monitor,* March, 1973.

Binet, A., and Simon, T. *The development of intelligence in children* (K. G. Kite, trans.). Vineland, N.J.: Vineland Training School, 1916.

Burks, B. S., Jensen, D. W., and Terman, L. M. *Genetic studies of a genius.* Vol. III. *The promise of youth: Follow-up studies of a thousand gifted children.* Stanford, Calif.: Stanford University Press, 1930.

Charles, D. C. Ability and accomplishment of persons earlier judged mentally deficient. *Genetic Psychological Monographs,* 1953, *47,* 3–71.

Dennis, W. The performance of Hopi children on the Goodenough Draw-A-Man Test. *Journal of Comparative Psychology,* 1942, *34,* 341–346.

Deutsch, M., and Brown, N. Social influences in Negro-white intelligence differences. *Journal of Social Issues,* 1964, *20,* 24–35.

Doll, E. A. *The measurement of social competence.* Minneapolis: American Guidance Service, 1953.

Forrester, B. J., and Klaus, R. A. The effect of race of the examiner on intelligence test scores of Negro kindergarten children. *Peabody Papers in Human Development,* 1964, *2*(7), 1–7.

Galton, F. *Hereditary genius.* London: Clay & Sons, 1869.

Garrett, H. E. The SPSSI and racial differences. *American Psychologist,* 1962, *17,* 260–263.

Goddard, H. H. *The Kallikak family.* New

York: Collier and Macmillan, 1912.

Goodenough, F. L., and Harris, D. B. Studies in the psychology of children's drawings: II, 1926–1949. *Psychological Bulletin,* 1950, *47,* 369–433.

Goodman, N. E. *Race awareness in young children.* Cambridge, Mass.: Addison-Wesley, 1952.

Harris, D. B. *Children's drawings as a measure of intellectual maturity: A revision and extension of the Goodenough Draw-A-Man Test.* New York: Harcourt, Brace & World, 1963.

Heber, R. A manual on terminology and classification in mental retardation. *Monograph Supplement to American Journal of Mental Deficiency,* 1959, *64* (No. 2).

Hollingsworth, L. S. *Children above 180 IQ.* Yonkers, N.Y.: World Book, 1942.

Horwitz, W. A., Kestenbaum, C., Person, E., and Jarvik, L. Identical twins — "idiot savants" calendar calculators. *The American Journal of Psychiatry,* 1965, *121,* 1075–1079.

Jensen, A. R. How much can we boost IQ and scholastic achievement? *Harvard Educational Review,* 1969, *39,* 1–123.

Kardiner, A., and Ovesey, L. *The mark of oppression.* New York: Norton, 1951.

Karon, B. P. *The Negro personality.* New York: Springer, 1958.

Kirk, S. A., et al. *Early education of the mentally retarded.* Urbana, Ill.: University of Illinois Press, 1958.

Klineberg, O. *Negro intelligence and selective migration.* New York: Columbia University Press, 1935a.

Klineberg, O. *Race differences.* New York: Harper, 1935b.

Klineberg, O. Negro-white differences in intelligence test performance: A new look at an old problem. *American Psychologist,* 1963, *18,* 198–203.

Lee, E. S. Negro intelligence and selective migration: A Philadelphia of the Klineberg hypothesis. *American Sociological Review,* 1951, *16,* 227–233.

McCurdy, H. G. The childhood pattern of genius. *J. Elisha Mitchell Scientific Society,* 1957, *73,* 448–462.

Merton, R. K. The self-fulfilling prophecy. *Antioch Review,* 1948, *8,* 193–210.

Shuey, A. M. *The testing of Negro intelligence.* (2nd ed.). New York: Social Science Press, 1966.

Terman, L. M. *Genetic studies of a genius.* Vol. I. *Mental and physical traits of one thousand gifted children.* Stanford, Calif.: Stanford University Press, 1926.

Terman, L. M., and Oden, M. H. *Genetic studies of a genius.* Vol. IV. *The gifted child grows up.* Stanford, Calif.: Stanford University Press, 1947.

Terman, L. M., and Oden, M. H. *Genetic studies of a genius.* Vol. V. *The gifted group at mid-life.* Stanford, Calif.: Stanford University Press, 1959.

Wechsler, D. *The measurement and appraisal of adult intelligence.* (3rd ed.). Baltimore: Williams & Wilkins, 1944.

Wechsler, D. *The measurement and appraisal of adult intelligence.* (4th ed.). Baltimore: Williams & Wilkins, 1958.

Wrightsman, L. S., Jr. Racial differences in intelligence. In L. S. Wrightsman, Jr. (Ed.), *Contemporary issues in social psychology.* Belmont, Calif.: Wadsworth Publishing Co., 1968.

SUGGESTED READINGS

Bodmer, W. F., and Cavalli-Sforza, L. L. Intelligence and race. *Scientific American*, 1970, *223*, 19–29.

Butcher, H. J. *Human intelligence: Its nature and assessment.* London: Methuen, 1968.

Guilford, J. P. *The nature of human intelligence.* New York: McGraw-Hill, 1967.

Kagan, J. Discussion: How much can we boost the I.Q. and scholastic achievement? *Harvard Educational Review,* 1969, *39*, 273–356.

Spuhler, J. N. (Ed.). *Genetic diversity and human behavior.* Chicago: Aldine, 1967.

Vernon, P. E. *Intelligence and cultural environment.* London: Methuen, 1969.

Photo by Lin Oakerson

E

Don't Bother Me,
I Can't Cope

Unit 18
Who's Who: The Labeling of Normal and Abnormal

He was a clean-cut young man, hardly the type one would notice in a crowd. His home life hadn't been too good, with his parents arguing and fighting too much. Neighbors said his mother was either mentally retarded or mentally disturbed. He was above average in intelligence and similar in many ways to millions of young men — except that he shot and crippled Governor George Wallace.

In the weeks preceding the assassination attempt, Arthur Bremer wrote frequently in his diary.

"I decided to go to a massage parlor. I looked up their ratings in *Screw* newspaper, checked the ones I wanted and was going to 3 or 4 that night. I couldn't do it. I walked past a place and then got lost (on porpose maybe). I felt like I was going to get raped. . . . "Fantasied killing Nixon while shooting right over the shoulder of that cop. . . .

"A woman, middle-aged, gave me an anti-war anti-Nixon leaflet. You stupid bitch, stop this useless accomplish-nothing form of protest, let the security slacken & I'll show you something really evective. . . . This will be one of the most closely read pages since the scrolls in those cave. I want something to happen. All my efforts and just another goddam failure. My fuse is about burnt. I've had it. I'm tired of writting about it, about what I was gonna do, about what I failed to do. What I failed to do again & again."

At his trial he pleaded not guilty by reason of insanity. The jury found him sane — and guilty. After sentencing he said that the prosecutor wanted society "to be protected from someone like me. But in my defense, I would sure like it if society had protected me from myself."

Time, 1972, pp. 22–23.

Was Bremer insane or immoral, demented or just dangerous? The issue of insanity as it relates to criminal behavior is an important one, for it reflects on the interpretation one gives to the behavior and has implications for how one deals with the criminal. If the behavior is viewed as bad, punishment is a reasonable solution. If the behavior represents maladjustment, confinement or punishment will not alter the basic cause of the behavior. Treatment of some kind would appear a better alternative.

The law defines insanity in terms of the ability of the criminal to be able to distinguish right from wrong at the time the crime was committed. In Maryland, where Bremer was tried and convicted, a person is considered insane only if unable to appreciate the criminal nature of the act committed. In this unit we shall examine the way in which psychology views abnormal behavior, comparing and contrasting it with the legal definition.

Approaches to Definition

The most fundamental problem we have to deal with is a problem of definition. How do we classify one person as normal and another as abnormal; one as adjusted and another as maladjusted?

SUBJECTIVE APPROACH

The *subjective approach* to definition leaves the classification of normality up to the individual's personal judgment and allows the person to use himself or herself as the standard of comparison. An individual says, "I am adjusted. If you are enough like me, you too are adjusted. If you are different, you must be abnormal." The problems with this approach are self-evident. It could lead to as many definitions of abnormality as there are people who care to define it. Using this definition, all criminals would be seen as abnormal, for they are clearly different from most of the population, which is never convicted of a serious crime. This approach often leads to a dichotomous, or twofold, categorization in which the individual is judged either normal or abnormal, with no middle ground.

STATISTICAL APPROACH

A second approach to the problem is the *statistical*, in which normality is based on the average, or mean, behavior. This is probably the most objective method of assessing abnormality, but it has serious flaws since it equates average behavior with most valued behavior. The behavior of the majority of people is not always the most normal or positive. The average behavior in Germany in the late 1930s and early 1940s was that which was in agreement with Hitler, but most of us would object to the classification of such behavior as normal.

Another problem with this approach is that there are two extremes surrounding the average. Let us take illegal behavior as an example. The average person has engaged in some illegal activity, most commonly traffic violations. The individual at the extreme who has committed many criminal acts might clearly be judged as maladjusted. But what about the people at the other extreme who seldom, if ever, violate the law? Are they also abnormal? According to this definition, the answer would have to be yes, for they do not represent the average — they deviate too much, although in a positive direction.

CULTURAL APPROACH

A third approach to the definition of abnormality is the *cultural approach*. Benedict (1934) has used this method of assessment. She points out that behaviors considered abnormal can be divided into three categories:

1. Behaviors which are abnormal in our culture but considered normal in other cultures
2. Behaviors considered normal in our culture but abnormal in other cultures
3. Abnormal behaviors that do not occur in our culture but do occur in other cultures

This approach stresses that there is no absolute definition of abnormal behavior. Rather, the concept of abnormality is seen as a culturally relative one. What is normal and abnormal may vary from culture to culture and may vary among subcultures within a given culture.

Although this approach seems much more flexible than the statistical, it does involve serious social ramifications. In practice, what is considered normal is also considered positive or valuable. As we have noted, the definition of normality or adjustment varies among subcultures. Unfortunately, the dominant subculture can and does impose its standards of normality on less dominant subcultures. White, middle-class, middle-aged Americans impose their standards of normal behavior on the subcultures of youth, of blacks, and of the poor.

As an example, let us look at the analysis of the urban black subculture made by Moynihan (1965). Normal in the white culture is a family headed by a male who earns the living and is the dominant figure in the family. In the black, lower-class, urban culture, a matriarchal family structure with the woman heading the family and a male adult often not even present is much more frequent than in the white, middle-class culture (see Figure 18-1). We won't go into the many reasons for the frequency of this family structure in black culture. What is more important for our purposes is that Moynihan, reflecting the views of many others, sees the black family structure as abnormal, not because it is bad in itself, but because "it is so out of line with the rest of American society" (1965, p. 29). To end the "tangle of pathology" within the black culture, the only thing that can be done, according to Moynihan, is to make efforts which "strengthen the Negro family so as to enable it to raise and support its members as do other families" (p. 47).

The problem with such an approach is that the black family structure has not been shown to be a cause of the problems of blacks in our society. Any pathology in the black subculture cannot be attributed to the simple fact that more families are headed by females (unless one wishes to invoke sexist arguments on the innate inferiority of women). The only thing that can be said about the two types

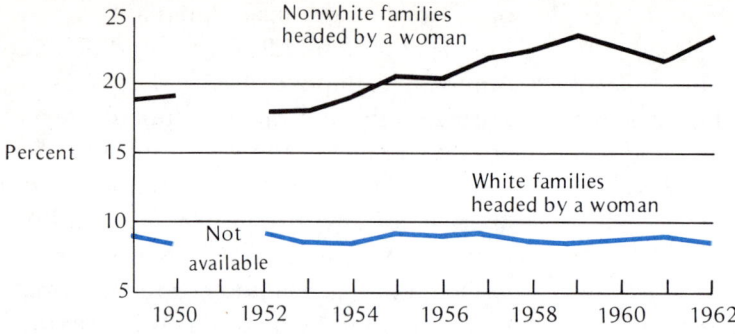

FIGURE 18-1 Percentage of white and nonwhite families headed by women

of family structure is that they are different — with no value judgment. The classification of the black family structure as pathological arises because it is different from the normal (good) structure found in the white subculture.

NORMATIVE APPROACH

The final approach to the problem of defining abnormality is the *normative approach*. This method stresses the establishment of an ideal against which a person is judged. Individuals are more or less normal depending on how closely they approach the ideal. One advantage of this system is that it does not involve a dichotomous, or twofold, categorization. Rather, it stresses that normality exists on a continuum, with people making greater or lesser approximations to the ideal. The disadvantage of this system is that the definition of normality is made on purely subjective, and often ethical and moral, bases.

As illustrative examples, two different normative systems will be presented briefly. Wegrocki (1939) defines abnormality as "the tendency to choose a type of reaction which represents an escape from the conflict-producing situation, instead of facing the problem" (p. 177). He argues that normality cannot be determined by simply looking at the behavior. One must examine the underlying purpose of the behavior to determine whether it represents a realistic attempt to face and solve the problem. The crucial determinant of abnormality in Wegrocki's system, then, is not the overt behavior but the function the behavior serves in the individual.

Coleman (1956) defines normality as "the maximal personal and social adjustment in keeping with long-term social welfare" (p. 15). This definition, as well as the preceding one, is based on what should be — i.e., the ideal behavior. Few people would argue with the value of either of these definitions, for they represent behaviors that most would consider positive. The problem arises when one attempts to clarify the terms within them. Although we might agree with the definitions, great differences of opinion would arise in deciding which behaviors truly reflected Wegrocki's "facing a problem" and what should be included in

154 *Don't Bother Me, I Can't Cope*

BOX 18-1 ON BEING SANE IN INSANE PLACES

A group of eight sane people faked psychiatric symptoms in order to gain admission to psychiatric hospitals. The eight included a graduate student, a psychiatrist, three psychologists, a painter, and a housewife. All were admitted to different hospitals of varying quality with the same complaint — they heard voices. Once admitted to the institutions, all behaved normally. They acted as they had before admission and said they no longer heard the voice. The purpose of their endeavor was to determine how long it would take the hospitals to recognize their "normality" and discharge them. It took an average of nineteen days for the patients to be discharged, with hospitalization time ranging from seven to fifty-two days. No member of the staff ever suspected that any of these "patients" had actually faked their symptoms to gain admission — although several of the hospitals' real patients did. At admission, all but one patient was labelled as schizophrenic. Upon discharge, they were diagnosed not as healthy, sane, or normal — but as schizophrenics in remission. The authors conclude that in psychiatric hospitals, the decision on normality or abnormality is not a function of the behavior of the patients themselves, but rests heavily on the environment in which the individual is observed. Once admitted, the individual is insane. If he behaves normally, his insanity is not gone — it is in remission (Rosenhan, 1973).

Coleman's "social welfare." Personal, moral, and ethical values, as well as political ideology, would act to give different content to these concepts.

The reader is probably wondering by now how any individual is ever classified as abnormal. It is quite clear that we have no neat, concise way of placing any individual in a normal or abnormal category. Agreement is fairly easy to obtain for those individuals who represent the extremes of adjustment or maladjustment. But there is a vast group in the middle ranges which is not so easily classified. In these cases, the decision is usually left up to the individual or the individual's family. That is, if the feeling of "abnormality" is strong enough, it will impel the individual or the family to seek professional aid. Occasionally society also intervenes to define abnormality through its laws, as it has done in the cases of homosexual and criminal behavior. But more and more we are getting away from such legal and social definitions of abnormality when the behaviors involved are not harmful and are not inflicted on nonconsenting adults.

Classification

Once one is classified as abnormal, one is further evaluated and placed in a diagnostic category. The standard diagnostic

> **BOX 18-2   MAJOR PSYCHOPATHOLOGICAL DIAGNOSTIC CATEGORIES**
>
> | Diagnosis | Symptoms |
> |---|---|
> | Neurosis | High level of anxiety |
> | | Excessive use of defense mechanisms to handle anxiety |
> | Psychosis | Disorientation |
> | | Delusions (beliefs contrary to objective reality) |
> | | Hallucinations (perception of objects or events not physically present) |
> | | Disturbance in emotions |
> | | Disturbance in verbal and nonverbal communication |
> | Psychophysiological disorders | Actual physiological disorder caused by psychological problems |
> | | Organic damage |
> | Brain disorders | Psychotic behavior resulting from damage to the brain |
> | Personality disorders | Maladaptive behavior patterns |
> | | Lifelong history of characteristic behavior |
> | | Patient unconcerned with problem |

classification system used by the American Psychiatric Association is given in the association's *Diagnostic and Statistical Manual of Mental Disorders* (1968). Box 18-2 lists the major categories and their symptoms. The usefulness of this system has been questioned, as will be discussed later when we consider the various categories. Nevertheless, the diagnostic categories continue to be widely applied, and it is perhaps of value for the student to be familiar with at least some of the terminology, for it is encountered in daily life — most dramatically in courtroom trials such as those of Arthur Bremer and Sirhan Sirhan.

DIFFICULTIES

Although the classification system is neatly divided into categories and subcategories, in actual practice the diagnosis is not so simple and clear-cut. Few patients, if any, are "pure neurotics" or "pure personality disorders." Behavior from a number of different disorders may be present within any one individual, making diagnosis less scientific than the categorization system would make it seem.

A second problem arises from the subjective judgments necessary on the part of the therapist. The case of Arthur Bremer provides a clear example of the different subjective interpretations psychiatrists can develop from interviewing and testing the same person. The psychiatrist for the prosecution described Bremer as a schizoid personality disorder. The psychiatrist for the defense diagnosed him as a schizophrenic. These are, as we shall see in the coming units, quite different disorders. From a legal point of view, the difference is important, for a schizophrenic is legally insane while a schizoid personality is not. What is Bremer? The best answer is probably that he is a unique human being whose individual behavior patterns, although clearly deviant, don't fit neatly into any category.

MEDICAL VS. BEHAVIORAL APPROACH

Problems such as these have led many psychologists to argue for the abandonment of this type of classification system, known as the *medical model*. It derives its name from the fact that it follows the pattern of physical medicine, which involves classifying the symptoms of the individual. The model works in physical medicine because the diagnosis of the symptoms allows the physician to identify the cause and the treatment. In psychological disorders, however, our level of knowledge does not allow us to point directly to cause and cure once the symptoms are described. Hereditary, constitutional, and environmental factors all operate in the development of various mental disorders. But the extent and type of their contribution to any specific illness is still a matter for speculation.

Many psychologists are turning from the medical model to a *functional* or *behavioral approach* (see Figure 18-2). This approach basically involves concentrating on the symptom; i.e., examining what is wrong with the individual. When an individual comes for treatment there is usually a specific complaint. There is some behavior that is bothering the patient or someone he or she associates with. The functional approach deals directly with this behavior, attempting to

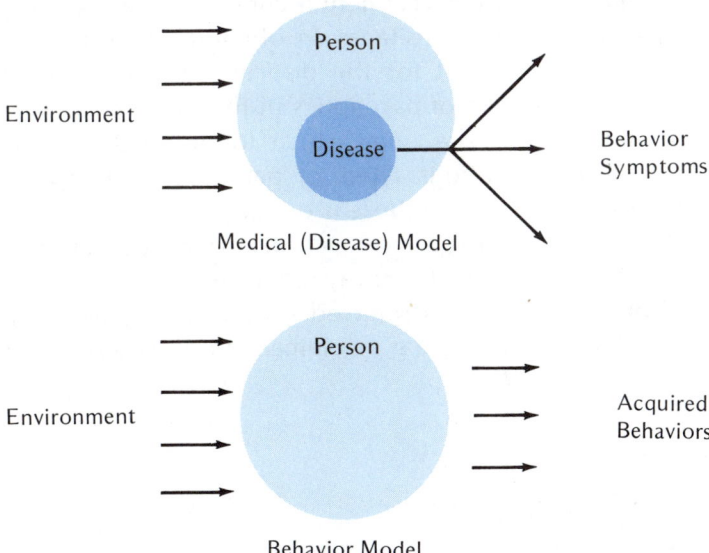

FIGURE 18-2 Conceptual differences between the medical model and the disease model

change it, usually through learning, so that the individual performs behaviors which reflect better adjustment. In the case of Bremer, functionalists wouldn't worry about whether he was schizoid or schizophrenic but would focus instead on his aggressive fantasies and aggressive behavior, as well as on methods of changing them.

The amount and type of mental illness have been found to vary with the social class of individuals. Gruenberg (1963) found that within New York City the amount of mental illness increased as the socioeconomic status decreased. Hollingshead and Redlich (1958) conducted extensive studies of the relationship between mental illness and social class, with social class determined by residence, occupation, and education. The results showed that neurotic disorders were more prevalent in the upper classes (I and II), while psychotic disorders were more frequent in the lowest class (V) (Figure 18-3). These different patterns of disorders among social classes are probably due to environmental differences. The lower classes are subjected to many more stresses due to overcrowding and economic privation. These stresses often are compounded by social and racial prejudice and discrimination. In addition, the lower classes are less likely to obtain psychiatric care for the milder disorders, such as neuroses, due to the expense of such treatment and because psychiatric care is viewed unfavorably in the lower classes. In many parts of the upper classes, such treatment is considered fashionable. The hesitancy in obtaining care may account for the disproportionate percentage of psychotics in the lower classes.

The units which follow deal with the various types of pathology. The discussion of these is of necessity brief, and not all types of each disorder are dealt with. The student who wishes further information is referred to abnormal psychology texts (e.g., Coleman, 1956; Kisker, 1972).

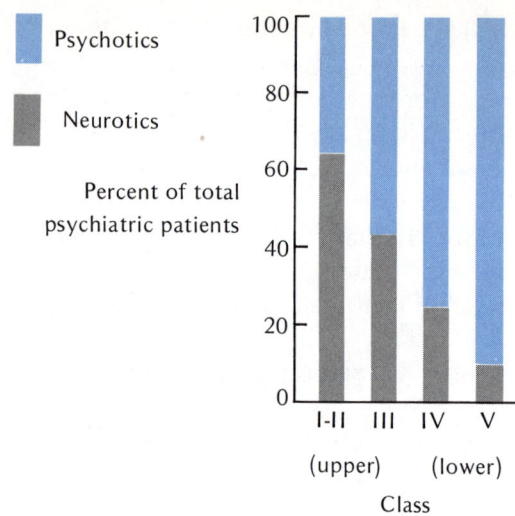

FIGURE 18-3 Prevalence of neurosis and psychosis according to social class

Unit 19
Neurotics: Builders of Dream Houses

The neurotic disorders are among the most common types of mental illnesses. The key factor in all neurotic disorders is anxiety. Although neurotics frequently need professional assistance, in most cases they do not require hospitalization. The neurotics do not show severe disturbances in thought patterns or lack of contact with reality. Rather, their illness is characterized by anxiety and the defense mechanisms they use to reduce it. The types of neurotics differ in the manner in which they deal with their anxiety. Box 19-1 describes the major behavioral patterns, or method of dealing with anxiety, used by each type of neurotic.

ANXIETY REACTION

Mrs. W., a thirty-seven-year-old Negro woman, sat in the clinic waiting room, stiffly upright in her chair, staring straight ahead, and rubbing a handkerchief between her hands . . . . When she was addressed, she jumped, startled, and caught her breath before responding. In the interview room she settled herself carefully in her chair and tried to smile pleasantly, but she looked obviously ill at ease. When asked what her complaint was she began to cry . . . . She said that many things made her jumpy, that tears came to her eyes readily, and that she often felt anxious without quite knowing why (Goldstein and Palmer, 1963, p. 58).

Mrs. W.'s case is typical of the anxiety reaction in which the anxiety is overtly and obviously expressed. The anxiety neurotic is nervous, upset, frequently cannot sleep, and may show increased pulse, sweating, and digestive upset. The person is "nervous," but with no reason that he or she can think of.

PHOBIC REACTION

Many of the symptoms shown by neurotics arise from directing the anxiety they feel toward some focal point, in the form of either specific fear or a specific psychological or physiological function.

I was riding in my husband's car and I suddenly became terrified. I felt as if I would die. I made him turn around and take me home. I ran into the house and suddenly felt safe. I could not understand what had happened. I had never been afraid of cars. The next day it happened again and it kept getting worse. Finally, just being on the street and seeing a car would bring on a terrible feeling. Now I just stay at home (de Nike and Tiber, 1968, p. 346).

> **BOX 19-1 TYPES OF NEUROTIC REACTIONS**
>
> | Type | Symptoms |
> |---|---|
> | Anxiety reaction | Overt anxiety, "nervousness" |
> | Phobic reaction | Excessive and apparently irrational fear |
> | Obsessive-compulsive reaction | Ideas that repeatedly intrude into the stream of thought (obsessions) |
> | | Repeated performance of a behavior or set of behaviors (compulsions) |
> | Hysterical reaction | |
> | Conversion reaction | Physical malfunction with no underlying physical or organic cause |
> | Dissociative reaction | Setting off or dissociating a portion of the personality; includes amnesia and multiple personality |
> | Hypochondriacal reaction | Excessive concern with body, worry about becoming sick, and belief he or she is sick |
> | Depressive reaction | Severe depression, feeling of hopelessness |

If one takes the general anxiety typical of the neurotic and directs it into an excessive fear of a specific thing, as in the case described above, it is called a *phobic reaction*. The fear is usually said to be irrational, since an observer can't see any real reason for it. There is nothing new about cars that should make the above patient suddenly terrified of them. There is no reason that the sight of the car should cause her fear — but she feels afraid.

If we closely examine the patient's background, we may find that the feared object is only a symbol for a real fear or that the feared object was in the past associated with a real objective fear. In the latter case, the phobic fear may be based on conditioning of the emotional reponse of fear. In the case of Little Albert discussed in Division C, Albert was conditioned to fear a white rat by repeatedly pairing the sight of the rat with a sudden loud noise. The fear of the rat then generalized so that the child was also afraid of fur coats, cotton, rabbits, and men with white beards. If we met Albert when he was twenty-one and saw him panic when we handed him a piece of cotton, we'd have serious doubts about his sanity. Once we knew his history, however, the behavior would seem much more reasonable.

Among the most common phobic fears are:

Claustrophobia: fear of small, closed places
Aichmophobia: fear of pointed objects
Agoraphobia: fear of open places
Acrophobia: fear of heights

OBSESSIVE-COMPULSIVE REACTION

Shirley K., a twenty-three-year-old housewife . . . had been disturbed by recurring thoughts that she might harm her two-year-old son, Saul, either by stabbing or choking him. She constantly had to check to reassure herself that Saul was still alive; otherwise she became unbearably anxious. If she read a report in the daily paper of the murder of a child, she would become agitated (Goldstein and Palmer, 1963, p. 25).

Shirley K. displays a type of behavior which is classified as an *obsessive-compulsive reaction*. The anxiety is directed into recurrent ideas *(obsessions)* or the need to keep performing the same acts *(compulsions)*. The repeated thought of harming her son was Shirley's obsession, while the repeated behavior of checking on him is a compulsion. Obsessive thoughts are not unusual in relatively normal individuals, as in the cases of persistent thoughts of an upcoming date or the inability to get a song "out of one's head." These obsessions represent a problem when they come to interfere with the normal flow of life. Compulsions are not uncommon either, as evidenced by the inability of some people to go to sleep before carefully checking all the doors and windows.

HYSTERICAL REACTION

A barber . . . complained that his hands were shaking continuously. He had feelings of dizziness, sweated profusely, and had a blurring of vision in his left eye. Sometimes, when he had eaten too much, he became covered with sweat, and occasionally he lost consciousness (Hutt and Gibby, 1957, p. 209).

Conversion reaction. The barber exemplifies one type of hysterical reaction known as the *conversion reaction*. As the name implies, this is a disorder in which the anxiety is "converted" into a physical malfunction. The symptoms may be sensory (blindness, deafness, lack of tactile sensitivity) or motor (paralysis). There is, however, no underlying physical or organic damage. The conversion reaction is most clearly distinguished by a total indifference of the patient to the physical problems, known as *la belle indifference*. The patient frequently seems totally unconcerned with the paralysis, blindness, or other disability. In addition, the symptom expressed may violate known neurological patterns (see Figure 19-1).

Conversion reactions should be clearly distinguished from the behavior of *hypochondriacal* neurotics. In the conversion reaction, the patient suffers a real loss of function — all of his or her behavior indicates an inability to see or walk — although no physical reason for the loss can be found. The hypochondriac, on the other hand, does not even suffer from loss of function. The individual is overconcerned with his or her body and the possibility of illness, in sharp contrast to the indifference of the conversion neurotic. The hypochondriac worries about getting sick, always thinks he or she is sick, but never actually has anything wrong. The apparent increase in hypochondriacs may be due in part to the overpublication of diseases. Although knowledge of disease symptoms and stress on the need to obtain preventive care are of great value, an exaggerated emphasis on such things in the mass media

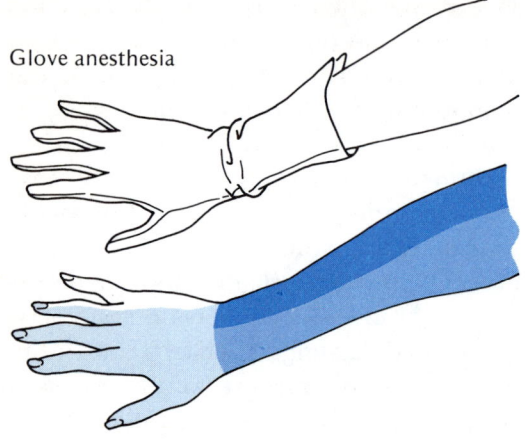

Glove anesthesia

Neural connections of the hand and arm

FIGURE 19-1 In the type of conversion reaction known as glove anesthesia, the person reports a lack of sensitivity in the same areas of the hand which would be covered by a glove. However, given the neural connections which actually exist in the hand it is extremely unlikely that this precise pattern of insensitivity could occur.

may stimulate overconcern for such factors.

Dissociative reaction. In addition to manifesting itself in the form of physical problems, as in the conversion reaction, the hysterical reaction may involve a problem in the psychological sphere only. This is a *dissociative reaction*. In this type of reaction, the individual attempts to control anxiety by "dissociating," or setting off, a portion of the personality. Those parts of the personality that are producing the anxiety are simply removed from consciousness.

Amnesia is a type of dissociative reaction that occurs when the individual is unable to recall parts or all of his or her past experience and identity. Amnesia can occur as a result of physical head injury, but in such cases the forgotten material is totally lost. Most cases of amnesia, however, are the result of psychological conflict. In these cases the material is repressed and can be recovered. The *fugue reaction* is a special case of amnesia. In this reaction, the individual not only forgets the past but leaves the location of the problems, going to another city or country. *Multiple personality* is another type of dissociative reaction and has received much attention due to its dramatic nature. Multiple personalities are formed when conflicting needs and desires are repressed, resulting in the formation of two or more personalities. The most famous case is that reported in *The Three Faces of Eve* (Thigpen and Cleckley, 1957), in which the patient developed three separate personalities. Although such cases are discussed extensively, they are quite rare.

DEPRESSIVE REACTION

One man who had recently been fired from his job commented about his situation as follows:

I don't know what I'm going to do. I know I can never get another good job again. No one will want me. I feel like my life is over. I just cannot begin again. I sit up all night knowing that I've failed and I don't know what to do about it. I wish I were dead (de Nike and Tiber, 1968, p. 350).

This disorder, also known as reactive depression, occurs when the individual reacts to problems and conflicts with a feeling of hopelessness, dejection, and depression. The depression often results from some specific event, such as the death of a loved one, but it continues for an excessively long period of time. This is probably the least serious of the neuroses, since there is a high probability that the patient will recover. The most serious danger is the possibility of suicide during the depression.

NEUROSIS AND SOCIAL CLASS

The type of neurotic symptom displayed by an individual has been shown to be related to the individual's social class. The conversion or hysterical reaction is shown more frequently by the lower class (V) than by any other class. The upper classes (I and II), however, tend to show the obsessive-compulsive reaction relatively more frequently than do other social classes (see Figure 19-2). Differences in living patterns among the social classes may account for the differences in symptoms shown. In the lower classes, concern for physical survival is a part of daily life, making it reasonable that mental illness would manifest itself through the body. The upper classes, due to their higher income, are freed from the struggle for

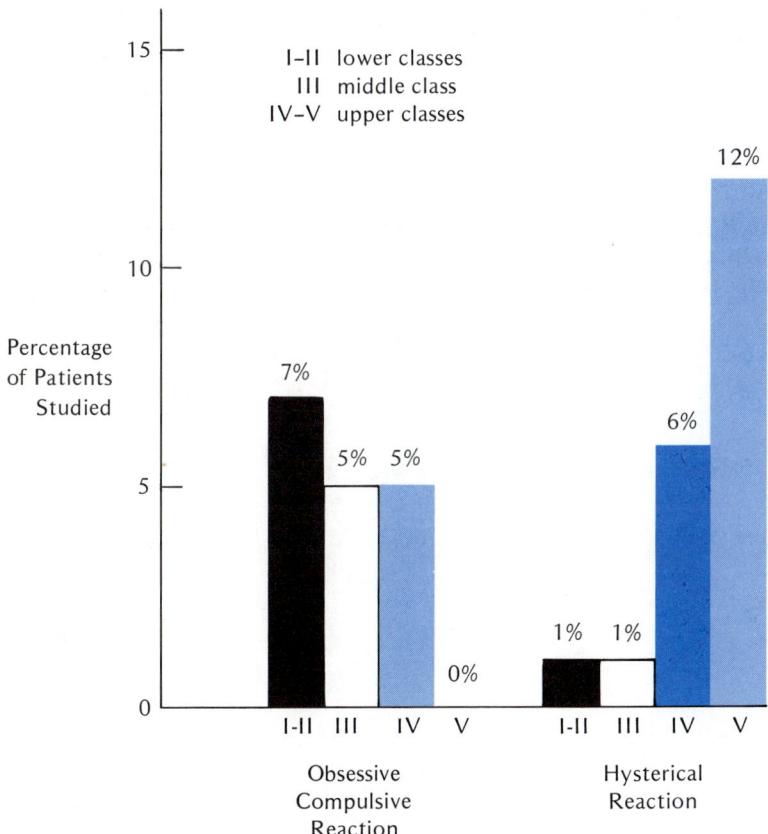

FIGURE 19-2 Percentage of patients studied in each diagnostic category by social class

physical survival and thus can center their attention on external factors in day-to-day life. Such concerns would, therefore, be more likely to surface in the symptom patterns of disturbed upper-class individuals.

These variations among social classes may be seen as different ways of adjusting to different demands. The stresses placed on members of the various classes are not the same, so the style of adjustment must vary also. This raises the question of the extent to which these "maladjustive" behaviors might be actually adjusted behaviors to a stressful or pathological environment. A behavior cannot be judged as maladjusted in isolation. One must examine it in its context. If one observes an individual sitting alone, flapping his hands around his face, one might classify him as "weird" — or, if one were better educated, as "psychotic." If on closer examination one observes that there are many gnats in the area, the behavior is seen as a normal and adaptive way to keep the gnats away from one's face.

WHO'S NEUROTIC?

Diagnosis of an individual as a neurotic is not a clear-cut decision. One must decide if the individual is displaying "too much" of these types of behaviors. In reading through the neurotic disorders, you probably said to youself at least once, "Hey — *I* do that!" Most of us can find in ourselves behaviors fitting into all neurotic categories. Does this make all of us neurotic? Or are most of us normal? The answer to both questions may be yes. We are all neurotic to the extent that we aren't perfectly well-adjusted. But, at the same time, most of us are normal since we are sufficiently well-adjusted so that these behaviors don't interfere with an effective and productive life. Diagnosis as a neurotic is, then, a determination of degree. When the behaviors are so pervasive that we feel maladjusted and feel that we can't cope effectively, help is needed. And if the behavior requires a label, neurotic is probably as good as any.

Unit 20
Psychotics: Occupants of Dream Houses

A person who is not very emotional is or could be mix up some with his love affair. Some people want more knowledge the they feel God want them to have. No man has a band on life by we have to live with others. Help me to show more love in the right direction and have more friend. And be able to live my life as I am able to make up my mind on som thing now.

Doctor help me to slow down a be content whe ever I am at. I want to go the thing to fast. Help me to slow down and think Mental illness is a emotion the person can not under why he did some things he or she did or craved and could not understand But with God help an a doctors help they can become well and never will be sick again.

Sinnett, 1964, p. 187.

The passage above was written by a psychotic man during a deeply disturbed phase of his psychotic experience. It reflects the thought processes, and the pain, that frequently characterize the psychotic.

Neurotics are characterized by high levels of anxiety, with categories of neurotics differentiated by the behaviors they adopt as protection from the anxiety. The psychotic is characterized by a loss of contact with reality. Psychotics are classified according to the behavior patterns demonstrated and the areas in which loss of contact with reality is most pronounced (see Box 20-1).

The psychotic reaction is one of the more severe mental disorders. As can be seen in Figure 20-1, it accounts for a high proportion of the admissions to mental hospitals. Although the severity of the psychotic disorder varies, it is generally more serious than the neurotic disorder because it involves loss of contact with reality, frequently preventing the individual from performing with even minimal effectiveness in a noninstitutional environment. The neurotic individual defends against the anxiety caused by unconscious material. In the psychotic, the

> **BOX 20-1 TYPES OF PSYCHOTIC DISORDERS**
>
> | Type | Symptoms |
> |---|---|
> | Schizophrenic reaction | Disturbance in reality relations
Disturbance in emotional processes
Disturbance in thought processes |
> | Simple schizophrenia | Withdrawal
Apathy
Emotional flatness |
> | Hebephrenic schizophrenia | Hallucinations and delusions
Shallow and inappropriate affect
Regression to childish behavior |
> | Catatonic schizophrenia | Alternation between stuperous and excited behavior |
> | Paranoid schizophrenia | Delusions, frequently involving persecution
Frequent hallucinations accompanying delusions |
> | Paranoid reaction | Logical, well-developed delusional system
Less personality disintegration than in schizophrenia |
> | Affective psychoses | Disturbance primarily in emotional sphere |
> | Manic-depressive reaction | Mood extremes in one of three patterns: manic (highly excited), depressive, or a cyclic manic-depressive pattern |
> | Involutional melancholia | Depression
Occurs during period of physiological changes of the involutional period |

defense mechanisms have broken down completely, allowing the unconscious material to fill the conscious mind.

The psychotic individual who performs a criminal act is far more likely to be found "innocent by reason of insanity" than are individuals with any other type of disorder. The often bizarre behavior and illogical thought pattern can easily convince a jury that the individual "didn't know what he was doing."

Symptoms of Psychosis

As is shown in Box 20-1, there are a number of different types of psychoses; but underlying all is a group of symptoms that sets the psychotic apart from other mentally disturbed individuals. Kisker (1972) lists six groups of symptoms that differentiate the psychotic reaction:

1. The patients show disorientation in the

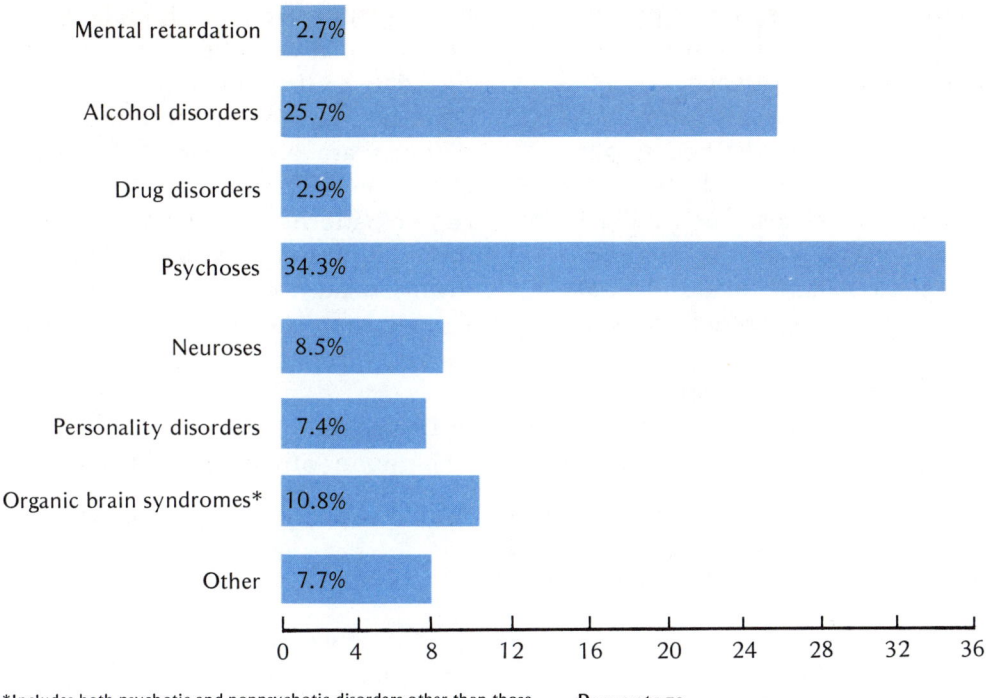

FIGURE 20-1 Percentage of admissions to public mental hospitals as a function of type of disorder

sense that they do not demonstrate knowledge of who they are or where they are. They fail to show any realistic orientation in time or space. The following excerpt from Kisker (1972, p. 313) gives an example of this disorientation:

Q: What is your name?
A: It is called fast colors.
Q: What is your father's name?
A: He put his head on the railroad tracks and see where he is today. He's in heaven.
Q: Do you have children?
A: How are you today?
Q: Where do you live?
A: I am not, and never was, foolish. I live in the barracks.
Q: What day is it?
A: According to my brain it is two weeks from tomorrow.
Q: What time of day is it?
A: It's sub-noon in Egypt.
Q: How old are you?
A: Diagram.
Q: What city is this?
A: I am out of my brain today. City in mind. You're not getting any more sense out of me than out of a turnip.

2. The patient typically shows delusions, which are beliefs that are contrary to objective reality. These beliefs are firmly held in spite of any rational argument that may be put forth against

them. Box 20-2 gives some of the different types of delusions which are found, and examples of each.

3. A psychotic patient may also show hallucinations, which are defined as perceptions of stimuli for which there are no objective correlates. Such hallucinations are usually visual or auditory, although some patients may show hallucinations involving other sensory systems.

4. The psychotic frequently shows disturbances in the emotional sphere involving either flat affect (lack of emotional responsiveness), impulsiveness, or emotional responses that are inappropriate to the situation.

5. Disturbances in verbal communication patterns are also typical of the psychotic. Verbalizations fail to show accepted patterns of grammar and logical thought, producing what is known as a "word salad." An example of such a verbalization is shown in the following excerpt (Pronko, 1963, p. 300).

Dear Dr.———
X=The phone with the dial. The dial is the

BOX 20-2   DIFFERENT TYPES OF DELUSIONS CHARACTERISTIC OF PSYCHOTICS (Kisker, 1972, p. 314)

Persecution

The cops are after me.
People spit at me.
They are going to horsewhip me.
Everybody I see is talking about me.
The milk delivered to my apartment has been poisoned.
Someone down the hall is chopping little children to pieces.

Power and Grandeur

I am the richest man in the world.
I am so powerful that the heads of people change when I look at them.
I own all the hotels in the world.
I have a hundred million dollars in the bank.

Somatic

I am sick because I swallowed a rock.
There are holes bored in my head.
My head is filled with cornflakes.
I've lost my skin.
I'm mangled inside.
My mouth is sewed closed.

Sexual

My neighbors accuse me of being a pervert.
The newspapers are going to release headlines saying that I am a "queer."
They insinuate that I am not a man.
My neighbors say I have syphilis.
They are whispering that I am a homosexual.
My husband made me insane so he would be free to commit adultery.

Religious

There is a devil in my ear.
I am God.
I have to shake the bed at night to get the devils out.
God is my husband.
I am Jesus Christ.

key to the door. The door is the door to Heaven. Only Angels Have Wings. The irritated dog has bitten the child. God bless that little girl that prayed for me.

6. Disturbances of nonverbal communication are also seen in psychotic patients. They may exhibit unusual gestures, body movements, or mannerisms. The content of both the verbal and nonverbal communications may be filled with important symbolic meaning.

These symptoms need not all be found in any one patient, but all are part of the general syndrome included in diagnosing a psychotic.

Schizophrenic Reaction

The schizophrenic group of psychotics is by far the most extensive (see Figure 20-2). The symptom pattern of the schizophrenic usually develops slowly, with the early symptoms quite different from the later, fully developed schizophrenic reaction. The early behavior usually involves neurotic symptoms. When fully developed, the schizophrenic reaction is characterized by disturbances in reality relations and in emotional and thought processes. The subject withdraws from reality and displays apathy and a flat affect. The schizophrenic also frequently has quite dramatic delusions and hallucinations. Various diagnostic categories, based on common symptom patterns, are used.

Simple schizophrenia. The *simple schizophrenic reaction* is characterized by withdrawal, apathy, and emotional flatness. The term *simple* is used because this group fails to show the bizarre hallucinations, delusions, and language disturbances found in other types of schizophrenia. Such individuals often appear retarded because of their lack of

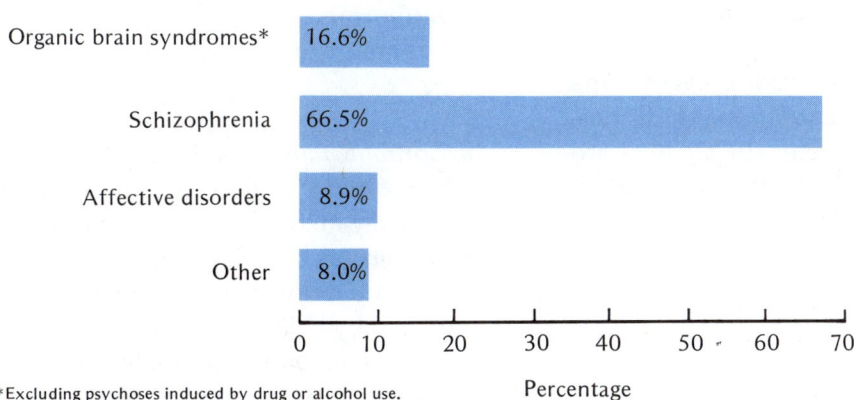

*Excluding psychoses induced by drug or alcohol use.

FIGURE 20-2 Relative incidence of various types of psychotic disorders as a percentage of the total number of psychotic patients admitted to public mental hospitals

responsiveness. Nonetheless, they are not intellectually deficient. The onset of the disturbance is usually very gradual and, due to its lack of dramatic symptoms, it may not be discovered until well advanced. This particular reaction accounts for only a small proportion of schizophrenic hospital admissions, since such patients can usually be adequately cared for at home.

Hebephrenic schizophrenia. The *hebephrenic schizophrenic reaction* can include the most severe personality disintegration of any of the schizophrenic reactions. The patient shows exaggerated delusions, hallucinations, and language disturbances. This type of schizophrenia commonly begins earlier in life than other types, with the patient showing a long history of unusual behavior. The hebephrenic schizophrenic not only demonstrates the shallow affect of the simple schizophrenic, but also shows affect inappropriate to the situation. The most typical symptom of the hebephrenic schizophrenic is regression to childish levels of behavior, exemplified by silliness, giggling, and making faces. The severe personality and thought disintegration and the characteristic silliness are shown in the following conversation (Suinn, 1970, p. 402):

Dr: I am Dr.———. I would like to know something more about you
Pt: You have a nasty mind. Lord, Lord! Cat's in a cradle.
Dr: Tell me, how do you feel?
Pt: London's bell is a long, long dock. Hee! Hee! Hee! (Giggles uncontrollably.)
Dr: Do you know where you are now?
Pt: D———n! S———t on you all who rip into my internals! The grugerometer will take care of you all! (Shouting) I am the Queen, see my magic, I shall turn you all into smidgelings forever!
Dr: Your husband is concerned about you. Do you know his name?
Pt: (Stands, walks to and faces the wall) Who am I, Who are we, Who are you, Who are they. (Turns) I . . . I . . . I . . . I!!! (Makes grotesque faces)

Catatonic schizophrenia. The *catatonic schizophrenic* alternates between stuporous and excited behavioral phases. In the stuporous stage the patient shows a general inhibition of motor activity. The patient may assume one position and either rigidly maintain it, resisting all changes in position, or show "waxy flexibility," maintaining any position in which he or she is placed.

During the excited phase, the catatonic may be dangerously violent. During this period the individual is restless, unable to sleep, and impulsive. Some patients alternate between the two states, while others may remain in one or the other. The stuporous state, however, is the more frequent of the two.

Paranoid schizophrenia. *Paranoid schizophrenics* are most clearly identified by their strong delusions. These delusions usually involve persecution but also may be sexual, religious, or somatic in content. The delusions are frequently accompanied by hallucinations. This type of schizophrenia appears at a later age than other types, most commonly between the ages of twenty-five and forty. The patient is usually quite verbal, and does not show the severe regression or deterioration evidenced by the hebephrenic. The characteristic delusional pattern of thought is seen in the following letter (Suinn, 1970, p. 386):

I'm a man 36 years of age, that in 1956–57 they changed the flag of the United States of America once by adding Alaska as a State to the Union and thus paving the way for Hawaii to become a state in 1959. That of course, gives me the "capacity of the flag itself" and therefore like any Congressional Medal of Honor winner, gives me the "capacity of the President of the United States of America," that's about as high an esteem capacity that a man can receive in any country. . . . in 1955-56 civil authorities . . . some "small time" politicians got together on me and sandbagged me and brainwashed me and bugged me with a "short-wave Radio grid center, with an ultra-Violet Cross Grid" called a "bug." Its sole purpose is to use a person's senses against himself, so as to perjure and distort him to no end of humiliation. . . . they vibrate your nerves physically with it and never ceases. . . . I'd been there several months before they gave me "ground privileges" and once on the grounds, they started frequencing my time all the more, vibrating the back of my neck, first flicking it to the front of my face, like a "whip" or a cat of 9 tails. . . .

Paranoid Reaction

This particular psychotic reaction is characterized by an intricate, logical, well-developed delusional system. The paranoid reaction is differentiated from the paranoid schizophrenic by its more systematic delusions, fewer hallucinations, and less extensive disorientation and general personality disintegration.

This particular disorder develops relatively late in life, generally between the ages of forty-five and fifty-five. The paranoid psychotic may function well in all areas of life except that concerned with the delusions. The delusional system usually centers on one theme, such as finances, a job, or an unfaithful spouse. The delusions typically take the form of persecution, although they may occasionally involve ideas of grandeur. Since the delusional system is well developed and very logical if one accepts the basic assumption, conversion of other individuals to these ideas sometimes occurs, leading to the development of religious, political, or social cults. When the delusional system is jointly held by a husband and wife or by other close relatives, it is referred to as *folie à deux*.

The patient resists all arguments against the validity of the delusional system and thus is extremely difficult to treat.

Affective Psychoses

Emotional disturbances are the main symptoms of this group of psychoses. Although there may be behavioral or thought disturbances, these remain secondary to the emotional distortions.

Manic-depressive reaction. The *manic-depressive* affective reaction is characterized by mood extremes which can show themselves in any one of three patterns. In the manic reactions, the patient is excited, optimistic, confident, and hyperactive. The hallucinations and delusions usually involve ideas of grandeur. The psychological aspects of the manic reaction are often accompanied by physiological changes such as increases in heart rate and blood pressure.

BOX 20-3 MANIC-DEPRESSIVE PSYCHOSIS

Madeline K. was a 60-year old widow who recently lost her second husband. She was initially hospitalized when she was 22, soon after her marriage to her first husband. On that occasion she showed manic symptoms, was treated and discharged, returned within a month with depressive features, was treated and released. She remained essentially normal until the recent breakdown.

The records show that she was suffering from an acute manic condition during her first hospitalization. Her husband had returned home to find her twirling around the living room bizarrely draped in her wedding gown tied with a bathtowel and wearing a lampshade. She gaily greeted him, laughed with an ear-piercing shrillness, and invited him to stay for the exciting "coming-out" party she was giving. Strewn on the table were a thousand handwritten invitations signed with a flourish and addressed to such dignitaries as the President of the United States, the justices of the Supreme Court, the Board of Trustees of the University of California, and the Emperor of Japan. She made incessant noises: singing her own ballads, shouting mottoes which she devised, reciting limericks, making rhyming sounds, and yelling obscenities. She had recorded her speech for presentation to the Library of Congress. The following is an excerpt:

(Singing) By yon bonny briefs — my briefs are entirely outrageous but God take me you'd best like it — (in normal voice) the world is round the world is crown'd — illusions of Georgie, once a porgie — can't you see? — I am worth more than all the cherries in the universe — red is beautiful, red is ripe — bow ye before me and receive my blessing — thank God I'm not the devil — the freshest thing on this earth is a newborn clod — to work is to win — twin is a twin does — I sing a song of sexpot — hand me your head on a platter and I will forgive you all your sins — my plan will earn you a hundred-thousand-fold — mishmoshmoneymash — slipperydickerypop — dam it all full speed abreast — my head is gold, my hands are silver, my tail is platinum — Where am I? What time is it? Who goes there? — Gee but it's marvelous to be alive. . . .

By contrast, her most recent commitment at age 60 involved a severely depressed condition. An acquaintance had noticed her gradual refusal to leave her apartment and her apathetic attitude toward herself and the world around her. She looked immensely weary and had not slept soundly for days. She seemed mute, but would occasionally reply if a question were repeated long enough. Through careful probing it was found that she believed herself responsible for the "epidemics of the world" which she said were her punishment for her earlier sickness. She felt an urge to do penance for a lifetime of sin but could not remember the exact nature of her sin. For the past three weeks she had remained indoors pondering her own evil nature, and fearful of going out and possibly infecting others through the sheer enormity of her evilness. Life looked hopeless, she felt as though she was living in a shadow of despondency, despair enveloped her very existence (Suinn, 1970, p. 367).

In the depressive reaction the patient appears sad, discouraged, and inactive. The hallucinations are characteristically those of self-degradation. The manic and depressive states are clearly seen in the case cited in Box 20-3.

In contrast to the manic and depressive syndromes, a patient may show a cyclical reaction and alternate between the manic and depressive phases (see Figure 20-3).

The manic-depressive reaction tends to be fairly brief, frequently ending without any therapy. The attacks, however, tend to be recurrent, with only 21 percent of the patients having a single attack (Coleman, 1956). The length of the attacks generally increases with such recurrence, with the original attack lasting an average of six and one-half months.

Involutional melancholia. This affective psychosis occurs fairly late in life, correlating with the physiological changes taking place in the involutional period. It was first thought to occur only in women during menopause. It is now clear, however, that it occurs in both sexes, although generally earlier in women (between ages forty-five and fifty-five) than in men (between fifty-five and sixty-five). The patient shows an agitated depression with feelings of hopelessness, apprehension, and self-pity. There are frequently accompanying paranoid thoughts. This disorder may be caused by the physiological changes of the involutional period, as well as by the psychological stresses created by impending old age.

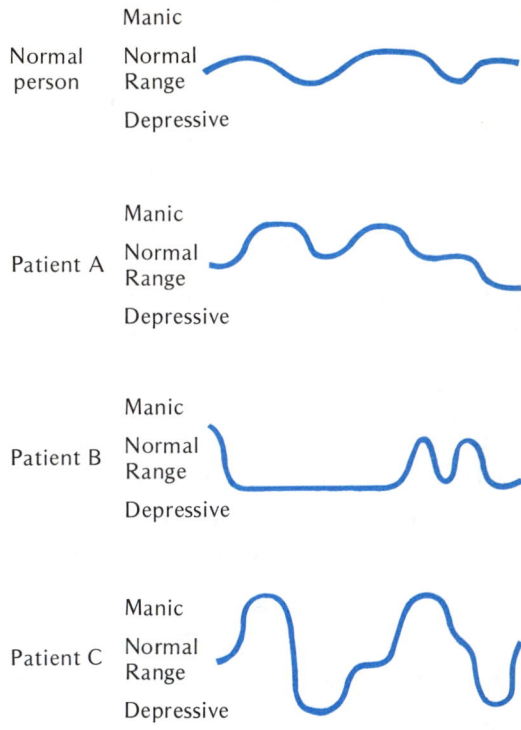

FIGURE 20-3 Pattern of moods in a normal individual and three manic-depressive psychotics. Patient A represents the manic reaction, Patient B exhibits the depressive reaction, and Patient C shows the cyclical manic-depressive reaction.

Psychotics: Occupants of Dream Houses

Unit 21
The Mind-Body Trap

John J. was the second of three children. . . . His mother died when he was twelve. He was a good student at high school and he helped his father, but after graduation he left home because he wanted to travel and see the world. . . . He was hard working and dependable. . . . For two nights a week John attended the local university, where he was taking three courses with the hope of getting a degree in engineering in four to six years. To get to his classes on time, he had to rush there straight from work, and he had no supper until he got home at ten o'clock. Often in class he had hunger pains and heartburn. . . . He was doing well in only two of his three courses and he was worried about this. . . . He also very much wanted to get married but seldom had time for a date. He was also troubled by the feeling that he ought to be at home helping his father. . . . A letter came from his father asking when he would be returning home, and in the evening, after a hasty supper, he sat down to try to write a cheerful reply . . . when he was struck by sudden agonizing abdominal pain. He felt it might be indigestion and waited some hours, but it was so severe that eventually he had to be taken to the hospital where it was found he had a perforated duodenal ulcer which required immediate surgery.

Treisman, 1968, pp. 498–499.

Bill W. was a bright student in junior high school, well-liked by his classmates and active in school athletics. His parents decided to send him to military school as a reward for being a "good" son. Shortly after this, there was a change in the boy's behavior. He began to show patterns of regression, loss of muscular control, stuttering, excessive masturbation, and extreme dependency. When a physical examination failed to show any organic problem, his behavior was diagnosed as a psychological disorder. His behavior continued to deteriorate until it reached the point at which he could no longer be cared for at home and had to be committed to a mental institution. Here the deterioration continued with further loss of muscular control, inability to converse with others, loss of bowel control, and stereotyped behavior. One night he became very ill and was rushed to a hospital, where he died. An autopsy showed that he had died of a brain tumor.

Personal communication, 1973.

The two cases cited above illustrate the close interaction between the mind and the body. The interaction between the two is so close that it is often difficult to differentiate their effects. In the case of John J., a primarily psychological problem produced physical destruction. In the case of Bill W., a physical problem produced psychological deterioration.

Psychophysiological Disorders

The case of John J. represents a psychophysiological disorder. These disorders, like the conversion reaction, involve physical symptoms of psychological origin. Unlike the conversion reaction, however, they involve real physical or structural damage to areas of the body. The physical symptoms show themselves in the organs and the viscera, which are under the control of the autonomic nervous system; those in the conversion reaction occur in parts of the body under the control of the central nervous system. Finally, the psychophysiological reactions conform to the known laws of physiology and anatomy. The conversion reaction may occur in a way that is inconsistent with these laws.

The wide range and variety of the psychophysiological disorders is seen by examining the formal classification system used by the American Psychiatric Association (1968), which includes skin, respiratory, gastrointestinal, and genitourinary reactions. These illnesses are not always the result of psychological factors. Rather, these are illnesses that *may* be caused by such factors.

Peptic ulcer and "executive" monkeys. One of the most extensively studied psychophysiological reactions is the peptic ulcer, often described as the disorder of executives. Brady (1958) performed an extensive study on the development of ulcers in monkeys. He used two monkeys, which were placed in an apparatus that could administer shock to both monkeys simultaneously (see Figure 21-1). The "executive" monkey had control of the shocks and could prevent the shock to both himself and his partner by pressing a lever according to a schedule. The partner could do nothing about the shock since the entire decision-making process was in the hands of the executive. The results showed that with a schedule of six hours' work and six hours' rest, the executive monkey developed an ulcer while the control monkey remained healthy. Other schedules of work-rest periods such as eighteen hours or thirty minutes did not lead to ulcers in either animal. The results indicate that it is not the stress alone that causes ulcers, but the timing and the cyclical nature of the stress and its relation to the production of stomach acid.

Stigmatization. One of the more dramatic examples of psychophysiological reactions is that of stigmatization. In one such case, a German woman, Teresa Neumann, developed marks of the crucifixion on her face, hands, and feet

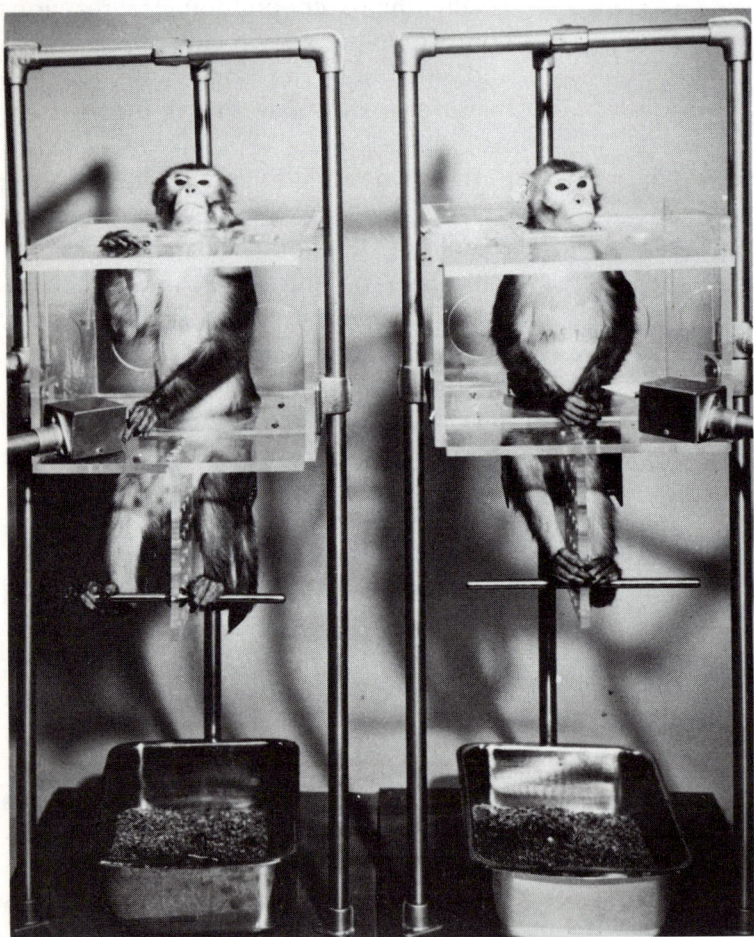

U.S. Army photograph; courtesy of J. V. Brady

FIGURE 21-1 Monkeys in the apparatus used for the "executive monkey" experiment

each Good Friday. Careful examination by physicians and psychiatrists demonstrated that these marks were not a hoax (Hynek, 1932).

Asthma. Asthma is another type of psychophysiological reaction, and it has been found to be associated with a certain type of personality. The "typical" asthmatic individual is insecure and has strong feelings of dependency and fear of losing his or her parents' love. These psychological problems and the attendant fears produce the difficulties of the respiratory system that are diagnosed as asthma.

Brain Disorders

In the psychophysiological disorders, the psychological stress is seen as a cause of the physical malfunctioning. The brain disorders represent the opposite causal relationship. In these disorders, the physical problem produces behavioral changes that are diagnosed as psychopathological. In the case of Bill W., discussed at the beginning of this unit, the psychopathology was caused by the brain tumor.

Senile psychosis. *Senile psychosis* occurs in the aged and includes patterns of both mental and physical deterioration. The patient may exhibit confusion, depression, or agitation. The line between normal senility and psychotic senility is not a clear one, as the conditions differ only in degree. The condition of senile psychotics rarely improves; usually, deterioration becomes increasingly severe.

Brain tumors. The behavioral symptoms resulting from *brain tumors* vary widely depending on the size and location of the tumor. There can be sensory disturbances, emotional changes, or intellectual deterioration. Although the syndrome, particularly in the early stages, may include physical symptoms such as headaches or drowsiness, the later behavioral and psychological changes may be far more dramatic and may lead to a psychiatric diagnosis. The presence of such organic bases for psychological disorders points to the need for full and complete physical examination in *all* cases of suspected psychiatric disorders. Such physical examination should take place before submitting the patient to psychiatric or psychological care.

Alcohol psychosis. The excessive and chronic use of alcohol can cause organic disorders and *alcohol psychosis*. The disorders resulting include delirium tremens, in which the subject shows disorientation, hallucinations, fear, suggestibility, and marked tremor; and *Korsakoff's syndrome,* or Korsakoff's psychosis. This syndrome is characterized by loss of memory, particularly for recent events. In attempting to fill in the memory gaps, the individual makes up memories. These fabrications are unrelated and make the individual seem disoriented. The disorder is not caused directly by alcohol, but rather by a vitamin B deficiency resulting from the improper diet of the alcoholic. The patient can be restored to a fairly normal life by a vitamin-rich diet, but some personality deterioration usually remains. With increasingly excessive alcohol intake, there may be degeneration of the cerebral and peripheral nerves.

The mind and the body may or may not be two separate entities. But it is clear from the examination of psychopathology that they cannot be treated separately. The interaction between the two is too close for one to be examined or understood in the absence of the other.

Unit 22
Personality Disorders: Violations of the Code

One of the earliest childhood memories of Hermann Goering, the Nazi, was of "bashing his mother in the face with both fists when she came to embrace him after a prolonged absence, at the age of three. This tendency to overt aggression manifested itself very early as one of his chief satisfactions in life." "During World War I Goering made the dangerous and fateful discovery that war could bring both glory and profit to one who was sufficiently reckless, unscrupulous, and amiable. After World War II, Goering was brought to trial. The experience did not seem painful to him. Rather, he seemed to enjoy the center stage. When films from the concentration camps were shown, other defendents were extremely upset. "As for Goering, he was apparently disturbed because it had spoiled his show. 'It was such a good afternoon too, until they showed that film. — They were reading my telephone conversations on the Austrian affair, and everybody was laughing with me. — And then they showed that awful film, and it just spoiled everything.'"

Gilbert, 1948, pp. 211, 215, 226.

Gilbert (1948) has argued that Goering was a psychopath, or what will be referred to here as an antisocial personality. Although this particular type of personality disorder is more dramatic than most, it has certain characteristics in common with the other types.

Personality disorders in general are "characterized by deeply ingrained maladaptive patterns of behavior" (American Psychiatric Association, 1968, p. 41). These patterns frequently show a lifelong history, as was true in Goering's case. In most cases these patients are unconcerned with their problems. If they obtain treatment it is due to the insistence of their families or as a result of clashes with society and the law.

The personality disorders differ from the neuroses and psychoses in that they seldom are characterized by thought disturbances, emotional disturbances, or anxiety. Rather, the maladjustment is expressed in overt behavior. Stated more simply, such individuals simply don't act as they "should." They have a whole way of life which may be described as deviant.

The personality disorders manifest themselves in a wide variety of different ways (see Box 22-1).

BOX 22-1   TYPES OF PERSONALITY DISORDERS

Types	Symptoms
Schizoid personality	Withdrawn, detached
Obsessive-compulsive personality	Rigid, meticulous, overly concerned with order
Passive-aggressive personality	
Passive-dependent	Extremely dependent, denies independence needs
Aggressive	Easily angered, has extreme dominance needs
Passive-aggressive	Expresses aggressive needs in passive, indirect ways
Antisocial personality	Has no moral values, acts on momentary impulses, fails to learn from experience
Dyssocial personality	Has strong moral code which differs from that of the dominant social or legal structure
Sexual deviations	
Pedophilia	Sexual desire for children
Voyeurism	Obtaining sexual pleasure from observing sex acts and objects
Exhibitionism	Obtaining sexual pleasure from exposing parts of the body in public
Homosexuality	Obtaining sexual pleasure from members of the same sex
Alcoholism	Use of alcohol as the preferred method of solving problems
Addiction	Use of drugs that cause increased tolerance with increased usage and produce withdrawal symptoms when use is discontinued

SCHIZOID PERSONALITY

When an individual demonstrates a lifestyle that is withdrawn and detached, one may describe the person as a *schizoid personality*. This is a person one simply can't get close to or communicate with.

OBSESSIVE-COMPULSIVE PERSONALITY

Most of us show somewhat excessive concern with order and correctness in some areas of our lives. When this concern pervades all aspects of life so that one is rigid, overinhibited, and meticulous, the person is characterized as having an *obsessive-compulsive* personality disorder. An example of such behavior comes from the following description by the patient:

> I am incessantly concerned over the fact that I am not going to get done all I want to. I always have several lists, some very extensive, and as I do the task I cross it off. I try to make a concise list of what I plan or want for the week. During the week I will add to it. Even on my day off, I get up early to do something on my list. I only wish there were more than twenty-four hours in a day (Kisker, 1972, p. 214).

PASSIVE-AGGRESSIVE PERSONALITY

A conflict between the need to be dependent and the need to be dominant, when it becomes the focus of a person's lifestyle, may lead to a *passive-aggressive* personality disorder. Since we all have the need to be dependent as well as the need to remain independent and autonomous, this is a conflict we all face. Our resolution of it varies and becomes a problem only when extreme solutions are adopted. Some people solve the problem by total denial of their independence needs and expression of the dependent needs only *(passive-dependent personality)*. The typical example of this is the wife who can do nothing without her husband's agreement and approval, the woman who takes no responsibility on herself. Her husband handles the money because it "confuses her." Their children wait for daddy to come home to be punished. She never buys a dress, a piece of furniture, or a can of soup without her husband's approval.

The reverse solution to the conflict is to deny all dependency needs and express only dominance needs, as occurs in the *aggressive personality*. This is most clearly typified by the easily angered man who is quick to respond to any insult, whether real or imagined, with some aggressive proof of his dominance. This man will fight at the slightest provocation and has no fear of telling anyone off.

The choice of a female to illustrate the passive-dependent personality and the choice of a male to illustrate the aggressive personality were not accidental — or sexist. Rather, this was done to illustrate the cultural effects on the definition of personality disorders. In our society, far more extreme dependency will be tolerated in a woman than in a man before the behavior is considered deviant. It is both "normal" and "good" for a female to be dependent. The reverse is true for expressed aggression. Men are supposed to be dominant and aggressive, so society tolerates far greater extremes of these behaviors in men than it will in women.

A third resolution of this conflict is

accomplished by passively or indirectly expressing one's strong aggressive needs *(passive-aggressive personality)*. Have you ever met a person who seemed kind, thoughtful, and considerate, yet always seemed to interfere with what you wanted to do? Who borrowed your math book the night before your exam without telling you — returning it with sincere apologies right after the exam? Who always seemed to appear at your door when you wanted to study, and remained in spite of all hints that you wanted to be alone? These people are aggressive in subtle, nondirect ways, pouting rather than shouting, passively obstructing rather than actively striking out.

ANTISOCIAL AND DYSSOCIAL PERSONALITIES

The next two types of disorders to be discussed represent behaviors that violate society's norms or laws. The two differ mainly in the underlying reasons for the behaviors. In one type, violation takes place because the individual has *no* internalized moral or ethical values *(antisocial personality)*. The other type of disorder *(dyssocial)* results in deviant behavior because the individual has a strong moral or ethical code which differs from the one endorsed by general society. Let us take as an example the crime of murder. The antisocial individual has no personal moral feelings about whether this is right or wrong. If he commits murder, it is an impulsive act done because someone got in the way of something he wanted. The dyssocial individual, when he commits a murder, does it because he feels it is right. The Cosa Nostra gang murders are examples of dyssocial behavior. Cosa Nostra gang members are men with a strong code of values that states that death is the right penalty for certain behaviors, such as violation of the code of secrecy.

The antisocial individual, because of his lack of values, will exhibit a kind of random production of immoral or illegal behaviors. He does what he wants when he wants to. He can't be taught his lesson, because the next time he wants to do something he will. He is directed by impulse, not past experience. An example of such behavior is cited by Kisker (1972, p. 217):

The total inability of the antisocial personality to profit from experience or to use good judgment is typified by a prisoner who thanked the warden profusely for his encouraging remarks at the time of his release from prison. However, on his way out of the office, the prisoner stole the warden's portable typewriter.

SEXUAL DEVIATIONS

The dominant moral code of society also functions in defining a wide range of sexual behaviors as abnormal. The "right" and "good" type of sexual behavior is heterosexual intercourse between married people — or, possibly, nonmarried consenting adults.

Some deviations from this norm clearly must be controlled, such as the expression of sexual desire for children *(pedophilia)*. Other types of sexual behavior create legal or social problems only in certain instances. Obtaining sexual enjoyment from observing sex acts and objects *(voyeurism)* clearly must be controlled when the object is a nonconsenting individual, as is true in the case of someone being watched by a "Peeping Tom." Yet the modification of voyeurism which is represented by reading *Playboy* or going to X-rated movies is generally not considered deviant. Showing in public parts of the body, particularly the genital organs, as a form of sexual stimulation *(exhibitionism)* may well fall within the range of deviance. But sexual display or exhibitionism in its more subtle form of telling dirty jokes is widely practiced in our society and is accepted as normal.

Homosexuality. This type of sexual behavior, classically defined as deviant, has recently come under careful scrutiny in regard to its acceptability. Historically, homosexuality has been viewed in a number of ways. The Bible condemns the practice as evil in the quotation from Leviticus 20:13: "If a man also lieth down with a man as he lieth with a woman, both of them have committed an abomination." The ancient Greeks, on the other hand, attributed positive value to the homosexual experience.

A third view of the homosexual holds that the individual is disturbed and is manifesting personality abnormalities. It assumes that the individual, if better adjusted, would automatically desire members of the opposite sex for sexual gratification. However, a number of studies have called this concept into question, for they have failed to find that homosexuals have significantly more personality disorders or neurotic behaviors than do heterosexual individuals (Freedman, 1968; McGuire, 1966). The only consistent difference between the two groups was the choice of sex object, and this alone led to homosexuals being classified as deviant.

The statistical surveys of Kinsey and his colleagues, by pointing to the extensiveness of homosexual practice in this country, have impugned the oversimplified classification of homosexuals as deviant. The survey found that 50 to 60 percent of the males sampled had engaged in some homosexual activity. The frequency for women was somewhat lower, only 28 percent, but the behavior was too prevalent to be considered highly unusual.

There is pressure at the present time to adopt a new view of the homosexual. This view stresses that the homosexual pattern of behavior should be seen as a social role rather than a medical or psychiatric problem (McIntosh, 1968). This is in accord with Freud's statement that homosexuality is a man-made perversion. The sexual drives of children, according to Freud, are not directed in a heterosexual manner, but are bisexual. The pressures toward heterosexuality come not from within the individual but from society. Homosexual behavior is, then, not a violation of nature, as is often claimed, but a violation of societal norms.

Such groups as the Mattachine Society are also changing attitudes toward homosexuality and attempting to gain social acceptance for the homosexual (Sagarin, 1968). The society increases pride and decreases self-doubts, enabling the homosexual to feel freer in identifying himself as a homosexual.

There is also a movement to point out and eliminate the discrimination against homosexuals, as typified by such groups as the Gay Liberation Front. Cory (1951) argues that the homosexual community represents a minority group. He notes that homosexuals, like many other minority groups, are subject to discrimination and are placed in a lower, unequal social status. There is a growing sentiment that homosexuality between consenting adults should no longer be considered deviant and that such individuals should not be discriminated against. Acceptance of homosexuals is not as widespread as acceptance of other minority groups, but a change in attitudes is taking place.

In arguing for the position of homosexuals as a minority group, Cory (1951) states that homosexuality is involuntary and unchangeable. Greenspan and Campbell (1945) even go so far as to state that homosexuality is due to a biological anomaly, rather than to environmental factors or one's relationship with one's parents. Current data do not support a biological basis for homosexuality, although such a causal factor should not be ruled out.

In spite of the pressures for a change in attitude, acceptance or tolerance of homosexual behavior by the society at large is still limited. In a survey by Rooney and Gibbons (1966), most subjects saw the homosexual as a sick person with personality pathology. If the current openness about homosexuality is not increasing acceptance, it may at least be serving to extinguish some of the existing stereotypes. Homosexuals are simply not all alike.

As pointed out by Simon and Gagnon (1967, p. 249):

It requires no great familiarity with this topic to appreciate that a similarity of the gender of sexual object choices masks a vast amount of variations in other dimensions that are crucial to living.

In summing up their study (p. 282), Simon and Gagnon point out that such behavior is obviously not fully natural but rather is

. . . unnatural in the way that all human behavior is unnatural, that is, it is without an absolutely predetermined and fixed shape and content, and it is a complex condition which derives from man's unique abilities to think, act, and remember his need to live with other humans.

In order to give due respect to the complexity of homosexual behavior, such an individual should not be dismissed as abnormal or disgusting. Rather, the civil and human rights of such individuals should be respected.

The final two categories of personality disorders include the addictions to alcohol and to drugs. We will not at this point be concerned with marijuana or LSD. These are generally considered to be nonaddictive and will be treated more fully in Division J.

ALCOHOLISM

The use of alcohol has become pervasive in our culture, and with it the presence of alcoholism. Although it is often difficult to determine exactly at what point an individual becomes an alcoholic rather than a heavy drinker, a general rule is to classify as alcoholics those who use liquor as the preferred method of solving their problems. Such an individual is unable to stop drinking and eventually runs into conflict with family and friends as well as with society.

Cultural determinants. The culture of which an individual is a part can have an important effect on the development of alcoholism. Moros (1942) found that the incidence of alcoholism was highest among those of Irish descent and among third generation Americans, while Jews showed a very low incidence of alcoholism. In an analysis of cultural differences by Bales (1946), the cultural influence was divided into three parts:

1. The degree to which the culture produces a strong need for adjustment and the amount of tension involved in living in the culture
2. The attitudes within the culture toward drinking
3. The degree to which the culture provides for its members suitable alternatives to alcohol

Bales makes a further subdivision in terms of the attitudes which the culture holds toward drinking. The attitude of *complete abstinence* is held by the Moslems. All alcoholic beverages are strictly forbidden. The *ritual* attitude is clearly exemplified by the Jews. Wine is used in this culture in the performance of religious ceremony, and the whole family is incorporated into the ritual drinking. Although many individuals would like to believe that the mere presence of alcohol causes alcoholism, the statistics on the incidence of alcoholism in Jews demonstrates the lack of validity of such a position. The *convivial* attitude stresses the use of alcohol for social unity, social ease, and relaxation. This type of drinking may occur in conjunction with a religious ceremony, such as a wedding, but is not an integral part of the ceremony. It is a totally secular activity. The *utilitarian* attitude stresses the use of alcohol for medication, self-interest, or purely personal satisfaction. This type of drinking is frequently, though not always, solitary. The drinking condoned by the convivial attitude is most likely to lead to utilitarian drinking. This is the category most likely to lead to alcoholism.

DRUG ADDICTION

The drug addict is similar to the alcoholic in using an external agent as a means to solve problems. Morphine and heroin, derivatives of opium, bring on a euphoric and peaceful state. This, perhaps, accounts in part for the high rate of use among the lower classes, for the drugs produce a psychological state far more pleasant than that evoked by the actual surroundings. These drugs are addictive: tolerance to them increases, and withdrawal symptoms are often severe. Excessive use of these drugs can cause serious illness or death. Chronic use can also lead to serious side effects.

The cost of the drug and its physical effect combine to prevent the addict from eating a proper diet and obtaining proper physical care. In addition, there is the ever-present threat of hepatitis arising from the use of unsterilized needles.

Treatment for addiction is difficult because it involves both physical and psychological attention. In addition, once released from institutional care, the addict frequently has no place to go except back to the environment that originally caused the addiction.

As has been noted, the definition of personality disorders rests heavily on the dominant values of the society. For this reason, great care should be exercised in assigning an individual to such a classification. Evaluation of the behavior must be done within the individual's actual life situation. Although a behavior might represent maladjustment abstractly, when viewed in the context of the individual's unique social and cultural environment it may be a well-adjusted response and one that is highly satisfying to the individual and those around him.

Individuals with personality disorders who commit criminal acts are unlikely to be judged insane. Their behavior and speech appear rational, and they seldom demonstrate the loss of control necessary to convince a jury that they didn't know right from wrong. Even the antisocial person, with no internalized moral values, "knows" what is right and wrong in the sense that if he is asked, he can tell you. But this knowledge has no effect on his behavior, since it has not been incorporated. Until there is some change in our legal definition of sanity, people with personality disorders will continue to take up a good proportion of the space in our prisons.

SUMMARY

The most basic problem in the classification of a person as normal or abnormal is the problem of definition. The law defines insanity in terms of ability to be able to distinguish right from wrong at the time of the crime. The *subjective approach* to definition leaves the classification of normality up to the individual's personal judgment, allowing each person to use himself or herself as the standard of comparison. The *statistical approach* defines normality as the average behavior. The *cultural approach* stresses that the concept of normality is a culturally relative one which may vary from culture to culture. The final approach to the definitional problem is the *normative approach,* which stresses the establishment of an ideal against which a person is judged. It is quite clear that we have no neat, concise way of placing any individual in a normal or abnormal category.

Once one is classified as abnormal, one is further evaluated and placed in a diagnostic category, most commonly according to the system used by the American Psychiatric Association. The usefulness of this system has been questioned due to problems such as the fact that diagnosis is not as simple and clear-cut as the categorization system makes it seem and the subjective judgment involved on the part of the therapist. These problems have led many psychologists to turn from this *medical model* of abnormality to a *functional* or *behavioral approach.* The latter approach concentrates on the behavioral symptom rather than its underlying causes and attempts to change it so that the individual performs behaviors which reflect better adjustment.

Neurotic disorders are among the most common types of mental illness and are characterized by anxiety and the defense mechanisms used to reduce it. Neurotics differ in the manner in which they deal with their anxiety. In the *anxiety reaction,* anxiety is overtly and obviously expressed. If the general anxiety typical of the neurotic is directed into an excessive and irrational fear, this is called a *phobic reaction.* In an *obsessive-compulsive reaction,* the anxiety is directed into recurrent ideas and repetitive behaviors. The *hysterical reaction* may manifest itself as a *conversion reaction,* a disorder in which the anxiety is converted into a physical malfunction, with no underlying physical or organic damage. The hysterical reaction may also involve a problem in the psychological sphere only, as in the *dissociative reaction,* in which the individual attempts to control anxiety by removing from consciousness those parts of the personality which are producing it. Examples of this reaction are *amnesia, fugue reaction,* and *multiple personality.* The *depressive reaction* occurs when the individual reacts to problems and conflicts with a feeling of hopelessness, dejection, and depression.

Whereas neurotics are characterized by high levels of anxiety, the *psychotic* is characterized by loss of contact with reality. Different types of psychoses are classified by the behavior pattern demonstrated and the areas in which loss of contact with reality is most pronounced. The psychotic reaction is one of the most severe mental disorders and accounts for a high proportion of the admissions to mental hospitals. Although there are different types of psychoses, there is a common group of symptoms underlying all. These symptoms include disorientation, delusions, hallucinations, and disturbances in emotions and in verbal and nonverbal communication.

The *schizophrenic reaction* (a psychosis) is made up of various diagnostic categories based on different symptom patterns. The *simple schizophrenic reaction* is characterized by withdrawal, apathy, and emotional flatness. The *hebephrenic schizophrenic reaction* is characterized by exaggerated delusions, hallucinations, language disturbances, and regression to childhood levels of behavior. The *catatonic schizophrenic* alternates between stuporous and excited phases. In the stuporous stage the patient shows a general inhibition of motor activity, while during the excited phase the patient may be dangerously violent. The *paranoid schizophrenic* is most clearly identified by the delusions, which frequently are accompanied by hallucinations.

The *paranoid psychotic reaction* is characterized by an intricate, logical, well-developed delusional system which is held to strongly, making treatment difficult. The paranoid psychotic may function well in all areas of life except that concerned with the delusion.

The *affective psychoses* involve disturbances primarily within the emotional sphere. The *manic-depressive reaction* is characterized by mood extremes which can show themselves in any one of three patterns: manic, depressive, or a cyclical reaction alternating between manic and depressive phases. *Involutional melancholia* occurs fairly late in life, correlating with the physical and psychological changes taking place in the involutional period. The patient shows an agitated depression with feelings of hopelessness, apprehension, and self-pity.

The *psychophysiological disorders* involve physical symptoms of psychological origin. Unlike the conversion reaction, this disorder involves real physical damage to the body which conforms to known laws of physiology and anatomy. Ulcers and asthma are examples of such disorders.

In *brain disorders,* a physical problem produces behavioral changes which are pathological. Among the disorders included in this category are senile psychoses, behavioral effects of brain tumors, and alcohol psychosis.

Personality disorders are characterized by deeply ingrained maladaptive patterns of behavior which frequently show a lifelong history. The patient is generally unconcerned with the problem and treatment is usually obtained involuntarily. The maladjustment is usually expressed in overt behavior rather than in thought disturbances, emotional disturbances, or anxiety. The personality disorders manifest themselves in a wide variety of ways. The *schizoid personality* demonstrates a life-style that is withdrawn and detached. The *obsessive-compulsive personality* has an excessive concern with order and correctness and is rigid, overinhibited, and meticulous. A conflict between the needs to be dependent and to be dominant, when they become the focus of the person's life style, may lead to a *passive-aggressive personality disorder.* Some solve the problem by total denial of their independence needs and expression of the dependency needs only *(passive-dependent personalities),* while others use the reverse solution and express only dominance needs *(aggressive personalities).* Still others resolve this conflict by passively or indirectly expressing aggressive needs *(passive-aggressive personalities).*

The *antisocial personality* and the *dyssocial personality* both represent behaviors that violate society's norms or laws. However, whereas the antisocial personality violates these codes because of an absence of internalized moral values, the dyssocial personality deviates because of a moral code which differs from the one endorsed by general society.

The dominant moral code of society also defines a wide range of sexual behaviors as abnormal, such as the expression of sexual desire for children *(pedophilia),* and obtaining sexual enjoyment from observing sex acts and objects *(voyeurism)* and from the display of parts of the body in public *(exhibitionism). Homosexuality* is also classically defined as deviant. The statistical surveys of Kinsey indirectly have called into question the oversimplified classification of homosexuals as deviants by pointing to the extensiveness of homosexuality among males. There is at present pressure to adopt a new view of homosexuality as a social role rather than a medical or psychiatric problem.

The final two categories of personality disorders include the addictions to alcohol and to drugs. One is generally classified as an alcoholic if one uses liquor as the preferred method of solving problems. The culture of which an individual is a part can have an important effect on the development of alcoholism. The drug addict is similar to the alcoholic in also using an external agent as a means to solve problems. Treatment for addiction is difficult because it involves both physical and psychological care.

The definition of personality disorders rests heavily on the dominant values of society. For this reason great care should be exercised to evaluate the individual's behavior within the actual life situation.

GLOSSARY

Addiction: use of drugs that cause increased tolerance with increased usage and produce withdrawal symptoms when use is discontinued

Affective psychosis: a psychotic disorder which involves disturbances primarily in the emotional sphere

Alcoholism: the use of alcohol as the preferred method of solving problems

Amnesia: a type of dissociative reaction in which there is memory loss for part or all of patient's past experience or identity

Antisocial personality: a personality disorder in which the individual has no moral values, acts on momentary impulses, and fails to learn from experience

Anxiety reaction: a type of neurosis characterized by overt anxiety or "nervousness"

Brain disorders: psychotic behavior caused by physiological or neurological malfunctions in the brain

Catatonic schizophrenia: a schizophrenic reaction characterized by alternately stuporous or extremely excited behavior

Conversion reaction: a neurotic reaction characterized by physical malfunction with no organic or physical cause

Compulsion: the need to repeatedly perform the same behavior

Cultural definition (of normality and abnormality): defining normal behavior in terms of the norms and standards of the culture in which it occurs

Delusion: ideas which have no objective or realistic basis

Depressive reaction: a neurotic reaction characterized by depression and feelings of worthlessness and hopelessness

Dissociative reaction: a neurotic reaction that involves setting off a portion of the personality in order to control anxiety; includes amnesia and multiple personality

Dyssocial personality: a personality disorder in which the individual has a strong code of moral values which is different from that of the dominant social or legal structure

Exhibitionism: obtaining sexual pleasure

and satisfaction from exposing parts of the body, particularly the genitals, in public

Fugue reaction: a type of amnesia that involves not only loss of memory, but flight from the environment which evokes the anxiety

Functional approach (to abnormal behavior): an approach focusing on behavior in dealing with psychopathology and attempting to change behavior directly in order to effect better adjustment

Hallucination: a perception which has no correlate in the external world

Hebephrenic schizophrenia: a schizophrenic reaction characterized by hallucinations, delusions, shallow and inappropriate affect, and childish behavior

Homosexuality: obtaining sexual pleasure and satisfaction from a member of the same sex

Hypochondriacal reaction: a type of neurosis characterized by excessive concern with the body, worry over being sick, and the belief that one is sick although there is no illness

Hysterical reaction: the type of neurosis that takes the form of a conversion reaction or a dissociative reaction

Involutional melancholia: a type of affective psychosis that occurs during the physiological changes of the involutional period and that is characterized by deep depression

Korsakoff's syndrome: a disorder characterized by loss of memory, fabrication, and disorientation; results from vitamin B deficiency associated with alcoholism

La belle indifference: the lack of concern shown by conversion neurotics in regard to their physical malfunctions

Manic-depressive reaction: an affective psychosis characterized by mood extremes in one of three patterns: manic (highly excited), depressive, or a cyclic manic-depressive pattern

Medical model: an approach to psychological disorders in which one focuses on the symptom and classifies the disorder in terms of the symptom on the assumption that the symptom is directly linked to the cause and treatment

Multiple personality: a form of dissociative reaction in which two or more complete and separate personalities are formed within the same individuals

Neurosis: a disorder characterized by high levels of anxiety and excessive use of defense mechanisms to reduce the anxiety

Normative definition (of normality and abnormality): defining what is considered to be ideal adjustment and normality and judging how closely the individual approaches the ideal

Obsession: an idea which repeatedly intrudes on one's stream of thought

Obsessive-compulsive personality: a personality disorder characterized by rigid and meticulous behavior and an overconcern with order

Obsessive-compulsive reaction: a type of neurosis characterized by the repeated intrusion of ideas into the stream of

thought (obsessions) and repeated performance of behaviors or sets of behaviors (compulsions)

Paranoid reaction: a psychotic reaction characterized by a logical, well-developed delusional system

Paranoid schizophrenia: a schizophrenic reaction characterized by delusions, commonly of persecution, and by hallucinations

Passive-aggressive personality: a personality disorder characterized by inadequate adjustment to conflicting dependence and independence needs

Pedophilia: sexual desire for children

Personality disorder: life-long maladaptive behavior patterns

Phobic reaction: a type of neurosis characterized by excessive and apparently irrational fear of some object or event

Psychophysiological disorder: physiological destruction caused by psychological stress

Psychosis: a disorder involving loss of contact with reality in which some or all of the following symptoms are present: disorientation, delusions, hallucinations, disturbances in emotions, and disturbances in communication

Schizoid personality: a personality disorder characterized by withdrawal

Schizophrenic reaction: a psychotic reaction involving disturbances in reality relations and in emotional and thought processes

Senile psychosis: psychotic behavior caused by aspects of the physical deterioration accompanying senility

Simple schizophrenia: a schizophrenic reaction characterized by withdrawal, apathy, and emotional flatness

Statistical definition (of normality and abnormality): defining normality as the statistically average or mean behavior

Subjective definition (of normality and abnormality): defining normality in terms of the individual's own judgment, using that person as the standard

Voyeurism: obtaining sexual pleasure and satisfaction from viewing sex acts and objects

REFERENCES

American Psychiatric Association. *Diagnostic and statistical manual of mental disorders*. (2nd ed.). Washington, D.C.: American Psychiatric Association, 1968.

Bales, R. F. Cultural differences in rates of alcoholism. *Quarterly Journal of Studies on Alcohol,* 1946, *6,* 480–499.

Benedict, R. Anthropology and the abnormal. *Journal of General Psychology,* 1934, *10,* 59–82.

Brady, J. Ulcers in "executive" monkeys. *Scientific American,* 1958, *199*(4), pp. 95–100.

Coleman, J. C. *Abnormal psychology and modern life*. (2nd ed.). Chicago: Scott, Foresman, 1956.

Cory, D. W. *The homosexual in America*. Philadelphia: Chilton, 1951.

de Nike, L. D., and Tiber, N. Neurotic behavior. In P. London and D. Rosenhan (Eds.), *Foundations of abnormal psychology*. New York: Holt, Rinehart and Winston, 1968.

Edwards, D. C. *General Psychology*. (2nd ed.). New York: Macmillan, 1972.

Freedman, M. J. Homosexuality among women and psychological adjustment. *Dissertation Abstracts,* 1968, *28*(B), 4294–4295.

Gilbert, G. M. Hermann Goering: amiable psychopath. *Journal of Abnormal and Social Psychology,* 1948, *43*, 211–229.

Goldstein, M. J., and Palmer, J. C. *The experience of anxiety*. New York: Oxford University Press, 1963.

Greenspan, H. G., and Campbell, J. D. The homosexual as a personality type. *American Journal of Psychiatry,* 1945, *101*, 682–684.

Gruenberg, E. M. A review of "Mental health in the metropolis": Midtown Manhattan study. *Milbank Memorial Fund Quarterly,* 1963, *42*, 77–94.

Hollingshead, A. B., and Redlich, F. G. *Social class and mental illness: A community study*. New York: Wiley, 1958.

Hutt, M. L., and Gibby, R. G. *Patterns of abnormal behavior*. Boston: Allyn & Bacon, 1957.

Hynek, R. M. *Konnersreuth: A medical and psychological study of the case of Teresa Neuman*. London: Burns, Oates & Washbourne, 1932.

Kinsey, A. C., Pomeroy, W. B., and Martin, C. E. *Sexual behavior in the human male*. Philadelphia: Saunders, 1948.

Kinsey, A. C., Pomeroy, W. B., Martin, C. E., and Gebhard, P. H. *Sexual behavior in the human female*. Philadelphia: Saunders, 1959.

Kisker, G. W. *The disorganized personality*. (2nd ed.). New York: McGraw-Hill, 1972.

McGuire, R. M. An inquiry into attitudes and value systems of a minority group: A comparative study of attitudes and value systems of adult male homosexuals with adult male heterosexuals. *Dissertation Abstracts,* 1966, *27*(4A), 1110–1111.

McIntosh, M. The homosexual role. *Social Problems,* 1968, *16*, 182–192.

Moros, N. The alcoholic personality: A statistical study. *Quarterly Journal of Studies on Alcohol,* 1942, *3*, 45–49.

Moynihan, D. P. *Negro Family: The case for national action*. U.S. Department of Labor, Office of Policy Planning and Research, 1965.

Pronko, W. H. *Textbook of abnormal psychology*. Baltimore: Williams & Wilkins, 1963.

Rooney, E. A., and Gibbons, D. C. Social reactions to "crimes without victims." *Social Problems,* 1966, *3*, 400–410.

Rosenhan, D. L. On being sane in insane places. *Science,* 1973, *179*, 1–9.

Sagarin, E. Structure and ideology in an association of deviants. *Dissertation Abstracts,* 1968, *29*(4A), 1305–1306.

Simon, W., and Gagnon, J. H. The lesbians: A preliminary overview. In J. H. Gagnon and W. Simon (Eds.), *Sexual deviance*. New York: Harper & Row, 1967.

Sinnett, E. R. The diary of a schizophrenic man. In B. Kaplan (Ed.), *The inner world of mental illness*. New York: Harper & Row, 1964.

Suinn, R. M. *Fundamentals of behavior pathology*. New York: Wiley, 1970.

Thigpen, C. H., and Cleckley, H. M. *The three faces of Eve*. New York: McGraw-Hill, 1957.

Time. One sick assassin. August 14, 1972, pp. 22–23.

Treisman, M. Mind, body and behavior: Control systems and their disturbances. In D. London and D. Rosenhan (Eds.), *Foundations of abnormal psychology*. New York: Holt, Rinehart and Winston, 1968.

Wegrocki, H. J. A critique of cultural and statistical concepts of abnormality. *Journal of Abnormal and Social Psychology*, 1939, *34*, 166–178.

SUGGESTED READINGS

Buss, A. H. *Psychopathology*. New York: Wiley, 1966.

Coleman, J. C., and Broen, W. E. *Abnormal psychology and modern life*. (4th ed.). Chicago: Scott, Foresman, 1971.

Redlich, F. C., and Freedman, D. X. *The theory and practice of psychiatry*. New York: Basic Books, 1966.

Rosenthal, D., and Kety, S. S. (Eds.). *The transmission of schizophrenia*. New York: Pergamon Press, 1968.

Ullmann, L. P., and Krasner, L. *A psychological approach to abnormal behavior*. Englewood Cliffs, N.J.: Prentice-Hall, 1969.

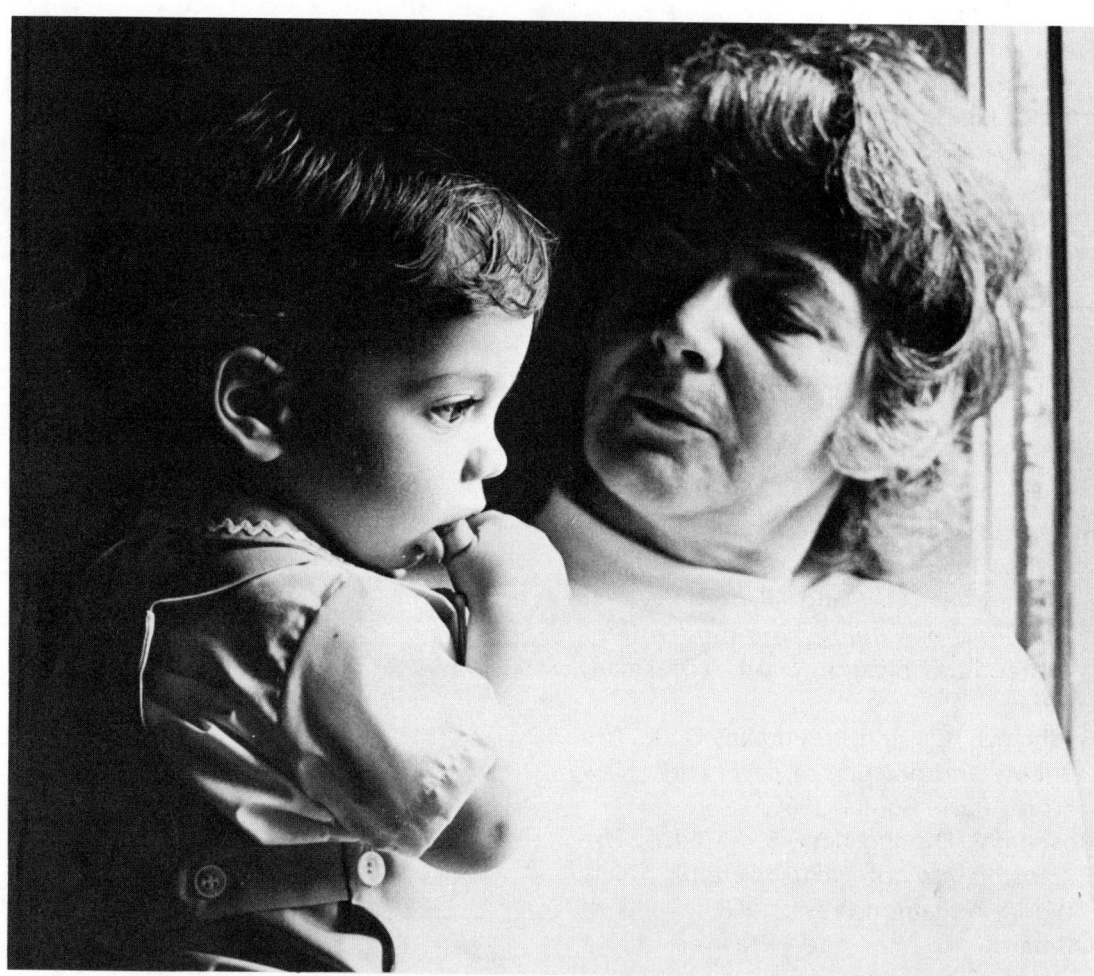
Photo by Julie Copeland

F

How Do We Cope?

Unit 23
The Number is the Meaning

One of the major problems in the area of personality disorders is assessment; that is, figuring out what is wrong with the individual. The area of assessment is beset by the same problems of definition which we met in the preceding division — what is adjusted behavior and what is maladjusted? Psychologists working in the area of assessment generally have sidestepped the issue by accepting the standard psychiatric classification discussed earlier and determining if their tests are useful for distinguishing people in these different categories.

There are many different assessment techniques, far more than could adequately be dealt with here. We have, therefore, somewhat arbitrarily selected two that are widely used and that represent very different approaches to personality testing. The student interested in a more detailed discussion of psychological testing is referred to Anastasi (1968).

The Minnesota Multiphasic Personality Inventory (MMPI)

ADMINISTRATION AND SCORING

The MMPI is known as a *self-report* inventory. The person taking the test is presented with a long list of statements and is asked to tell whether or not they are personally applicable. The person is to give one of the following answers to each statement: true, false, cannot say. The answers are then scored on a number of different scales, producing for each individual a pattern of scores (Box 23-1).

The items do not necessarily reflect on the surface what the scale measures. This is because the items were chosen and scored not according to how different types of people were expected to answer, but according to the way they actually did answer. For example, by testing samples of individuals diagnosed as normal and individuals diagnosed as hysterics, it was found that normals report liking to read newspaper articles on crime significantly more frequently than do hysterics. Therefore the item can be used to differentiate the two.

The individual scores are recorded on a profile sheet (Figure 23-1) and it is this pattern, rather than any individual score, which is the basis for diagnosis. The pattern is then compared to norms which have been established by testing groups of individuals in different normal and diagnostic categories. Average patterns of

BOX 23-1 THE VALIDITY AND CLINICAL SCALES OF THE MMPI (Kleinmuntz, 1967, p. 220)

Scale	Sample Item	Interpretation
?	No sample. It is merely the number of items marked in the "cannot say" category.	This is one of four validity scales, and a high score indicates evasiveness.
L	I get angry sometimes (FALSE).*	This is the second validity scale. Persons trying to present themselves in a favorable light (e.g., good, wholesome, honest) obtain high L Scale elevations.
F	Everything tastes the same (TRUE).	F is the third validity scale. High scores suggest carelessness, confusion, or "fake bad."
K	I have very few fears compared to my friends (FALSE).	An elevation on the last validity scale, K, suggests a defensive test taking attitude. Exceedingly low scores may indicate a lack of ability to deny symptomatology.
Hs	I wake up fresh and rested most mornings (FALSE).	High scorers have been described as cynical, defeatist, and crabbed.
D	At times I am full of energy (FALSE).	High scorers usually are shy, despondent, and distressed.
Hy	I have never had a fainting spell (FALSE).	High scorers tend to complain of multiple symptoms.

responses have been obtained from each of these groups, and the score of each individual taking the test is compared to these patterns to see to which group his or her scores are most similar. If the response pattern is more similar to a normal than to any other group, the person is classified as normal. If the responses are most similar to those of the standard group of hysterics, the person is classified as a hysteric.

This discussion is an oversimplification of the scoring of the MMPI, but it should give a general idea of how an individual's scores are evaluated. It should be kept in mind, however, that diagnosis is rarely if ever based on the results of a single test. The diagnosis that is suggested by the test scores is compared with diagnostic interpretations that have been obtained

Scale	Sample Item	Interpretation
Pd	I liked school (FALSE).	Adjectives used to describe some high scorers are adventurous, courageous, and generous.
Mf	I like mechanics magazines (FALSE).	Among males, high scorers have been described as aesthetic and sensitive. High-scoring women have been described as rebellious, unrealistic, and indecisive.
Pa	I am happy most of the time (FALSE).	High scorers on this scale were characterized as shrewd, guarded, and worrisome.
Pt	I am certainly lacking in self-confidence (TRUE).	Fearful, rigid, anxious and worrisome are some of the adjectives used to describe high Pt scorers.
Sc	I believe I am a condemned person (TRUE).	Adjectives such as withdrawn and unusual describe Sc high scorers.
Ma	I am an important person (TRUE).	High scorers are called sociable, energetic, and impulsive.
Si	I enjoy social gatherings just to be with people (FALSE).	High scorers: modest, shy, and self-effacing. Low scorers: sociable, colorful, and ambitious.

* The True or False responses within parentheses indicate the scored direction of each of the items.

from interviews and from a number of other tests.

CRITICISMS

There are several problems with the MMPI. The first is that the test is based on and developed within the framework of psychiatric diagnosis discussed above. Therefore, all the problems with these diagnostic categories are incorporated into the test.

Secondly, there are cultural and subcultural differences in the way individuals respond to the test and in how their responses are interpreted. People in different cultures and subcultures may interpret questions differently, and their answers may be based on these different interpretations. In addition, as noted previously, behaviors normal (in the statistical sense) in one culture may be considered abnormal in another. And, it will be recalled, scores on the MMPI are compared with norms or averages for a group of individuals. If the scores of a Puerto Rican male from the ghetto are compared with norms derived from normal white middle-class males and it is found that his score is different, can we assume that this Puerto Rican male is "abnormal"? To the extent that adequate and representative norms are available for the individual being tested, this problem does not arise. But a failure to use the appropriate norms can result in an inaccurate diagnosis of the individual.

A final problem with the MMPI is determining the truthfulness of the individual's answers. If a man says it is false that he is worried about sex matters, can we believe him? The MMPI has scales incorporated into the test to detect and correct for lying, as indicated in Box 23-1, but whether they are completely successful is open to question.

The Rorschach

ADMINISTRATION AND SCORING

The Rorschach is a projective test that represents an approach to personality assessment totally different from that of the MMPI. In the Rorschach, the individual is presented with a series of inkblots, one at a time (Figure 23-2). The individual is asked to describe what he sees in each inkblot. After all cards have been shown, the psychologist presents them all again for a more detailed inquiry into the original answers. The responses are scored according to a number of different criteria, such as location of response (where on the inkblot the response is centered) and content of response. Interpretation of the test is far more subjective than that of the MMPI. The psychologist examines all the information given by the patient and attempts to integrate it into one unified, global picture of the individual's personality.

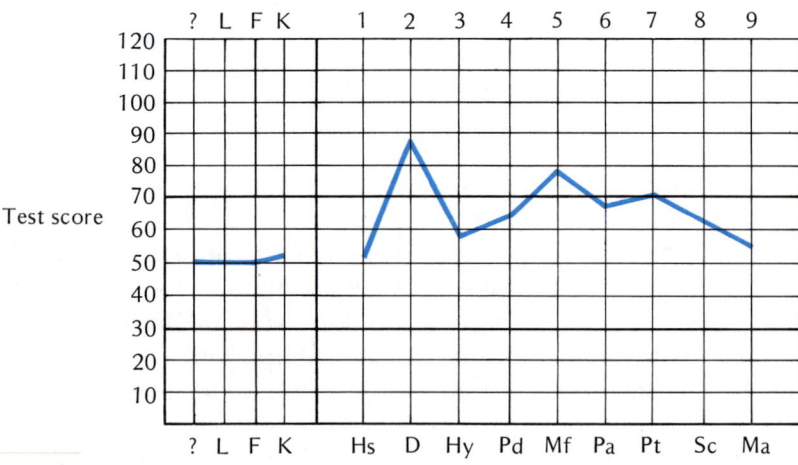

FIGURE 23-1 An MMPI profile

200   How Do We Cope?

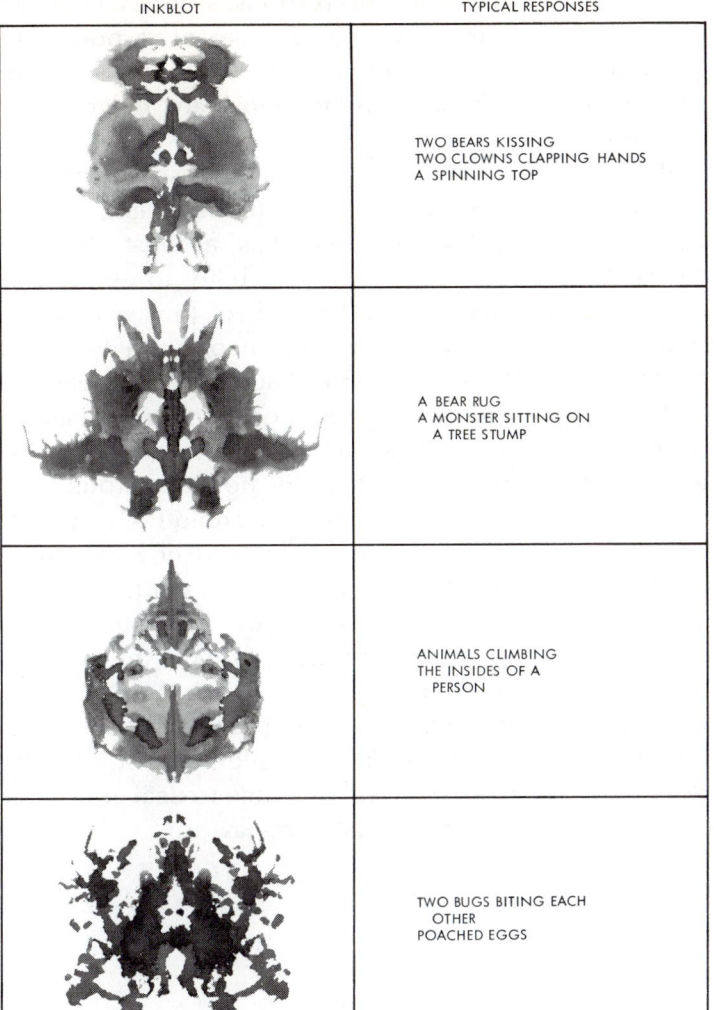

Copyright © 1967 by Dorsey Press

FIGURE 23-2 Some typical responses to four inkblots

The Rorschach, like other *projective techniques,* is based on the assumption that when faced with an ambiguous and unstructured stimulus and asked to structure or describe it, individuals will give a response that reflects basic aspects of their own personalities. There are no facts or objective cues to tell them what the inkblot is, because it is nothing but an inkblot. So in identifying what it appears to be, individuals must go inside themselves and use their own unique experiences and personalities as sources of information.

CRITICISMS

There are difficulties in the administration and scoring of the Rorschach as there are with the MMPI. Although faking is much more difficult on the Rorschach than on the MMPI, it is still possible. Secondly, the quality of the responses to the test are highly dependent on the relationship between the examiner and the patient. During the testing, the two are working in a close interpersonal relationship and it is clear that how they feel about each other will affect the kinds of responses obtained. Reasonably good rapport is necessary to obtain valid responses. Finally, the Rorschach may be criticized due to the subjectivity of its scoring. There are few norms, and most evaluation is done by the therapist. The subjectivity of the scoring is shown clearly in the case of Arthur Bremer (George Wallace's unsuccessful assassin). Both defense and prosecution psychiatrists gave the Rorschach to Bremer, and both noted certain deviant patterns in his responses; for example, an extremely large number of responses to each card. Yet the two came up with different interpretations and diagnoses.

This brief review of assessment may leave the student with the feeling that the techniques are weak at best. Yet the weaknesses in our ability to assess and diagnose merely reflect the weaknesses in the whole area of personality study. That is not to say that the area is useless or should be ignored or abandoned. Rather, there are so many vital unanswered questions that there is no firm ground on which assessment techniques can rest. Until we can understand how disorders occur, what we can do to correct them, and what criteria we want to use in defining adjustment, work in this area will continue to be confusing and of questionable value. But only through continued work and exploration of a variety of aspects will we come to deal effectively with maladjusted behavior.

Unit 24
Meaning Explained

The bit of truth . . . is that men are not gentle, friendly creatures wishing for love, who simply defend themselves if they are attacked, but that a powerful measure of desire for aggression has to be reckoned as part of their instinctual endowment (Freud, 1930, p. 85). . . . Our intellect is a feeble and dependent thing, a plaything and tool of our impulses and emotions. . . . all of us are forced to behave cleverly or stupidly according as our attitudes and inner resistances ordain.

Freud, quoted by Jones, 1955, p. 368.

[The person] moves in the direction of limited expansion through growth, expansion through extending itself by means of its tools, and expansion through reproduction . . . moves in the direction of greater independence or self-responsibility . . . moves through struggle and pain toward enhancement and growth.

Rogers, 1951, pp. 488, 490.

We must expect to discover that what a man does is the result of specifiable conditions and that once these conditions have been discovered, we can anticipate and to some extent determine his actions.

Skinner, 1953, p. 26.

The views of the three theorists quoted above represent the drastically different theoretical approaches that have been adopted in an attempt to explain personality. We cannot hope to make the introductory student an expert in personality theory. We merely wish to present a variety of theories so that the student will understand their various approaches and will be aware of the ways in which different people deal with the problem of adjustment. The student interested in more detailed information is referred to Hall and Lindzey (1970), Maddi (1968), and Pervin (1970) and to original works by the various theorists.

WHAT IS A THEORY?

There is frequently confusion about exactly what is meant by a *theory*. In order to clarify what we are talking about when we talk of theories, a brief discussion of the concept seems in order. First of all, a theory is never factual or "true." This misconception often arises due to the enthusiasm with which a theory is presented by its proponents. They obviously believe the theory to be accurate or they would not write about it and use it. Therefore, they often state it as though it were indeed a fact. Nonetheless, as pointed out by Hall and Lindzey (1970), "theories are never true or false, although their implications or derivations may be either" (p. 10). Once all aspects of a theory are proved true, if such a time should ever arrive, the theory is no longer a theory — it is a law.

On the other hand, a theory is not a blind guess, unsubstantiated by any knowledge. In developing a theory, one gathers information and observations, formulating general principles on the basis of this knowledge. The information may be gathered systematically in a laboratory or may be obtained from experience with patients. But theories, at least in the area of personality, don't come out of isolated thinking. A theory might be best seen as an educated, carefully thought out "guess."

In the area of personality we are a long way from understanding all facets of the individual and having all the facts on how people function. Nevertheless, we must deal with personality and its problems. We simply can't say to a patient coming in for treatment, "Sorry, but I don't know why you have this disorder and I'm not sure exactly what is the best treatment for you, so please go home until we have a scientific breakthrough." If this approach were taken, no one would be treated, because there is no sure cure for any known psychological disorder. The personality theorist fills the gap between our limited factual knowledge and the pressing need to help people now.

In reading the following discussion, therefore, students should keep their minds open and should not uncritically accept or reject any of the theories. Rather, they should reserve judgment until each has been carefully evaluated. None of the following theories is accepted by everyone. Each has its vigorous proponents and its equally vigorous opponents. Perhaps the best criterion for judgment is that discussed by Hall and Lindzey (1970): whether or not the theory is useful.

Freudian Psychoanalytic Theory

Freudian theory is doubtless the best known of all personality theories. It is both the most highly praised and the most strongly criticized. The widespread familiarity with this theory is probably due to two factors. First, it is fairly easy to summarize and simplify so that nonprofessionals can grasp some of the basic concepts. This aspect of the theory has probably been the cause of much of the misunderstanding and lack of appreciation of the theory. Such simplification omits its complexity and the careful, brilliant thought which went into its development. A second factor contributing to its popularity is that Freud dealt with sex, a topic which invariably creates interest. Here again there is much misunderstanding of Freud. By sex, he was referring not simply to genital sex, but rather to any activity which leads to physical pleasure. When Freud refers to the erotic desires of the infant, he is not necessarily implying that the infant has a desire for intercourse with the mother. Rather, he is pointing out that the sucking behavior of the infant is physically pleasurable and is therefore erotic or sexual in nature.

STRUCTURE OF PERSONALITY

There are three major functional components of personality in Freudian theory: the *id,* the *ego,* and the *superego*. These are not actual structures, nor do they occupy any physical space. They are merely theoretical concepts, each describing a different group of functions and properties. The three components, although separate in function, are constantly interacting.

The Id. The id is the basic instinctual component of personality. This is the part of personality with which the human infant is born, and it is the driving force of all the infant's behavior. The id operates according to the *pleasure principle:* its only consideration is obtaining pleasure and reducing pain. It does not take into account any social conventions, moral principles, or practical considerations. Observation of the infant makes clear the strength of the id's demands and the immediacy of these demands. A hungry child cries until fed. One cannot explain to the infant that this is not the appropriate time or place for eating. As characterized by Pervin (1970, p. 227), the id is "demanding, impulsive, blind, irrational, asocial, selfish and narcissistic, omnipotent and, finally, pleasure loving." The id approaches the world with only one thought, "I want, *now.*" This, then, is the basic force that directs all of man's behavior. It is a force which comes in conflict with society, necessitating the development of the other two portions of the personality.

The ego. The ego develops out of and becomes differentiated from the id due to the demands of the real world. As time goes by, more and more pressure is exerted on the infant to control his demands in keeping with the existing social restraints. The ego operates according to the *reality principle,* which exerts controls on the immediate demands of the id so that behavior does not run counter to objective reality. The ego, in other words, serves the role of saying to the id, "You can't eat now because you are in a department store and there is no food," or, "You must wait to urinate for society demands that such functions be performed in the bathroom." Needless to say, the id and the ego are in constant conflict, for few of our physiological demands can be immediately gratified.

The superego. The third portion of the personality is the superego, which contains the basic values transmitted to the child by the parents, and the person's idea of all the things he or she would like to be *(ego ideal)*. In most cases, these values are similar to the traditional values of the society. However, they need not be. This portion of the personality may also fail to develop if the parents fail to transmit values, leading to an individual without conscience. This is the type of individual we have previously characterized as exhibiting an antisocial personality disorder.

The superego exerts its influence on both the id and the ego. It attempts to stop the impulses of the id, particularly those dealing with sexual behavior. In addition, it attempts to influence the decisions of the ego, arguing for behavior that takes into consideration only the moral aspects of the act, rather than the realistic aspects.

As an example of the functioning of the three personality components in a simple situation, consider an individual walking past a fruit stand displaying oranges. The id says, "I'm hungry. Take an orange and eat it now." The superego quickly imposes, "Thou shalt not steal." The ego, "executive" of the personality, says, "Now hold it. You've got money in your pocket. Pick up an orange, go in and pay for it, then eat it." The ego has thus satisfied the demands of the id, the superego, and reality. Few situations are this simple, however, so there is much conflict within the individual. The well-developed, "successful" ego is one which can find compromise solutions to conflicts which will create the minimum amount of tension.

PERSONALITY DEVELOPMENT

In the course of development, the individual goes through several stages of *psychosexual* development. Each stage is characterized by a different source of erotic pleasure, and involves a certain amount of conflict and anxiety. If these problems are not resolved, the individual is said to be *fixated* at that stage. In effect, this means that the individual has not fully transferred all energy to the next developmental level, retaining some of the behaviors from the fixated stage.

Oral stage. The first stage of psychosexual development is the *oral stage*. During this time, the main source of erotic pleasure is the mouth. Sucking is the primary means of obtaining oral pleasure at first, followed by biting at a later age. An individual fixated at this stage, according to Freudian theory, engages in such behaviors as smoking, nail biting, and the expression of "biting" sarcasm as an adult.

Anal stage. The *anal stage* begins when the child is ready for toilet training, and is characterized by erotic pleasure obtained from release or retention of the feces. This is an important stage for two reasons. First, it is the first time that strict controls are placed on the child's instinctual desires in order that the child conform with society's requirements. Secondly, it is a time when the infant learns to exercise personal power. By withholding feces while on the toilet or by expelling into his diapers, the child can cause much parental agitation. He now sees clearly that what he does can affect the behavior of others. Fixation during this stage may lead to such personality traits as stinginess, messiness, or cruelty.

Phallic stage. During the *phallic stage* the child becomes interested in his or her genital organs. Erotic pleasure is obtained from masturbation and fantasy. One of the most important aspects of this stage is what Freud called the *Oedipus complex*. This involves a strong positive attachment to the opposite sex parent and a negative feeling toward the parent of the same sex. The young boy, for example, somewhere between the ages of three and five becomes strongly attached to his mother. According to Freud, he wishes to possess his mother sexually and to replace his father. At the same time he is aware that such feelings are not acceptable and that his father has the power to punish him for such feelings. In the normal course of development, the result of the conflict is for the boy to *identify* with the father. By being like the father, in effect becoming the father, he may avoid the punishment for incestuous thoughts. This identification is a crucial process, for it involves the incorporation of values and ideals of the same sex parent, and these become part of the superego.

Latency stage. Freud identified the period from the end of the phallic stage to sometime in early adolescence as the *latency stage*. He believed that during this time there was a lessening of sexual behavior in the child. This is probably not true. Rather, there are just no dramatic new developments during this time. The child is, instead, obtaining further knowledge of those erogenous zones already dealt with by Freud in the three earlier psychosexual stages; interest and sexual drive are not diminished.

Genital stage. The final stage of psychosexual development is the *genital stage*. During this stage the individual shifts from a self-orientation in erotic pleasure to an outward orientation. The individual, if fully socialized, at this stage becomes interested in heterosexual relations.

DEFENSE MECHANISMS

During the course of one's life, one is faced with much anxiety. When the anxiety leads to too much stress, the ego sets up what are known as *defense mechanisms*. These are methods of protecting the individual against anxiety. These defense mechanisms are not realistic and operate at an unconscious level (the individual is not aware of using them). It should be noted that defense mechanisms represent an unrealistic approach to problems and are not a "healthy" method for coping with anxiety. Nonetheless, they are probably present in all individuals. They lead to serious psychological disorders when used to excess.

Repression. This defense mechanism involves an unconsciously motivated forgetting. Quite simply, if some experience or idea is fear-producing to the individual, it is forgotten. Theoretically, if the repression is complete, there will be no residual anxiety. Most commonly, however, the repression is not complete, leaving the individual with some anxiety but no memory of its cause.

Reaction formation. When using this defense mechanism, the individual replaces the unacceptable desire or emotion with its opposite. A father, for example, cannot accept the fact that he hates his child. He therefore replaces this feeling with a conscious statement of his great love for his child. How, then, can one tell if a parent really loves the child? Reaction formation is usually marked by excessiveness. If a mother can do nothing but praise her child, constantly asserting her love and admitting to no weakness in her child nor in her love, the love is probably not genuine. In the same way, a husband who cannot stop extolling the virtues of his "perfect" wife has probably hidden some negative and hostile feelings toward his wife by means of reaction formation.

Projection. In this defense mechanism, the individual's unacceptable desires are attributed to someone else. For example, if a man finds within himself sexual desires that go contrary to his moral values, he simply attributes them to someone else, thus removing from himself the source of anxiety. In the same way, if he feels aggressive toward another individual and yet cannot accept this aggression in himself, he changes the statement "I want to harm him" into "He wants to harm me." Projection may be the basis for some of the stereotypical behavior attributed to minority groups by individuals prejudiced against them. The sexual "deviancy" attributed to both Jews and blacks may indicate the projection of certain sexual desires to these minority groups by the prejudiced individual.

Regression. An individual in regression returns to an earlier form of behavior in an attempt to cope with stress. The six-year-old only child who suddenly finds a new baby in the house may begin to show such behaviors as pants-wetting or thumb-sucking. The stage to which an individual regresses is usually determined by the earlier progress through the various stages of psychosexual development.

Rationalization. When this defense mechanism is used, the individual creates a socially acceptable reason for behavior that was actually motivated by unacceptable drives. A student who fails to study for a test due to laziness or disinterest will claim a headache prevented studying; once having failed the test, the student will often claim that the professor is unfair. More dramatic behaviors are also sometimes dealt with by rationalization. Some of the greatest atrocities committed during the course of human history have been cloaked in such slogans as "preservation of democracy," "Christian love," and other equally noble ideals. They represent a socially acceptable explanation for socially unacceptable behavior.

Denial. This defense mechanism involves simply denying that certain unacceptable emotions or ideas exist. The difference between a true denial of something and denial as a defense mechanism is that in the latter case the denial is excessive.

CONTRIBUTIONS OF THE THEORY

Whether or not the preceding section has caused the student to decide that Freudian theory is valuable, it should be kept in mind that Freud has made some extremely important contributions to psychology. These contributions stand regardless of whether the theory is rejected. The three most important are:

1. Stress on the importance of infant and childhood experiences in personality development. Although the extent of influence of early experience on later personality development is still in question, it is now generally agreed that the early years of the individual's life are important. It is accepted that what happens to a child in the first five years can, and often does, have substantial effect on the adult personality.
2. Stress on the importance of unconscious factors. Freudian theory led to the widespread acceptance of the idea that we are not totally conscious beings. We do things without knowing why; we have wants and desires of which we are unaware; we have emotions of which we are not conscious.
3. Stress on the importance of sexual behavior. Freud's stress on sexual behavior, particularly adult genital sex, was an important factor in freeing this behavior from Victorian restraints and enabling free discussion of the topic. He may be seen, in fact, as the "father" of the current sexual revolution in the sense that he encouraged more openness about sex. It should be noted that Freud did not advocate freedom of sexual behavior, only freedom of discussion. Morally, he was quite puritanical, believing the only "proper" sexual behavior was that between man and wife for the purpose of having children. In essence, Freud said that when you take any aspect of human behavior which is of crucial importance and bind it with layers of ethical, moral, and religious restraints, it is bound to cause problems. The sex drive is strong, the restraints against sexual behavior are equally strong — and an obviously stressful conflict will therefore be created.

Rogers's Self Theory

Sharply contrasting the instinctually driven individual in Freud's theory is the view of man expressed in Rogerian theory (Rogers, 1959). In this humanistic approach to personality, people are seen as basically rational, socially oriented beings.

The sum of what a person is, everything psychological and physical, is called the *organism*. As the individual develops, a part of these physical and psychological experiences becomes differentiated within the organism as the *self*. In other words, an individual sees a portion of all his or her experiences as "me," and these are incorporated into the self-concept.

In Rogers's system there is only one drive or motive, the *actualizing tendency*. This is an inborn tendency of the organism to achieve full realization of its capacities and potentialities, both physical and psychological. In the same way that the self-concept becomes differentiated out of the organism, a *self-actualizing tendency* becomes differentiated out of the actualizing tendency. The goal of this "subdrive" is to fulfill the capacities and potentialities of the *self*, of what the individual thinks he or she really is.

In fulfilling the actualizing tendency, the organism evaluates its experiences through a *valuing process,* with an experience being good or bad to the extent to which it helps actualize the organism. The self, however, due to the child's early training, may develop as its evaluation criteria what are called *conditions of worth.* Stated simply, these are the things the child has learned he or she must do in order to be loved (or obtain *positive regard*). The parents' behavior teaches the child that their love is conditional, not unconditional; i.e., they love him only if he is good. Behaviors are then performed which produce positive regard and the corresponding self-regard.

The problem is that behaviors that lead to positive regard, or evaluation as "good" according to the conditions of worth, may be rated as bad by the organism's valuing process if they don't fulfill the actualizing tendency. Behaviors that are "bad" according to the conditions of worth cause anxiety to the individual since they do not fill the individual's need for self-regard. Therefore, the individual denies or distorts them, and this is the start of the trouble. Things are experienced by the person that are not allowed to become conscious or that enter consciousness in a distorted form. For Rogers, an adjusted person is one who can openly accept and evaluate all his or her experiences, one whose actualizing tendency and self-actualizing tendency work toward the same goal of fulfillment. This state is called *congruence* between self and experience.

Learning Theories

As the name implies, this group of theories stresses the importance of learning in the behavior of the individual. This group of theorists concentrates on the study of behavior because it takes the approach that individuals *are* what they *do*. Although it is accepted that some behavior is genetically determined or influenced, most behaviors are seen as learned in accordance with man's basically hedonistic or pleasure-seeking nature.

An important corollary of this statement is that if a behavior is performed, the person doing it must be getting something positive out of it. In the classic example of the man beating his head against the wall, the man is not doing it because it hurts (pain), but because it feels so good when he stops (pleasure).

In Skinner's approach, the basic assumption is that all behavior is lawful. The personality is understood by examination of the behavior, the causes of the behavior in terms of external stimulus conditions, and the consequences of the behavior (i.e., what follows it). This approach to personality makes in-depth analysis of the individual unnecessary. To understand behavior, a Skinnerian would say, the probing of early childhood experience is not required. One need merely isolate the stimuli that cause the response and the reinforcers that follow it in order to understand why it occurs.

The three theories discussed here represent only a sampling of the theories that have been advanced. None of them is true — or false. They are simply different attempts by different people to move toward a fuller understanding of that complex concept, personality.

Unit 25
Change: Communication with the Psyche and the Soma

One of the tasks of psychoanalysis . . . is to lift the veil of amnesia which hides the earliest years of childhood and to bring to conscious memory the manifestations of early infantile sexual life which are contained in them.

Freud, 1966, p. 497.

For the client . . . therapy would mean an exploration of increasingly strange and unknown and dangerous feelings in himself. . . . He finds himself experiencing these feelings fully, completely, so that for the moment he *is* his fear, or his anger, or his tenderness, or his strength. . . . He finds his behavior changing in constructive fashion in accordance with his newly experienced self. He approaches the realization that he no longer needs to fear what experience may hold, but can welcome it freely as a part of his changing and developing self.

Rogers, 1961, p. 185.

One need not be aware of one's behavior or the conditions controlling it in order to behave effectively. . . . Behavior is shaped and maintained by its consequences.

Skinner, 1971, pp. 183, 16.

Corresponding to the widely divergent approaches to personality theory are the above three approaches to therapy. Each of these therapeutic approaches derives from the concept of personality held by the particular theorist. As was the case with the theories discussed in the preceding unit, none of these therapies is the "right" or "true" approach to the correction of personality maladjustment. Their effectiveness varies widely and depends on many factors, such as characteristics of the therapist and the nature of the patient's problem. The relative effectiveness of each will be evaluated at the end of this unit.

Psychoanalysis

Psychoanalytic, or Freudian, therapy involves the analysis of the individual's total life experience. Therapies are frequently classified as directive or nondirective, depending on whether the therapist takes an active part in guiding and influencing the patient *(directive)* or merely acts as a passive observer, letting the patient bring out material and work through the problem with little interference *(nondirective)*. It is difficult to classify Freudian therapy in either of these categories, for psychoanalytic therapy involves a good deal of freedom on the part of the patient yet has very specific rules set down by the therapist.

ADJUSTMENT AND MALADJUSTMENT

In Freudian theory, adjustment is defined in terms of balance among the three parts of the personality: id, ego, and superego. As an example, let us look at one type of patient frequently treated by Freud: the neurotic filled with guilt and anxiety. The guilt often arose because the patient did things that were censored by the superego, such as having fantasies about unacceptable sexual behavior. The anxiety arose from fear that the sexual desires of the id, so tightly held in check, would somehow break through and become actual behavior rather than fantasy. In Freudian terms, the problem may be seen as an ego which is too weak coupled with a superego which is too strong. To treat the individual and to help the person achieve a better adjustment, all the conflicts would gradually be brought into the open. Adequate adjustment would involve making the superego less stringent in its demands and the ego stronger in effecting compromises between the id and the superego. According to Freudian theory, there is nothing wrong with the behavior (e.g., sexual fantasies). What is maladjusted is an ego faced with a conflict that it cannot handle.

TECHNIQUES

Free association. The primary rule one must follow as a patient in psychoanalysis is to say anything and everything which comes into one's mind. The technique used is *free association*. When free associating, the patient says whatever is thought of, without ordering, censoring, or attempting to make the sequence of thought logical or acceptable. The therapist, for the most part, merely sits and listens, encouraging the patient if he or she seems unable to talk and occasionally offering tentative interpretations of the material discussed by the patient. Freud explains his approach as follows (1949, p. 63):

[The therapist and patient] form a pact with each other. The patient's sick ego promises us the most complete candor, promises, that is, to put at our disposal all of the material which his self-perception provides; we, on the other hand, assure him of the strictest discretion and put at his service our experience in interpreting material that has been influenced by the unconscious. Our knowledge shall compensate for his ignorance and shall give his ego once more mastery over the lost provinces of his mental life.

Dream analysis. The analysis of dreams is an important part of psychoanalysis. Freud believed that much of the unconscious material within the individual is brought to consciousness during dreaming and that dream analysis therefore could offer much information about the individual and the individual's problems. The dream, according to Freudian theory, has two content components. The *manifest content* is the actual, conscious content of the dream. The *latent content* is the hidden meaning of the dream. During analysis the patient becomes able to both relate the manifest content of the dream and interpret it in terms of its symbolic meaning.

TRANSFERENCE

Another important aspect of psychoanalysis is the process of *transference*, in which "the patient sees in his analyst the return — the reincarnation — or some important figure out of his childhood or past" (Freud, 1949, p. 66). The therapist is responded to in the way the patient would respond to this earlier important figure. There is both positive and negative transference. In the former, the patient feels all the warm and loving feelings toward the therapist that were felt toward the original individual. In the case of negative transference, all the feelings of hostility and hatred are expressed.

Transference may help the analytic process by bringing out important emotions which must be dealt with for successful treatment. Transference can also hinder the therapeutic process. During positive transference, the patient may say and do things simply to please the therapist, rather than seriously trying to solve the problem. During negative transference, there is the possibility that the feelings of hatred will lead the patient to terminate therapy.

Basic to psychoanalysis is the belief that the symptom — whether it is overt anxiety, compulsive handwashing, or a snake phobia — is only a surface manifestation of the real problem. The solution to the patient's problem can be achieved only through in-depth analysis, by revealing long-term and deep-seated conflicts, and by strengthening the ego's ability to deal with conflict.

Client-Centered Therapy

Rogerian, or client-centered, therapy has as its goal the opening up of individuals to all of their experiences. The therapy is a nondirective one in which the therapist listens and occasionally restates or focuses on what the patient says. There is no interpretation in terms of underlying conflicts as occurs in Freudian therapy. Rather, the therapist reflects back the meaning of the statement as he or she perceives it in an attempt to help the patient see the problem more clearly (Box 25-1).

The basic problem, according to Rogers, is that the patient isn't a full experiencing person and there is a conflict between actual behavior and what is permitted into the self-concept. The therapist, to be successful, must give the patient accurate empathy, or understanding of how the patient feels. He or she must also give the patient nonpossessive warmth, which is an affection given without implying ownership or the necessity to return the affection. This gives the patient a feeling of being valued. In this atmosphere of trust and safety, the patient can bring out all those excluded experiences for reevaluation and incorporation into the self. The patient feels safe in talking about them, for the empathy and warmth of the therapist will eliminate any threat of losing positive regard by admitting to "doing bad things." The basic atmosphere set up by the therapist is one which says to the

---

BOX 25-1 CLIENT-CENTERED THERAPY: AN ILLUSTRATION

Patient: . . . I guess I do have problems at school. . . . You see, I'm Chairman of the Science Department so you can imagine what kind of a department it is. . . .

Therapist: You sort of feel that if you're in something that it can't be too good. Is that . . . .

P: Well, it's not that I . . . it's just that I'm . . . I don't think that I could run it.

T: You don't have any confidence in yourself?

P: No confidence, no confidence in myself. I never had any confidence in myself. I — like I told you that like when even when I was a kid I didn't feel I was capable and I always wanted to get back with the intellectual group.

T: This has been a long-term thing, then, it's gone on a long time. . . .

P: Yeh, the feeling is — even though I know it isn't it's the feeling that I have that — that I haven't got it, that — that — that people will find out that I'm dumb or — or . . . .

T: Masquerade . . . .

P: Superficial, I'm just superficial. There's nothing below the surface. Just superficial generalities, that . . . .

T: There's nothing really deep and meaningful to you.

P: No — they don't know it, and . . . .

T: And you're terrified they're going to find out.

P: My wife has a friend, and — and she and the friend got together so we could go out together with her and my wife and her husband. . . . And this guy, he's an engineer and he's, you know — he's got it, you know; and I don't want to go, I don't want to go because — because if — if we get together he's liable to start to — to talk about something I don't know, and I'll — I won't know about that.

T: You'll show up very poorly in this kind of situation.

P: That I — I'll show up poorly, that I'll — that I'll just clam up, that I . . . .

T: You're terribly frightened in this sort of thing.

P: I — I'm afraid to get around people who — who I feel are my peers. Even in pool — now I — I play pool well and — if I'm playing with some guy, that I — I know I can beat, psychologically, I can run fifty, but — but if I start playing with somebody that's my level, I'm done. I'm done. I — I — I'll miss a ball every time.

T: So the . . . fear of what's going on just immobilizes you, keeps you from doing a good job (Hersher, 1970, pp. 29–32.)

patient, "You are of value. This value you have will not be destroyed by anything you say or do. I may not like what you do, but I will still value you."

Basic to client-centered therapy is the idea that patients can solve their own problems. The job of the therapist is to create the kind of environment in which patients feel safe enough to bring out their problems and to make themselves fully functioning persons.

Behavior Therapy

The therapeutic technique known as *behavioral therapy* involves the replacement of a deviant or unacceptable behavior with one that is acceptable, using the process of learning.

TECHNIQUES

Several different techniques are used in teaching the subject a new response.

Counterconditioning. In *counterconditioning*, the individual learns a new response to the old stimulus. The new response which is learned is incompatible with the old, so that the two cannot be performed simultaneously. Some of the techniques used to stop the cigarette smoking habit are illustrative of this approach. Let us say, for example, that each time a woman inhales the smoke, a large amount of smoke is blown directly into her face or she is given an electric shock. In time the smoke in the face or the shock replaces with unpleasant feelings the previously pleasant feelings associated with inhalation. The woman's response to a cigarette is now negative rather than positive, and she should give up smoking.

Desensitization. Another therapeutic technique, used largely with patients who experience some specific fear or phobia, is Wolpe's *desensitization*. In this technique the patient is trained to induce a relaxed state. Once able to relax completely, the patient is gradually introduced to the anxiety-producing stimulus, first through imagination and then by gradually closer contact. Since one cannot feel both relaxation and anxiety at the same time and the relaxation response has become associated with the stimulus, the response of anxiety is no longer felt in the presence of the stimulus.

Operant training. In the *operant training* approach, the appropriate behavior is trained through a series of reinforcements. The patient is given some type of reward every time an "adjusted" behavior is performed and is given no reinforcement (extinction) for behaviors that are undesirable. As an example of operant approaches, let's look at a procedure known as a *token economy*. This is frequently used in hospital settings where a number of people are to be dealt with simultaneously. The patients are told that they can earn tokens (chips, slips of paper), which they can then use to buy the things they want. Each time a patient does something that has been determined to be positive, one of these tokens is given. The behavior to be rewarded may vary from patient to patient, with a withdrawn schizophrenic being given a token for talking and a violent patient receiving a token for a period of calm.

Operant techniques can also be used in self-management (see Box 25-2).

Other Therapeutic Techniques

In addition to the therapies discussed, there are several therapeutic techniques that are not associated with any specific personality theory. These include shock therapy, psychosurgery, and chemotherapy.

SHOCK THERAPY

Shock therapy is generally administered in one of two ways: by insulin or by electricity. In insulin shock, the insulin is injected into the patient's system, inducing convulsions and deep coma. In order to bring the patient out of coma, an intravenous solution of glucose is injected. Electroshock therapy involves sending a current of electricity through the patient's brain. Here, too, convulsions and coma result; however, consciousness is recovered spontaneously with no additional treatment necessary.

There is much controversy over the use of shock as a therapeutic technique. Its proponents claim it is useful with certain types of patients. Opponents point to the sometimes irreversible damage inflicted on the patient and question the useful-

---

BOX 25-2 SELF-MANAGEMENT TECHNIQUES IN BEHAVIOR MODIFICATION

One woman who wanted to quit smoking came to [the behavior modification therapist] for help. He put her on a self-management program using the response-cost method. He first instructed her to record the number of cigarettes she smoked each day. Moving in small steps, she was then required to record each cigarette in a book at the time she smoked it, and also to record the time and place.

Later she added to this procedure by recording the time she started smoking it, the time she finished, and any companions while puffing.

Next she had to record the smoking behavior fully, and save each cigarette butt in an envelope. Already the procedure had become awkward and embarrassing in some situations, such as parties. Her smoking dropped off.

In the next step the woman was to start quitting cigarettes in certain places, beginning with the places she smoked the least — in the car, at the supermarket. Then permitted smoking areas for the woman were eliminated, one at a time. She was limited until she smoked in only one room in her house. Still she hung on to the last few weeds.

The woman limited herself to smoking in one favorite chair. She was not allowed to do anything else in that chair — no reading, no TV, no talking.

Then the final coup was delivered. The favorite chair was moved from the living room to the basement laundry room (Hilts, 1973, p. 21).

ness of the technique. In addition, there is a humanitarian argument against the administration of such treatment. Shock therapy can involve severely unpleasant subjective experiences, far too severe, some argue, for the unreliable results achieved.

At this time there is no conclusive answer to this problem. It would seem that, given the severity of the method, shock therapy should be used only with the greatest of caution. In addition, far more research is needed on the physiological effects of the techniques. It hardly seems possible to alter the human system to the point of inducing convulsions and coma without also inducing some lasting physiological effects. Discovery of these effects is necessary before a full evaluation of shock therapy is possible.

PSYCHOSURGERY

Psychosurgical techniques involve performance of surgery on the brain. Many thought processes are known to be localized in the frontal lobes of the brain; many emotional behaviors are tied to the thalamus. It was thought at one time that by cutting the connection between these two sections of the brain one could break down the abnormal behavior patterns associated with certain psychological disorders. Such an operation is known as a *lobotomy*. The operation results in a decrease in intellectual abilities, lessened abstract capacities, reduced learning ability, emotional flatness, and a general lethargy. The technique was originally conceived for use only with severely disturbed patients whose care was exceptionally difficult and on whom other therapeutic techniques had had little effect. But lobotomies became common, and the operation was performed in many cases in which it was probably unwise. After the introduction of drugs that control behavior, the technique was seldom used. However, very recently psychosurgery has become a fairly widespread procedure again and is being advocated by some as an effective technique for controlling criminal and other undesirable behavior. (See Unit 34 for a more detailed discussion of these recent trends.)

CHEMOTHERAPY

Chemotherapy involves the use of drugs to control a patient's behavior so that care is simplified and there is a greater chance for therapeutic contact. Stimulants such as Benzedrine have been used to help bring patients out of deep depression. Tranquilizers such as chlorpromazine and reserpine have been used to calm patients in emotionally excited states.

It should be noted that the therapies mentioned here are probably not true cures or solutions to problems. They are better considered as methods of controlling behavior, permitting additional therapeutic intervention which can help effect a real and lasting adjustment.

Which Theory is Right?

As was pointed out previously, all theories by their very nature are open to question and criticism. As would be expected, there is constant controversy among the proponents of the various theories. The limits of this text do not permit a review of all the controversies. We will here cover only one, which involves behavioral therapists and the more traditional psychotherapists.

Eysenck (1952) reviewed the literature on cures of neurotic patients. He found that 44 percent of the patients treated by psychoanalytic techniques and 64 percent of the patients treated by eclectic methods (those using whatever psychotherapeutic technique seemed most relevant to the patient's problem) were cured. These figures do not look bad until one compares them to the spontaneous cure rate (cure with *no* treatment), which Eysenck claimed was 72 percent. What his review apparently demonstrated was that a neurotic patient if left alone has a greater chance of recovery than if treated by any psychotherapeutic method. Eysenck (1952, p. 323) concluded that the "figures fail to support the hypothesis that psychotherapy facilitates recovery from neurotic disorders."

Needless to say, such a contention was followed by a strong rebuttal from the psychotherapeutic camp (Rosenzweig, 1954). The Eysenck paper was criticized for its definitions of neurosis and psychotherapy. In addition, the equality of the psychotherapeutic group and the nontherapeutic group in severity of illness and criteria for recovery was questioned. Rosenzweig concluded that the data were too limited to make any generalizations as to the effectiveness of psychotherapeutic techniques.

In his answer to Rosenzweig's critique, Eysenck (1955) pointed out that he was not attempting to demonstrate that psychotherapy was useless. The data, he claimed, merely failed to show that such therapeutic techniques facilitate recovery. In a later review of the literature, Eysenck (1960) found that patients who underwent psychotherapy showed about the same cure rate as did untreated neurotics. However, patients who were treated by behavioral therapy improved significantly more quickly.

The battle still rages and probably will for some time. The student would be wise to keep in mind that there are good arguments for and against each theory, as well as data which support each. Knight (1949), in discussing psychotherapy, lists several characteristics important in a good psychotherapist, including extensive training, willingness to use whatever method seems most useful for the individual patient, and personal integrity, sincerity, and lack of rigidity. Knight (1949, p. 106) noted that if his criteria for a good therapist are valid, "those psychotherapists who have a fixed system of treatment for all patients who come to them are practicing poor psychotherapy." We simply do not yet have enough data to answer the question of which theory, if any, is "right."

The statement by Knight about psychotherapists applies to students of psychology and psychologists as well. Those who accept only one theory at this stage of limited knowledge, totally rejecting all others, are unnecessarily limiting their own range of knowledge, psychological sophistication, and usefulness.

SUMMARY

One of the major problems in the area of personality disorders is the problem of assessment. Two of the many different assessment techniques are the *Minnesota Multiphasic Personality Inventory* (MMPI) and the *Rorschach Inkblot Test*.

The MMPI is a self-report inventory in which the individual is presented with statements and asked to tell whether they personally apply. A number of different scales are scored, producing a pattern of scores which is compared to established norms for different normal and diagnostic categories. There are several problems with the MMPI. First, the test is based on the standard psychiatric diagnostic system, incorporating all the problems of this system. Second is the problem of cultural and subcultural differences. A final problem is that of discerning the truthfulness of the answers given.

The Rorschach is a projective test. The individual is presented with a series of inkblots and asked to describe what he or she sees. Interpretation of the scores is based on a number of different response factors. The Rorschach, like other projective tests, is based on the assumption that responses to ambiguous stimuli will reflect the individual's basic personality characteristics. There are difficulties with the Rorschach as well. Faking is possible, although more difficult than on the MMPI. Secondly, the quality of the responses is highly dependent on the relationship between the examiner and the patient. Finally, the scoring is highly subjective.

Many different theoretical approaches have been adopted in an attempt to explain personality. We are a long way from understanding all facets of the individual. Nevertheless, we must deal with personality problems now. Theory attempts to fill the gap between limited knowledge and the need to help people now.

Freudian psychoanalytic theory is probably the best-known theory. There are three major functional components of personality: (1) The *id* is the basic instinctual component. It operates on the *pleasure principle*, which involves seeking pleasure and avoiding pain. It is in conflict with society, necessitating the development of the other two portions of the personality. (2) The *ego* operates on the *reality principle*, which involves exerting controls on id demands so that behavior conforms to objective reality. (3) The *superego* contains the individual's basic values, usually transmitted to children by their parents. The superego exerts its influence on both the id and the ego, arguing for behavior which takes into consideration only the moral aspects of the act.

In the course of development the individual goes through several stages of *psychosexual development*. If the problems at each stage are not resolved, the individual is said to have *fixated* in that stage. The first stage of psychosexual development is the *oral stage*, during which the mouth is the main source of erotic pleasure. The *anal stage* is closely associated with toilet training and is characterized by erotic pleasure obtained from the release or retention of feces. During the *phallic stage*, children become interested in their genital organs and obtain pleasure from masturbation and fantasy. It is during this stage that the *Oedipus complex* occurs. The period from the end of the phallic stage to the beginning of puberty is the *latency stage,* during which there is a lessening of sexual behavior in the child. The final stage is the *genital stage,* during which the individual shifts from self-oriented erotic pleasure to outward orientation and interest in heterosexual relationships.

In response to anxiety, the ego sets up *defense mechanisms.* These are unconscious and unrealistic methods which reduce anxiety. They are probably used by everyone, becoming problematic only when excessive.

The three most important contributions of Freudian theory are: (1) stress on the importance of infant and childhood experiences in personality development, (2) stress on the importance of unconscious forces, and (3) stress on the importance of sexual behavior.

Rogers's self theory is a humanistic approach to personality in which people are seen as basically rational and socially oriented. The *organism* is the totality of individual experiences, while the *self* is made up of the individual's experiences of "me." The only drive is the *actualizing tendency,* which has as its goal fulfilling the capacities and potentialities of the organism. Experiences of the organism are evaluated by the *valuing process.* Self experiences may be evaluated in the same way or by socially imposed *conditions of worth.* The adjusted person in this theory is one who has achieved *congruence* between self and experience.

Learning theories stress the importance of learning and reinforcement. Personality is made up of learned behaviors and is understood in terms of external stimuli which cause behavior and of the consequences of behavior.

Corresponding to the widely divergent approaches to personality are various approaches to therapy. *Psychoanalytic therapy* involves the analysis of the individual's total life experiences. All of the individual's conflicts are gradually brought into the open. The primary rule one must follow as a patient in psychoanalysis is to say anything which comes into one's mind, using *free association.* The analysis of dreams is an important part of psychoanalysis. Another important aspect is the process of *transference,* in which the patient responds to the therapist as he or she would to some important figure out of the patient's past. This process may either help or hinder therapy. Basic to psychoanalysis is the belief that the symptom is only a surface manifestation of the real problem.

Rogerian, or *client-centered,* therapy has as its goal the opening up of the individual to all experiences. The therapy is a nondirective one in which the therapist creates an atmosphere of warmth, understanding, and trust in which the patient will be able to bring out denied and distorted experiences for reevaluation and incorporation into the self. Basic to this therapy is the notion that the patient can solve the problems independently.

The therapeutic technique known as *behavior therapy* involves the replacement, through learning, of a deviant or unacceptable behavior with one that is acceptable. Several different techniques are used. In *counterconditioning,* the individual learns a new response to an old stimulus. The new response is incompatible with the old, so that the two cannot occur simultaneously. In *desensitization,* the patient is trained to relax completely in the presence of a previously anxiety-producing stimulus until only the relaxation response is associated with the stimulus. In the *operant training* approach, the appropriate behavior is trained through a series of reinforcements. The patient is given some type of reward for performing desired behaviors and no reward for undesirable behaviors. *Token economy* is an example of the operant approach.

In addition to the above therapies, there are several techniques which are not associated with any specific personality theory. *Shock therapy* may be administered either by insulin or electric shock, producing convulsions or coma, or both. *Psychosurgical techniques* involve operating on the brain to alter behavior. A *lobotomy* involves cutting the connection between two sections of the brain to break down abnormal behavior patterns. *Chemotherapy* involves the use of tranquilizing and energizing drugs to control a patient's behavior so that care is simplified and there is a greater chance of therapeutic contact. Chemotherapy, psychosurgery, and shock therapy have not yet been shown to be true cures. Rather, they frequently serve as methods of controlling behavior, enabling additional therapeutic intervention.

GLOSSARY

Actualizing tendency: in Rogers's theory, the inborn tendency to fully realize physical and psychological potential

Anal stage: the second stage of psychosexual development in Freudian theory, in which the child gains erotic pleasure from release or retention of feces

Behavior therapy: therapy which changes behavior through learning and reinforcement

Chemotherapy: therapy in which the patient is treated with drugs which control behavior

Conditions of worth: in Rogers's theory, an evaluation standard derived from childhood when the individual felt he or she had to do certain things and avoid others in order to be loved

Congruence: consistency between experiences and the way they are symbolized in the self, according to Rogers's theory

Counterconditioning: behavior therapy that involves the learning of a new response to a stimulus. The new response is incompatible with the maladaptive response previously given to the same stimulus, and thus the old response is not likely to occur.

Defense mechanism: in Freudian theory, an unrealistic method used to handle anxiety; it operates on an unconscious level

Denial: defense mechanism in which the person states that unacceptable emotions, ideas, or behaviors do not exist

Desensitization: therapy in which the patient is trained to relax in response to anxiety-producing stimuli so that in time the anxiety is replaced by a relaxation response

Directive therapy: therapy in which the therapist is active in guiding and influencing the patient

Ego: the learned component of personality in Freudian theory, which attempts to handle the demands of the id and superego according to the restrictions of external reality

Ego-ideal: in Freudian theory, the portion of the superego that contains the individual's ideas of all that is good and all that he or she would like to be

Fixation: to leave energy in a particular Freudian stage of psychosexual development so that behaviors characteristic of that stage remain part of the individual's behavior pattern

Free association: saying whatever comes into one's head without ordering or censoring; verbalized stream of consciousness

Genital stage: the last stage of psychosexual development in Freudian theory, characterized by heterosexual relationships and a concern for giving pleasure

Id: the inborn component of personality in Freudian theory, which is the source of all biological drives. It is irrational and unconscious and operates according to the pleasure principle

Identification: the process of taking over characteristics of another person, becoming like the other

Latency stage: the fourth stage of psychosexual development in Freudian theory, in which no dramatic new erotic pleasures are obtained but information and experiences from earlier stages are integrated

Latent content: unconscious or hidden meaning of a dream

Lobotomy: a psychosurgical technique involving cutting the connection between the frontal lobes of the brain (locus of many thought processes) and the thalamus (locus of many emotions)

Manifest content: actual conscious content of a dream

Nondirective therapy: a type of therapy in which the patient brings out material and solves the problem with support from, but little intervention by, the therapist

Oedipus complex: in Freudian theory, a strong positive attachment to the parent of the opposite sex and a strong negative feeling toward the parent of the same sex which occurs during the phallic stage of psychosexual development. Resolution involves identification with the same sex parent and incorporation of his or her values to form the superego.

Oral stage: the first stage of psychosexual development in Freudian theory, in which the child obtains erotic pleasure from oral stimulation

Phallic stage: the third stage of psychosexual development in Freudian theory, in which the child obtains erotic pleasure from self-stimulation of the genital areas

Pleasure principle: a desire to obtain that

which is pleasant and avoid that which is painful; the principle by which the id operates in Freudian theory

Projection: a defense mechanism in which one attributes one's own unacceptable desires to another person while denying their presence in oneself

Projective technique: a psychological testing method in which subjects are asked to respond to ambiguous stimuli on the assumption that responses in such unstructured situations will reflect the subject's personality characteristics

Rationalization: a defense mechanism in which socially acceptable reasons are given for unacceptable behavior

Reaction formation: a defense mechanism in which unacceptable desires or emotions are replaced with their opposites; characterized by excessiveness of expressed emotion

Reality principle: the principle on which the ego operates in Freudian theory; its goal is to satisfy the id and the superego while being guided by realistic considerations

Regression: a defense mechanism in which the individual returns to an earlier, more primitive form of behavior

Repression: a defense mechanism in which threatening material is unconsciously forgotten

Self: the portion of all experiences that is perceived as "I" or "me" in Rogers's theory

Self-actualizing tendency: in Rogers's theory, the tendency to fulfill all potentials and capacities of the self

Superego: the component of personality in Freudian theory that contains all the basic learned values of the individual

Token economy: a form of behavioral therapy in which the desired behavior is positively reinforced by use of tokens which can be exchanged for valued objects

Transference: a process in which the patient sees and reacts to the therapist with behavior that would be characteristic in response to some important figure in the patient's past

Valuing process: in Rogers's theory, the organism's method of evaluating experiences in terms of whether they are actualizing

REFERENCES

Anastasi, A. *Psychological testing*. (3rd ed.). New York: Macmillan, 1968.

Dahlstrom, W. G., Welsh, G. S., and Dahlstrom, L. C. *An MMPI handbook*. Vol. I. *Clinical interpretation*. Minneapolis: University of Minnesota Press, 1972.

Eysenck, H. J. The effects of psychotherapy. *Journal of Consulting Psychology*, 1952, 16, 319–324.

Eysenck, H. J. The effects of psychotherapy. *Journal of Abnormal and Social Psychology*, 1955, 50, 147–148.

Eysenck, H. J. The effects of psychotherapy. In H. J. Eysenck (Ed.), *Handbook of abnormal psychology*. New York: Basic Books, 1960.

Freud, S. *Civilization and its discontents.* London: Hogarth, 1949. (Originally published: 1930.)

Freud, S. *An outline of psychoanalysis.* New York: Norton, 1949.

Freud, S. *The complete introductory lectures on psychoanalysis.* Edited and translated by G. Strachey. New York: Norton, 1966.

Hall, C. S., and Lindzey, G. *Theories of personality.* (2nd ed.) New York: Wiley, 1970.

Hersher, L. (Ed.). *Four psychotherapies.* New York: Appleton-Century-Crofts, 1970.

Hilts, P. J. Mastering yourself. *Potomac,* April 29, 1973.

Jones, E. *The life and work of Sigmund Freud.* Vol. 2. New York: Basic Books, 1955.

Kleinmuntz, B. *Personality measurement.* Homewood, Ill.: Dorsey, 1967.

Knight, R. P. A critique of the present status of the psychotherapies. *Bulletin of the New York Academy of Medicine,* 1949, *25,* 100–114.

Maddi, S. R. *Personality theories: A comparative analysis.* Homewood, Ill.: Dorsey, 1968.

Pervin, L. A. *Personality: Theory, assessment and research.* New York: Wiley, 1970.

Rogers, C. R. *Client-centered therapy.* Boston: Houghton Mifflin, 1951.

Rogers, C. R. A theory of therapy, personality, and interpersonal relationships as developed in the client-centered framework. In S. Koch (Ed.), *Psychology: A study of a science.* New York: McGraw-Hill, 1959.

Rogers, C. R. *On becoming a person: A therapist's view of psychotherapy.* Boston: Houghton Mifflin, 1961.

Rosenzweig, S. A. A transvaluation of psychotherapy: A reply to Hans Eysenck. *Journal of Abnormal and Social Psychology,* 1954, *49,* 298–304.

Skinner, B. F. *Science and human behavior.* New York: Macmillan, 1953.

Skinner, B. F. *Beyond freedom and dignity.* New York: Bantam Books, 1971.

SUGGESTED READINGS

Freud, A. *The ego and the mechanisms of defense.* London: Hogarth, 1937.

Mischel, W. *Personality and assessment.* New York: Wiley, 1968.

Rabin, A. I. *Projective techniques in personality assessment.* New York: Springer, 1968.

Rogers, C. R. *On becoming a person: A therapist's view of psychotherapy.* Boston: Houghton Mifflin, 1961.

Waelder, R. *Basic theory of psychoanalysis.* New York: International Universities Press, 1960.

Wolpe, J., and Lazarus, A. A. *Behavior therapy techniques: A guide to the treatment of neuroses.* New York: Pergamon Press, 1966.

Photo by Agnes M. Fromer

G

To Be Or Not To Be . . . Affected By Others

Unit 26
Obey!

He was a tall man who looked slim and fit in his spotless uniform. What a contrast to us, who were untidy and grimy after our long journey! He had assumed an attitude of careless ease, supporting his right elbow with his left hand. His right hand was lifted, and with the forefinger of that hand he pointed very leisurely to the right or to the left. None of us had the slightest idea of the sinister meaning behind that little movement of a man's finger, pointing now to the right and now to the left, but far more frequently to the left.

It was my turn. Somebody whispered to me that to be sent to the right side would mean work, the way to the left being for the sick and those incapable of work, who would be sent to a special camp. I just waited for things to take their course, the first of many such times to come. My haversack weighed me down a bit to the left, but I made an effort to walk upright. The SS man looked me over, appeared to hesitate, then put both his hands on my shoulders. I tried very hard to look smart, and he turned my shoulders very slowly until I faced right, and I moved over to that side.

The significance of the finger game was explained to us in the evening. It was the first selection, the first verdict made on our existence or non-existence. For the great majority of our transport, about 90 percent, it meant death. Their sentence was carried out within the next few hours. Those who were sent to the left were marched from the station straight to the crematorium. This building, as I was told by someone who worked there, had the word "bath" written over its doors in several European languages. On entering, each prisoner was handed a piece of soap, and then

— but mercifully I do not need to describe the events which followed. Many accounts have been written about this horror.

We who were saved, the minority of our transport, found out the truth in the evening. I inquired from prisoners who had been there for some time where my colleague and friend P——— had been sent.

"Was he sent to the left side?"

"Yes," I replied.

"Then you can see him there," I was told.

"Where?" A hand pointed to the chimney a few hundred yards off, which was sending a column of flame up into the gray sky of Poland. It dissolved into a sinister cloud of smoke.

"That's where your friend is, floating up to Heaven," was the answer. But I still did not understand until the truth was explained to me in plain words.

Frankl, 1963, pp. 17–19.

This rather delicately phrased passage of horror is a partial accounting of Viktor Frankl's experience in the first of several German concentration camps. Many such accounts of man's capability of abusing his fellow man have been recorded in history. That this phenomenon is not peculiar to the German or Nazi mentality can be seen from scenarios in American history.

In the first seconds of violence, the firing of carbines was deafening, filling the air with powder smoke. Among the dying who lay sprawled on the frozen ground was Big Foot. Then there was a brief lull in the rattle of arms, with small groups of Indians and soldiers grappling at close quarters, using knives, clubs, and pistols. As few of the Indians had arms, they soon had to flee, and then the big Hotchkiss guns on the hill opened up on them, firing almost a shell a second, raking the Indian camp, shredding the tepees with flying shrapnel, killing men, women, and children.

"We tried to run," Louise Weasel Bear said, "but they shot us like we were a buffalo. I know there are some good white people, but the soldiers must be mean to shoot children and women. Indian soldiers would not do that to white children."

... When the madness ended, Big Foot and more than half his people were dead or seriously wounded; 153 were known dead, but many of the wounded crawled away to die afterward. One estimate placed the final total of dead at very nearly three hundred of the original 350 men, women and children. The soldiers lost twenty-five dead and thirty-nine wounded, most of them struck by their own bullets or shrapnel (Brown, 1970, p. 444).

The massacre at Wounded Knee closed an important chapter in the quest for an Indian Nation. It was also only one such atrocity in a history including many broken promises and treaties.

In other instances, man's inhumanity to his fellow man has been equally violent and brutal. The lynching of thousands of blacks by white Americans in both the North and the South in the United States lacked only the scientific precision of the Nazi's "final solution." As was the case with the extermination of the Jews and the Indians, members of the mob usually felt it their rightful duty to perform the acts in question — often mock trials were held or confessions were forced from the victims.

Recent newspaper accounts have revealed a horror story that approximates the brutality of the Nazi efforts in genocide. In 1932, Dr. J. R. Heller, then assistant surgeon general in the venereal disease section of the Public Health Service in Alabama, began a study of syphilis in which blacks were used as human guinea pigs. Males infected with syphilis were recruited to participate by being promised free treatment for any other illness, free hot lunches, and free burial after autopsies were performed. The object of the study was to determine the effect of the disease on the human body.

The study, which began ten years before penicillin was found to be a cure for syphilis, enlisted approximately six hundred black males who were mostly poor and uneducated. The abuse indicated here "in the name of science" was compounded by the deliberate withholding of curative drugs when they became available. Doctors had some form of treatment (injection of bismuth, arsenic, and mercury) as early as 1936 but deliberately withheld it so autopsies could be performed on those who died. A recent review of 125 of these cases indicated that half had syphilitic heart valve damage and 28 had died of cardiovascular or central nervous system (CNS) problems related to syphilis.

A common thread in these incidents is that the victims in all cases were assaulted or abused for no reason except the accident of their birthright. And in all cases those responsible for the violent acts were obeying an authority (military) or a social morality which was not necessarily consistent with their personal or private convictions. That obedience comes so easily and often in these situations makes it an issue of extreme psychological significance.

Authoritarian Personality

In a classic study performed at the University of California at Berkeley, Adorno et al. (1950) were guided by the hypothesis that the political, economic, and social convictions of an individual often form a broad and coherent pattern and that this pattern is an expression of deep-lying personality traits. The major concern was with "potentially fascistic" individuals, those whose structure is such as to render them particularly susceptible to antidemocratic propaganda. Because anti-Semitism had been so strongly related to fascism in Hitler's Germany, Adorno et al. (1950) hypothesized that people who were anti-Semitic would be high in their potentiality for fascism. Accordingly, they devised what they called the "implicit antidemocratic trends or potentiality for fascism (F) scale."

On the basis of Freudian theory and social psychological evidence, these investigators hypothesized that the potential fascist would have the following personality pattern. First, he or she would adhere rigidly to all conventional values, especially those involving authority and traditional morality. Second, the individual would believe that any deviation from the conventional practices should be strongly punished. Third, he or she would have a preoccupation with power and toughness in human relations, coupled with a destructive, cynical attitude about human beings. Fourth, he or she would project his unconscious emotional impulses outward and would resist serious introspection.

A subsequent analysis of the internal consistency of the F scale confirmed the researchers' hypothesis that these characteristics do fit together to form a personality pattern — highly conventional, obsessed with power, subservient to authority, and unanalytical. Further, people who were anti-Semitic were also found to be ethnocentric and possessed a number of personality characteristics associated with the authoritarian personality. From interviews and other clinical data, the researchers found the picture of the authoritarian personality to be consistent with that presented by the F scale. The subjects with authoritarian personalities rejected any possible negative comments about themselves or their parents and engaged in what was termed "self-glorification." Self-reports indicated that neither they nor their parents ever experienced fear, aggression, or laziness. Their parents were concerned about status, were cold and unloving, severely punished deviations from what they considered acceptable behaviors, and were not reluctant to use physical punishment to force their particular point of view. The interview and questionnaire data also showed that persons who were highly anti-Semitic were also generally prejudiced toward other "non-American" groups, possessed highly distinctive personality traits, came from harshly disciplined home environments, and had rigid cognitive styles.

Copyright © 1969 The Chicago Sun-Times. Reproduced by courtesy of Wil-Jo Associates, Inc., and Bill Mauldin.

"My client is not a war criminal! He was one of the silent majority, merely following orders."

This research, generally referred to as the "Berkeley Study," was the model for countless studies to determine the make-up of the authoritarian personality. Although the original work had some methodological flaws, the original pattern of relationships has been obtained in a number of replications. However, the question of accounting for the pattern of relationships is still very much an open one.

Obedience

C. P. Snow (1961) has suggested that more hideous crimes have been committed in the name of obedience than in the name of rebellion. Obviously, humanity can also be served by acts of kindness that result from obedience. Nonetheless, the focus here is to examine acts of destruction to human life in the context of obedience.

MILGRAM'S STUDY

Milgram (1963) has studied this problem in its most general form: If X tells Y to hurt Z, under what circumstances will Y obey and under what circumstances will Y refuse?

Imagine yourself responding to an ad in a local newspaper offering payment ($4.50) for participation in a psychological study. Upon arriving at the psychology laboratory at Yale University, you are greeted by a scientist in a laboratory coat who informs you that the experiment in which you will participate is concerned with the effects of punishment upon memory. The experiment requires a teacher and a learner. You and one other subject who arrived at approximately the same time are allowed to pull slips of paper from a hat to determine who will be the teacher and who will be the learner. Assume you draw the slip containing the word *Teacher*. You and your partner (the learner) are taken to another room, where he is strapped into an "electric chair" apparatus. Electrodes are attached to the learner's wrist, and an electrode paste is applied to prevent blisters and burns. As the teacher you are told that your job is to read a list of word pairs to the learner and test his ability to recall the second word in the pair after hearing the first word repeated. Each time the learner makes a mistake you are to shock him, and with each mistake you are to move one level higher on the shock generator.

The voltage levels on the shock apparatus (see Figure 26-1) range from 15 to 450 volts. This range is labeled from "Slight Shock" to "Extreme Intensity Shock" and finally to "Danger, Severe Shock." The experiment is designed so that the learner will eventually receive the strongest shock on the generator.

As you increase the shock level, cries of agony and increasingly insistent demands to stop the experiment are heard from the learner. However, the experimenter orders you to continue with the procedure, in disregard of the learner's protest. Thus, mutually incompatible demands place you in severe conflict. Should you obey the experimenter's demands and continue to deliver the shock, or should you respond to the learner's pleas and stop? The transcript from an obedient teacher indicates the way the conflict was resolved by 65 percent of the subjects:

150 Volts Delivered. You want me to keep going?
165 Volts Delivered. That guy is hollering in there. There's a lot of them here. He's liable to have a heart condition. You want me to go?
180 Volts Delivered. He can't stand it! I'm going to kill that man in there! You hear him hollering? He's hollering. He can't stand it. What if something happens to him? . . . I'm not going to get that man sick in there. He's hollering. Too many left here. Geez, if he gets them wrong. There's too many of them left. I mean who is going to take responsibility if anything happens to that gentleman? (The experimenter accepts responsibility.) All right.
195 Volts Delivered. You see he's hollering. Hear that. Gee, I don't know. (The experimenter says: "The experiment requires that you go on.") I know it does, sir, but I mean

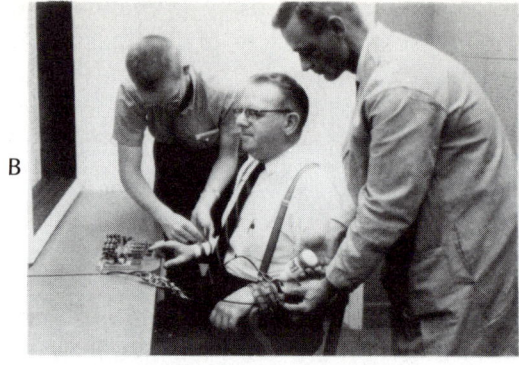
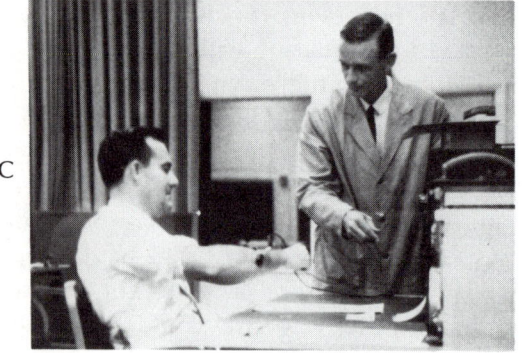

Copyright 1965 by Stanley Milgram. From the film *Obedience,* distributed by the New York University Film Library.

FIGURE 26-1 The shock generator used in Milgram's experiment on obedience is shown in *A*. In *B*, the victim is being strapped into the "electric chair." In *C*, a subject is receiving a sample shock before starting the "teaching session." The subject in *D* is refusing to go on with the experiment any longer.

—huh—he don't know what he's in for. He's up to 195 volts.
210 Volts Delivered.
225 Volts Delivered.
240 Volts Delivered. Aw, no. You mean I've got to keep going up with the scale? No sir. I'm not going to kill that man! I'm not going to give him 450 volts! (The experimenter says: "The experiment requires that you go on.") I know it does but that man is hollering in there, sir (Milgram, 1965).

Despite his numerous, agitated objections, this subject unfailingly obeyed the experimenter. The shocks were fake and the learner was a paid accomplice of the experimenter. But this was unknown to the "teachers" who were noted to sweat, tremble, stutter, bite their lips, and dig their fingernails into their flesh. Of the forty subjects who served as teachers, none stopped short of administering 300 volts (Severe Shock) to the learner, and 65 percent administered 450 volts to the learner.

MY LAI MASSACRE

This compelling example of man's ability to respond to authority rather than to a sense of individual morality antedated a real and more dramatic example of the same phenomenon: Lt. William Calley's massacre of unarmed Vietnamese civilians at My Lai. Kelman and Lawrence (1972), in analyzing American response to the trial of Lt. William Calley (three-fourths of all respondents thought the sentence of life in prison was too harsh), provide some insights into the dynamics of obedience to authority. Data from 989 respondents over the age of 18, gathered from responses to questions about the trial, the Vietnam war, and Calley's actions at My Lai, indicated two patterns of response: (1) those who approved of the trial on the grounds that each individual soldier is responsible for his acts, and (2) those who disapproved of the trial on the grounds that the government was responsible — a good soldier follows orders. The two groups differed in their assessment of who specifically should be held responsible. Among those who approved of the trial, only 6 percent felt that only Calley was responsible; 80 percent felt that higher authorities should share the blame. Respondents who disapproved of the trial generally felt that neither Calley nor other military authorities should be held responsible.

Over one-third (37 percent) of the respondents thought Calley's actions were justified if his victims, regardless of age or sex, were Communists. This is consistent with previous psychological findings that people justify aggression toward others by projecting; i.e., by attributing negative traits to them. Forty-seven percent justified Calley's behavior on the grounds that "it is better to kill some South Vietnamese civilians than to risk the lives of any American soldiers." However, only 17 percent of those who approved of the trial agreed with this sentiment.

Kelman and Lawrence (1972) remind us that both social scientists and laymen generally have recognized that the concept of individual responsibility implies that persons act deliberately in bringing about behavioral outcomes (i.e., individuals who intentionally cause an act are held responsible for its consequences). The precedent for this tradition in our culture stems from an 1843 decision in British law (M'Naghten's rule) and results in the legal interpretation that all crimes are intentionally motivated. Nonetheless, all the instances cited above would suggest that the perpetrators or aggressors relaxed or dismissed this consideration so that the link between causation and responsibility was broken. Having done so, it probably became easier to respond to authority or other external pressures irrespective of the departure from their own personal morality. Kelman and Lawrence summarize the negative public reactions to the Calley trial by suggesting that the public did not view Calley's behavior as a mere aberration, but as to some extent a "product of a political ideology that exempts authoritative orders from the demands of individual conscience."

Unit 27
Follow the Leader: Conformity and Social Influence

Have you ever noticed that people will look up at the sky simply because others are doing so? This is an example of conformity to a group norm. College students wear denim jeans and long hair to conform to group norms. Norms serve to regulate members' behavior in organized and coherent ways. In many societies, for example, strict traffic regulations help considerably in reducing accidents. Ordinarily, members accept as legitimate the standardized rules imposed as norms. What are the reasons for this?

Consequences of Nonconformity

Groups usually dispense rewards to members who conform, and there may be severe consequences for deviations. Berkowitz and Howard (1959) and Sampson and Brandon (1964) found that groups tend to direct increased communication toward deviates. This effort is made, however, only when group members think there is a reasonable probability of influencing or pressuring the deviant to conform. A more powerful form of punishment is reserved for those who seem unlikely to shift away from their deviancy: rejection.

Schachter (1951) included three accomplices in a group discussion experiment in which one accomplice remained consistently deviant from the group viewpoint; of the other two accomplices, one initially disagreed with the group and gradually shifted to the group's position, while the other consistently took the same position as the group. After trying to change the position of the two deviants, the group, when given the opportunity by the experimenter, voted to reject the unyielding deviant accomplice. Although this study produced only a weak effect when repeated with high school students (Emerson, 1954), it has been replicated in seven European nations. Emerson suggested that his high school students, who tended to yield more to the deviants, were probably not as firm in their convictions on the issues they were discussing as an older college population would be. The replication of this effect in seven European countries suggests the probable universality of the phenomenon.

Most cultures seem to have strong negative consequences for members who deviate from their accepted practices. No doubt this fact is transmitted to individuals by various socializing agents (e.g., parents and teachers). New ideas often require a departure from the traditional. Nevertheless, history shows many examples of men and women who have had to pay tremendous consequences for stepping outside the norm in making their contributions. Dr. Ignaz Phillip Semmelweis was ostracized by the medical profession in 1863 because of his efforts to get doctors to wash their hands in an antiseptic solution between digital examinations of pregnant women. And Ayn Rand (1943) has suggested through one of her characters that the first person to discover fire was probably burned at the stake. In both instances, the acts were threatening to existing group standards or practices.

There is considerable evidence of group pressures toward uniformity despite individual beliefs. Past research has indicated that several important functions are served by pressures to uniformity in groups: (a) group goals are achieved more easily, (b) group survival is greater, (c) groups can serve as a source of confirmation of opinions and abilities (Festinger, 1954) and the appropriateness of an emotion or bodily state (Schachter and Singer, 1962), and (d) groups can facilitate members in their efforts to define their relations to their social surroundings.

A common observation of most social groups is the regularity of the patterns of social interaction. Close examination of these situations reveals that a good deal of this regularity is simply due to conformity. There is a paradox in the pervasiveness of conformity in our culture despite our seeming reverence for independence or nonconformity. For example, John F. Kennedy's book *Profiles in Courage* (1955) details numerous instances in which political heroism was identified with defiance of one's colleagues and constituents — in other words, with independence or, perhaps, nonconformity. The price of nonconformity, as Emerson points out, is to be misunderstood: "Pythagoras was misunderstood, and Socrates, and Jesus, and Luther, and Copernicus, and Galileo, and Newton, and every pure and wise spirit that ever took flesh." Perhaps our lot is to admire nonconformity at the safe distance of conforming to the group.

Research on Group Behavior

SHERIF'S STUDIES

A pioneer in the laboratory investigation of group behavior was Sherif (1936). Sherif's subjects viewed a stationary pinpoint of light in an otherwise totally dark room; under these conditions, after awhile, a light will *appear* to move *(autokinetic effect)*. The instructions to the subjects required them to estimate in inches the distance the light moved. In this situation, subjects in a group typically start out making independent and somewhat discrepant judgments. In time, however, their judgments converge so that a group norm is established. Although individuals are not aware that they are being influenced by others in the group, the norm remains consistent for the group and for individuals in the group when tested separately.

In Sherif's experimental setting, the nature of the stimulus was fairly ambiguous; therefore, any conflict in the subject's mind between physical reality (perceived movement) and social reality (group judgment) is easily resolved in the direction of social reality (i.e., verifying one's judgment against the group consensus). Such a consideration naturally raises the question of the probable outcome when the stimulus objects being judged are more structured.

ASCH'S STUDIES

The research of Solomon Asch (1956) provides us with a response to this question. In this study, a college student volunteers to participate with several others in what is supposedly an experiment in visual perception. Lines of varying lengths are to be presented and compared with a standard line. On each of several trials, the subjects are required to identify the comparison line whose length equals the length of the standard line and to state their choices aloud, one at a time. Our volunteer subject always responds last.

On the first few trials, the judgments are easy and there is perfect agreement within the group. Eventually, the first subject gives a response that appears to be obviously wrong to our volunteer subject. However, to our volunteer's dismay the other subjects unanimously give the "wrong" answer also. (Unknown to our volunteer subject, the other subjects are confederates of the experimenter who have been trained to disagree with the volunteer subject about two-thirds of the time.) How is the conflict typically handled?

Results (see Figure 27-1) indicate that about one-third of the individuals facing this conflict yield completely to the erroneous judgments of the others more

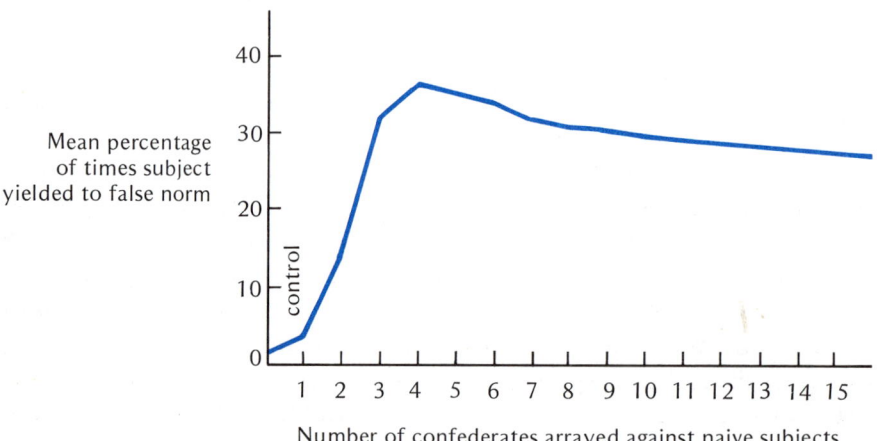

FIGURE 27-1 Percentage of agreement with a false norm on the part of naive subjects in Asch's study

than half the time. Most persons suffer a great discomfort under such circumstances, and few can completely ignore the pressure from the group and maintain the conviction of their own perceptions.

CRUTCHFIELD'S STUDIES

Variations of the Sherif and Asch experiments have been conducted in an effort to explore the extent of conformity with different kinds of stimuli and, further, to investigate personality predispositions to conformity. Notable among these investigations is the work of Crutchfield (1955) at the Institute of Personality Assessment and Research (IPAR) at the University of California, Berkeley. Crutchfield's procedure is essentially an automated modification of the Sherif and Asch paradigms. Five experimental subjects are seated at adjacent electrical panels, shielded from one another, and are led to believe that they can communicate with each other by pushing any of eleven switches on their panels. Each subject's panel contains five rows of eleven signal lights. The rows are lettered A, B, C, D, and E, with each row corresponding to one of the subjects, and each light corresponding to one possible answer to the particular question.

Slides requiring various kinds of judgments (e.g., lengths of lines, areas of figures, number completion series, vocabulary items) are presented in plain view of each subject. Each subject is required to indicate answers by pushing the appropriate switch on the panel at his or her designated turn in the group. A responds first, B second, C third, and so on. The sequence is rotated by the experimenter so that all subjects give judgments in each serial position. In reality, the situation is contrived: there is no connection between the subjects' panels. They are actually wired to the experimenter's panel, and it is the experimenter who sends information simultaneously and identically to each of the panels. In effect, all five subjects are in the same position on each trial. The experimenter electrically creates the group and on certain "critical" trials creates a unanimous contradictory consensus.

This procedure should be viewed as more than simply an automated version of the Sherif or Asch technique. Rather, it is a powerful research tool that permits an investigator to simulate group interaction without the use of confederates and simultaneously preserve standardized procedures for presenting stimulus materials and for maintaining the rigorous requirements of good measurement techniques.

Personality Correlates of Conformity

Among the findings on personality predisposition to conformity is the somewhat obvious and expected relatiomship between authoritarianism and conformity. Crutchfield (1955) found a positive correlation between authoritarianism and conformity. Additionally, he found nonconformers (or independents) to be more intellectually effective and to have more ego-strength, more leadership ability, and greater maturity. These subjects also reflected a conspicuous absence of inferiority feelings, rigid and excessive self-control, and authoritarian attitudes.

Other investigations have found conformers to be persons with low self-esteem and acute symptoms of neurotic anxiety (Janis, 1954) and compulsiveness (Hoffman, 1953). Barron (1953) identified the following self-descriptions among conformers: obliging, optimistic, efficient, determined, patient, and kind. Conformers also described themselves as practical-minded and group-oriented. These findings suggest that conformity has two nonrelated components: pathological dependency and social responsibility.

Norms

The studies by Sherif, Asch, and Crutchfield provide strikingly similar findings regarding the nature of conformity and group consensus. However, Sherif (1936, 1966) specifically focuses on the development of norms as an underlying dynamic of conformity. He describes a basic process operating in the formation of accepted standards of judgment that might elsewhere be referred to as values or attitudes. However, his emphasis seems consistent with the definition of social norm offered by Secord and Backman (1964): "a standard of behavioral expectation shared by group members against which the validity of perceptions is judged and the appropriateness of feelings and behavior is evaluated" (p. 323).

As discussed earlier, groups tend to control and regulate the "permissible" behaviors of their members. In the process norms are established, and these in turn operate as constraining forces on individual members. There is pressure to conform and a strong reluctance to deviate from that norm. According to McGrath (1964), group norms include (1) a frame of reference, (2) a prescribed right attitude or behavior, (3) affective feelings about the rightness of attitudes and tolerance of norm violations, and (4) positive and negative sanctions by which proper behavior is rewarded and improper behavior is punished.

Needless to say, all conformity does not necessarily lead to acts of violence or destruction. Some conformity simply serves as the way in which some groups achieve social solidarity. And in some instances, conforming behaviors have resulted in a greater tolerance for others. For example, Newcomb (1943) found that women students at Bennington College from 1935 to 1939 became less conservative and more progressive as they moved from their freshman year to their senior year. This effect was strongest for those who were most fully assimilated into college life and who identified with its leaders most strongly. Nevertheless, our purpose here has been to explain destructive behavior, and the dynamics of social power and conformity seem a useful way to do that.

Unit 28
Forces that Compel: Social Power

> We sometimes induce a man to behave by prompting him (for example, when he is not able to solve a problem), or by suggesting a course of action (for example, when he is at a loss as to what do do). Prompts, hints, and suggestions are all stimuli, usually but not always verbal, and they have the important property of exerting only partial control. No one responds to a prompt, hint, or suggestion unless he already has some tendency to behave in a given way.

Skinner, 1971, p. 87.

An important source of social influence, as seen in many of the examples in Units 26 and 27, is the power relationships among group members. In considering these relationships, two questions arise: What determines the behavior of the person who exerts power? What determines the reactions of the person being influenced? Some answers to these questions are provided in a formulation of social power by French and Raven (1959). These authors see power as a pervasive, complex, and often disguised source of social influence.

French and Raven's Formulation of Social Power

Power is defined as the maximum force which an individual (person A) can induce on another (person B) minus the maximum resisting force which the other (person B) can mobilize in the opposite direction.

BASES OF SOCIAL POWER

French and Raven delineate five bases of social power: (1) reward power, (2) coercive power, (3) legitimate power, (4) referent (attraction) power, and (5) expert power. These sources of power derive from the nature of the relationship between A and B, where B is the person being influenced and A is another person or a role, a norm, or part of a group. In this framework, the psychological change in B must be related clearly to A so that other effects can be ruled out. When the effect of the influence is in the direction advocated by A, it is said to be positive; when it is in the opposite direction, it is said to be negative.

Reward Power. The basis of reward power lies in A's ability to reward B for compliance with desired behavior patterns. Reward may be in the form of administering positive effects or simply removing (or decreasing) negative effects. The reward must cause pleasure and be seen as a reward to B. A common example of reward power is the case of a bonus offered by one's employer. Acts performed by members of the military are surely influenced by promotions, medals, and other incentives.

Coercive Power. In contrast to reward power, coercive power results from the ability of A to influence the attainment of bad outcomes for B. In this particular relationship, there is an expectation on the part of B that A will punish him for failure to comply or conform with A's efforts to influence him. Coercive power, in other words, is a function of A's *capacity* to inflict negative outcomes. One confusing aspect of coercive power is whether the withholding of a reward is punishing; and, similarly, whether the withdrawal of punishment is rewarding. There is disagreement on the answer to this question. The outcome of coercive power is further complicated when the less powerful person, in order to avoid punishment, resorts to alternatives rather than accomplishing outcomes desired of him. For example, an employee can lie about his attendance when the boss is away to avoid incurring his wrath.

Legitimate Power. Legitimate power is a function of B's internalizing of group norms that give A the right to exert influence on him; concomitantly, B's role behavior is such that he feels obligated to yield to A's influence. The establishment of legitimate power is based on (1) cultural values, (2) acceptance of social structure, and (3) designation by a legitimate agent. In all cases, there is a feeling of "oughtness" on the part of B. In a large number of instances, A's power is the direct result of an election process. Some exceptions to this are the military, governmental agencies, and most industrial organizations. In the final analysis, legitimacy is a relationship among values within a situation. The blacks who volunteered to participate in the syphilis study mentioned in Unit 26 were probably responding to the legitimacy of medical personnel.

Referent Power. The basis for referent power lies in B's identification with A. The feeling of oneness resulting from the attractive nature of identification provides for A's influence on B. This type of relationship is seen in charismatic leaders who "inspire" others to follow their direction. Another instance of referent power is evidenced in Festinger's theory of social comparison (1954). Festinger asserts that social influence stems from the "drive for self-evaluation" — based on a comparison with a similar other. In other words, an individual's needs for reality testing in groups become a source of influence. The correctness or incorrectness of opinions and beliefs, in the absence of objective nonsocial criteria, is seen as a function of the opinions of others. When there is disagreement, pressures toward uniformity emerge. This type of apparent or real "collective wisdom" of a group is the basis for a good deal of conformity.

Expert Power. Expert power is derived from B's perception of A's knowledge or ability. The expertise is generally judged to be relevant to some goal. For example, a person may seek out a psychologist or psychiatrist for help with personal troubles, or an attorney for advice on legal matters. The expertise need not require any specialized training or skills, as in the case of the native who gives directions to a stranger who is lost. There must, however, be an element of cooperation if expert power is functioning. A man may lose his property if he doesn't cooperate with (follow the advice of) his attorney. Similarly, a student's learning may be jeopardized if he doesn't cooperate with his teacher.

WEAKNESSES OF THE SYSTEM

These conceptualizations of social power are useful for examining some of the sources of social influence in groups. However, this schema contains some basic weaknesses:

1. These conceptions of power were not derived empirically and are therefore somewhat speculative.
2. Research evidence suggests that the various forms of power do not occur independently of one another. Hence, combinations of these forms are usually present in any single instance.
3. The framework does not provide for an analysis or clarification of the resistant forces.

Nonetheless, studies have shown that most leaders tend to emphasize the legitimacy of their positions while simultaneously utilizing reward and coercive power. Others, however, employ referent and expert power, and these lead to a higher-quality product.

Unit 29
Folkways and Stateways: Prejudice and Racism

Reports written by doctors in charge of a public health syphilis study (see Unit 26) show that at least twenty-eight of the Alabama black men used in the study died as a direct result of untreated syphilis. Charges of racism and abuse were directed at the medical personnel responsible for this project. Similar questions regarding Eichmann's attitudes toward Jews were raised by the Israelis; yet it was never established that Eichmann was anti-Semitic. Were the Public Health Service physicians prejudiced against blacks? Or were they just dedicated scientists? The answers to these questions are not easy and in a sense may be less important than the behavioral outcome. Part of the difficulty in answering these questions can be attributed to inconsistencies between stated attitudes and observed behavior.

In the present unit, we are concerned with reported attitudes and how they relate to observed behavior. More specifically, our focus is on prejudice and racism. In Unit 26, examples of brutality to Jews, Indians, and Blacks were discussed. These examples were designed to convey the pervasive and almost universal nature of the destructive outcomes associated with negative attitudes — especially prejudice and racism.

Many years of effort by behavioral scientists in seeking a remedy for the ill effects of prejudice in our society have met with frustration, partially because of the truth of the pronouncement made at the turn of the century by the prominent sociologist William Graham Sumner: "Stateways cannot change folkways." More simply put, Sumner was suggesting that you cannot legislate against prejudice. We will discuss the merits of Sumner's argument later in this unit; at this point, it seems possible that an understanding of attitudes could help in clarifying the nature of prejudice and racism.

Attitudes

Attitudes carry expectancies regarding behavior. That is, an attitude is a positive or negative feeling about some person, object, or phenomenon that predisposes us to some action. For example, we hold attitudes toward long-haired hippies, policemen, college professors, and girls in bikinis. These attitudes serve to orient our behavior toward these individuals. We may be attracted to girls in bikinis and repelled by long-haired hippies. A collection of organized attitudes forms a value system within which decisions are made and further attitude development occurs.

Through the socialization process, value systems are passed on from generation to generation. Hence, attitudes are learned and become relatively enduring as a way of adapting to one's environment. At the same time, the environment serves as a source of attitude formation. It is reasonable to assume that attitudes affect behavior and that behavior affects attitudes.

Attitudes cannot be seen or observed. We infer attitudes from other behaviors that can be observed (e.g., answers on a questionnaire, facial expressions). Because attitudes are inferred constructs, there will always be a question of validity and consistency. For example, to what extent does a stated attitude represent what it is supposed to (the underlying attitude), and how related is the stated attitude to an overt behavioral act? In 1934, R. T. LaPiere, a sociologist, traveled across the United States with a Chinese couple, stopping at hotels and restaurants and receiving service at all of them except one. Later, he wrote letters to these same hotels and restaurants asking if they would serve Chinese. Of those that responded, approximately 90 percent indicated that they would not serve Chinese — a response that was clearly inconsistent with their past actions. A similar study conducted by Kutner, Wilkins, and Yarrow (1952), using three women, one black and two white, produced approximately the same outcome. Restaurants that had accommodated the interracial party subsequently refused to accept reservations for an interracial party over the telephone. These studies bring up questions of which is the correct expression of the attitude — the overt behavior (serving racial minorities) or written and verbal statements (refusal to accept reservations from racial minorities).

COMPONENTS OF ATTITUDES

The inconsistencies in attitude expression described above can be better understood by examining the three components of attitudes: cognitive, affective, and behavioral (see Figure 29-1). The *cognitive* component of an attitude refers to the belief-disbelief or information aspect one holds about an attitude object. For example, some persons believe that blondes are dumb, or that blacks are lazy. These beliefs have been called stereotypes. More generally, one could believe that one's country is always right and, accordingly, become irritated when another citizen criticizes it. Indeed, it is possible for an individual to hold contradictory beliefs (cognitions): the person who says that "integration is a noble goal but blacks do not have a right to move into my community" is holding contradictory beliefs.

In contrast to the cognitive aspect of attitudes, the *affective* component deals with emotions and feelings, such as likes and dislikes. This component is perhaps most central in attitudes and underlies a great number of observed inconsistencies. Imagine the conflict you would experience if you were committed intellectually to a given attitude to which your gut

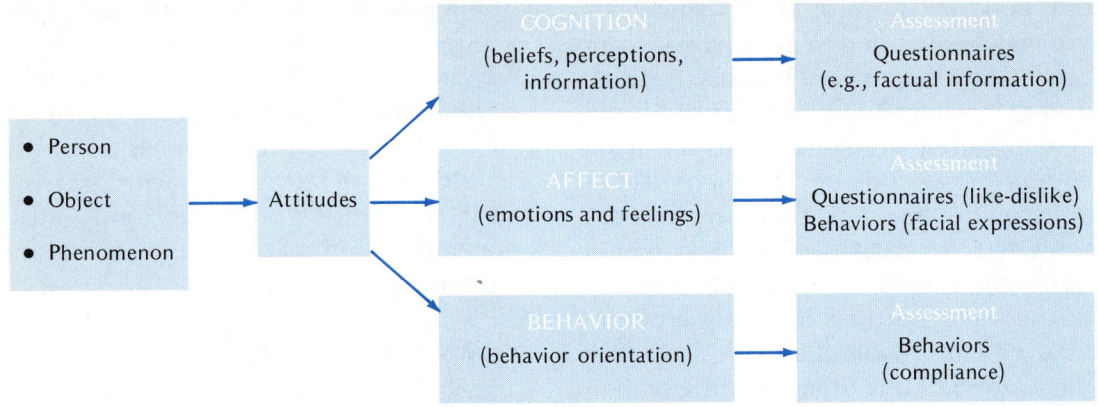

FIGURE 29-1 The schematic structure of attitudes

feelings were not supportive. If you believe the surgeon general's report stating the relationship between cancer and smoking, yet you continue to smoke because of the pleasure you derive from that habit, there is a strong probability that you will occasionally experience conflict or tension.

The third component of an attitude is *behavior* orientation. Here we are concerned with how a person would respond in a given context. To state publicly an attitude is one thing; to engage in behaviors designed to produce changes consistent with the stated attitude is quite another.

COGNITIVE DISSONANCE

The theory of cognitive dissonance (Festinger, 1957) provides a rather detailed explanation of cognitive inconsistencies and how they are handled by the individual. Physically, dissonance is defined as an inharmonious or harsh sound; discord; disagreement or incongruity. Festinger introduced the term to represent an inconsistency among two or more cognitive elements within an individual — that is, differences or inconsistencies among opinions, beliefs, knowledge of the environment, and knowledge of one's own actions and feelings.

Two cognitions are in dissonant relation if they do not fit together, i.e., if they are inconsistent. For example, the belief that all human beings are equal in God's eye and the belief (or practice) that blacks should not be allowed to worship in one's church are in dissonant relation, since the opposite of the second follows logically from the first. The man who smokes cigarettes and believes that smoking is harmful to his health has an opinion that is dissonant with the knowledge that he is continuing to smoke.

The theory further holds that dissonance is psychologically uncomfortable and will therefore motivate the person to try to reduce dissonance and achieve consonance. Strategies that can be used to try to reduce dissonance are:

(1) change the belief or the behavior, (2) search for other evidence supporting the belief, (3) reject present evidence supporting the belief, and (4) recruit social support for the belief.

The utility of this theory for our purposes is that it provides some explanation for the observed inconsistencies and discrepancies in attitudes and behavior. Further, it details strategies that individuals may employ in dealing with tensions that arise from contradictions.

Prejudice and Racism

One very strong effect of group norms is that they produce climates that are ripe for the growth of attitudes. In conforming and identifying with one's group, one often develops a distrust for all others. In a mild form this phenomenon is referred to as *ethnocentrism*. In its strongest form, this phenomenon is called *prejudice*. Because of its pervasiveness, it has been suggested that prejudice may be learned and reinforced as a by-product of identification and socialization into one's own group. The phenomenon is so strong that it has led Pettigrew (1960) to postulate that conformity may be the sociopsychological key to analyzing desegregation. Knowledge and understanding of how conformity facilitates the development of norms which in turn lead to prejudiced behaviors may help us to understand how to reduce or irradicate racial prejudice.

CONFORMITY

If conformity is the key to understanding desegregation, then it is also the key to understanding prejudice and racism. It has been pointed out that the height of irony in racial conformity occurred in Panama, where the Canal Zone side of a street was racially segregated and the Panamanian side was racially integrated. Biesanz and Smith (1951) have observed that most Panamanians and Americans appeared to accommodate without difficulty as they went first on one side of this racial barrier and then on the other. This kind of duality has its parallels in some situations in American life in which whites accommodate integration in one aspect of their lives and bitterly oppose it in others.

Obviously, this pattern does not generalize to all in any group; there are those whose attitudes are constant regardless of where they are. Of interest here are those individuals with less well defined attitudes that shift as a function of the situation — conformists. Pettigrew (1960) found more racial prejudice in groups he classified as conforming (e.g., females, church attenders) than in their counterparts (e.g., males, non–church attenders). Further, there is less racial prejudice in communities in which minority group members constitute a small percentage of the population. The fact that these findings obtain in southern communities and not in northern communities was interpreted as substantiation for attitudinal and behavioral conformity. The extreme sanctions (verbal and written intimidation, burned crosses, and bomb threats) employed in the South resulted in greater adherence to white supremacy values.

Kelman (1958, 1961) describes three types of conformity: (1) *compliance:* conformity based on one's need for a favorable reaction from the group, (2) *identification:* acceptance of influence because one wants a satisfying relationship with others, and (3) *internalization:* acceptance of influence because the behavior engaged in is satisfying in and of itself. In this last case, individuals are very likely to engage in behaviors they perceive to be expected of them even when they are not being monitored. A good deal of behavioral and attitudinal racism occurs in this manner.

RACISM

Definition. Behavioral and attitudinal racism implies hate or aversion directed at denying equal rights and opportunities to persons because of their racial origin.

Billingsley and Giovannoni (1972, p. 8) provide a more comprehensive definition of this phenomenon:

Racism is a social force deeply imbedded in the fabric of the society in which we live. It is the systematic oppression, subjugation, and control of one racial group by another dominant or more powerful racial group, made possible by the manner in which the society is structured. In this society, racism emanates from white institutions, white cultural values, and white people. The victims of racism in this society are Black people and other oppressed racial and ethnic minorities.

Similarly, Jones (1972, p. 117) utilizes the concepts of social power, race prejudice, and ethnocentrism to define racism as follows:

Racism results from the transformation of race prejudice and/or ethnocentrism through the exercise of power against a racial group defined as inferior by individuals and institutions with the intentional or unintentional support of the entire culture.

Types. Jones describes three kinds of racism: individual racism, institutional racism, and cultural racism. The first, *individual racism,* is embodied in the definitions above. *Institutional racism,* on the other hand, is (1) a deliberate manipulation of institutions to achieve racist objectives and (2) the by-product of institutional practices resulting in restrictions of a racial nature to the access and privileges of institutions. It is not necessary to demonstrate intention or deliberateness in institutional practices. Finally, *cultural racism* contains elements of both individual and institutional racism and is actually their combined expressions of the superiority of one cultural heritage over that of other races (see Figure 29-2).

As Jones points out, the conceptualization of individual racism is very similar to classic definitions of prejudice. The first expansion to institutional racism had its origin in the important work of Carmichael and Hamilton (1967) and departs considerably from a concern with attitudes and attitude change. Instead, it focuses on more objective criteria reflected in racial inequities. An important distinction is being made here between *intentions* and *consequences.* An analysis of individual racism, as does an analysis of prejudice, requires one to deal with inferences, value judgments, and conjecture. An analysis of institutional racism, however, simply requires one to examine prevailing patterns that demonstrate racial inequities.

For example, a coalition of black,

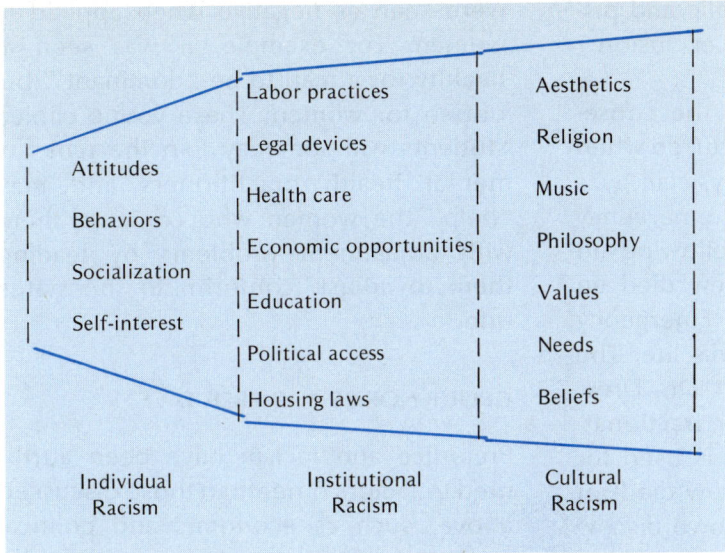

FIGURE 29-2 Through a telescope widely—a model for the analysis of racism

Mexican-American, and women's groups in California (including the regional NAACP chapter, the Mexican-American Political Association, and the National Organization for Women) surveyed the decision-making structures of the sixty-seven largest California corporations as listed in *Fortune* magazine. The coalition discovered that of the corporation's 1008 directors, not one is black; none of the 1008 directors is Mexican-American; 1 is Spanish-surnamed (he won the Nobel Prize in physics); 6 of the 1008 directors are female, and of these, 3 are married to presidents or chairmen of companies and 1 is the daughter of a company's founder. None of the top 1268 officers and executives of the sixty-seven corporations is black; none of the top 1268 officers is Mexican-American; only 6 of the top officers and executives are women (one is married to the company president, one to the chairman). This type of situation, which is widespread throughout the country, is typically accepted as *prima facie* or *de facto* evidence of institutional racism.* To argue otherwise would require us to speculate about the possible inferior capabilities or genetic differences of the members of these excluded groups.

Cultural racism is manifested in practices that deny, ignore, or distort the accomplishments and achievements of a race of people. Individuals and institutions collectively, through custom and law, have engaged in practices that discourage social contact between the races (miscegenation laws and restrictive covenants), have selectively reported news in a way that is unfavorable to minorities, and have adopted hiring and promotion policies that result in few minority group

---
*As is clear in this example, prejudice and discrimination can be generalized to groups other than blacks; women too are affected by these practices.

Folkways and Stateways: Prejudice and Racism 249

members participating in public and private institutions — or in total exclusion.

Effects. A tragic example of the consequences of such practices occurred when Dr. Charles Drew, a black physician, was refused admittance to the emergency room of a white hospital following an automobile accident. Dr. Drew died en route to another hospital. Emergency treatment might have saved his life. The tragedy of this event is that Dr. Drew discovered the technique for fractionating blood into plasma which is used for emergency treatment. Dr. Drew died for the lack of application of his own discovery.

Such an outcome seems to be the legacy of a prejudiced society. Some years ago Clark and Clark (1947) provided experimental evidence of additional negative effects of racism. In a study designed to test the preference for dolls among black children, it was discovered that black children not only favored white dolls over black dolls, but thought that white dolls were prettier and superior. These findings were interpreted as evidence of a diminution of self-esteem among the victims of prejudice (racism). In more recent experimental studies, Goldberg (1971) discovered that female judges rated an essay less favorably when it was attributed to a female author. Studies by Rosenkranz (1968) give us some clues as to the development of negative sex role stereotypes among women. Clinical judges, asked to rate adjectives when applied to males and females, gave different ratings for the same adjective when applied to each sex. Adjectives judged as positive for men were seen as negative when applied to women. For example, it was seen as healthy for a man to be "dominant," but not so for women. These young clinical students will someday join the ranks of mental health practitioners and may "help" the women who come to them with adjustment problems by leading them to adjust (conform) to the status quo.

GROUP NORMS AND PREJUDICE

Prejudice and racism have been attributed to factors other than those discussed above, such as economic and political competition, displaced aggression, and personality needs. However, in this unit we are focusing primarily on explanations relevant to conformity to social norms. As we have suggested, all groups encourage adherence to standards and certain beliefs as a matter of loyalty. These standards and beliefs in time become codified and require members to work against individuals who violate these codes (enemies). It has also been noted that justification for these acts is often achieved by disparaging the victim.

At the beginning of this division, several examples of destructive behavior were cited. An analysis of the dynamics of the events suggested that individuals were obedient to superiors above everything else. It is easy to argue that these extremes represent exceptional cases. However, such arguments are weakened by the data from Milgram's study of destructive obedience (65 percent obeyed completely) and the seemingly ubiquitous nature of these behaviors. It seems that if one has a creed or ideology in which one believes, there are sometimes few extremes (if any) that one will not go to in order to maintain commitment to and good standing in the group. For example, in *Teahouse of the August Moon* (Patrick, 1952), Col. Purdy asserts, "But my job is to teach these natives the meaning of democracy, and they're going to learn democracy if I have to shoot every one of them" (p. 23). American whites killed Indians under the banner of manifest destiny; Nazi Germany exterminated six million Jews to preserve the master race; white Americans lynched thousands of black Americans in the name of white supremacy; and white physicians left hundreds of blacks with untreated syphilis in the name of science. Light-skinned blacks have been observed to discriminate against dark-skinned blacks; and in the name of black power, blacks have engaged in destructive acts against whites — and other blacks.

Remedy. Some time ago, it was felt that improvement between the races could come about only through favorable attitude change. Despite William Graham Sumner's notable comment that "stateways cannot change folkways," a good deal of research has been addressed to finding ways to effect favorable attitude change through increased contact. The shifting emphasis from the concept of prejudice to a concern with the various kinds of racism has helped us to focus on a different approach: behavioral change.

The *equal-status contact hypothesis* (Allport, 1954) cast light on the possibility that changes in behavior could effect changes in attitude (see Figure 29-3). Starting with the assumption that "by assembling people without regard for race, color, religion, or national origin, we can thereby destroy stereotypes and develop friendly attitudes," Allport reviewed research covering several kinds of contact.

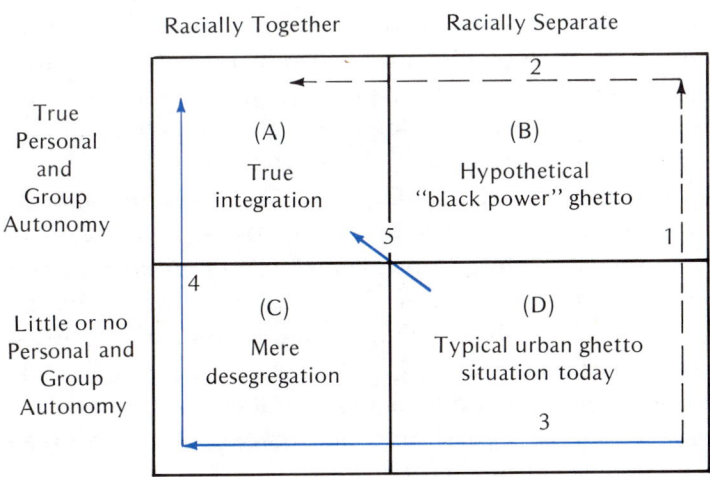

FIGURE 29-3 Autonomy and contact-separation

In each instance, there was evidence for increased liking and favorable attitudes with increased frequency of personal contact. However, in none of the studies was any evidence presented that would suggest a change in subsequent behavior patterns of whites toward blacks. Typical of the results of these studies are the data cited by Allport on reactions by white soldiers to the idea of integrating army platoons. In this instance, white soldiers in platoons that already had blacks were most favorable to the innovation and thought it a good idea. In a somewhat unusual setting, Deutsch and Collins (1951) obtained similar findings. Studying attitude change in two public housing projects, they found more favorable attitude change in the project where blacks and whites lived in the same building than where buildings within the project were either all black or all white.

Efforts to generalize these data must be made with caution. First of all, the studies deal only with reports of attitude change. None focus on behavior change. Additionally, the pervasiveness of racial prejudice in northern communities where there is a good deal of integration suggests that the reported attitude changes in these studies may be quite limited. Rarely are situations as ideal as those found in a public housing project or the military. There are many situations in which blacks and whites come in contact that do not meet the requirements of *equal status*. Additionally, it may be too simplistic to conclude that stereotypes and biases are automatically reduced or irradicated by contact, no matter how ideal it is. In summarizing these studies, Allport (1954, p. 267) concluded that:

Prejudice (unless deeply rooted in the character structure of the individual) may be reduced by equal status contact between majority and minority groups in the pursuit of common goals. The effect is greatly enhanced if this contact is sanctioned by institutional supports (i.e., by law, custom or local atmosphere), and if it is of a sort that leads to the perception of common interests and common humanity between members of the two groups.

Much of the racial prejudice in our society seems to be deeply rooted in the character structure of individuals. Also, institutional support of integration has not been effective in our culture. The experimental evidence most supportive of Allport's formulation is found in the Robber's Cave study by Sherif (1966). After tension and hostility had been produced between two groups of boys in a summer camp by putting them into direct conflict and competition with each other, hostility reduction was not possible simply by bringing them together under equal status and more favorable circumstances. Tension reduction and favorable relations were produced only by creating an emergency situation (damaging the water system) which compelled the two groups to cooperate.

Expanding on Sherif's and Allport's conclusions, it seems that favorable intergroup relations (diminution of racism) will come about through system changes that facilitate cooperation, mutual trust, and sharing of power. Perhaps the whole system (leaders, policies, and rank and file) should be changed so as to create new group norms.

Unit 30
Contagious Behaviors

I wish to use my body as a torch
To dissipate the darkness
To waken Love among men
And to bring Peace to Viet Nam.

Why do Americans burn themselves?
Why do non-Vietnamese demonstrate all over the world?
Why does Viet Nam remain silent
And not dare to utter the word "Peace"?

I feel helpless
And I suffer
If being alive I cannot express myself,
I will offer my life to have my aspirations known.

Is appealing for Peace a crime?
Is acting for Peace communism?
I am appealing for Peace
In the name of Man.

I join my hands and kneel down;
I accept this utmost pain in my body
In the hope that the words of my heart be heard
Please stop it, my fellowmen!

This poem was written by a Vietnamese school teacher who poured three gallons of gasoline over her clothes and burned herself to death in the presence of newsmen she had invited to witness the "ritual." She recited the poem as the fire consumed her body.

The self-immolation of this Vietnamese school teacher, Nhat Chi Mai, mirrored the actions of both Norman Morrison, the American pacifist who burned himself in front of the Pentagon on November 2, 1969, and Thich Quang Duc, the Buddhist monk who burned himself to death. In 1963, the practice of self-immolation achieved international visibility when it was instrumental in bringing about the fall of South Vietnam's President Ngo Dinh Diem. Of note is the fact that many similar incidents followed this dramatic event, including a young woman college student from a small eastern college burning herself to death on campus in response to a disappointing love affair.

Nhat Chi Mai indicated that she was imitating the behaviors of others in order to dramatize her feelings about war. Were others who burned themselves to death also imitating acts that had been highly publicized?

This imitation phenomenon has been observed in other areas of behavior. The nation witnessed a series of mass killings following the publicity around the Speck murders.* For example, soon after this event a young man carried a rifle into the tower of a building on the campus of the University of Texas in Austin and killed and injured several persons before being captured.

Political assassination became so prevalent in the 1960s that a presidential commission on violence was convened. The commission formulated a "profile on an archetypal assassin": (1) comes from a broken home, with the father absent or unresponsive to the child; (2) has a withdrawn personality, is a loner, has no girlfriends, is unmarried or a failure at marriage; (3) has been unable to work steadily in the last year or so before the assassination; (4) is a zealot for a political, religious, or other cause, but not a member of an organized movement; (5) kills in the name of a specific issue related to the principles or philosophy of his cause; and (6) selects a moment when his target is appearing amid crowds.

Despite the accuracy of this assessment, we all must know individuals who fit this bill of particulars who have not, and never will, kill anyone. But the decade of the sixties witnessed a long sequence of such behaviors: In 1962 an assassin shot down Medgar Evers, field secretary for the NAACP in Mississippi, as he left his car to enter his home; in 1963 Lee Harvey Oswald killed President John F. Kennedy as the presidential motorcade rode through Dallas; in 1965 Malcolm X was cut down by a volley of bullets from the guns of unidentified assassins; Sirhan Sirhan shot Senator Robert Kennedy on June 5, 1968, at the jubilant climax of his presidential primary victory in Los Angeles, California; two months before, on April 4, 1968, Dr. Martin Luther King was assassinated by James Earl Ray as he stood on the balcony of a Memphis motel. Once again, on May 15, 1972, four bullets cut down the governor of Alabama, George C. Wallace, as he campaigned for the Democratic presidential nomination in Laurel, Maryland. The governor is paralyzed from the waist down due to spinal cord damage, and doctors say his condition may be permanent.

Professor Hilsinger of Temple University inadvertently became involved in another activity which has gained international attention and concern: hijacking (see Box 30-1). A study by a team of psychologists from Ohio State University indicates that this once isolated and not too serious practice has become a political instrument of war (see Figure 30-1). From 1968 to the middle of 1971, there were 106 incidents of aerial piracy of United States aircraft alone. Eighty of these incidents were successful (Boltwood et al., 1972). Although twenty-eight of these hijackers have been convicted by courts and sentenced to terms totaling

---

*Richard Speck was convicted of killing eight student nurses in their dormitory at a Chicago hospital.

BOX 30-1 HIJACKED — AND ALIVE TO TELL THE TALE

The seat-belt sign clicks off and seven hijackers, scattered throughout the plane, stand up.

Hilsinger, a Temple University professor, looks up and there's "a guy 5 feet away from me with a gun. He shoots the guy in front of me. I guess he knew it was a security guard. Next to me, at my shoulder is another hijacker with a gun and a hand grenade.

"The hijacker who shot the man in front of me turns to face everyone in the tourist section. It's crowded, 94 people.

"As soon as the hijacker turns his head, the security man — who was only shot in the arm — jumps up and shoots the hijacker. He falls at the feet of three British people on a bird watching expedition — they were all in their 70s.

"Then the security man pumps a few more shots in him and runs down the aisle, shooting as he goes. Those security guys (four of them) are crack shots. One shoots twice down the aisle and drops some guy down there.

"Right then, the hijacker at my shoulder pulls the pin on the grenade. The first security guy runs back up the aisle again and sees the first hijacker trying to crawl on the floor. A girl hijacker runs up and throws her body over this guy. The security man bends down and one at a time, blows the head off both of them.

"Another security guard runs up the aisle and shoots the hijacker holding the live hand grenade." Hilsinger watches the man crumple and the grenade rolls toward his feet. The thought flashes: "I've got to get this son of a bitch the hell away from me" ("Hijacked — and Alive To Tell the Tale," 1973).

over 350 years in prison, hijacking continues to be a major source of danger and harassment to passengers and airline officials alike.*

Theory of Behavioral Contagion

It could be asked how contagion differs from the types of social influence already discussed: conformity, "pressure toward uniformity," social facilitation, and imitation. In *conformity* a conflict exists between one's personal reality and social reality as defined by others. The conflict is created by the actions of others but must be resolved by the individual alone. In contagion, however, conflict exists prior to the presence or influence of others and is resolved by their presence. The examples cited in this unit probably represent instances of troubled individuals who sought ways of resolving their difficulties but who experienced conflict in doing so. This conflict was reduced or eliminated only after these individuals had witnessed or become aware of others engaging publicly in "unacceptable" behaviors (hijacking airplanes, self-immolation, and mass murder). *Pressures toward uniformity* are

---

*As this unit was being prepared, five United States aircraft were hijacked.

Contagious Behaviors   255

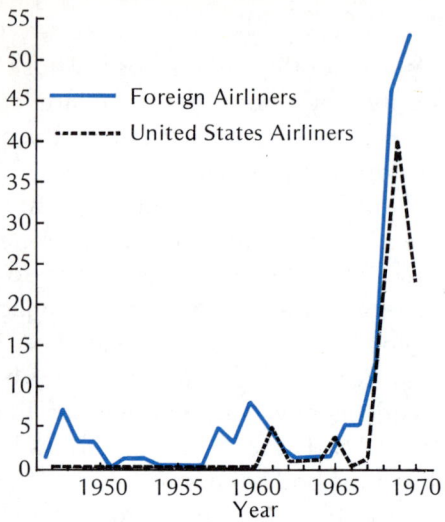

FIGURE 30-1 Foreign and United States airline hijackings, 1950–1970

explained by the same set of dynamics that explained conformity and are therefore conceptually different from contagion. *Social facilitation,* on the other hand, is a mechanism that explains how an observed behavior acts as a releaser for that same behavior in others. It differs from contagion in that there is no apparent conflict. Finally, *imitation* is the mere matching or copying of the behavior of a model. This is said to come about through the punishment of nonmatched responses between a leader (model) and a follower, or through the reward of matched behaviors. To some extent the term *imitation* may be considered basic to the various kinds of social influence. However, as will be seen, a theory of behavioral contagion attempts to explain the eliciting effect of a model by a unique set of dynamics.

Wheeler (1966) has developed a theory of behavioral contagion that helps us to understand these behaviors. Wheeler's theory attempts to explain the effect of a "model" upon the behavior of an observer. Behavioral contagion is said to occur when: (1) a behavior or incident occurs which serves as a source of instigation to an observer, (2) the behavior exists in the observer's response repertoire and there are no physical barriers or restraints to prevent the behavior from occurring, (3) the behavior is not being performed by the observer, and (4) the behavior is perceived and recognized by the observer. If an individual is instigated to perform a behavior in the absence of physical restraint and doesn't, it is assumed that a conflict exists between internal restraints and the instigation to perform.

Wheeler argues that the observation of a model performing a behavior reduces the observer's restraints against performing that and similar behaviors. Noting that aggression is one of the behaviors in our culture subject to numerous restraints led Wheeler to select aggression as a dependent variable in most of his research. Wheeler and Caggiula (1966) found increased overt interpersonal aggression in subjects who were allowed to observe an aggressive model. This focus fits well with the examples of contagious behaviors (self-immolation, murder and assassination, and hijacking of airplanes) cited above. Acts of aggression played a prominent role in each instance.

While it is not safe to generalize laboratory findings into a wide variety of social situations, the evidence does seem

BOX 30-2 THE EPIDERMIS EPIDEMIC: STREAKING

In his May, 1974, commencement address, University of Maryland President Wilson H. Elkins cited a list of milestones for the university during the year. Most of these citations were for accomplishments in the usual athletic endeavors — football, basketball, soccer. However, a loud roar and applause from the graduates and the audience greeted the citation for "streaking." The reference was to an increasingly popular activity in which men and women shed their clothes and run in the nude.

Psychologists and others disagree on when and why streaking became such a popular activity. However, most agree that it is nonsexual or even antisexual. The nonsexual aspect of the streaking phenomenon may explain why the reaction of society has been rather mild and good-humored. Streakers themselves claim just to be having fun. Others have characterized streaking as simply an attention-getting device or, more seriously, as an irreverence or attack on societal values. While each of these explanations may be valid, it seems equally compelling that the visibility of the streaking phenomenon in the media provides a modeling experience for individuals observing these events.

Reprinted by permission of Don Wright, The Miami News

"—They say streaking is a phenomenon directly related to the pressures and frustrations of our society. Was that who I thought it was?"

to provide reasonable support for restraint reduction as an explanation of the behavioral contagion witnessed in the acts of self-immolation, killing, and hijacking. In all cases, the wide coverage provided by the news media permitted individuals to observe or become aware of someone else engaging in behaviors against which there usually are strong internal restraints. Assuming that a given individual is instigated by aspects of his or her life to engage in antisocial or illegal behaviors, to be informed of someone else engaging in a similar activity undoubtedly makes it easier for that behavior to be performed.

Summarizing research by Kimbrell and Blake (1958) and Freed et al. (1955) in which greater amounts of contagion occurred under conditions of weak motivation, Wheeler (1966) concludes that the probability of behavioral contagion is greatest when the restraints against engaging in antisocial behaviors are just slightly greater than the desire to do so. Background and self-report information from individuals engaging in the antisocial and illegal behaviors cited above provide a basis for assuming instigation to engage in those or similar behaviors. Finally, Wheeler and Levine (1967) found that the similarity between the subject and the model did not affect the amount of aggression. Hence, it is not necessary for there to be any similarity between the actor in one situation and the actor in a subsequent incident of similar character. The profile of a typical assassin or hijacker may aid only in capturing suspects. The profile will have no bearing on the eliciting effect of the behavior once the act is committed and publicized.

Prosocial Behaviors and Bystander Intervention

Thus far we have concentrated on negative forms of behavior. It should also be pointed out that generous or altruistic models have been shown to elicit prosocial behaviors in a wide variety of situations. Rosenhan and White (1967) found that donating behavior in children was enhanced by observation of a generous adult model. Bryan and Test (1967) and Wagner and Wheeler (1969) obtained similar findings in adults observing adult models. Similarly, Wagner and Wheeler showed that helping decreases in the presence of a selfish model.

Berkowitz and Daniels (1964) have suggested that these prosocial behaviors are a matter of conditioned response to a norm of social responsibility. However, it could be that a model increases pressure toward or reduces restraints against positive behaviors. This is an issue that will certainly require more research. Evidence suggests that while people are deeply and constantly motivated toward prosocial behavior, they are simultaneously aware of the social norm to "mind their own business."

In March 1964, Kitty Genovese was attacked as she came home from work at three o'clock in the morning. From their individual apartments, thirty-eight of her neighbors stared out of their windows at what was going on and none came to her assistance. Even though her assailant took over half an hour to murder her, no one helped or even called the police.

This incident created sensational newspaper headlines and became the impetus to laboratory and field research by behavioral scientists on public apathy. While newspaper headlines cried "apathy" and "indifference," and others labeled the incident "moral callousness" or "loss of concern for our fellow man," Latané and Darley (1968) viewed the situation as similar to crowd behavior in other emergency situations, such as car accidents. As these authors point out, many emergency situations attract fascinated spectators who do not involve themselves in the action. Perhaps the conflict mentioned earlier between assisting others in emergencies and minding your own business is responsible for the failure to help. It certainly suggests a strange departure from the way conflict is resolved in the conformity studies discussed earlier in this division.

LABORATORY RESEARCH

Latané and his colleagues conducted a series of studies designed to provide some understanding of the type of situation typified by the Kitty Genovese murder, which is not uncommon:

Eleanor Bradley tripped and broke her leg while walking on Fifth Avenue in New York. Forty minutes passed and no one came to help.

A 17-year-old youth was stabbed in the stomach while riding the subway in New York. Although his assailants fled, eleven passengers sat and watched the youth bleed to death — none came to help.

An 18-year-old switchboard operator who was raped and beaten managed to escape from her assailant and rushed into the street naked and bleeding. Forty persons gathered and watched as the rapist attempted to drag her back into the building. No one made an effort to help.

Latané and Darley (1968) created an emergency situation by introducing non-toxic smoke into a room where subjects were responding to questionnaires. Would subjects report the smoke to someone, and if so, how soon? About half of the subjects who were in the room by themselves reported the situation to the experimenter within two minutes; 75 percent responded within six minutes. Although smoke so completely filled the room that subjects could barely see what they were doing, in group situations there was a tendency not to report the incident.

This same tendency was in evidence when subjects were waiting alone or with others and heard sounds from an adjacent office that suggested that someone was in distress (Latané and Rodin, 1969). After listening to two minutes of what sounded like someone falling off a chair and hurting her ankle, 70 percent of subjects waiting alone in an adjacent office rushed in to help. However, with two strangers in the same situation, 40 percent helping behavior occurred; and when a passive confederate was present, the number that would help was reduced to 7 percent. These same patterns of helping behavior occurred in a "shoplifting" situation and when the victim was presumably having a "seizure." In the latter case, 83 percent helping behavior in a situation in which the subject was alone decreased to 31 percent helping behavior in a group of four persons.

These studies have led to the conclusion that helping behavior becomes less likely as the number of bystanders increases. In attempting to understand this phenomenon further, Latané and his colleagues developed a model of the intervention process which states that persons go through a series of four decision points before deciding whether to act. First, the bystander has to (1) *notice* that something is happening; and then he or she must (2) *interpret* the situation. If the bystander decides that something is wrong or that an emergency exists, the next decision is (3) to determine his or her *responsibility* and, finally, (4) to determine what *form of assistance*, if any, is necessary. Besides the possible embarrassment of making the wrong decision and acting stupidly, "diffusion of responsibility" — someone else will do it — has been advanced as a reason why people don't help others in emergency situations.

FIELD RESEARCH

Most of the studies discussed above were conducted in the laboratory. A field study, however, produced strikingly different results. Bystanders in a New York subway faced with a staged "emergency" situation — a drunk or a handicapped victim of a fall — helped overwhelmingly in both situations; individuals appearing to be ill were more likely to receive help than those who appeared to be drunk. More important, however, there was no "diffusion of responsibility." That is, help was not less frequent or slower in larger groups than in smaller groups (Piliavin, Rodin, and Piliavin, 1969). The authors of this study are developing a model which handles their results and perhaps accounts for the difference between this and the previous studies. The model assumes that emergency situations create states of emotional arousal which are interpreted differently as a function of the situation. Empathy, similarity to victim, and possible rewards (praise from victim and others) or costs (embarrassment, physical harm) are suggested as determinants of helping behavior in emergency situations.

The implication of these apparently divergent outcomes regarding bystander behavior is that a good deal more research and investigation of real-life crises is needed. Milgram (1970) has suggested that we might also pay attention to factors external to individuals: large numbers, density, and heterogeneity. These factors certainly play some role in people's attempts to deal with their fellow human beings.

SUMMARY

There are numerous examples of people's tendency to respond to authority rather than to a personal sense of morality. In the name of obedience, individuals will perform acts of destruction, as has been demonstrated both in Milgram's laboratory experiment and in the nonexperimental case of Lt. Calley at My Lai. Analysis of public response to such acts indicates that it is believed that the perpetrators or aggressors dismiss considerations of individual responsibility. Thus, it becomes easier to respond to authority or other external pressures.

Group norms serve to regulate an individual's behavior in some organized way as the group pursues its goals or objectives. Groups usually dispense rewards to members who conform, and there may be severe consequences for deviation. Research has indicated that several important functions are served by pressures to uniformity in groups: (1) group goals are achieved more easily; (2) group survival is greater; (3) groups often serve as a source of confirmation of opinions, abilities, and appropriateness of emotional and bodily states; and (4) groups facilitate members in defining their relations to their social environment. Lab studies have been performed by Sherif and Asch, who have studied conformity in judgments of autokinetic movement (Sherif) and length of lines (Asch). Most subjects facing a conflict between their own judgments and those of others suffer great discomfort, and few can completely ignore the group pressure. Crutchfield has also studied conformity using an automated modification of the Sherif and Asch paradigms. His approach has the advantage of avoiding the use of confederates, of allowing more efficient testing of subjects, and of permitting a wider range of stimulus materials.

An important source of social influence is in power relationships. Power is defined as the maximum force which person A can exert on person B, minus the maximum resisting force which person B can mobilize in the opposite direction. French and Raven delineate five bases of social power: (1) reward power: A's ability to reward B for compliance with desired behavior; (2) coercive power: the ability of A to influence the attainment of bad outcomes for B; (3) legitimate power: a function of B's internalizing group norms that give A the right to exert influence on him; (4) referent power: A's ability to influence B as a result of B's identification with A; and (5) expert power: A's ability to influence B as a result of B's perception of A's knowledge or ability. Although this schema contains some basic weaknesses, these conceptualizations of social power are useful for examining some of the sources of social influence in groups.

The destructive outcomes associated with negative attitudes, especially racism and prejudice, are of a pervasive and universal nature. Thus, an understanding of attitudes might be helpful in clarifying the nature of prejudice and racism. An attitude is a positive or negative feeling about some person, object, or phenomenon that predisposes us to some action. Attitudes are learned and are relatively enduring ways of adapting to one's environment. Attitudes cannot be observed and, therefore, must be inferred from observable behaviors, causing problems of validity and consistency.

There are three components of attitudes: (1) cognitive: the belief-disbelief or information aspect; (2) affective: emotions and feelings; and (3) behavioral: how one responds to the attitude object.

Festinger's theory of cognitive dissonance provides an explanation of cognitive inconsistencies and how they are handled. The term *dissonance* refers to an inconsistency among two or more cognitive elements within an individual. The theory holds that dissonance is psychologically uncomfortable and will motivate the person to reduce dissonance and achieve consonance.

Conformity to and identification with one's group may create a distrust for nonmembers, forming the basis for racism and prejudice.

Jones describes three kinds of racism: (1) individual; (2) institutional; and (3) cultural. The conceptualization of individual racism is similar to classic definitions of prejudice. Institutional racism is (a) a deliberate manipulation of institutions to achieve racist objectives and (b) the by-product of institutional practices resulting in restrictions of a racial nature to the access and privileges of institutions. Finally, cultural racism is seen as the combined expression of individual and institutional racism in terms of superiority of one's cultural heritage over that of other races.

In seeking a remedy for the problems of prejudice and racism, the emphasis has shifted from attitude change to behavioral change. Allport's equal-status contact hypothesis suggests that contact among individuals of equal status will reduce prejudiced attitudes. However, there are many situations in which racial contacts do not meet the requirements of equal status. Additionally, it may be too simplistic to conclude that the stereotypes and biases are automatically reduced by contact, no matter how ideal. Much racial prejudice seems to be deeply rooted in the character structure of individuals and in social institutions. It seems that favorable intergroup relationships will come about through system changes that facilitate cooperation, mutual trust, and sharing of social power.

Wheeler has developed a theory of behavioral contagion which attempts to explain the effect of a "model" upon the behavior of an observer, arguing that observation of a model performing a behavior reduces the observer's restraints against performing that and similar behaviors. The theory has been applied to contagious behaviors such as self-immolation, political assassination, and airplane hijacking. On the other hand, generous or altruistic models have been shown to elicit prosocial behaviors.

Many emergency situations attract fascinated spectators who do not involve themselves in the action. Latané and his colleagues conducted a series of studies designed to provide some understanding of such situations. These studies have concluded that the larger the number of bystanders, the less likely helping behavior is to occur, due to "diffusion of responsibility." However, a field study showed that bystanders faced with a staged "emergency" in a New York subway helped overwhelmingly with no "diffusion of responsibility." In an attempt to account for these apparently divergent outcomes, a model is being developed which assumes that emergency situations create states of emotional arousal which are interpreted differently as a function of the situation. A good deal more research and investigation are needed.

GLOSSARY

Affective component: that part of an attitude that deals with emotions and feelings

Attitude: an inferred construct, assumed to be acquired through experience, involving a set of beliefs and affects concerning some class of people, events, or actions

Authoritarianism: a basic personality style that includes a set of organized beliefs, values, and preferences, including submission to authority, identification with authority, denial of feelings, and cynicism

Autokinetic effect: the tendency for a stationary light, when viewed in an otherwise completely darkened room, to appear to move

Behavior orientation: the component of an attitude determining how a person will respond in a given context

Causation: a cause-and-effect relationship among two or more variables; one variable directly affects the other

Coercive power: the ability of an individual to influence the attainment of bad outcomes for another

Cognitive component: that part of an attitude which includes its belief-disbelief aspects

Cognitive dissonance: a state in which a person holds two beliefs, or cognitions, which are inconsistent with each other

Collective wisdom: opinions of a group used to evaluate one's own behavior; the basis for a good deal of conformity

Compliance: conformity based on one's need for a favorable reaction from the group

Conformity: behavior that is in agreement with that of the others in a group

Consistency: correspondence between a stated attitude and an overt behavioral act

Correlation: the statistical relationship between two or more variables

Cultural racism: the combined individual and institutional expressions of superiority of one cultural heritage over that of other races

Destructive obedience: acts of destruction to human life carried out in the name of obedience to authority and not necessarily consistent with personal or private convictions

Deviation: nonconformity to group norms; behavior directly antithetical to the normative group expectations

Discrimination: behavior that treats certain individuals unfairly and is based upon their membership in a specific group

Ego: according to Freud, that part of the personality oriented toward acting reasonably and realistically

Ethnocentrism: a rejection of foreigners, aliens, and all outside groups and a belief that one's group or nationality is the best in all respects

Expert power: the ability of an individual to exert influence on another as a result of that other's perception of the individual's knowledge or ability

Group norm: a standard or behavioral expectation shared by group members against which the validity of perceptions is judged and the appropriateness of feelings and behavior is evaluated

Group norm theory of destructive behavior:

a theory stating that adherence to certain beliefs of groups which may become codified can require members to work against individuals who violate these codes

Identification: acceptance of influence because one wants a satisfying relationship with others

Individual racism: a belief in the superiority of one's own race over another, and the behavioral acts that maintain those superior and inferior positions

Institutional racism: the conscious and unconscious manipulation of institutions to achieve racist objectives, and the byproducts of certain institutional practices which operate to restrict on a racial basis the choices, rights, mobility, and access of groups of individuals

Internalization: acceptance of influence because the behavior engaged in is satisfying in and of itself

Legitimacy: a relationship among values within a situation

Legitimate power: ability of an individual to exert influence on another as a function of that other's internalization of group norms

Norm: a socially defined and enforced standard concerning the way an individual should interpret the world or behave in it

Perception: one's immediate experience of other persons or objects, gained through the sense organs but somewhat modified by one's personal characteristics and by social influences

Prejudice: a strong negative attitude based upon overgeneralization, lack of information, or misinformation about a group

Projection: a defense mechanism in which one seeks to alleviate conflict by seeing in others the motives or attributes that one sees in oneself and which cause anxiety

Racism: systematic oppression, subjugation, and control of one racial group by another dominant or more powerful racial group

Reality testing: evaluating one's own attitudes and abilities by comparing them with those of other people

Referent power: ability of an individual to exert influence on another as a result of that other's identification with the individual

Reward power: influence resulting from the ability of an individual to reward another for compliance with desired behaviors

Role conflict: a situation in which an individual is expected to play two roles that involve competing or antagonistic responses

Scientific precision: a quality of a statement or theory that has been derived empirically through experimental methods

Social-comparison theory: a point of view that states that one evaluates one's own attitudes and abilities by comparing them with those of other, particularly similar, people

Socializing agents: those individuals and situations responsible for the "growing-up" process, in which the child acquires distinctive values, attitudes, and personality characteristics

Social power: the maximum force which an individual can exert on another minus the maximum resisting force which the other can mobilize in the opposite direction

Social reality: the group consensus or judgment used to verify one's own judgment

Social solidarity: the result of all the forces acting on all the members of a group to remain in the group

Stereotype: a simplified and standard image, often highly evaluative, inaccurate, and rigidified, of a group of people

Validity: the accuracy or correctness of measurement; the degree to which a stated attitude represents what it is supposed to (the underlying belief)

Value: a standard that influences one's decision making

REFERENCES

Adorno, T. W., Frenkel-Brunswick, E., Levinson, D. J., and Sanford, R. N. *The authoritarian personality.* New York: Harper & Row, 1950.

Allport, G. W. *The nature of prejudice.* New York: Doubleday, 1954.

Asch, S. E. Studies of independence and submission to group pressure: I. A minority of one against a unanimous majority. *Psychological Monographs,* 1956, *70*(9, Whole No. 416).

Barron, F. K. Some personality correlates of independence of judgment. *Journal of Consulting Psychology,* 1953, *21,* 287–297.

Berkowitz, L., and Daniels, L. R. Responsibility and dependency. *Journal of Abnormal and Social Psychology,* 1964, *66,* 427–436.

Berkowitz, L., and Howard, R. Reactions to opinion deviates as affected by affiliation need and group member interdependence. *Sociometry,* 1959, *22,* 81–91.

Biesanz, J., and Smith, L. M. Race relations of Panama and the Canal Zone. *American Journal of Sociology,* 1951, *77,* 7–14.

Billingsley, A., and Giovannoni, J. M. *Children of the storm: Black children and American child welfare.* New York: Harcourt Brace Jovanovich, 1972.

Boltwood, C. E., Cooper, M. R., Fein, V. E., and Washburn, P. W. Skyjacking, airline security, and passenger reactions: Toward a complex model for prediction. *American Psychologist,* 1972, *27,* 539–545.

Brown, Dee. *Bury my heart at Wounded Knee.* New York: Holt, Rinehart and Winston, 1970.

Bryan, J. H., and Test, M. A. Models and helping: Naturalistic studies in aiding behavior. *Journal of Personality and Social Psychology,* 1967, *6,* 400–407.

Carmichael, S., and Hamilton, C. V. *Black power: The politics of liberation in America.* New York: Free Press, 1967.

Clark, K., and Clark, M. Racial identification and preference in Negro children. In T. Newcomb and E. Hartley (Eds.), *Readings in social psychology.* New York: Holt, 1947.

Crutchfield, R. S. Conformity and character. *American Psychologist,* 1955, *10,* 191–198.

Deutsch, M., and Collins, M. E. *Interracial*

housing: A psychological evaluation of a social experiment. Minneapolis: University of Minnesota Press, 1951.

Emerson, R. Deviation and rejection: An experimental replication. *American Sociological Review*, 1954, *19*, 688–693.

Festinger, L. *A theory of cognitive dissonance*. Evanston, Ill.: Row, Peterson, 1957.

Festinger, L. A theory of social comparison processes. *Human Relations*, 1954, *7*, 117–140.

Frankl, V. E. *Man's search for meaning: An introduction to logotherapy*. New York: Washington Square Press, 1963.

Freed, A. M., Chandler, P. G., Blake, R. R., and Mouton, J. S. Stimulus and background factors in sign violation. *Journal of Personality*, 1955, *23*, 499.

French, J. R. P., Jr., and Raven, B. H. The bases of social power. In D. Cartwright (Ed.), *Studies in social power*. Ann Arbor: University of Michigan Press, 1959.

Goldberg, P. A., Pheterson, G. I., and Kiesler, S. B. Evaluation of the performance of women as a function of their sex, achievement, and personal history. *Journal of Personality and Social Psychology*, 1971, *19*, 114–118.

"Hijacked — and Alive to Tell the Tale." *The Washington Post*, January 21, 1973.

Hoffman, M. L. Some psychodynamic factors in compulsive conformity. *Journal of Abnormal and Social Psychology*, 1953, *48*, 383–393.

Janis, I. L. Personality correlates of susceptibility to persuasion. *Journal of Personality*, 1954, *22*, 504–518.

Jones, J. M. *Prejudice and racism*. Reading, Mass.: Addison-Wesley, 1972.

Kelman, H. C. Compliance, identification, internalization: Three processes of attitude change. *Journal of Conflict Resolution*, 1958, *2*, 51–60.

Kelman, H. C. Processes of opinion change. *Public Opinion Quarterly*, 1961, *25*, 57–78.

Kelman, H. C., and Lawrence, L. H. American response to the trial of Lt. William L. Calley. *Psychology Today*, June 1972, p. 41.

Kennedy, J. F. *Profiles in courage*. New York: Franklin Watts, 1955.

Kimbrell, D., and Blake, R. R. Motivation factors in the violation of prohibition. *Journal of Abnormal and Social Psychology*, 1958, *56*, 132–133.

Kutner, B., Wilkins, C., and Yarrow, P. R. Verbal attitudes and overt behavior. *Journal of Abnormal and Social Psychology*, 1952, *47*, 649–652.

LaPiere, R. T. Attitudes vs. actions. *Social Forces*, 1934, *13*, 230–237.

Latané, B., and Darley, J. M. Group inhibition of bystander intervention in emergencies. *Journal of Personality and Social Psychology*, 1968, *10*, 215–221.

Latané, B., and Rodin, J. A lady in distress: Inhibiting effects of friends and strangers on bystander intervention. *Journal of Experimental and Social Psychology*, 1969, *5*, 189–202.

McGrath, J. E. *Social psychology: A brief introduction*. New York: Holt, Rinehart and Winston, 1964.

Milgram, S. Behavioral study of obedience. *Journal of Abnormal and Social Psychology*, 1963, *67*, 371–378.

Milgram, S. Some conditions of obedience and disobedience to authority. In I. D. Steiner and M. Fishbein (Eds.), *Current studies in social psychology*. New York: Holt, Rinehart and Winston, 1965.

Milgram, S. The experience of living in cities. *Science,* 1970, *167,* 1461–1468.

Newcomb, T. M. *Personality and social changes.* New York: Holt, 1943.

Patrick, John. *Teahouse of the August Moon.* New York: Van Rees Press, 1952.

Pettigrew, T. F. Social distance attitudes of South African students. *Social Forces,* 1960, *38,* 246–253.

Piliavin, I. M., Rodin, J., and Piliavin, J. A. Good Samaritanism: An underground phenomenon? *Journal of Personality and Social Psychology,* 1969, *13,* 289–299.

Rand, Ayn. *The Fountainhead.* New York: Bobbs-Merrill Co., 1943.

Rosenhan, D., and White, G. M. Observation and rehearsal as determinants of prosocial behavior. *Journal of Personality and Social Psychology,* 1967, *5,* 424–431.

Rosenkranz, P. The effect of sex role stereotypes on clinical judgments of mental health. Paper presented at the meeting of the New England Association of Social Psychology, Hanover, New Hampshire, October 1968.

Sampson, E. E., and Brandon, A. C. The effects of role and opinion deviation on small group behavior. *Sociometry,* 1964, *27,* 261–281.

Schachter, S. Deviation, rejection, and communication. *Journal of Abnormal and Social Psychology,* 1951, *46,* 190–201.

Schachter, S., and Singer, J. E. Cognitive, social and physiological determinants of emotional state. *Psychological Review,* 1962, *69,* 379–399.

Second, P. F., and Backman, C. W. *Social psychology.* New York: McGraw-Hill, 1964.

Sherif, M. *In common predicament.* Boston: Houghton Mifflin, 1966.

Sherif, M. *The psychology of social norms.* New York: Harper, 1936.

Skinner, B. F. *Beyond freedom and dignity.* New York: Bantam Books, 1971.

Snow, C. P. Either-or. *Progressive,* February 1961, p. 24.

Sumner, W. G. *Folkways.* Boston: Ginn, 1906.

Wagner, C., and Wheeler, L. Model, need, and cost effects in helping behavior. *Journal of Personality and Social Psychology,* 1969, *12,* 111–116.

Wheeler, L. Toward a theory of behavioral contagion. *Psychological Review,* 1966, *73,* 179–192.

Wheeler, L., and Caggiula, A. R. The contagion of aggression. *Journal of Experimental Social Psychology,* 1966, *2,* 1–10.

Wheeler, L., and Levine, L. Observer similarity in the contagion of aggression. *Sociometry,* 1967, *30,* 41–49.

SUGGESTED READINGS

Allport, G. W. *The nature of prejudice.* New York: Doubleday, 1954.

Freedman, J. L., Carlsmith, J. M., and Sears, D. O. *Social psychology.* Englewood Cliffs, N.J.: Prentice-Hall, 1970.

Jones, J. M. *Prejudice and racism.* Reading, Mass.: Addison-Wesley, 1972.

Sherif, M. *The psychology of social norms.* New York: Harper, 1936.

Wheeler, L. *Interpersonal influence.* Boston: Allyn & Bacon, 1970.

Zimbardo, P. H., and Ebbesen, E. B. *Influencing attitudes and changing behavior.* Reading, Mass.: Addison-Wesley, 1969.

Photo by Lin Oakerson

H

Environment:
Outside and Inside

Unit 31
The "Behavioral Sink"

There could be no escape from the behavioral consequences of rising population density. By the end of 27 months the population had become stabilized at 150 adults. Yet adult mortality was so low that 5,000 adults might have been expected from the observed reproduction rate. The reason this larger population did not materialize was that infant mortality was extremely high. Even with only 150 adults in the enclosure, stress from social interaction led to such disruption of maternal behavior that few young survived.

Calhoun, 1962, p. 3.

The larger implication of this work is that density should not be viewed as necessarily a social evil. Although having many people in a small area presents great problems in logistics, organization, potential pollution, noise, etc., it may not automatically have a negative effect on the people involved. Density per se is not a simple negative, aversive stimulus; and more particularly, there is no evidence that it produces a decrement in performance. High density should be considered in terms of the problems it presents, but should, for the moment, not be considered inherently evil. Thus, if the problems of a logistical nature can be solved, it may be that we will want to encourage or at least allow high density rather than discourage it. This is not to say that we want to allow or encourage population growth; but given a particular population, we may want to encourage concentration rather than, as is the fashion now, rail against the evils of urban concentrations and blame them on negative effects of density per se. This is, of course, all speculative; but for the moment, this research indicates

> that density per se is not inherently evil. That is all we know for the moment.
>
> Freedman, Klevansky, and Ehrlich, 1971, p. 24.

These are obviously not the last words on overcrowdedness and population control; but they do appear in the context of widespread concerns regarding improved technology and its inevitable impact on both the destruction and the expansion of life. Improvements in medical science have given people a greater amount of control over their life spans. However, in the absence of effective birth control, we are becoming overpopulated. In not quite two thousand years, the world population has grown from 250 million to approximately 3 billion. And with still more anticipated improvement in medicines — and longer life spans — we are surely in for overcrowdedness, economic stresses, and increasing governmental control. DDT, penicillin, and better drinking water will continue to make possible an annual increase in population of many million people.

In this division, we are concerned with improvements in technology that contribute to increasing the quality of life but that simultaneously have undesirable byproducts: noise and pollution, and excessive or unwanted behavior control and destruction. To understand these factors as they relate to crowdedness and overpopulation, it might be well to discuss population theories and their explanations for survival and adaptation.

POPULATION THEORIES

Environmental. This approach attempts to relate animal cycles to physical and biological events. Temperature, rainfall, diseased organisms, lunar cycles, and sun spots are all thought to cause increases and decreases in population size. Very simply, this theory suggests that environmental factors such as temperature and epidemics control reproductive activities. Extremely warm weather is likely to lead to a reduction in behaviors that result in higher birth rates; the opposite is probably true in extremely cold climates. Similarly, widespread disease will most likely have a negative or adverse effect on population growth.

Interaction. The interaction explanation describes relationships between animal populations and aspects of the biological environment that control population growth and decline. Examples of these interactions are prey and predator, herbivore and plant, and parasite and host. In all cases, population survival is a function of the availability of food supply. If organisms eat all available food they will starve to death; however, food supply will regrow in a number of years and the cycle will repeat itself. Cycling can only be stopped by regulating population according to food supply.

Self-regulation. This theory, also referred to as self-limitation, states that forces which promote population increase are strongest when population is at its lowest point and weakest when population is at its highest. This explanation has been likened to the concept of feedback: behavioral output affects subsequent behavior in the same way that temperature changes affect the thermostat in your home. The number of animals in a given species at one time is a function of *birth rate*, *death rate*, and *movement* from place to place. The impact of birth rate and death rate on population size is obvious. However, movement and its implications for density are a bit more complicated. Population density (or crowdedness) has been related to various social stresses (fighting, interference with maternal behaviors, and antagonist behaviors) which in turn have resulted in population decline or instability.

Behavioral Sink

It has been observed that most animals in a reproducing population reach an equilibrium with conditions in the environment. The distribution of food, water, and other environmental resources necessary for survival sets limits on the amount of population growth. Temperature, for example, has been related to variations in size of the English sparrow in the United States. Large size is of survival value in extremely cold climates, and small size is of survival value in extremely warm climates. Since temperature controls or regulates an important aspect of the survival of English sparrows (i.e., their physical size), temperature has an indirect effect on the size of their population. Disruption of maternal physiology, such as a lowering of fetal nutrition, can also limit population growth.

John B. Calhoun (1947, 1948, 1962) has demonstrated on numerous occasions that when laboratory rats in a confined space are allowed to reproduce without limits to the point of overcrowding, abnormal patterns of behavior develop which can lead to extinction of the whole population. Animals were observed to engage in behavioral patterns that led to the development of what was called a *behavioral sink*. That is, animals would crowd together in greatest numbers in one small part of their total living space which was interconnected to other living areas (see Figure 31-1). As many as sixty of the eighty rats in each of several experimental populations would assemble at one time in this compartment to eat. As a result, extreme population densities developed in the area where the animals were fed. Individual rats rarely ate unless they were in the presence of other rats. Eating in social groups is atypical in rats. However, the animals began to perform their eating and other biological activities in this one compartment as though these activities were primarily social.

While these habits did not interfere with the nutritional needs of the animals, they did disrupt other equally vital behaviors such as the courting of sex partners, the building of nests, and the nursing and care of the young. Other disturbances that have been noted include damage to various internal organs, notably the adrenals. Extreme crowdedness produced social stresses that caused enlarging of the adrenals, which rendered the rats susceptible to additional stress and strain. Enlarged adrenals require increases in hormonal output from the

FIGURE 31-1 Effect of population density on the behavior and social organization of rats was studied by confining groups of 80 animals in a room divided into four pens. Development of a "behavioral sink," which further increased population in one pen, is reflected in the lower right pen.

Copyright © 1962 by Scientific American, Inc.

pituitary, which in turn bring about a decrease in hormones serving the reproductive organs. The net result of these internal chemical changes is a decline in birth rate and the birth of unhealthy offspring.

Females were most affected by these abnormal changes. Many were unable to carry pregnancy to full term or to survive delivery of their litters. Infant mortality ran as high as 96 percent among the most disoriented groups. Those mothers who survived pregnancy and delivery were often unable to perform their maternal functions. Among the males, the behavioral disturbances ranged from overactivity to pathological withdrawal.

In still other studies, animals were observed to arrange themselves in dominance hierarchies and engage in aggressive behaviors toward one another. Wounds received from these fights contributed to the animals' becoming socially inhibited. The socially dominant families weaned as many as ten litters from twelve pregnancies, whereas the socially inhibited individuals weaned only one litter. These experiments indicate very clearly that overcrowdedness produces aggressive behaviors and physiological disturbances which have negative effects on population growth through either poor fetal nutrition, breakdown in maternal behavior, or abnormal sexual patterns on the part of males (Calhoun, 1949, 1962).

It is interesting to speculate on the implications of these developments for human ecology. Many authors have associated declining birth rates and increasing death rates with crowded inner city living conditions — especially conditions found in ghetto areas. While it is tempting to associate profound physiological effects with overcrowded human conditions, this relationship must remain speculative at present because of the lack of solid evidence. It should also be pointed out that human populations show alarming growth rates, primarily in densely populated urban communities.

Conflict and Aggression

The many instances of aggression and violence in our country represent additional ways in which our viability is being threatened. It is often suggested that aggression and conflict in humans are best understood in the context of animal aggression and overcrowdedness. Animals fight among themselves to establish dominance, to establish territorial rights, or both. Humans purportedly engage in aggression for both reasons. Konrad Lorenz in *On Aggression* (1966) and Robert Ardrey in *The Territorial Imperative* (1966) both describe aggression in animals as a ritual with the function of species preservation. That is, animal populations distribute themselves over territories so that the food supply will be adequate to assure the survival of its members. Typically, animals defend these territories against intrusion, primarily against members of their own species. These acts are referred to as a ritual because physical contact rarely occurs — violence is even more infrequent. Animals simply mark the boundaries to their territory by releasing glandular secretions, making vocal sounds, or assuming body postures that signal "intended" violence to the invading animal. These are usually sufficient to drive the would-be invader away without any violence.

It is easy to oversimplify or inappropriately extend these findings to humans. Several authors have done just that in attempting to understand conflict and aggression in human societies. Specifically, gang rivalry in densely populated cities has often been attributed to territorial disputes; internationally, it has been noted that most wars have been fought over border disputes and disagreements over land. These comparisons, however, do not take into account that territorial behaviors in animals are instinctive and related to food-gathering behaviors. Man, on the other hand, has a highly developed central nervous system (CNS) and therefore engages in few if any instinctive behaviors. Additionally, man enjoys a greater versatility of social roles and holds simultaneous membership in a variety of primary, secondary, and reference groups, such as the family, fraternities, and professional group membership, respectively. Therefore, understanding aggression in man requires a broader perspective.

Unit 32
It's All in Your Head

PROTEST POSTPONES VIRGINIA BRAIN SURGERY

Brain surgery to modify the behavior of a 22-year-old mental patient from Arlington who partly blinded himself — scheduled for today at the Medical College of Virginia in Richmond — was postponed yesterday after a friend, who may be a fellow patient, protested to authorities.

Protest postpones Virginia brain surgery, 1973.

The controversy behind this story includes a widespread debate over the use of surgical techniques to control behavior (psychosurgery). Psychosurgery is a medical procedure for removing carefully located areas of the brain known to be associated with specific behaviors. The procedure is accomplished with scalpel, electrical current, or other means. In the case cited above, the area to be removed is called the amygdala, part of the limbic system (center of attention, emotion, and memory). Electrical stimulation of the amygdala causes flight and defense responses. Surgical removal of the amygdala brings about a reduction in aggressive behavior — even to the point of taming a wild animal.

In its earlier form, prefrontal lobotomy, the operative procedure involved simply cutting nerve fibers in the frontal lobe of the brain. A prefrontal lobotomy was usually recommended to calm the more combatant or physically aggressive patient. With the advent of psychoactive drugs (tranquilizers), the prefrontal lobotomy became a rarely used technique. With the recent discoveries in brain localization, some neurosurgeons now believe they can more precisely control behavior through surgery.

Various behaviors and their relationship to specific areas of the brain will be covered in the remainder of this division. Much information has been gathered on brain functioning through the use of both electrical stimulation and surgical lesions.

Electrical stimulation of the brain has produced behaviors as general as muscular tremors and visual sensations and as specific as eating responses and copulation. These techniques date back to 1870, when two German scientists, Fritsch and Hitzig, applied electrical currents to the exposed cortices of dogs. When a dog was stimulated in the left hemisphere of the brain, muscular movement in the right leg occurred; similar stimulation in the right hemisphere produced muscular movement in the left leg.

Other researchers have demonstrated that specific behavior changes occur when a portion of the brain is removed. For example, removal of damaged tissue in the temporal lobes has produced a cessation of seizure activity. This research, generally performed on lower animals, has produced an abundance of information relating the anatomy of the brain to specific behaviors. The kind of psychosurgery mentioned above is an outgrowth of this research history. To understand better the relationship between the central nervous system and complex behavior requires a knowledge of the structure of the brain.

The Human Brain

The brain has approximately 14 billion nerve cells, called neurons, which transmit and receive impulses to and from one another. In most instances these neurons behave according to the *all-or-none principle,* which states that if a neuron is stimulated it will either become fully activated or will not respond at all. If there is only a slight activation, the impulse will move a small distance and then diminish in its capacity to continue its activity. Impulses being transmitted to the central nervous system clearly obey the all-or-none principle.

The interconnecting neurons of interest in this discussion are located in the brain and the spinal cord. The brain is that portion of the central nervous system encased in the skull. During embryological development, three enlargements occur in the head region. These enlargements eventually become the major parts of the human brain: the forebrain, the midbrain, and the hindbrain (see Figure 32-1).

THE FOREBRAIN

The *cerebrum* or *cerebral cortex* is the main portion of the brain, as well as the largest. It occupies the upper part of the skull and consists of two equal portions called *hemispheres.* In recent years, most of the research conducted on the brain has studied the subcortical structures of the forebrain. The first structure of importance here is the *corpus collosum,* which consists of a bundle of fibers that connects the left hemisphere with the right hemisphere. This connection accounts for the coordination between the two halves of the brain.

The remaining parts of the subcortex compose the *diencephalon:* the *thalamus*

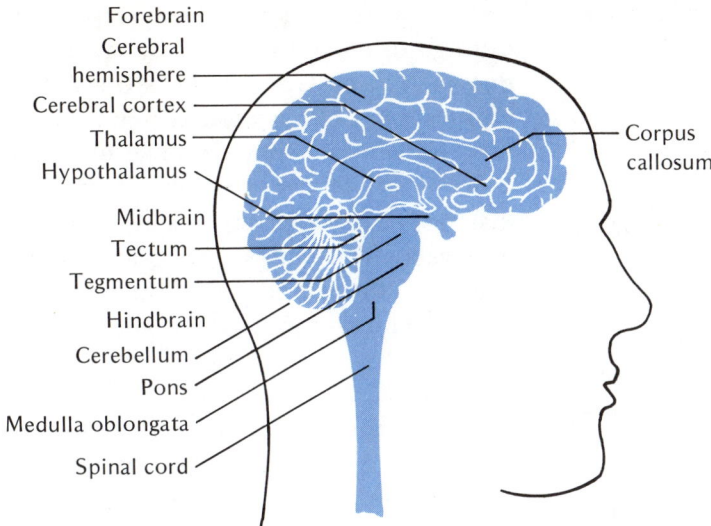

FIGURE 32-1 The principal parts of the human brain

and the *hypothalamus*. The thalamus functions as a relay station for neural transmission and coordination between the lower brain centers and the cerebral cortex.

Perhaps no other structure of the brain has received in recent years as much experimental attention as the hypothalamus. The hypothalamus, about the size of a walnut, has been identified in conjunction with the pituitary gland as an important controller of voluntary behavior, emotion, and thinking. It is instrumental in the bodily expression of emotion and governs internal organs. The hypothalamus, septal area, amygdala, and cingulate gyrus are important structures of the *limbic system* and have played a critical role in psychosurgery and electrical stimulation of the brain (ESB). Stimulation of these areas has produced feeding behavior, sleep, pupil dilation, and sexual behavior. Olds and Milner (1954) identified the septal area as the site of pleasure; electrical stimulation of the amygdala has produced violent outbursts of a type associated with epilepsy; and surgical destruction of the cingulate gyrus has led to improvement in patients suffering from manic-depressive psychosis. While these experimental findings are highly exciting and significant, it should be remembered that the limbic system varies from species to species and therefore we must be cautious in relating these outcomes to attempted applications in man.

Peripheral Nervous System

The peripheral nervous system is made up of nerves that connect the central nervous system (CNS) with receptors (sense organs) and effectors (organs of response — muscles and glands). This system is divided into two components: (1) a *somatic component* which controls the skeletal system and (2) a *visceral component* which controls glands and smooth muscles.

SOMATIC COMPONENT

The somatic component consists of sensory and motor neurons that produce body movement. This is a highly developed relationship, one which results in the ability to move parts of the body with precision. For example, we can move a given part (leg, finger, arm, etc.) without moving any of the adjacent parts. The precision involved here helps explain such finely coordinated behaviors as painting, sewing, and walking on a tightrope.

VISCERAL COMPONENT

The visceral component, referred to as the *autonomic nervous system,* consists of nerves that come directly from the brain and the spinal cord and control internal and external signs of emotion. The activity here is more diffuse and primitive than the activity of the somatic component. The visceral component is further divided into the *sympathetic* and *parasympathetic* nervous systems (see Figure 32-2). These two systems act in opposition; when one controls the actions of a given organ, the other acts to inhibit or stop that action.

Sympathetic nervous system. The sympathetic system is activated most commonly when an individual is in an emergency situation; for example, when the individual's life is threatened. Victims of automobile accidents and similar crisis situations often report engaging in extraordinary behaviors that seem impossible during normal times. These behaviors are due in part to sympathetic arousal. The famous physiologist Cannon noted the way in which certain bodily functions prepare organisms for emergencies. In instances of fear or rage, we experience increased heart rates, the liver releases sugar to the muscles, and an increased flow of adrenalin stops the digestive functions.

Parasympathetic nervous system. In contrast, the parasympathetic system regularizes the body and controls vital functions such as digestion and elimination. Its chief function is to conserve body energy. This is accomplished by a slowing of the heart rate. For purposes of restoring energy, there is an increase in activity in the gastrointestinal tract.

Detecting emotions. Occasionally, these emotional or bodily states cannot be detected simply by observing individuals. Emotional reactions can be small changes that do not show easily, or we may deliberately control facial expressions in order to hide our emotions from others. Perhaps you can recall the embarrassment of asking or being asked for a first date and the effort put forth to control and not reveal the awkwardness of the situation. Suspected criminals being questioned by the police usually make strong efforts to hide or disguise any emotional reaction that may incriminate them.

While most of us are fairly successful at disguising external signs of emotion under these circumstances, there are instruments that can detect bodily changes

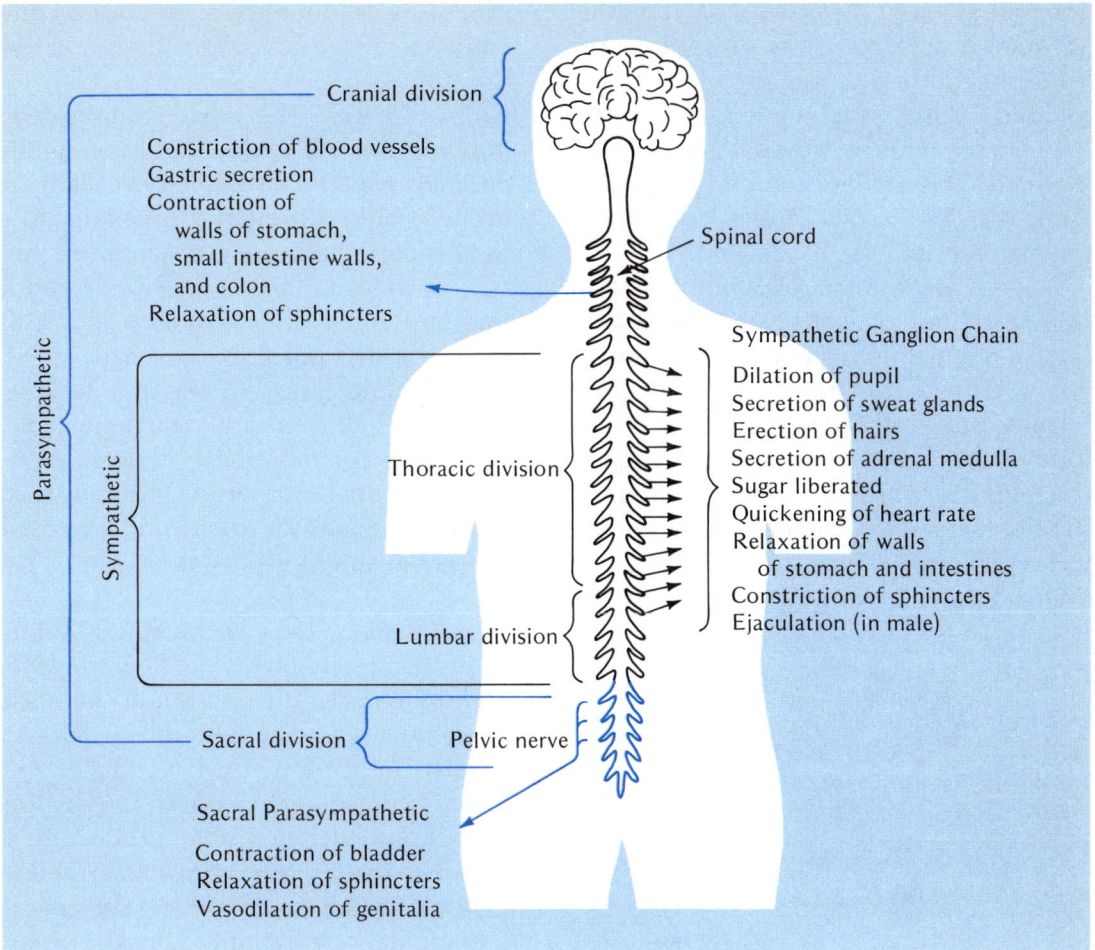

FIGURE 32-2 Simplified portrayal of the sympathetic and parasympathetic divisions of the autonomic nervous system. Structures of both divisions occur on both sides of the body.

representative of emotions. Increased blood pressure and pulse rate are common indexes of emotional arousal. In some emotional states the sweat glands are activated, and the galvanic skin response (GSR) is frequently used to detect this reaction. The so-called lie detector is based upon this relationship. If we lie when being questioned we react emotionally, and our bodies betray this emotion through autonomic nervous system reactions. Hence, what is being detected is not lying itself but changes in bodily states produced by lying.

The Endocrine System

The nervous system is only part of an internal network that affects behavior. We single it out and give it a good deal of focused attention because it plays a critical role in the processing of information from the outside world. An equally important system was discovered by the nineteenth-century physiologist Claude Bernard. This system, the endocrine system, carries bodily substances (hormones) through the bloodstream.

The endocrines are a ductless system the secretions of which are pumped directly into the bloodstream and carried to every part of the body. The endocrine glands are distributed throughout the body (see Figure 32-3), and each gland secretes a different hormone or combination of hormones which regulates chemical reactions within the body (bodily metabolism). An important aspect of this process is its influence on motivation and emotion.

Pituitary gland. The most complex and important of the endocrine glands is the *pituitary gland*. The pituitary, called the master gland, is located in the brain close to the hypothalamus. The anterior portion of the pituitary secretes a hormone that influences other glands responsible for the body's reaction to external stress. The posterior lobe of the pituitary secretes hormones that directly regulate the physiology of the body. A decrease in the hormonal output of the posterior pituitary results in dwarfism; excessive outputs result in giantism.

Thyroid gland. One of the glands stimulated by the pituitary is the *thyroid gland*. The thyroid gland is located in the neck, near the Adam's apple, and produces a substance called thyroxin. Normal thyroid functioning is necessary for proper growth. A deficiency in the production of thyroxin results in cretinism, an abnormality characterized by stunted growth and mental retardation.

Parathyroid gland. Located just above the thyroid is the *parathyroid gland;* its secretions control the levels of calcium and phosphate in the body. Additionally, the parathyroid affects the excitability of the nerve cells.

Adrenal glands. The *adrenal glands*, located above the kidneys, secrete adrenalin and noradrenalin (also called epinephrine and norepinephrine). These secretions come from a portion of the adrenals called the medulla, which has a

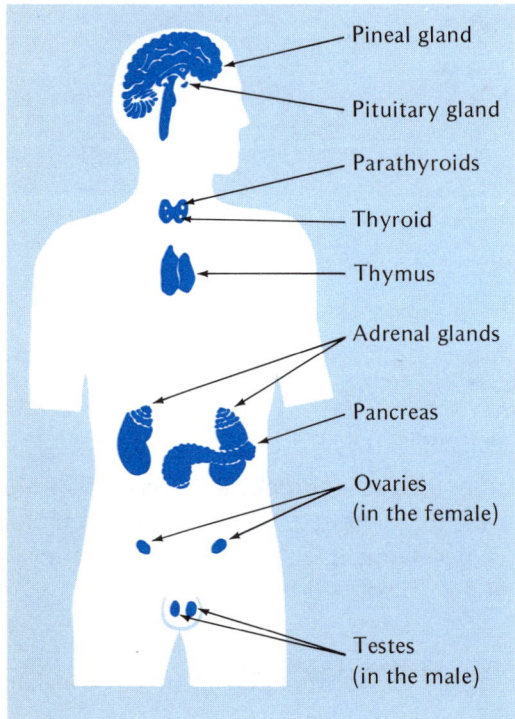

FIGURE 32-3 The endocrine glands and their location in the body

close relationship to the autonomic nervous system and is important to emotional arousal. The other part of the adrenals, the adrenal cortex, secretes substances that have an indirect effect on the chemical balance within the body's cells.

Pancreas. The commonly known disease diabetes results from too high a blood-sugar level. The blood-sugar level is controlled by insulin secretions from the *pancreatic gland,* or pancreas. If there is a deficiency of insulin, the blood-sugar level becomes too high. Persons suffering from diabetes usually control their blood-sugar level by taking regular injections of insulin.

Gonads. The *gonads* (testes in the male and ovaries in the female) secrete hormones responsible for secondary sex characteristics (e.g., body hair, deep voice in the male, and enlargement of certain organs) and, subsequently, for adult reproductive behavior. The gonads are one of the several endocrine glands stimulated by the pituitary.

As this brief overview indicates, the endocrine system, in conjunction with other parts of the nervous system, exerts a range of influences on body functioning and emotional behaviors. The hormones released by the endocrines stimulate either other organs or parts of the central nervous system. While this relationship is not yet fully understood, this summary gives us some idea of how these systems (central nervous system and endocrine system) work both jointly and independently in influencing behavior. Having a brief knowledge of these relationships should help us to understand better many of the issues relating to psychosurgery, brain stimulation, and other forms of behavior control.

Unit 33
Brain Control and Genetic Engineering

Well, is it true that you can put wires in so that you can feel pleasure? Intense pleasure....

It's really true, Morris said.

... I want the operation, I'm volunteering.... in the article it said that one jolt of electricity was like a dozen orgasms. It sounded really terrific.

And you want this operation performed on you?

Yeah, Beckerman said, nodding vigorously. Right.

Why?

Are you kidding? Wouldn't everybody want it? Pleasure like that?

Perhaps, Morris said, but you're the first person to ask for it.

What's the matter? Beckerman said. Is it really expensive or something?

No. But we don't perform brain surgery for trivial reasons.

Oh, wow, Beckerman said. So that's where you are. Jesus.

And he got up and left the room, shaking his head.

Crichton, 1972, pp. 94–96.

The preceding dialogue occurs between young Craig Beckerman (a potential patient) and Dr. Morris in *The Terminal Man*.

If the future lives up to the present, our expanding technology in the area of brain research will provide humanity with yet another technique by which it can expand its pleasures — or destroy itself. As we have mentioned in Division C, some years ago James Olds and Peter Milner accidentally discovered that rats conditioned to press a bar would do so repeatedly to the point of exhaustion when the bar presses resulted in small shocks of electricity to the brain (see Figure 33-1). These investigators had implanted tiny electrodes in the septal region of the rat's brain which could deliver electrical stimulation to this region if the animal pressed a bar or lever in its cage. Observations indicated that the animals preferred engaging in bar pressing to receive electrical shocks to eating. Since its accidental discovery, the effect has been repeated with dogs, cats, sheep, dolphins, goldfish, monkeys, and human beings. One scientist noted that tropical fish would repeatedly swim between electrodelike goalposts when that behavior would activate a small pulse of electricity. This continuous swimming activity, which was not noted when the electricity was turned off, led to speculations regarding pleasure experiences for these fish. Researchers now conclude that the brain's pleasure areas (septal region) can be turned on either by electrodes or by the senses.

More recent applications of electrical stimulation of the brain have included relief of pain for terminal cancer patients through stimulation by electrodes implanted in the head. In other instances, patients wearing control boxes on their belts can stimulate the brain's pleasure center in order to counteract anxiety and depression. And finally, a homosexual was made to enjoy his first heterosexual experience after repeated stimulation of the brain (Newsweek, 1971).

Successful research in the area of brain stimulation coupled with progress in other biomedical sciences have provided people with the capacity not only to alter and modify their behavior but to predetermine the decision-making prerogatives of future generations. Needless to say, this outcome has produced cries of alarm from many. Scientific applications that result in efforts to "improve" the nature of the human species have been referred to as *genetic engineering*. We need only reflect for a moment on some of the atrocities mentioned in Division G to appreciate why some people would be frightened by recent advances in science that have implications for tampering with or altering human behavior. Questions that naturally arise are: "What criteria are used in improving humanity?" "Who determines or selects the criteria?" "What variations, if any, are permitted?" and "At what stage in the developmental sequence should one intervene?" These issues have both political and scientific implications. In Stanley Kubrick's film version of Anthony Burgess's novel *A Clockwork Orange*, these issues are made salient. Alex, leader of a quartet of young ruffians, has a forty-year prison sentence commuted by agreeing to be a guinea pig in a new psychological process for rehabilitating criminals. Strapped in a chair with his eyes clamped open, he is forced to watch violet films while electroshock is administered by electrodes implanted in his head. The shocks are designed to make him sick as he watches the violence.

FIGURE 33-1 The rat's reward for pressing the bar is receiving stimulation through the electrode that has been implanted in its brain.

This is simply a classical conditioning procedure (see Unit 10). The process works! However, this is just the beginning of a new set of problems for Alex. He has obviously been denied choice, which prohibits him from engaging even in defensive violence, and he is further victimized by political forces which are using his case to advance their own cause.

A most dramatic instance of mind control occurs in Michael Crichton's *Terminal Man,* in which a team of surgeons connects a patient's brain to a computer which regulates his behavior. The patient, Harold Benson, suffers from psychomotor epilepsy which presumably causes purposeful aggressive behaviors often resulting in serious harm to others. The operation essentially involves implantation of electrodes into the right temporal lobe. These electrodes are then connected to a computerized charging unit which stimulates limbic areas. In theory, the computer can detect the start of a seizure and deliver a countershock to stop it. This should produce fewer and fewer seizures. However, Harold Benson "likes" the shocks and begins to initiate seizures in order to experience the pleasure. And as was the case for young Alex above, this is just the beginning of a new set of problems for Harold Benson.

A different kind of brain control is used in *The Manchurian Candidate.* It is, however, just as effective. American soldiers are "brainwashed" or hypnotized in a classical conditioning-like setting in Korea. Through posthypnotic suggestion, these men are induced to engage in behavior not of their choosing — including political assassination back home. These fictional (but highly possible) accounts of consequences of brain control procedures offer ample justification for the fear so many people have of scientific advances in this area.

Recent research on brain function has produced three important techniques, and their significance in the understanding of human behavior cannot be overestimated.

1. *Psychosurgery,* an outgrowth of the frontal lobotomy, is a technique which involves operative procedures designed to destroy areas of the brain thought to be responsible for certain undesirable reactions. Some measure of success with this technique has been achieved with patients with severe manic-depressive psychoses.
2. *Electrical stimulation of the brain (ESB).* Since the accidental finding of Olds and Milner, psychologists have discovered a large number of brain areas in the hypothalamus that regulate behaviors when electrically stimulated. Experimental animals have been made to eat, have sex, drink water, and perform many other behaviors simply by pressing a button connected to electrodes in the animals' heads (see Box 33-1). In an experimental demonstration, Dr. Jose Delgado of Yale University was able to stop a charging bull by stimulation of the brain with remote control radio waves.
3. *Biofeedback* is a technique which permits mastery over the brain such that patients can regulate functions previously thought to be involuntary, like heart rate and blood pressure. Experimentation in this area may lead to the identification of the best time to

BOX 33-1 BIOFEEDBACK: ELECTRODES FOR PLEASURE

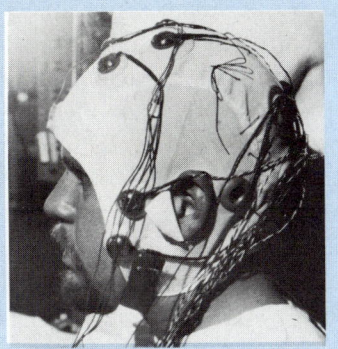
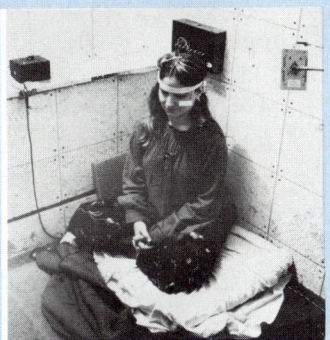
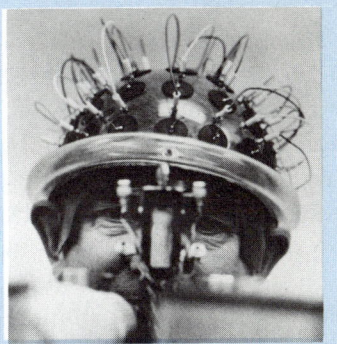

Newsweek — Lester Sloan   Newsweek — J. D. Wilson   Newsweek — Lester Sloan

subject the brain to inputs (e.g., for studying). College students are also participating in experiments that condition them to induce new brain sensations approximating a drug "turn-on."

Chemical Controls Over Behavior

The procedures discussed above have contributed to our ability to identify and understand specific brain areas that control emotions and other functions. Additionally, we are becoming more knowledgeable about how the brain stores information and the chemistry involved in the process. These discoveries have also led to an increasing understanding of and control over the chemical processes underlying many behaviors. Scientists have concluded that protein plays a role in memory and that RNA (ribonucleic acid), which affects the formation of protein, is found in increased amounts following training. It has been claimed that injections of RNA from trained animals to untrained ones result in a transfer of skills. Flatworms (planaria), when conditioned and then cut in half, were able to retain as much learning in each half (head half and tail half) of the original animal as a comparable conditioned group that was not cut in half (McConnell, Jacobson, and Kimble, 1959). In pursuing the implications of this finding, McConnell and others reasoned that these animals' body cells undergo a change in RNA during learning such that if ground-up bodies of trained animals are fed to untrained animals the latter should show the sophistication of the trained ones. Subsequent experimenters trained animals, extracted RNA from their brains, and then injected this brain extract into untrained ones. These injected untrained animals then behaved as if they had learned the task. The findings from these experiments have provoked speculation that students may some day acquire knowledge without studying by receiving injections of RNA brain extract from experts. Unfortunately, a large number of investigators have found contradictory evidence or at least failed to find support for this mode of transfer in learning (Byrne, 1966; Jacobson, Kales, Lehmann, and Zweizig, 1965; Jensen, 1965).

Dr. George Unger of Baylor College of Medicine conditioned rats to fear darkness. He then isolated a compound in their brains called "scotophobin" (fear of darkness). When this compound was injected into unconditioned animals, they too showed fear of darkness.

These highly interesting but unusual findings regarding chemical processes in the brain and their influence on behavior suggest that some day it will be possible to alter and influence behavior through brain chemistry. Some scientists have already begun to talk about a pill to improve the mind. Not too long ago, many doubted that people would someday walk on the moon. It is not farfetched to anticipate the same remarkable rate of development in the technology of brain functioning and genetic engineering as has occurred in our space program.

Due to the already sizable impact of development in the biomedical sciences, questions of ethics and law have been raised. Various experimental techniques, to be used at different stages of development, are being offered to cope with an increasing number of genetic defects. As the population expands, the mutation rate also grows. Hence, humanity is increasingly facing the need to change itself. Abortion, genetic screening, gene therapy, and artificial insemination are just a few of the techniques that are available or becoming available which will allow people on the one hand to correct genetic disorders and on the other to alter or control humanity in some fundamental way.

Unit 34
The Brave New World: Medicine for our Leaders

The army is attempting to develop electronic machines to control the behavior of others (enemies, persons engaged in civil disturbances, etc.). The control will be exercised through a devilish complex of flickering, steady, and unseen light rays, audible sounds and other tones too high for the human ear to hear. The main problem is that the "novel and unique devices/systems must be constructed so they will cause no permanent damage to target personnel and to innocent bystanders. . . . the ultrasonics, audible aversive stimuli, unique communications techniques and methods of speech interruption" are part of the army's physiological/psychological studies.

In plain English, the devices described above are:

Flickering light of varying itensity which can throw off the normal electric rhythms of the brain. This leads to confusion and can even break down the brain's ability to control the body.

Sound outside the human hearing range which can cripple a person's ability to function. Audible sound, some of it so loud as to cause unendurable pain, can have the same general effect.

Electronic sound devices which can interrupt, distort, or mask speeches by troublemakers at demonstrations.

To perfect the electronic behavior machines, army scientists are spending $50,000 this year and asking $200,000 over the next two years. Ultimately, human guinea pigs will be used to test the devices.

George Orwell's *1984*? No. The above was quoted from a classified army memorandum by Jack Anderson in *The Washington Post* in August 1972. While the development of these behavior control devices clearly suggests how our expanding technology can be used deliberately to interfere with our freedom, there is also evidence that sounds coming from modern machines and other sources constitute serious health hazards.

Technology: Effects on Health

In some cities, the noise level at a busy intersection has been measured at 120 decibels — about fifty decibels louder than the highest level considered to be safe. Some authorities say that such intensities can cause permanent loss of hearing that cannot be corrected by surgery or hearing aids. Others cite heart damage and other negative physiological changes. Yet, as a byproduct, our expanding technology and new life-styles expose us to noise levels that seemingly increase every year: the radio, talking movies, the loudspeaker, riveting machines, hot rods, sirens, discotheques, and the screeching fighter bombers that characterize modern warfare. In addition to threatening our health, many of these noise-making devices are polluting the environment as well. Automobiles, airplanes, and power plants represent a few of the major sources of pollution to our land, waters, and air.

The examples cited above give some evidence of the ways in which expanding technology is contributing accidentally and deliberately to the control and destruction of both the environment and humanity itself. Included in any examples of technological advancement should be

Copyright 1972 by Herblock in The Washington Post

"Deep breathing, now — That's it — Out goes the bad air — In comes the bad air —"

290 Environment: Outside and Inside

evidence of how we have extended our life span and as a result created other kinds of hazards. Improvements in medical science, for example, have given us greater amounts of control over our life span but simultaneously have left us prey to a larger variety of diseases.

Technology: Effects on Aggression and Violence

Early efforts at understanding aggression led to the postulation of the frustration-aggression hypothesis, which states that "aggression is always a consequence of frustration" and that "the existence of frustration always leads to some form of aggression" (Dollard, Doob, Miller, Mowrer, and Sears, 1939, p. 1). Many years later Leonard Berkowitz (1962) argued for a revision of the frustration-aggression hypothesis, suggesting that: (1) frustration does not always lead to aggression, but rather creates a readiness for aggression; (2) necessary cues must be present for aggression to occur; and (3) frustration is not a necessary antecedent to aggression.

Berkowitz's formulations point to a possible relationship between viewed violence (films, television) and subsequent aggression. The introduction of television into the home offered promise of improved educational opportunities and better-quality entertainment. Instead, television, along with other media (newspapers, movies, etc.), has been embroiled in heated controversy regarding its influence on violence and aggression. The growing impact of television on our culture indicates both improved technological advances and serious implications for behavior control. Television is seen largely as a medium that entertains or provides information. However, an indirect effect of television is that it molds opinions and attitudes and often produces increases in aggressive behavior. For example, a boy was knifed in a reenactment of the knife fight scene from "Rebel Without a Cause" following a television rerun of the movie. In another instance, youths throughout a western city began stealing car radio antennas and constructing zip guns from them after the showing of the movie "City Across the River," which demonstrated such construction.

These incidents, however, prove nothing about the general effect of television aggression on most viewers. Some have argued that viewing television violence serves as a safety valve which enables us to reduce our aggressive impulses (catharsis). Others argue that viewed violence serves to increase aggression (see Box 34-1). A surgeon general's commission after several years of research concluded that there is a relationship between television violence and aggression among children.

These conclusions, however, are not shared by the total scientific community. There is still considerable controversy over the effect of television violence on viewers' subsequent behavior. In all probability, both stimulation to engage in aggressive behaviors and catharsis of aggressive impulses are possible — more research is needed to determine under what conditions each occurs. The important point here is that widespread aggression and violence have caused some to

BOX 34-1 EFFECTS OF AGGRESSIVE MODELS

Observation of adults displaying aggression not only facilitates the learning of new aggressive responses but also weakens competing inhibitory responses in subjects, thereby increasing the probability of occurrence of previously learned patterns of aggression. Therefore, Bandura, Ross, and Ross (1963) predicted that subjects who observed aggressive models would display significantly more aggression when subsequently frustrated than subjects who were equally frustrated but who had no prior exposure to models exhibiting aggression (the control group).

In a test of this prediction, one group of experimental subjects observed real-life aggressive models, a second group observed these same models portraying aggression on film, and a third group viewed a film depicting an aggressive cartoon character. Following the exposure treatment, subjects were mildly frustrated and tested for the amount of imitative and nonimitative aggression they would exhibit in a different experimental setting.

The results confirmed the prediction that exposure of subjects to aggressive models increases the probability that subjects will respond aggressively when instigated on later occasions. Subjects who had observed the real-life models and the film-mediated models exhibited considerably more imitative physical and verbal aggression than did subjects in the control group.

The prediction that imitation is positively related to the reality cues of the model was only partially supported, however. While subjects who had observed the real-life aggressive models exhibited significantly more imitative aggression than did subjects who had viewed the cartoon model, no significant differences were found between those who had viewed the live and the filmed models, nor between those who had seen the film and the cartoon. The three experimental groups did not differ significantly in total aggression or in the performances of only partially imitative behavior.

Boys exhibited significantly more total aggression, more imitative aggression, more aggressive gun play, and more nonimitative aggression than did girls. Male models, as compared to female models, elicited significantly more aggressive gun play.

These results provide strong evidence that exposure to filmed aggression heightens aggression in children. Filmed aggression not only facilitated the expression of aggression, but also effectively shaped the form of the subjects' aggressive behavior. It is also apparent from the results of the experiment that a good deal of human imitative learning can occur without any reinforcers delivered either to the model or to the observer.

come to accept these negative behaviors as a way of life and have caused still others to speculate on our eventual fate. Robert Ardrey (1966, p. 63) writes:

Any species must risk extinction when aggressiveness finds its fences in ruin and violence an ever available entertainment. But the social species risk most. For beings who are biologically dependent on the group, whose existence is impossible without the cooperation of one's fellows, the violent solution of natural disagreement becomes a form of suicide.

Biochemical Control

I would prefer man to blow up the world if that is his natural inclination rather than have civilization become automatons existing in the sordid Orwellian world which you suggest.

In reference to your advocacy of character control drugs being administered to public office holders: You're sick! Incurably sick! And a convincing example of what free men have to fear from the practitioners of modern psychology. (American Psychological Association *Monitor*, 1972, pp. 1, 6.)

These are two of the responses to Dr. Kenneth Clark's presidential address to the American Psychological Association, in which he advocated the administration of pills to world leaders to curb aggression and the abuse of power. The origins of Clark's proposal date back to his concern with Hiroshima and Nagasaki as well as the horrors attributed to Adolph Hitler. Clark has summarized his position in a letter to one of his colleagues in which he states:

I suppose, in effect, what I am asking my fellow human beings now is that they not be afraid to use the knowledge and the methods of science to reinforce human morality and reduce the chances that non-rational and immoral decisions will destroy the human species.

While much of the scientific community shares the skepticism of Clark's critics, psychologist-philosopher Arthur Koestler argues that biochemical manipulation of human behavior can't begin too soon. Like most inventions or discoveries, techniques that permit the mastery and control of behavior can be used for good or evil purposes. Yet the nagging question to which no answer has been forthcoming is "Who will control the controllers?"

The underlying dynamics of behavior control can be traced back to Galton's observation of the tendency for genius and eminence to run in families. This observation produced a focus on family histories in efforts to understand behavior patterns. The infamous Jukes family, for example, was noted to have produced several generations of criminal, diseased, and feeble-minded individuals (Galton, 1870). Other efforts traced two lines of descent from the Kallikak family: the illegitimate son of a feeble-minded girl was feeble-minded and antisocial, whereas children born in wedlock to a "normal" woman were normal and socialized individuals. These studies do not allow a separation of the effects of hereditary and environment, however, and are therefore of limited value. Specific breeding procedures have been tried in animals other than man in an attempt to separate these factors.

SELECTIVE BREEDING

Experimental studies in selective breeding provide information on traits that are clearly attributable to inherited or genetic factors. In these studies, animals with desired traits are selected and mated through several generations, producing a new strain. As early as 1940, Tryon selectively bred "dull" and "bright" rats over seven generations and produced two distinct populations. Since bright and dull were defined as a function of maze-learning only and not other measures of intelligence, the dull rats were able to out-perform the bright rats on some other tasks. Additionally, it was discovered that environmental influence could overshadow the effect. That is, bright rats raised in a restricted environment became dull.

In another example of selective breeding, Hall and Klein (1942) bred two distinct populations of rats ("fearful" and "fearless") and discovered that when they were mixed in cages the fearless rats initiated five times as many attacks as the fearful and these attacks were more severe than those of the fearful.

Extensions of experimental breeding techniques to humans has led to questions regarding the rights of test-tube babies. Scientists have either developed techniques or are at the breakthrough stage with a number of procedures that fall under the heading of "genetic engineering." These practices obviously raise theological, philosophical, and legal considerations that challenge our tendencies to cope with an increasing number of genetic defects through technological intervention.

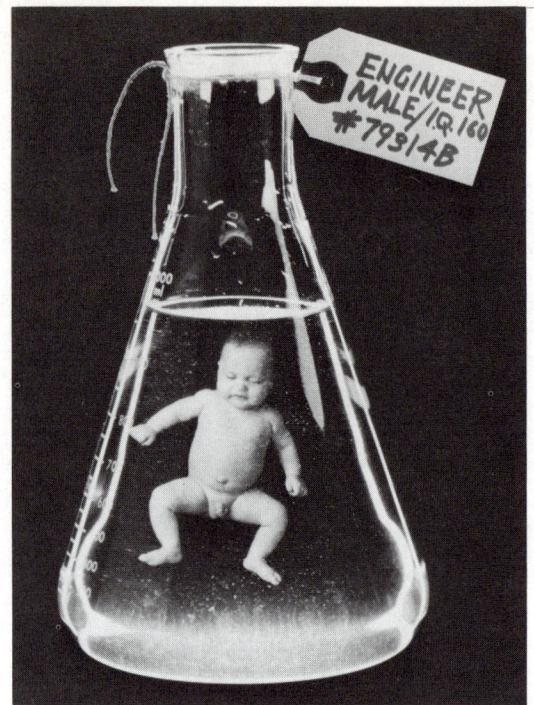

Photo by Ken Kay

Techniques now available to scientists include: the sampling of prenatal fluid and abortion; creation of life in a test-tube; and artificial insemination as well as reimplantation (placing a fertilized egg in the uterus and allowing it to develop). Genetic screening and therapy seem to be at the point of breakthrough. These advances and new ones being discovered every day give us the power to choose and control our destiny and that of future generations to a degree never known in the history of the human species. The temptation to breed selectively in order to eradicate mongolism, criminality, and other undesirable traits is great. There is little question about the possibility of a race of superhumans with superbrains resulting from these efforts. The question is whether we want such a superrace and what the alternatives are. Our expanding technology offers great benefits — if we make the right choices — but simultaneously yields destructive and undesirable by-products (noise, pollution, etc.).

The significant advances in the evolution of the human brain are now being out-paced by cultural and technological changes creating what sociologist Alvin Toffler calls "future shock." Our challenge is to bring rigorous interdisciplinary attention to these issues. Dr. B. F. Skinner of Harvard University advocates the use of operant conditioning and control of the environment as a way of improving humanity and the social community (Skinner, 1971). Perhaps the answer to improving the quality of life can be found within the context of scientific developments, but the need for caution and safeguards must be emphasized.

Individuals obviously must assume some of the responsibility for safeguarding their own lives. Here, too, advances in scientific technology can be of benefit. For example, our control of births is an outgrowth of medical science. The surgeon general's report on the relationship between cancer and cigarette smoking has generated some caution regarding smoking habits and the advertising of cigarettes in the media. Extensions of the concern about cigarette smoking and the focus on environmental pollution have produced some rather novel approaches to controlling the habits of cigarette smokers. Consider the approach being taken by a hotel firm in the Washington, D.C. area:

Three Marriott Hotels in the Washington area have set aside 69 rooms for nonsmokers. All

Drawing by Raden. Copyright © 1973 Chicago Tribune.

"I don't spit in your water; so don't pollute my air!"

ashtrays and matches have been removed; all the curtains, rugs and bedding thoroly [sic] cleaned; and nonsmoking maids and housemen have been assigned to these rooms. (Nonsmokers fight to clear the air, 1973.)

Other examples of efforts to control the behavior of smokers can be seen in regulations directed at airline and train passengers. Smokers and nonsmokers are now segregated on most public conveyances. Similarly, concerns with diet and nutrition represent individual responses to potential hazards in the farming and processing of foods. In the next unit, we will deal with some of the concerns regarding the potential hazards in food growing and handling.

Unit 35
We Are What We Eat

According to a 1972 *Parade* article, the Soviet news agency, Tass, claims to have a 167-year-old citizen living in a small mountain settlement west of the Caspian Sea. Shirali Mislimov is said to have been born on May 19, 1805. According to Alexander Katkow of Tass, the amazing aspect of the story is that Mislimov is not exceptional. Katkow suggests that in two other Soviet republics many citizens live to be at least 100 years old. It is further suggested that life expectancy in other parts of Russia and in America is not as long because we burn ourselves out.

Our efforts to survive and live healthy lives are in some measure a function of our dietary habits. The United States leads the world in the incidence of coronary heart disease. Approximately five hundred thousand cases are discovered each year; whereas in Japan and Italy the incidence is much lower. These differences seem to be traceable to diet. Medical science, for example, has uncovered the following facts relating diet and coronary disease: (1) Japanese and Italians live on diets containing much less animal fat than do ours; (2) there is a greater incidence of high blood fat and high blood cholesterol in the United States than in Japan or Italy; (3) autopsies of persons who die of coronary disease reveal fatlike deposits in their blood vessels. While these factors offer strong evidence that diet is at least partly responsible for the high incidence of coronary heart disease, some authorities feel that it is totally responsible.

One of our major activities is the winning of food; and it is in this capacity that sources of potential threat to our well-being exist. Success in the growth and production of food may be creating an ecological crisis. In the past two thousand years, more than one hundred species of animals and birds have been exterminated by pesticides, which also destroy other things in the environment upon which a sufficient food supply is dependent. Advances in technology have changed humanity from a part of nature to an exploiter of nature. Many of the animal forms that are destroyed for food are necessary to maintain the ecological balance.

Damage to the environment is caused by other factors also, such as radioactive dust in the atmosphere, DDT, and contamination by waste products from factories, kitchens, and lavatories. When the elements and forces of nature are no longer in balance, air will no longer support life, but will poison it. Foods that have been dusted with pesticides will threaten our health. This destruction to our environment has been called "terracide" and poses one of the greatest challenges to our survival since the Industrial Revolution.

Early systems of nutrition required abstinence from wine and meats, and recommended foods such as fruit, nuts, honey, and milk. This practice still has some support, and coupled with the destruction to the environment cited above forms the basis for vegetarianism. The practice of omitting meat from the diet as a means of improving health, however, is based on a mixture of facts and faith.

Scientists have been able to trace goiter* in rabbits to a diet of cabbage. Similarly, toxic materials have also been found in turnips, mustards, kale, brussels sprouts, and broccoli. Additionally, rhubard and spinach have been found to contain poison which lowers mineral ions (calcium) in the bloodstream. Overprocessing and faulty cooking methods remove needed vitamins from our foods.

The man mentioned above whom the Soviet Government discovered in the mountainous Caucasus region was 167 years old. All of the people in his village had also enjoyed a long life span. Another woman from the village, age 124, claimed her father had been as healthy as the rest of the villagers and died at 103. Scientists investigating the villagers' longevity attributed it to a variety of cultured milk in their diet. It was theorized that lactic acid bacteria are responsible for generating new cells and this in turn curbs the aging process. Comparable milk culture products are now commercially available (see Box 35-1).

Health Foods

Fact or fiction, the increasing concerns about hazards to health due to diet have resulted in Americans' spending from $40 to $80 million in one year on organically grown foods (foods produced without pesticides, artificial fertilizer, or additives). Grocers responding to this change in dietary habits are opening health food stores from New York to California and Hawaii. To protect consumers and legitimate organic farmers, two California legislators have introduced bills legally defining organic foods, requiring farm inspections, and extending the "truth-in-labeling" laws to this expanding farm industry. Additionally, businessmen and

---

*Goiter results from a deficiency of iodine in the thyroid gland.

businesswomen are joining an organization called Organic Merchants which requires the following oath:

I recognize my kinship to the brotherhood known as Organic Merchants. I understand that the purpose of our brotherhood is to provide information to the public regarding agriculture, the food industry, and nutrition and that this information shall be provided without profit.

I understand that the purpose of our brotherhood is to set quality control standards, making them in the form of a public contract that validly demonstrates a serious commitment. Therefore, I agree not to sell any food products containing: white sugar — "raw" sugar — turbinado sugar — corn syrup — bleached white flour — hydrogenated fats — artificial flavor — artificial color — cottonseed products — monosodium glutamate — synthetic vitamins — synthetic sugar substitutes — synthetic salt substitutes — synthetic preservatives, emulsifiers, or other synthetic food chemicals.

I also agree not to sell refined salt, refined oils and refined flours (white flour, degerminated corn meal, gluten flour, white rice flour) and to begin gradual elimination of products containing these items.

These activities obviously represent commitment and efforts toward stricter quality control standards. However, in the final analysis consumers must understand and act to protect their environment — and their health. Whether or not we can escape these dangers is an open

---

BOX 35-1

Why Continental Acidophilus...

Continental Acidophilus is a centuries old natural lactic bacteria milk culture. It has been manufactured and developed into the most viable strain available by the same family for generations. It helps provide a necessary bacteria balance in our digestive tract which is called a favorable intestinal flora. The friendly bacteria must overwhelm the unfriendly bacteria for proper digestion and assimilation of all foods and vitamins. Acidophilus assists in the growth and replacement of valuable intestinal bacteria.

Continental Acidophilus is the best seller on the West Coast. Make it your best seller too.

Continental Culture Specialists

Glendale, California

Reprinted through the courtesy of Continental Culture Specialists

question, for what we consider nutritional excellence is confounded with custom, tradition, feelings and religion and is not just decided on the basis of health.

From the psychologist's point of view, much of the current focus on health foods relates to at least two phenomena. On one hand, there is a good deal of fadism in the retreat to health foods. Hence, there are implications for conformity and group norm formation. On the other hand, custom and religious tradition may dictate diet practices. In some instances, abstinence from pork has a religious basis. Yet drinking wine with meals may simply reflect tradition or social custom. For the psychologist, however, these reasons are less important than the possibility of group differences in significant behaviors due to dietary habits or practices.

Much of the movement to health foods, as indicated earlier, was caused by chemical additives to foods and contamination resulting from pesticides. In part, there is strong justification for this movement. However, reliance on organic or health foods simply to avoid chemical poisoning could be misleading. A blight or other serious problems could result in organic crops being sprayed. However, the dangers of accumulation of pesticides are well recognized by regulatory agencies. Consequently, progress is being made in preventing abuse of chemical pesticides. Not only are regulations stricter, some chemicals are available only to licensed professionals. These professionals are more skilled in application techniques and are more easily controlled by regulatory agencies.

Some of the attack on additives by proponents of health foods is exaggerated and unjustified, while in other cases these critics are right on target. For example, some additives offer protection against natural toxins and microbiological organisms (e.g., botulism and salmonella) in some foods. No doubt, we would all agree that this is a valuable thing. On the other hand, some foods are simply sugar, additives, and synthetic vitamins; still others contain additives which are used to delude consumers about their quality and value. In some instances, these practices can have adverse effects on our health. An allergist in California has claimed that a diet free of artificial food flavoring and coloring can eliminate the symptoms of hyperactivity, a sometimes serious behavioral and learning disorder affecting an estimated five million children in the United States alone. Thickeners are used to make dairy products like canned milk, baby formula, and some ice creams thick and smooth. Food coloring is used solely to dye foods. These additives probably cause little or no harm to the consumer. Some critics suggest that preservatives such as nitrates and nitrites used in frankfurters and other cured meats are often used excessively in order to provide the pink coloring associated with freshness. There is growing evidence that such practices are contributing to cancer in humans.

One source of protection we have from these deceptive schemes is the GRAS (Generally Regarded as Safe) list. This list consists of substances with which there has been considerable experience and which are considered safe by the scientific community. However, some of the substances on this list, which was created in 1960, have turned out to be harmful. Hence, the list is under further scientific scrutiny. Our best protection from any of these dangers is to be well informed and to select carefully among health foods and foods declared safe by health experts.

Caffeine

Caffeine is just one example of the widespread danger associated with normal dietary habits. The coffee break is as American as apple pie; several hundred thousand cups are probably consumed daily by Americans. Additional sources of caffeine intake are tea, cola drinks, and cocoa. However, coffee contains the most caffeine — 100 to 150 milligrams per cup (the amount considered a therapeutic dose). Tea leaves contain more caffeine than coffee beans, but prepared tea is less concentrated than coffee — approximately 90 milligrams per six-ounce cup. A 12-ounce bottle of Coca-Cola contains about 55 milligrams of caffeine, and a six-ounce cup of cocoa contains about 50 milligrams of caffeine. The caffeine content of milk chocolate is considerably less, but some authorities indicate that milk-chocolate bars can be quite troublesome when ingested by children. Children react to caffeine more strongly than do adults. Caffeinated drinks are not as good for children as fruit sodas. According to some authorities, caffeine causes insomnia and hyperactivity among children. In adults, caffeine is a stimulant that allays drowsiness and fatigue, allows a person to sustain intellectual effort for longer time, and produces a clearer flow of thought.

Severe negative effects of high caffeine intake have been recognized by medical experts for some time. In addition to insomnia, large quantities of caffeine produce low-grade fever, irritability, and arrhythmias (abnormal rhythms of the heart). Studies have also determined that caffeine can cause cancer, birth defects, and other types of mutations. Researchers at the Harvard School of Public Health found that heavy coffee drinkers were more susceptible to cancer of the lower urinary tract; in Japan, studies showed that caffeine injections in pregnant mice, in amounts equivalent to 50 to 100 cups of coffee per day for a woman, resulted in birth defects in 6 to 20 percent of the offspring.

Caffeine consumption is just one example of the many dietary habits that pose threats to our health, particularly when engaged in excessively. Again, a good rule of thumb for a healthy diet is to select carefully the foods we eat, and eat moderately. Our body condition is a reflection of what we eat.

Hunger

Psychologists and physiologists have studied hunger perhaps more than any other drive. Since most animals can recognize the bodily states that signal hunger and respond appropriately to them, this activity has been the focus of much research in motivation. By depriving an animal of food and then using food as a goal to regulate its behavior, scientists have been able to study a large number of behaviors and many of the related motivational dynamics exercised

Copyright 1973 by United Features Syndicate, Inc.

in overcoming aroused biological states. These studies have relied on the observation that animals will go to great extremes to restore or maintain the constancy of their internal physiology. This process is called *homeostasis*. Homeostasis refers to the tendency of the body to maintain itself in a state of physiological equilibrium. For example, when body temperature increases, the sweat glands are activated. The perspiration generated from this process acts as a coolant to the body surface, thereby reducing the body temperature to a normal level. Similarly, internal physiological cues signal hunger, which in turn results in eating behaviors that reduce internal tissue needs as well as maintain levels of sugar in the blood.

Animal and human studies (Davis, 1928) have produced the rather interesting finding that organisms who are given a free choice of a variety of foods will balance their intake so as to eat needed food substances. Food intake tends to vary with changes in bodily needs for a particular substance. Richter and Eckert (1938) provided an experimental demonstration of this phenomenon. Rats deprived of their adrenal glands (see Unit 32) drank water solutions with much heavier concentrations of salt than normal rats who did not have their adrenal glands removed.

A rather sad account of the death of a three-year-old boy provides an example of how specific hungers operate in humans. In this particular case, the little boy hated anything sweet but craved anything salty. He often licked the salt off crackers and other foods. On one occasion he was observed to consume nearly the entire contents of a salt shaker. Ultimately his parents began to put tremendous quantities of salt in his food as a way of getting him to eat his meals. In addition to these unusually large quantities of salt in his food, he also ate a teaspoon of salt daily.

Eventually the boy's parents brought him to the hospital due to certain physical abnormalities. On the well-regulated diet of the hospital, he died within a week. An autopsy indicated that his adrenal glands were defective, which caused his body to lose salt faster than it was possible to replace it on a normal diet (Wilkins and Richter, 1940).

This sad and rather extreme case illustrates how individuals engage in food-seeking and consumatory behaviors that aid in maintaining balance among internal physiological conditions (homeostasis). Not all biological needs associated with food can be satisfied so simply. In addition to detecting cues associated with hunger, many animals can also anticipate certain needs prior to cue arousal. For example, some animals store food for the winter or simply bury it for a later time. These same anticipatory behaviors have in humans taken on a more sophisticated and complex form — refrigerated and chemical means of storage and preservation, international trade, and various agricultural practices (e.g., organically grown foods).

The survival of humanity is more than a specific response to internal biology. It is a much larger effort to establish a total environment (physical and social) that not only sustains life but ensures evolution. Many of the concerns with ecology, dietary habits, and agricultural practices discussed above can be seen as part of this process.

SUMMARY

Improvements in technology contribute to increasing the quality of life, but simultaneously have undesirable by-products. To explain this in relation to *crowding* and *overpopulation,* several population theories have been proposed:

1. The *environmental approach* attempts to relate physical and biological events to animal cycles.
2. The *interaction* explanation describes activities between animal populations and aspects of the biological environment that control population growth and decline.
3. The *self-regulation theory* states that the forces which promote population increase are strongest when population is at its lowest point and weakest when population is at its highest.

John Calhoun has demonstrated that overpopulation and overcrowding can produce abnormal patterns of social behavior and physiological changes that can lead to extinction of the whole population. Although it is interesting to speculate on the implications of these findings for human ecology, this relationship must remain speculative because of the lack of solid evidence.

Aggression and *violence* also pose a threat to our viability. It is suggested that such behaviors in humans are best understood in the context of animal aggression. Animals fight to establish dominance and *territorial rights.* Humans purportedly engage in aggression for the same reasons. However, these comparisons do not take into account that territorial behaviors in animals are instinctive and relate to food-gathering behaviors. Human beings have few if any instinctive behaviors and are not limited to single group membership. Therefore, understanding aggression in human beings requires a broader perspective.

There is controversy over the use of surgical techniques to control behavior (psychosurgery). *Psychosurgery* is a medical procedure for changing behavior by altering specific portions of the brain. To understand the relationship between the central nervous system (CNS) and behavior requires a knowledge of brain structure. The *cerebrum* or *cerebral cortex* is the main portion of the brain. The *hypothalamus,* in conjunction with the *pituitary gland,* has been identified as an important controller of voluntary behavior, emotion, and thinking. This and other structures of the *limbic system* have been found to relate to eating behavior, sleep, pupil dilation, and sexual behavior.

The peripheral nervous system is made up of nerves that connect the CNS with receptors (sense organs) and effectors (organs of response). This system is divided into two components: (1) the *somatic component,* which consists of sensory and motor neurons that produce movement and (2) the *visceral component* or *autonomic nervous system,* which controls internal and external signs of emotion. The visceral component is further divided into the *sympathetic* and *parasympathetic nervous systems.* The sympathetic system is activated when an individual is in an emergency situation. The parasympathetic system regularizes the body and controls vital functions such as digestion and elimination.

Another important part of the body's internal network is the *endocrine system.* The endocrine glands are distributed throughout the body, and each secretes a different hormone or combination of hormones which regulate chemical reactions (metabolism) in the body, influencing motivation and emotion.

Successful research in brain stimulation and other biomedical sciences has provided the capacity to alter and modify behavior and determine options for future generations in the form of genetic engineering. Research on brain function has produced three techniques of behavior change: *psychosurgery, electrical stimulation of the brain* (ESB), and *biofeedback.* These have contributed to our understanding of how specific brain areas control specific behaviors.

Our increasing knowledge about brain chemistry has behavior implications as well. Protein appears to play a role in memory, and RNA, which influences protein formation, is found in increased amounts following learning. Such findings suggest that some day brain researchers may be able to alter and influence learning through brain chemistry.

Many examples give evidence of how expanding technology contributes to the control and destruction of the environment and of humanity itself. The introduction of television offered improved educational opportunities and better-quality entertainment. However, it also molds opinions and attitudes and may produce increased aggression. While some argue that television violence increases *aggression,* others argue that it serves as a safety valve which enables us to reduce aggressive impulses *(catharsis).*

Increased understanding of genetics also has increased implications for control. Experimental studies in selective breeding provide evidence that aspects of intelligence may be attributable to genetic factors. Extension of such findings to human beings raises serious theological, philosophical, and legal considerations.

Our efforts to survive and live a healthy life are partially a function of our dietary habits. One of our major activities is the winning of food; yet success in the growth and production of food may be creating an ecological crisis. The multifactor destruction to our environment has been called *terracide*. The increasing concern about health hazards due to chemical additives and pesticide contamination have resulted in an increase in the consumption of health foods and efforts toward stricter quality control.

Caffeine consumption is one example of a dietary habit that contains threats to health. Severe negative effects of high caffeine intake have been long recognized, yet several hundred thousand cups of coffee are probably consumed daily by Americans.

Hunger has perhaps been studied more than any other drive. Most animals can recognize bodily states that signal hunger and respond appropriately. Animals will go to great lengths to maintain or restore *homeostasis* (equilibrium of internal physiology). Organisms given a free choice of a variety of foods will balance their intake so as to eat needed foods and make up for nutritional deficits. In addition, many animals can anticipate certain needs prior to arousal. The sophistication and complexity of these anticipatory behaviors in man provide evidence of the large effort to establish a total environment that not only sustains life but ensures evolution.

GLOSSARY

Adrenal glands: the pair of endocrine glands located over the kidneys; the adrenal medulla secretes adrenalin and noradrenalin, and the adrenal cortex secretes the adrenocortical hormones

Aggression: in animals, a ritual the function of which is species preservation

All-or-none principle: the principle stating that an impulse sufficient in strength to travel over a nerve cell occurs at full strength or not at all

Amygdala: a structure in the forebrain that is important in emotional arousal; it is closely connected with the hypothalamus

Arrhythmias: abnormal rhythms of the heart

Autonomic nervous system: the peripheral nervous system which innervates the smooth muscles and glands

Behavioral sink: a situation characterized by the crowding together of animals in greatest numbers in one small part of their total living space

Biofeedback: a technique which permits mastery over the brain such that patients can regulate involuntary functions such as heart rate

Brain: that portion of the central nervous system encased in the skull

Brain stem: the area of the brain which controls blood pressure, respiration, and other involuntary functions essential to life

Catharsis hypothesis of aggression: the position that viewing violence serves as a safety valve which enables us to reduce our aggressive impulses

Central nervous system: that part of the nervous system including the brain and spinal cord

Cerebellum: that portion of the brain concerned with the coordination of fine movements

Cerebral hemispheres: the two symmetrical halves of the cerebral cortex

Cerebrum (cerebral cortex): the main portion of the brain, occupying the upper part of the skull and controlling emotions and basic drives

Corpus callosum: a structure that consists of the fibers connecting one cerebral hemisphere with the other

Effectors: the organs of response: muscles and glands

Endocrine glands (ductless glands): glands that discharge their secretions directly into the bloodstream

Environmental population theory: an approach which attempts to relate physical and biological events with animal cycles

Feedback: the concept that behavioral output affects subsequent behavior

Forebrain: the most anterior of the three principal divisions of the brain; it includes the cerebrum, the thalamus, and the hypothalamus

Frustration-aggression hypothesis: the position that aggression is always a consequence of frustration and the existence of frustration always leads to some form of aggression

Galvanic skin response: the change in electrical resistance of the skin which occurs in response to external stimulation

Genetic engineering: scientific applications that are efforts or attempts to improve the nature of humanity

Goiter: condition resulting from a deficiency of iodine in the thyroid gland

Gonads: the sexual endocrine glands: ovaries in females and testes in males

Homeostasis: the tendency of the body to maintain itself in a state of physiological equilibrium

Hypothalamus: a structure at the base of the forebrain containing centers important in the control of motivational and emotional components of behavior

Interaction population theory: theory that describes activities between animal populations and aspects of the biological environment that control population growth and decline

Limbic system: a group of closely related structures in the brain, important to emotion and motivated behavior

Metabolism: the processes of cellular activity in an organism, including the assimilation of nutriments, the storage and utilization of energy, the repair of tissue, and tissue growth

Neocortex: the part of the brain responsible for movement, senses, and acquisition of new skills

Neuron: the nerve cell; the unit of the nervous system

Organic foods: foods produced without pesticides, artificial fertilizers, or additives

Pancreatic gland (pancreas): endocrine gland which secretes insulin

Parasympathetic system: a subdivision of the autonomic nervous system which acts reciprocally with the sympathetic division and tends to preserve ordinary metabolic functions of the body

Parathyroid gland: the endocrine gland responsible for regulating calcium metabolism

Peripheral nervous system: that part of the

nervous system lying outside the brain and the spinal cord and comprising in general the peripheral nerves and such ganglia as occur in the retina and sympathetic chain

Pituitary gland (the master gland): a gland located near the hypothalamus and having neural connections to it; the pituitary gland secretes a number of hormones which regulate the secretion of other glands in the body

Psychosurgery: surgical procedures designed to destroy areas of the brain thought to be responsible for certain psychotic reactions

Receptors: sense organs

RNA: ribonucleic acid; one of the substances in cell nuclei known to be a source of genetic transmission and which is possibly important in memory as well

Self-regulation population theory: theory stating that forces which promote population increase are strongest when population is at its lowest and weakest when population is at its highest

Septal area: one of the structures in the old forebrain that is part of the limbic system; important in emotion and feeling

Somatic: the component of the peripheral nervous system which controls the skeletal system

Sympathetic system: a subdivision of the autonomic nervous system; it acts reciprocally with the parasympathetic division and mobilizes the body for action; its activity is facilitated by the release of adrenalin

Temporal lobe: the lateral portion of the cerebral hemispheres, which lies below the lateral fissures and contains auditory projection areas

Terracide: destruction to the environment caused by advances in technology

Thalamus: a center in the forebrain containing the major relay junctions for nerve impulses passing to and from the cerebral cortex

Thyroid gland: the endocrine gland which is mainly responsible for controlling metabolism and metabolic rate

Vegetarianism: the practice of omitting meat from the diet

Visceral: the component of the peripheral nervous system which controls glands and smooth muscles; the autonomic nervous system

REFERENCES

Ardrey, R. *The territorial imperative*. New York: Atheneum, 1966.

Bandura, A., Ross, D., and Ross, S. Imitation of film-mediated aggressive models. *Journal of Abnormal and Social Psychology*, 1963, 66, 3–11.

Berkowitz, L. *Aggression: A social psychological analysis*. New York: McGraw-Hill, 1962.

Burgess, A. *A clockwork orange*. New York: Norton, 1962.

Byrne, W. L., et al. Memory transfer. *Science*, 1966, 153, 658.

Calhoun, J. B. The role of temperature and natural selection in relation to the variations in the size of the English sparrow in the United States. *The American Naturalist,* 1947, *81,* 203–227.

Calhoun, J. B. The development and role of social status among wild Norway rats. *Anatomical Record,* 1948, *101,* 694.

Calhoun, J. B. Population density and social pathology. *Scientific American,* 1962, *206*(2), 139–150.

Cannon, W. B. *Bodily changes in pain, hunger, fear and rage.* New York: Appleton-Century, 1929.

Clark, K. Clark's "peace pill" proposal — a year later. *American Psychological Association Monitor,* April, 1972.

Condon, R. *The Manchurian candidate.* New York: McGraw-Hill, 1959.

Crichton, M. *The terminal man.* New York: Bantam Books, 1972.

Davis, C. M. Self-selection of diet by newly weaned infants. *American Journal of Diseases of Children,* 1928, *36,* 651–679.

Delgado, Jose. Electrical stimulation of the brain. *Psychology Today,* 1970, *3*(12), 48–53.

Dollard, J., Doob, L. W., Miller, N. E., Mowrer, O. H., and Sears, R. R. *Frustration and aggression.* New Haven: Yale University Press, 1939.

Freedman, J. L., Klevansky, S., and Ehrlich, P. R. The effect of crowding on human task performance. *Journal of Applied Social Psychology,* 1971, *1*(1), 7–25.

Fritsch, G. and Hitzig, E. Ueber die elektrische Erregbarkeit des Grosshirns. *Arch. Anat. Physiol.* 1870, 300–332. Cited by E. G. Boring, *A history of experimental psychology.* (2nd ed.). New York: Appleton-Century-Crofts, 1957. P. 29.

Galton, F. *Hereditary genius: An inquiry into its laws.* New York: D. Appleton and Co., 1870.

Hall, C. S., and Klein, S. J. Individual differences in aggressiveness in rats. *Journal of Comparative Psychology,* 1942, *33,* 371–383.

Is this man 167 years old? *The Washington Post,* September 24, 1972.

Jacobson, A., Kales, A., Lehmann, D., and Zweizig, J. R. Somnambulism: All night EEG studies. *Science,* 1965, *148,* 975–977.

Jensen, D. D. Paramecia, planaria and pseudo-learning: Learning and associated phenomena in invertebrates. *Animal Behavior Supplement,* 1965, *1,* 9–20.

Koestler, A. *The act of creation.* New York: Macmillan, 1964.

Lorenz, K. *On aggression.* New York: Harcourt, Brace & World, 1966.

McConnell, J. V., Jacobson, A. L., and Kimble, D. P. The effects of regeneration upon retention of a conditioned response in the planarian. *Journal of Comparative and Physiological Psychology,* 1959, *52,* 1–5.

Nonsmokers fight to clear the air: Sawing clean Zzzs. *Chicago Tribune,* March 25, 1973.

Olds, J., and Milner, P. Positive reinforcement produced by electrical stimulation of septal area and other regions of rat brain. *Journal of Comparative and Physiological Psychology,* 1954, *47,* 419–427.

Olds, J., and Milner, P. Self-stimulation of the brain. *Science,* 1958, *127,* 315–324.

Probing the brain. *Newsweek,* June 21, 1971, pp. 60–67.

Protest postpones Virginia brain surgery. *The Washington Post,* March 27, 1973.

Richter, C., and Eckert, J. F. Mineral metabolism of adrenalectomized rats studied by the appetite method. *Endocrinology,* 1938, *22,* 214–224.

Skinner, B. F. *Beyond freedom and dignity.* New York: Knopf, 1971.

Surgeon General's Office, United States Department of Health, Education and Welfare. *Smoking and health: Report of the advisory committee to the Surgeon General of the public health service.* USPHS Publication No. 1103. Washington, D. C.: United States Government Printing Office, 1964.

Toffler, A. *Future shock.* New York: Random House, 1970.

Tryon, R. C. Genetic differences in maze learning in rats. In *National Society for the Study of Education: The thirty-ninth yearbook.* Bloomington, Ill.: Public School Publishing, 1940.

Wilkins, L., and Richter, C. P. A great craving for salt by a child with corticoadrenal insufficiency. *Journal of the American Medical Association,* 1940, *114,* 866–868.

Sheer, D. (Ed.). *Electrical stimulation of the brain.* Austin, Tex.: Hogg Foundation and University of Texas Press, 1961.

Toffler, A. *Future shock.* New York: Random House, 1970.

SUGGESTED READINGS

Buss, A. H. *The psychology of aggression.* New York: Wiley, 1961.

Fawcett, J. T. *Psychology and population.* New York: Population Council, 1970.

Fuller, J. L., and Thompson, W. R. *Behavior genetics.* New York: Wiley, 1960.

Landauer, T. K. *Readings in physiological psychology.* New York: McGraw-Hill, 1967.

Photo by James P. Jenkins

I

Feelings

Unit 36
Why Do I Feel This Way?

A forty-four-year-old married male sought treatment because of twitches over his eye, heart, and solar plexus. He was particularly worried about "pressure points" over his right eye. These pressure points were being interpreted as being caused by a "spirit" that was helping him to make decisions. The "messages," however, had begun to impart conflicting information, which troubled the client. When he was admitted to the hospital, "his speech was described as tangential, with loose associations, its content concerned with grandiose schemes and persecutions by others, but centering around information from his pressure points. There was no evidence of hallucinations."

Valins and Nisbett, 1971, p. 4.

The bodily states described by the client in the passage above are comparable to sensations experienced by most of us at one time or another. Emotion is so prevalent in our lives that it would be difficult to imagine existence without emotion or feeling. Fortunately, we are usually able to describe fairly accurately — or at least to our own satisfaction — that particular feeling or emotion associated with a particular bodily state. For example, if you are driving your car in excess of the speed limit and notice a police car in your rear-view mirror or hear a siren, the chances are good that you will have a strong emotional response. Perhaps the bottom of your stomach will drop a little. Undoubtedly there would be high agreement that this strong emotional response is one of fear or anxiety (a negative feeling). On the other hand, if you have been away from someone you love or care for very much, a phone call indicating that that person will be with you very soon will similarly produce a strong emotional response. Again, there would be fairly consistent reports of agreement that this strong emotional response is one of love or pleasure (a positive feeling).

Almost all of us have been excited, afraid, elated or alarmed at one time or another. Common to all of these experiences are certain internal bodily changes such as a rapidly pounding heart, a dry throat, and tense stomach muscles. While these experiences are fairly universal, there is very little agreement as to which specific internal cues or bodily states correspond with a particular emotion or feeling. An example of the complexity of attempting to identify bodily processes underlying a particular emotional state can be seen in reports from fliers on missions in the Second World War (Shaffer, 1947). The most frequently mentioned symptoms of fear were a pounding heart, rapid pulse, and tense muscles. On the other hand, some fliers reported symptoms of fear that included confusion, nausea, and loss of bladder control.

The wide range of internal bodily states associated with a single emotion has created a certain amount of difficulty for the psychologist and physiologist. Because of the difficulty of determining with precision which emotion is being experienced, there is a lack of agreement among psychologists regarding a satisfactory definition of emotion and feeling. Some have suggested that emotion has no distinguishing characteristics, while others suggest that the term should be abandoned or that it will eventually disappear from the psychologist's vocabulary. Despite these problems, the study of emotions continues to be of central importance to psychology. Consequently, we should arrive at an acceptable definition for purposes of this division.

In general, psychologists do agree upon two components of emotions: (1) a state of individual feeling or experience and (2) expressive behaviors. The concept of feeling is usually applied to mild emotional experiences perceived only by individuals themselves, whereas the term *emotion* is used to refer to strong and widespread reactions. Therefore, the definition of emotion that we would offer is: "a mental state or experience often expressed in overt behavior."

Learned Versus Innate Components of Emotion

Once we have defined emotion, it is reasonable to raise the issue of where emotions come from. Are we born with emotions and feelings, or are they acquired? A good deal of animal behavior has been attributed to instincts (innate drives), whereas the behavior of human beings is thought to be more a function of reasoning and therefore something that has been learned. As a result of Darwin's theory of evolution, human beings came to be viewed as merely an extension of lower animals. This new perspective led to the belief that people, like lower animals, could be characterized by innate or instinctive behaviors. Eventually, this view was opposed on the basis that the term *instinct* did not provide an explanation of any given behavior but simply a restatement of that behavior.

Current thinking on the issue is that both learned and innate mechanisms are essential components of emotion. Consequently, there is a need to understand better their individual and combined influence on emotional experiences. The learning of emotional expressions is largely a function of experiences each individual has and is influenced by values, attitudes, and other aspects of one's cultural surroundings. For a more detailed review of these learning processes, the reader should reexamine Division C. Additionally, Unit 38 will deal with fear as an acquired drive. The innate aspects of emotion are related to brain structures and chemical processes (the endocrine system) that are primarily influenced by genetic factors. Many of these relationships were explored in Division H. As we indicated at the beginning of this unit, key aspects of emotion are the bodily sensations produced by internal aroused states. The part of the nervous system responsible for these internal bodily changes is the autonomic nervous system, which derives its name from the fact that the bodily changes it controls are autonomous and automatic. The autonomic nervous system has two divisions: the *sympathetic* and the *parasympathetic*. These two divisions usually play opposing roles in their control over emotions. The *sympathetic* division, on the one hand, generally prepares the body for aroused states by causing an increase in heart rate and blood pressure, and sends blood to the muscles. The *parasympathetic* division, on the other hand, aids in the calming and relaxing of the body by bringing about a decrease in heart rate, a reduction in blood pressure, and by sending blood to the digestive system. These activities also build up and conserve bodily energy.

The action of the autonomic nervous system in conjunction with the endocrine system account for the bodily states that we label feeling and emotion. The observation of the relationship between bodily states and felt emotion has formed the basis of theorizing about emotion.

Theories of Emotion

THE JAMES-LANGE THEORY (1884–85)

One of the earliest efforts at explaining the relationship between emotional feeling and corresponding bodily states was developed by William James, the American psychologist, and independently by the Danish physiologist Carl Lange. The theory contradicted the common assumption that emotion precedes the stirred-up bodily states which are caused by autonomic changes. Typically, we think of the emotional sequence as an initial experiencing of emotion followed by an experiencing of the bodily changes that accompany the emotion. For example, we see a bear, are frightened, and run. The James-Lange theory reverses this sequence: according to this theory, first we see a bear, then we experience internal bodily changes (increased heartbeat, etc.) and possibly run (which increases the bodily reaction). Only at this point, in response to this stirred-up bodily state, do we feel fear. The theory thus argues that first we run, then we are afraid. In other words, the James-Lange theory of emotion states that bodily changes occur before there is any conscious awareness of the emotions which correspond to the changes.

THE CANNON-BARD THEORY (1927)

Walter Cannon, an American physiologist, and his student Phillip Bard suggested an alternative theory of emotion. The major focus of the Cannon-Bard theory is on the role of the cortex and lower brain centers (thalamus and hypothalamus) in the experiencing of emotion. For example, according to this theory, if we see a bear, we consciously engage in a decision process as to the potential danger; at the same time, the hypothalamus is in a state of readiness to stimulate various bodily organs. If the bear is not perceived as dangerous, discharges from the hypothalamus to bodily organs will be inhibited. On the other hand, if the bear is considered dangerous, the cortex will signal the hypothalamus to release impulses to bodily effectors, bringing about such reactions as increased heart rate and running. The interaction between the hypothalamus and the cortex produces the feeling of emotion — in this case, fear.

In opposition to the James-Lange theory of emotion, the Cannon-Bard theory suggests that emotional feeling and aroused bodily states occur at the same time and are initiated by lower brain centers (thalamus and hypothalamus), not the autonomic system. However, both theories indicate that the cortex plays an important part in the experiencing of feelings and emotions.

SCHACHTER'S THEORY OF COGNITIVE LABELING (1964)

In contrast to the James-Lange formulation of emotion, Schachter has proposed that cognitive (mental) factors may be major determinants of emotional states. When an individual is in a state of autonomic arousal, there is a need to explain the arousal. When the explanation of the arousal is in agreement with the perception of events in the social environment or with past experiences, the individual will experience the defined emotion. According to this formulation, it is the cognition (mental state) which determines whether the aroused bodily state will be labeled positively or negatively, or more specifically as happiness or fear, or some other emotion. These formulations are stated in three theoretical propositions (Schachter, 1964, p. 53):

1. Given a state of physiological arousal for which an individual has no immediate explanation, he will "label" this state and describe his feelings in terms of the cognitions available to him.
2. Given a state of physiological arousal for which an individual has a completely appropriate explanation (e.g., "I feel this way because I have just received an injection of adrenalin"), no evauative needs will arise, and the individual is unlikely to label his feelings in terms of the alternative cognitions available.
3. Given the same cognitive circumstances, the individual will react emotionally or describe his feelings as emotions only to the extent that he experiences a state of physiological arousal.

In order to test these propositions, Schachter and Singer (1962) injected subjects with epinephrine (adrenalin), a drug that produces aroused bodily states. Subjects were then placed with confederates (trained companions of the experimen-

TABLE 36-1 Measures of Emotional State in Euphoric and Anger Conditions as a Function of Assigned Emotional States

Arousal Condition	Measure of Emotional State	
	Euphoria	Anger
Epinephrine-informed	.98	−.18
Epinephrine-ignorant	1.78	2.28
Epinephrine-misinformed	1.90	Not tested
Placebo	1.61	.79

(After Schachter and Singer, 1962.)

ters) who created one of two situations: "euphoria" — by doodling, flying paper airplanes, and playing basketball by throwing wads of paper into the wastebasket, or "anger" — by complaining about the experiment, ripping up the experimental questionnaire, and stomping out of the room.

Variations in arousal condition were achieved by informing some subjects of the side effects of epinephrine (accelerated heartbeat and involuntary tremor); this was the Epinephrine-Informed group. Others were given no information about possible side effects — the Epinephrine-Ignorant group; some subjects were misinformed about the side effects of the drug (itching and headaches) — the Epinephrine-Misinformed group. Finally, there was a placebo group which was given neutral saline injections and treated exactly like the Epinephrine-Ignorant group.

Two types of measurement of emotional state were obtained: (1) observer ratings and (2) a self-report questionnaire. The results of the self-report measure (see Table 36-1) were in agreement with the predictions. As can be seen, subjects in the informed conditions expressed far less euphoria and anger than subjects in any of the other manipulated states of arousal. Indeed, individuals who experience stirred-up bodily states with no apparent explanation will tend to label the accompanying felt emotion in accordance with past learning and their definition of the situation (see Figure 36-1).

Attribution. Valins (1967) in a somewhat related manner has provided evidence of how individuals use perception of their own physiological responses to interpret how emotional a stimulus situation is. This process, according to Valins, is called *attribution*. Very simply, attribution is a process an individual uses to explain his or her world. While social consensus is often used as a criterion in validating an individual's explanations, there are occasions when one must rely solely on one's own judgment. Following Schachter's development of cognitive labeling, Valins and Nisbett (1971, p. 6) propose that:

Wide World Photos

FIGURE 36-1 It is quite possible that John Kennedy, Jr., in witnessing the funeral procession bearing his father's casket, labeled his emotion in accordance with past White House ceremonial events—for example, parades with flags and soldiers. Therefore, the appropriate behavior seemed to be to salute.

A *stimulus attribution* occurs when an individual attributes his reaction (e.g., visceral arousal, subjective fear, avoidance behavior) in the presence of a particular salient stimulus to the stimulus itself (for example, electric shock). A *circumstance attribution* occurs when an individual attributes his reaction to some aspect of the situation other than the particular salient stimulus (e.g., to a drug taken before the electric shock is given).

In an earlier study, Valins had male subjects listen to a supposed recording of their heartbeats while viewing seminude photographs of young women. The recorded heartbeat was actually a phony. Nonetheless, when subjects viewed seminude pictures in the presence of a strong heartbeat, the pictures were judged to be more emotionally arousing than they were by subjects who heard less pronounced heartbeats. When subjects were correctly informed regarding the heartbeats (control group), their judgments were not affected by the irrelevant recordings of random heartbeats.

The above discussion makes it abundantly clear that efforts to formulate a theory of emotion cannot rely solely on physiological responses. We now have evidence that the central nervous system and the autonomic nervous system play important roles in emotion. However, it is now clear that situational cues and learning experiences play equally important roles.

Unit 37
Excitement

On one occasion my dentist injected a considerable amount of adrenalin into my blood, in the course of administering a local anesthetic. I turned pale and trembled, and my heart beat violently; the bodily symptoms of fear were present, as the books said they should be, but it was quite obvious to me that I was not actually feeling fear. I should have had the same bodily symptoms in the presence of a tyrant about to condemn me to death, but there would have been something extra which was absent when I was in the dentist's chair. What was different was the cognitive part: I did not feel fear because I knew there was nothing to be afraid of.

Russell, 1927, p. 226.

This rather insightful comment by Bertrand Russell on the epinephrine-induced state of arousal provides some evidence of the difficulty psychologists are having in making distinctions among the various emotions. Because of the fairly consistent bodily changes associated with strong emotion, a good deal of effort has been directed toward differentiation between bodily states and corresponding emotional changes. Only a mild degree of success has been achieved. There is minimal evidence that fear and anger can be distinguished from each other on the basis of physiological changes associated with each. However, given the meager evidence in support of this distinction and the rather firm indications that surrounding context is important in distinguishing among emotions, many theorists have turned to a concern with the general state of excitement or arousal underlying strong emotional responses. States of arousal in human beings and other animals form a continuum that ranges from understimulation (sensory deprivation or monotony) to the stressful conditions in life that produce disease and exhaustion.

STRESS

When individuals are subjected to stress, their state of arousal is at the high end of the continuum. Since most of us are subjected to some form of stress at one time or another, it is important to know and understand the effects of such pressures.

Studies of the physiological consequences of stress indicate that it disrupts the body's homeostatic mechanisms (internal physiological balance). In such instances, coping behaviors attempt to restore the loss of internal balance. Often these behaviors result in coping behaviors that are categorized as psychosomatic disorders (e.g., ulcers, high blood pressure).

The Canadian physician Hans Selye (1956) has studied the physiological reactions to stress probably more extensively than anyone else. From his studies he has developed what is called the *General Adaptation Syndrome* (GAS), which is a descriptive model of the stages in an organism's attempt to cope with physiological stresses (e.g., starvation, severe burns, freezing). Three consecutive but distinct stages characterize an organism's response to chronic stress:

1. *Alarm.* The initial response to severe stress is a slowing down of autonomic activity, followed by an increase in functioning of the sympathetic division of the autonomic nervous system. Thus, there is an increase in heart rate, blood pressure, and production of sweat.
2. *Resistance.* This stage is characterized by increased output of hormones that increase body metabolism, making high levels of energy output more possible. During this stage, some of the endocrine glands become enlarged as a function of the increased activity.
3. *Exhaustion.* In this final stage, the organism collapses due to the overworked autonomic and endocrine systems. In other words, the prolonged defenses employed during the resistance stage burn themselves out. In most instances, even if the original stress is removed at this point, the system may not be able to recover; the consequence is often severe psychosomatic illness or death.

SOCIAL EFFECTS ON PHYSIOLOGICAL AROUSAL

Somewhere beneath the point of harmful overstimulation is a range of optimal functioning. This range of events is probably more characteristic of our existence than either of the two extremes. The concept of homeostasis provides the best explanation of our ability to function in this optimal range. Because of the natural homeostatic tendency of the body to maintain an internal steady state, there is little possibility of suffering from negative physiological states. Homeostatic devices automatically monitor and correct departures from essential physiological levels. We are therefore free to explore and pursue our world without having the burden of monitoring our bodily processes. And in the absence of severe environmental intervention, this arrangement proves to be quite satisfactory. However, as the reader may recall, the Schachter (1964) formulation of emotion suggests that some monitoring of or tuning in to bodily states is a part of understanding and learning to distinguish emotion. Since this process also relies heavily upon an interpretation of one's environmental context, emotional expression undoubtedly is a function of learning.

Many believe that the only distinguishable emotion at birth is excitement. Yet the growing child learns very quickly how to use emotional expressions to get what it wants. Tears and crying can be used to gain attention, to get food, or to receive comfort from adults. Not only are appropriate emotional expressions learned, evidence suggests that the child also learns which expressions are appropriate to the particular culture.

The famous study cited in Unit 11 of how a child learned fear reveals the typical way in which emotion is learned. Albert was first conditioned to fear rats, then the fear was generalized to all white objects with fur. This application of the classical conditioning model is an example of the way in which many irrational fears can be acquired. Similarly, it has been demonstrated that gentling or handling rats can have positive conditioning effects. Research by Bovard (1954, 1959) indicates that the internal physiological damage generally associated with stress is minimized when animals are subjected to stress in the presence of familiar others. Is it possible that gentling or handling rats produces positive outcomes as a result of the association between this type of touching and the physical proximity of another member of the same species? Male albino rats which have been gentled and handled show increased body size and weight. These changes have been shown to be due to better utilization of food, not to an increase in food consumption. Additionally, when these same animals are subjected to severe stress they do not show as much heart and stomach damage as nonhandled rats.

SENSORY DEPRIVATION AND MONOTONY

At the lower end of the arousal continuum (inactivity), individuals experience as much difficulty as at the other extreme (stress). A minimum level of stimulus input to the brain seems to be essential to our well-being.

Isolation. An early clue to the effects of low levels of stimulation was provided by observation of feral children (children reared in the wildnerness without human contact). In the few reported instances of such children, who were usually discovered in their preteens, language and intellectual development showed signs of retardation. These deficiencies were attributed to a lack of stimulus input during early developmental years.

A rather significant case of poor language development due to isolation involved a girl named Isabelle, an illegitimate child who lived alone with her deaf-mute mother until she was discovered at the age of six and one-half (Davis, 1947). Upon discovery, Isabelle acted like a wild animal. Unable to speak, she made only strange croaking sounds. Her I.Q. was assessed by the Stanford-Binet and she was given a chronological age of nineteen months, placing her in the low-grade intellectual category.

After approximately two years of specialized training, Isabelle had overcome most of her deficits and possessed a vocabulary of about two thousand words. By the time she reached the sixth grade in public school she was behaving quite normally. One explanation for Isabelle's intellectual deficit is that there was a lack of stimulation (verbal and nonverbal) in her environment. Some, however, argue that it is only an absence of opportunity to learn verbal language that explains the stunted mental development of isolated and feral children.

Observations made by René Spitz (1945, 1946) of children in foundling homes seem to support the "lack of general stimulation" interpretation for stunted mental development in isolated children. According to Spitz, symptoms observed in children living in foundling homes where they had little or no personal attention indicated severe psychological disturbance.

Sensory deprivation studies. These observations received more recent support following the Second World War (Bexton, Heron, and Scott, 1954). Canadian college students at McGill University in Montreal were paid handsomely (twenty dollars per day) to do nothing for twenty-four hours a day. All students who participated in the study were required to lie alone in rooms on cots. Their eyes were covered with goggles to prevent form vision, and their arms and legs were covered with padding to minimize tactile sensation. Background and outside noises were blocked out by the monotonous noise of a room air conditioner or fan.

Typically, subjects quickly developed a need for stimulation of almost any kind: listening to outdated stock-market reports, or a low-level recorded talk on the dangers of alcohol, and pursuing experimental tasks, regardless of how boring. Despite the strong incentive to remain in the situation as long as possible, few subjects could tolerate it for more than eight hours. In addition, some subjects reported experiencing hallucinations, while most reported restlessness and an inability to think clearly.

It seems safe to conclude from these studies that organisms need stimulus input for effective brain functioning and healthy development. Further, social isolation and sensory deprivation are unpleasant experiences and individuals will engage in activities that are often mean-

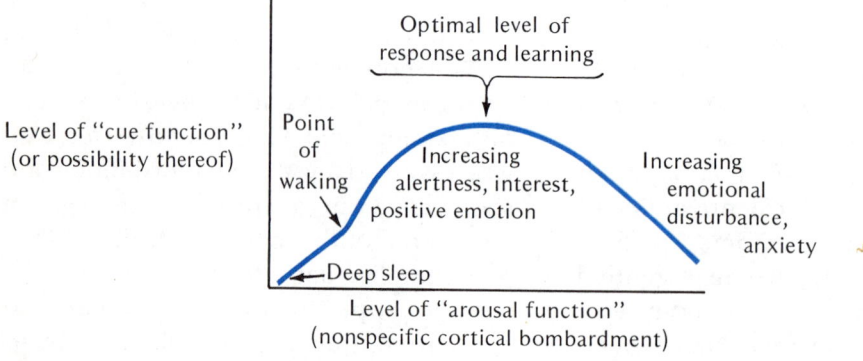

FIGURE 37-1 Arousal curve

ingless or boring to overcome their ill effects.

Too much or too little arousal is not good; some optimal level (or range) between these two extremes is probably most conducive to maximum functioning. This conclusion is consistent with Hebb's (1955) formulation of arousal and cue function (see Figure 37-1). Hebb has concluded that performance is at its best when the level of arousal is moderate. Too low a level of arousal coincides with deep sleep, whereas too much arousal can produce anxiety or actual emotional disturbance. The significance of this formulation lies in its importance for motivation: there is an optimal level of arousal for effective behavior. In the next unit, we will deal with negative states of arousal — fear and anxiety.

Unit 38
Fear and Anxiety

So Freud concluded that anxiety is useful. That shouldn't be surprising, when you consider anxiety's prominent role in the development of the human race. Only within our lifetimes has mankind been affluent enough in substantial areas of the world even to think seriously of abandoning negative (mainly fear-arousing) incentives, and of relying only on positive motives to get the necessary work of the race performed. Nor has affluence changed the picture that much. Men still find short-range benefits, including the fleeting luxury of sheer laziness, to be powerful incentives for doing nothing. If fear were not there to get them moving, to energize and guide their unpleasant choices and painful efforts to save themselves, soon no one would be left to insist that love and kindness are always more effective. Even social psychologists would find it hard to stick to their jobs very long for the sake of sheer intellectual delight; they too need the motivations of economic worry, of nagging concern about the fate of a psychologically naive, but technologically sophisticated human race. As long as man lives in a real, unperfected world with other real, unperfected human beings, fear will play a valuable role.

Elms, 1972, p. 311.

It seems that fear and anxiety can operate as positive incentives. Most commonly, however, fear and anxiety are associated with unpleasant emotional states which we attempt to remedy or avoid. It is in this context that Schachter has pursued an understanding of the relationship between anxiety and affiliation (Schachter, 1959).

ANXIETY AND AFFILIATIVE BEHAVIOR

In the last unit, we pointed out the relationship between isolation and heightened arousal. Schachter proposed that this heightened arousal is comparable to anxiety and hypothesized that heightened anxiety would lead to a greater desire for affiliation. To test this assumption, Schachter (1959) performed an experiment in which female subjects were shown a monstrous-looking piece of apparatus which they were led to believe would deliver shocks to them in an effort to study the physiological effects of electric shock. These women were also told that the shocks would be intense and painful. These subjects constituted the high-anxiety condition. In a low-anxiety condition, the setting was exactly the same except there was no shock apparatus present and the women were told that the shock would be a mild tickle or tingle and that they would enjoy the experiment.

The women in both conditions were then told that there would be a ten-minute delay to get the room in order. At this time the women were given a choice of waiting alone or with some of the others. Each subject gave her preference on a questionnaire that listed three choices: "I prefer being alone," "I prefer being with others," and "I really don't care."

The results indicated that a larger proportion of the women in the high-anxiety condition preferred to wait in the presence of others (see Table 38-1). Of thirty-two women in the high-anxiety group, twenty wanted to wait with others, whereas only ten of the thirty subjects in the low-anxiety group preferred to wait with others. These results were interpreted as indicating that highly anxious subjects chose to be in the company of others because affiliative needs were aroused — "misery loves company."

In a second experiment only the high-anxiety condition was employed. However, again each subject was given an opportunity to wait alone or in the company of others. Half of the women were given the choice of waiting alone or with others who were waiting to take part in the same shock experiment — the same-state condition. The remaining women were given a choice of waiting alone or with other women who were not waiting to be shocked but were waiting to see their faculty advisors — the different-state condition.

The findings indicate that affiliative choices are highly directional. In the same-state condition, six out of ten subjects chose to wait with others who were also waiting to participate in the experiment. In the different-state condition in which a choice to be with others meant being with women who had nothing to do

TABLE 38-1   Relationship of Anxiety to the Affiliative Tendency

Anxiety	Waiting Conditions Chosen			
	Together	Don't Care	Alone	Total
High Anxiety	20	9	3	32
Low Anxiety	10	18	2	30

(After Schachter, 1959.)

with the experiment, none of the ten subjects chose this option. These results were interpreted as clearly indicating that needs aroused by manipulating anxiety require the presence of others in a similar situation to achieve satisfaction — "misery loves only miserable company."

Sarnoff and Zimbardo (1961) appropriately identified a confounding factor in Schachter's study. Schachter had failed to make the distinction between anxiety and fear. Freud distinguished between realistic or objective anxiety and instances in which there is no real danger present. Realistic or objective anxiety is equated with fear; there is an objective danger. Anxiety, in contrast, is a kind of a vague fear with only a vague object or no known object at all. According to this distinction, then, Schachter manipulated fear, *not* anxiety. Accordingly, Sarnoff and Zimbardo repeated Schachter's experiment with one important difference — both fear and anxiety were manipulated. One group of subjects (the high-fear group) was led to anticipate severe shocks in a situation similar to that in Schachter's study. Subjects in a second group were made anxious by being required to suck on a number of objects such as rubber nipples and whistles. While this requirements in no way instilled fear or presented the subjects with any objects to fear, it was posited that it would cause the subjects anxiety and discomfort. When given the choice of waiting alone or with others, only those subjects anticipating shock (the high-fear group) chose to wait with others. The highly anxious subjects chose to wait alone. Thus, affiliation needs increased in the presence of fear and decreased in the presence of anxiety.

The findings suggest that other people can be both a source of comfort and a source of discomfort or embarrassment; when we are aroused, we seek out others if they are perceived as comforting and avoid them when we see them as a possible source of discomfort or embarrassment.

FEAR AROUSAL AND PERCEPTION

A classic study demonstrating the relationship between fear arousal and subsequent perceptual behavior was performed by Henry Murray in 1933. Little girls at a birthday party were asked to rate the maliciousness of a set of photographs. The ratings were performed both before and after a frightening game played in the dark called "Murder." Analyses of the girls' responses indicated that ratings of maliciousness increased after the game, which led to the conclusion that fear arousal produced the perception of danger in the environment which was attributed to the photographs.

Feshbach and Feshbach (1963) replicated this study by inviting neighborhood children to a Halloween party in which "spooky" events were also employed to create fear arousal. The children formed a circle in the dark and told ghost stories, and then they played the game of "Murder," also in the dark. After these fear-arousal experiences, the children attributed greater maliciousness ratings to a set of photographs than did a control group of children who did not attend the party. The findings were identical to those reported by Murray and confirm the interrelationship between fear arousal and subsequent perceptual responses. The perceptions in this case are not unlike the cognitive labeling phenomenon described by Schachter (1964) and discussed earlier in this division.

FEAR AS AN ACQUIRED DRIVE

In understanding fear it is necessary to know both how it comes about or is acquired and what impact it has on behavior. We have explored studies that describe to some extent what happens when we become afraid. Now, let us consider how fear is acquired.

There are some unlearned fears that are caused primarily by strangeness or sudden and unexpected events. For example, a sudden loud noise or strange object will elicit a fear response in most individuals. However, this is probably most characteristic of small children. In later life other factors such as humiliation or social and physical threats produce fear.

Since fear usually produces some behavioral outcome, it has the property of a drive. That is, individuals are usually motivated to escape or otherwise avoid fear situations. Knowing how the drive process develops has implications for understanding the development of more complex drives and motivations such as power, prestige, and vocational pursuits. At the present time we do not fully understand the developmental sequences in these more complex pursuits; but the answers may lie in our understanding of acquired drives in a laboratory experimental situation.

In a well-known experiment studying learned drives, Miller (1948) demonstrated how animals could be motivated to escape a fearful situation. Miller used a two-compartment box in which animals could be shocked in a white compartment and escape to a safe compartment, which was black. Escape could be accomplished by turning a wheel located above the escape door (see Figure 38-1).

Rats were initially tested for symptoms of fear — extreme defecation, crouching, and excessive urination — in the white compartment. Once it was determined

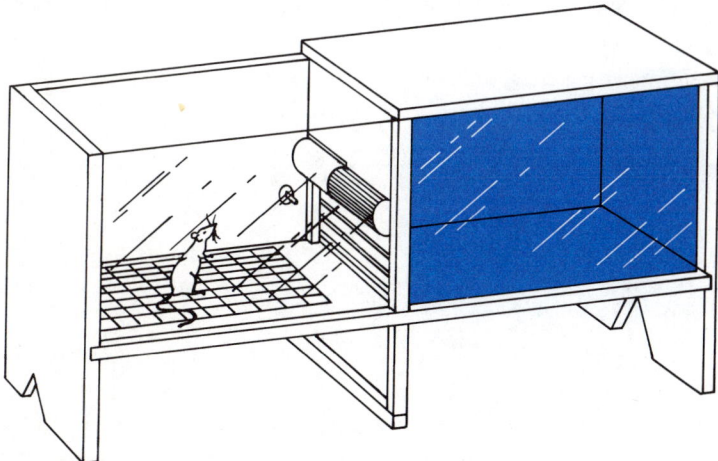

FIGURE 38-1 The apparatus used in studying fear as an acquired drive

that no fear existed, the animals were then conditioned to fear the white comparment by being given a series of electric shocks. Subsequent to this treatment, whenever the animals were placed in the white compartment they demonstrated the fear responses. By accident they soon discovered that the wheel located above the door permitted them to enter a compartment where they had not been shocked. After this accidental discovery, whenever rats that had been shocked in the white compartment were placed there, they immediately opened the door and escaped to the black compartment.

This experiment demonstrates how animals that were made tense and agitated (fearful) were able to learn a behavior which brought about relief — escape to a safe place. Many human behaviors and motivations are acquired in this same way. That is, we learn as a function of experience to engage in behaviors that will remedy or avoid unpleasant situations. In most instances, it is a signal from our viscera, representing our internal physiological state, that alerts us to the fearful situation. Psychologists have called this behavior a conditioned emotional response (CER). In the next unit we will examine similar processes of a more positive nature.

Unit 39
Love

The late Gordon Allport wrote: "The human hunger to give and to receive love is insatiable. No one ever feels that he can love or be loved enough. Yet this root fact of human nature is seldom acknowledged or studied by psychologists" (1960, p. 199). Allport goes on to suggest that one of modern psychology's failures is its omission of serious study of human affiliative desires and capacities. This "flight from tenderness," he suggests, might be related to psychologists' need to be tough-minded. That is, psychology has deliberately and selectively concerned itself with a rigorous scientific pursuit of observed behaviors. Somehow aggression and violence have fared better than love as forms of interpersonal behavior suitable for study by psychologists.

A second reason cited by Allport for the lack of emphasis or treatment of love by psychologists is the strong interest in fundamental and overt behaviors; in this particular context, psychologists have mainly studied attraction. After all, other interpersonal emotions, such as hate, frustration, and aggression, are usually only possible because of initial motives of attraction. However, the more negative emotions have tended to be more salient in human events. Consequently, psychologists have dealt with the universal events of positive attachments largely in the contexts of affiliation and attraction. An exception to the tendency to overlook love as an appropriate study of psychology can be found in the work of Harlow and his colleagues.

MOTHER LOVE

At the primate laboratory at the University of Wisconsin, psychologist Harry Harlow noted that baby monkeys reared within sight and sound of other monkeys but with no physical contact experienced behavior problems once they reached adolescence. Among these problems was sexual inadequacy.

As part of a program to assess minimal rearing requirements, monkeys were reared with their mothers and then separated from them. The separation produced quiet withdrawal in the baby monkeys. The infants withdrew to the corners of their cages and remained there for weeks. (This behavior is almost identical to the patterns of depression seen in young children separated from their parents by hospitalization.) In an effort to determine whether the negative effects of separation were a function of separation from the mother or simply of separation from any important social object, infant monkeys were reared together in small groups without their mothers, then separated. The separation from their peers was as devastating as separation from their mothers.

Surrogate mothers. In what is perhaps the best known of these studies, Harlow (1958) observed newborn monkeys that were immediately separated from their mothers and placed in cages with substitute or surrogate inanimate mothers. One of these substitute mothers was made of uncovered wire mesh; the other was essentially the same except it was covered with soft terry cloth. Both mothers were outfitted with bottles of milk with nipples on them to provide opportunities for nursing. Of primary importance was the amount of time spent in contact with each mother. The results were compelling. The baby monkeys spent more time with the cloth mothers regardless of where they were fed. On some occasions when feeding was only possible from the wire mother, the infant monkeys would climb upon the cloth mother and reach over to nurse from the wire mother.

When placed in strange and frightening situations, the monkeys would cling to the cloth mother. If there was no cloth mother present, fearful situations tended to produce emotional behaviors, i.e., crouching, sucking, and the like. Harlow interpreted these results to indicate that contact and warmth were more important to baby monkeys then being fed. The cloth mother provided this *contact comfort* in reducing the infant monkey's fears and providing routine pleasure. Despite the strong attraction and subsequent attachment to the cloth mother, infant monkeys reared by surrogate mothers were nonetheless sexually inadequate as adults. In the few cases in which pregnancy did occur, the monkeys reared by surrogate (wire or cloth) mothers were very poor mothers themselves. They rejected and pushed away their infants and in some instances beat them so savagely that the infant monkeys had to be taken away from their mothers. Harlow concluded that intimate physical contact with a mother figure (mother love) is essential to secure and healthy development in infant monkeys.

SOCIAL PENETRATION

The attraction component of love is the aspect of positive interpersonal relations that psychologists have spent most time studying. A typical approach to interpersonal attraction is the theory of social penetration (Altman and Taylor, 1973), in which individuals are likened to a series of concentric circles or "layers" of personality representing increasing levels of intimacy. Getting to know or becoming acquainted with someone is seen as a matter of penetrating these layers. Moving through the layers is a function of likes and dislikes which develop through interaction. The general framework for this theoretical position comes from what is called social exchange theory, in which attraction in relationships develops when rewards exceed costs. That is, interpersonal attraction and relationship development occur as a result of individuals' comparing or weighing the good things about others against the bad things. This comparison or evaluation process occurs within relationships and between relationships.

What is rewarding and what is costly can often be a personal matter. However, there are at least two theoretical positions that can clarify what psychologists know about attraction. Newcomb (1956) has constructed a theory of interpersonal attraction based on the assumption that individuals with similar attitudes and the opportunity to interact frequently are generally more attracted to each other. In a study of college roommates, he found general support for his formulation. Friendship pairing was primarily a function of living on the same floor with another individual and having similar attitudes.

From a contrasting point of view, Winch (1952) argues that attraction is a function of an individual's personality meeting your needs. In many instances, need matching is only possible when opposite traits are involved. For example, dominant individuals usually select submissive partners for marriage. It is quite possible, however, that need matching can occur on the basis of either similar or opposite traits as long as they are complementary.

ROMANTIC LOVE

Zick Rubin's (1973) studies of romantic love are an exception to Allport's assertion that psychologists lack interest in the subject. As stated earlier, attraction is a component of love, and Rubin reminds us that the equation of love with a physical or emotional need can be traced back to the sixth century B.C. Even then love was characterized as a powerful desire to be in the other's presence, to make physical contact, to be approved of, and to be cared for. The Greeks have called this form of love *eros* — a passionate desire to possess and to be fulfilled by another person.

Yet Rubin's efforts must be seen as a breakthrough for psychologists, for as Berscheid and Walster (1969) point out, as recently as the 1920s the study of love was virtually taboo and led to the dismissal of two college professors at a state university.

Rubin's approach to the study of love was to treat it like an attitude rather than an emotion or need: "Love is an attitude held by a person toward a particular other person . . ." (1970, p. 265). While this choice of definition was a deliberate one in order to keep the approach comparable to that used in assessing attraction, there may be a shortcoming in the omission of need or emotion.

As a first step, Rubin developed "liking" and "love" scales (see Box 39-1) which he administered to 158 dating couples. All subjects had responded to a poster (see Box 39-2) soliciting dating couples to respond to confidential questionnaires for which they would be paid one dollar. They were required to complete the questionnaire twice: once with respect to their date, and a second time with respect to a close friend of the same sex.

BOX 39-1 LOVE-SCALE AND LIKING-SCALE ITEMS (Rubin, 1973, p. 216.)

Love Scale

1. If _____ were feeling bad, my first duty would be to cheer him (her) up.
2. I feel that I can confide in _____ about virtually everything.
3. I find it easy to ignore _____'s faults.
4. I would do almost anything for _____.
5. I feel very possessive toward _____.
6. If I could never be with _____, I would feel miserable.
7. If I were lonely, my first thought would be to seek _____ out.
8. One of my primary concerns is _____'s welfare.
9. I would forgive _____ for practically anything.
10. I feel responsible for _____'s well-being.
11. When I am with _____, I spend a good deal of time just looking at him (her).
12. I would greatly enjoy being confided in by _____.
13. It would be hard for me to get along without _____.

Liking Scale

1. When I am with _____, we almost always are in the same mood.
2. I think that _____ is unusually well-adjusted.
3. I would highly recommend _____ for a responsible job.
4. In my opinion, _____ is an exceptionally mature person.
5. I have great confidence in _____'s good judgment.
6. Most people would react favorably to _____ after a brief acquaintance.
7. I think that _____ and I are quite similar to one another.
8. I would vote for _____ in a class or group election.
9. I think that _____ is one of those people who quickly wins respect.
10. I feel that _____ is an extremely intelligent person.
11. _____ is one of the most likable people I know.
12. _____ is the sort of person whom I myself would like to be.
13. It seems to me that it very easy for _____ to gain admiration.

As can be seen in Table 39-1, love scores for men (for girlfriends) and women (for boyfriends) are almost identical. There is a slight tendency for women to like their boyfriends more than they are liked in return. No such differences occurred for love. An interesting finding, however, is that women tend to love the same sex friend more than men love the same sex friend. This finding is consistent with our cultural stereotype in which it is more acceptable for women to refer to themselves as "loving" one another than it is for men. This finding is also consistent with other data that indicate that women are more open in expressing their feelings than are men. This difference has been described as lethal to the male role based on the assumption that there is greater mental health associated with openness. Finally, the difference between love for partner and love for friend was much greater than the difference between liking for partner and liking for friend.

As a final phase of this investigation and as a validation of the love scale, partners who scored high on the love scale (strong love) and partners who scored low on the love scale (weak love) were invited back to the laboratory to participate in what they thought to be a "study of communication among dating and unacquainted couples." Half of these couples were asked to report to the laboratory together and were run as pairs in the experiment. The other half were asked to report to the laboratory individually (the apart group) and were each matched with someone else's boyfriend or girlfriend.

While the subjects participated in the "communication task" the experimenter

---

BOX 39-2   POSTER USED TO SOLICIT SUBJECTS (Rubin, 1973, p. 218.)

ONLY *DATING COUPLES* CAN DO IT!

GAIN INSIGHT INTO YOUR RELATIONSHIP
BY PARTICIPATING IN A UNIQUE SOCIAL–PSYCHOLOGICAL STUDY
. . . AND GET PAID FOR IT TOO! !

Who can participate?
All Michigan student couples (heterosexual only) who are dating regularly, going together, or engaged. (Married couples are not eligible.)

What do you have to do?
Simply show up with your boyfriend or girlfriend at one of the times and places listed. You will be asked to fill out a confidential questionnaire, and each of you will be paid $1 for the one-hour session.

Then what?
All those who fill out the questionnaire will have a chance to be selected as subjects for a subsequent experiment, which (if you agree to participate) should be both exciting and lucrative.

BOTH MEMBERS OF A COUPLE MUST TAKE PART

TUESDAY, OCTOBER 29, 7:30 P.M. — AUDITORIUM C
WEDNESDAY, OCTOBER 30, 7:30 P.M. — AUDITORIUM C

TABLE 39-1 Love and Liking for Date and Same Sex Close Friend

| | Mean scores | |
Condition	Women	Men
Love for partner	89.46	89.37
Liking for partner	88.48	84.65
Love for friend	65.27	55.07
Liking for friend	80.47	79.10

(Rubin, 1970, p. 268.)

recorded the amount of time they spent looking into each other's eyes. As can be seen from the results in Table 39-2, couples in which both members score high on romantic love spent much more time looking into each other's eyes than do any other pairing of experimental subjects. In interpreting these findings, Rubin (1970, p. 272) states:

This pattern of results is in accord with the assumption that gazing is a manifestation of the exclusive and absorptive component of romantic love.... One way in which this oblivious absorption may be manifested is through eye contact. As the popular song has it, "Millions of people go by, but they all disappear from view — 'cause I only have eyes for you."

This rather novel and interesting research approach is just a modest beginning to our understanding of love. Nevertheless, we have moved the topic out of the taboo category of researchable issues. Consequently, we will see more and more future efforts in this direction.

SUMMARY

Because of the many different internal bodily changes associated with any single emotion, it is difficult to determine with precision which emotion is being experienced. Therefore, there is a lack of agreement among psychologists regarding a satisfactory definition of emotion. In general, psychologists do agree upon two components of emotions: (1) a state of individual experience and (2) expressive behaviors. Therefore, the definition that is offered here is "a mental experience often expressed in overt behavior."

Where do emotions come from? Current thinking on the issue of learned versus innate factors in emotion stresses that both are important. The innate aspects are related to brain structure and chemical processes which are primarily influenced by genetic factors. The action of the autonomic nervous system in conjunction with the endocrine system accounts for the bodily states that we label emotion. The relationship between bodily states and felt emotion forms the basis of theorizing about emotion. One of the earliest efforts at explaining this relationship was the *James-Lange theory,* which argues that bodily changes occur before there is any conscious awareness of the

TABLE 39-2 Mutual Eye-Gazing (in seconds)

Group	Mean
Strong love (together)	56.2
Weak love (together)	44.7
Strong love (apart)	46.7
Weak love (apart)	40.0

(Rubin, 1970, p. 271.)

emotions. Alternatively, the *Cannon-Bard theory* suggests that emotional feeling and stirred-up bodily states occur at the same time.

Schachter's *theory of cognitive labelling* proposes that cognitive (mental) factors may be major determinants of emotional states. According to this formulation, given a state of physiological arousal for which an individual has no immediate explanation, the individual will "label" this state and describe his or her feelings in terms of the cognitions available. This theory and supporting research make it clear that efforts to formulate a theory of emotion must include situational and learning experiences as well as physiological responses.

In studying emotion, many theorists have turned to a concern with the general state of excitement underlying strong emotional responses *(arousal)*. States of arousal form a continuum that ranges from understimulation (sensory deprivation or monotony) to the stressful conditions in life that produce disease and exhaustion. Stress places a strain on the body such that the homeostatic mechanisms are disrupted. In such instances, coping behaviors are used in an attempt to restore the loss of internal balance. Hans Selye has developed what is called the *General Adaptation Syndrome (GAS)*, describing three stages in an organism's attempt to cope with stress: alarm, resistance, and exhaustion.

Individuals experience as much difficulty at the lower end of the arousal continuum as at the upper extreme. A minimum level of stimulus input seems to be essential for effective brain functioning and healthy development. Social isolation and sensory deprivation are unpleasant experiences, and individuals will engage in normally meaningless or boring activities to overcome the ill effects of these experiences. Neither too much nor too little arousal is good; some optimal level between these two extremes is probably most conducive to healthy functioning.

Fear and anxiety are most commonly seen as unpleasant emotional states which we attempt to remedy or avoid. It is in this context that Schachter has studied the relationship between anxiety and affiliation. In experiments performed to test the assumption that heightened anxiety would lead to a greater desire for affiliation, Schachter found that anxiety increases one's desire to be with others, but only if the others are facing the same stressful situation. Sarnoff and Zimbardo, in a later study distinguishing between fear and anxiety, found that fear increases affiliation, whereas anxiety decreases affiliation.

Fear affects not only affiliation, but also perception of others. It has been demonstrated that fear arousal in children causes them to attribute greater maliciousness to photographs of strangers.

An important consideration in understanding fear is in knowing how it is acquired. There are some unlearned fears that are caused primarily by strangeness or sudden, unexpected events. Inasmuch as fear usually produces a behavioral outcome, it has the property of a drive. In a well-known study, Miller demonstrated how such drives could be learned. Rats shocked in a situation learned a new response to escape from that situation. Even with the shock removed, the rats persisted in the learned behavior whenever placed in the same situation — demonstrating a learned fear of the situation. Many human behaviors and motivations are acquired in a similar manner.

One emotion to which psychologists have given little attention is love. This neglect has occurred primarily because it was felt that the concept of love did not lend itself to the rigorous scientific approach. An exception can be found in the work of Harlow and his colleagues. They have shown that baby monkeys reared without physical contact with other monkeys experienced behavior problems once they reached adolescence. In what is perhaps the best known of these studies, Harlow observed newborn monkeys who were separated from their mothers and placed in cages with substitute mothers made of wire or of terry cloth. The preference shown for the terry cloth mother over the wire mother, particularly in frightening situations, led Harlow to conclude that contact is an important factor in development. However, these monkeys showed some abnormalities in adulthood, leading to the speculation that social interaction is also necessary for normal development.

Another approach to interpersonal attraction is depicted in the *social penetration theory*, in which individuals are likened to a series of concentric circles or layers of personality. Penetrating these layers, from superficial to intimate levels, is a function of likes and dislikes which develop through interaction. The general framework for social penetration theory comes from *social exchange theory*, in which attraction in relationships develops when rewards exceed costs. Even though what is rewarding is often a personal matter, two theories provide some clarity. Newcomb's *theory of interpersonal attraction* is based on the assumption that individuals with similar attitudes and the opportunity to interact frequently are generally more attracted to each other. From a contrasting point of view, Winch argues that attraction is a function of the two individuals' filling each other's needs or forming a complementary relationship.

Zick Rubin's interest in romantic love is another exception to the lack of interest in the study of love by psychologists. Rubin describes love as an attitude rather than as an emotion or need, thereby keeping its assessment comparable to that of attraction. Rubin developed a "liking" and a "love" scale which he administered to 158 dating couples. Results indicated: (1) love scores for men and women are almost identical; (2) women tend to love a same sex friend more than men do; (3) the difference between love for partner and love for friend was much greater than the difference between liking for partner and liking for friend; and (4) couples in which both members score high on romantic love spend much more time looking into each other's eyes than do any other pairing of experimental subjects. This rather novel and interesting research approach, although just a modest beginning to our understanding of love, has moved the topic out of the taboo category of researchable issues.

GLOSSARY

Affective: pertaining to emotions and feelings; often used in contrast to cognitive

Affiliation: a basic social need; the desire to be with other people

Arousal: a general state of excitement underlying strong emotional responses

Attribution: according to Valins, a process in which an individual uses perception of his or her own physiological responses to interpret how emotional a stimulus situation is

Cannon-Bard theory: theory postulating that a stimulus sets off a general physiological pattern and also cortical responses, which serve as a preliminary basis for the subjective state, followed by an integration of these components

Cognitive: relating to what are also called intellectual processes: reasoning, judging, and defining

Conditioned emotional response (CER): a reaction to an emotional stimulus based on a person's interpretation of the situation on the basis of learned responses from past experience with that stimulus

Drive: an aroused condition of the organism based upon deprivation or noxious stimulation of specified internal or external events

Emotion: a state of excitement or tension which may be sensed as pleasant or unpleasant, depending on how the stimulus is perceived

Epinephrine: a drug which affects the sympathetic nervous system, producing a state of physiological arousal: increases in heart rate, blood pressure, etc.

Eros: a passionate desire to possess and to be fulfilled by another person; love as needing

Fear: the awareness of a threatening situation that calls for flight or escape; differs from anxiety in being realistic and objective

Feeling: a mild emotional experience perceived only by the individual

General Adaptation Syndrome (GAS): a model developed by Hans Selye describing three stages in an organism's attempt to cope with physiological stresses: alarm, resistance, and exhaustion

Insatiable: unable to achieve need satisfaction of an aroused state

Instinct: the name given to an unlearned, patterned, goal-directed behavior

James-Lange theory: theory holding that a stimulus evokes visceral and motor responses, the awareness of which leads to the subjective experience of emotion

Placebo: a false (but to all appearances real) preparation given the subjects in a control group of an experiment concerned with testing the effect of certain drugs or chemicals on behavior

Romantic love: as defined by Zick Rubin, the sort of love that may exist between unmarried, opposite-sex partners, as distinguished from such other related forms as love between children and their parents, close friends, and human beings and God.

Sensory deprivation: reduction of external stimulation by means of isolation or by

Social penetration: theory describing the range of interpersonal exchanges that occur in growing interpersonal relationships

Stress: conditions, either intrinsic or extrinsic, which impose special difficulties for a person such that homeostatic mechanisms are disrupted

Surrogate mother: wire or terry-cloth "mothers" used by Harlow in his research with infant rhesus monkeys to demonstrate the dramatic effects of early experiences; the monkeys raised with the wire surrogate displayed disturbances in socioemotional development

Theory of cognitive labeling (Schachter): given a state of physiological arousal for which an individual has no immediate explanation, the individual will "label" this state and describe his or her feelings in terms of the cognitions available

insulation from stimulation; leads to many disturbances in cognitive and perceptual functioning, accompanied by emotional reactions

REFERENCES

Allport, G. *Personality and social encounter.* Boston: Beacon Press, 1970.

Altman, I., and Taylor, D. A. *Social penetration: The development of interpersonal relationships.* New York: Holt, Rinehart and Winston, 1973.

Berscheid, E., and Walster, E. H. *Interpersonal attraction.* Reading, Mass.: Addison-Wesley, 1969.

Bexton, W. H., Heron, W., and Scott, T. H. Effects of decreased variation in the sensory environment. *Canadian Journal of Psychology,* 1954, *8,* 70–76.

Bovard, E. W., Jr. A theory to account for the effects of early handling on viability of the albino rat. *Science,* 1954, *120,* 187.

Bovard, E. W. The effects of social stimuli on the response to stress. *Psychological Review,* 1959, *66,* 267–277.

Cannon, W. B. *Bodily changes in pain, hunger, fear and rage.* (2nd ed.). New York: Appleton-Century-Crofts, 1929.

Davis, K. Final note on a case of extreme isolation. *American Journal of Sociology,* 1947, *52,* 432–437.

Elms, A. C. *Social psychology and social relevance.* Boston: Little, Brown, 1972.

Feshbach, S., and Feshbach, N. Influence of the stimulus object upon the complementary and supplementary projection of fear. *Journal of Abnormal and Social Psychology,* 1963, *66,* 498–502.

Harlow, H. F. The nature of love. *American Psychologist,* 1958, *13,* 673–685.

Hebb, D. O. The mammal and his environment. *American Journal of Psychiatry,* 1955, *111,* 826–831.

James, W. *The Principles of Psychology.* New York: Henry Holt and Company, 1890.

Miller, N. E. Studies of fear as an acquired drive: I. Fear as motivation and fear-reduction as reinforcement in the learning of new responses. *Journal of Experimental Psychology,* 1948, *43,* 227–231.

Murray, H. A. The effect of fear upon the estimates of the maliciousness of other personalities. *Journal of Social Psychology,* 1933, *4,* 310–329.

Newcomb, T. M. The prediction of interpersonal attraction. *American Psychologist,* 1956, *11,* 575–586.

Rubin, Z. Measurement of romantic love. *Journal of Personality and Social Psychology,* 1970, *16,* 265–273.

Rubin, Z. *Liking and loving: An invitation to social psychology.* New York: Holt, Rinehart and Winston, 1973.

Russell, B. *An outline of philosophy.* London: George Allen and Unwin, 1927.

Sarnoff, I., and Zimbardo, P. Anxiety, fear, and social affiliation. *Journal of Abnormal and Social Psychology,* 1961, *62,* 356–363.

Schachter, S. *The psychology of affiliation.* Stanford, Calif.: Stanford University Press, 1959.

Schachter, S. The interaction of cognitive and physiological determinants of emotional state. In L. Berkowitz (Ed.), *Advances in experimental social psychology.* Vol. 1. New York: Academic Press, 1964.

Schachter, S., and Singer, J. E. Cognitive, social, and physiological determinants of emotional state. *Psychological Review,* 1962, *69,* 379–399.

Selye, Hans. *The stress of life.* New York: McGraw-Hill, 1956.

Shaffer, L. F. Fear and courage in aerial combat. *Journal of Consulting Psychology,* 1947, *11,* 137–143.

Spitz, R. A. An inquiry into the genesis of psychiatric conditions in early childhood. *Psychoanalytic Study of the Child,* 1945, *1,* 53–74.

Spitz, R. A. Hospitalism: a follow-up report. *Psychanalytic Study of the Child,* 1946, *2,* 113–117.

Valins, S. Emotionality and information concerning internal reactions. *Journal of Personality and Social Psychology,* 1967, *6,* 458–463.

Valins, S., and Nisbett, R. E. *Attribution processes in development and treatment of emotional disorders.* New York: General Learning Press, 1971.

Winch, R. F. *The modern family.* New York: Holt, Rinehart and Winston, 1952.

SUGGESTED READINGS

Altman, I., and Taylor, D. A. *Social penetration: The development of interpersonal relationships.* New York: Holt, Rinehart and Winston, 1973.

Glass, D. C. (Ed.) *Neurophysiology and emotion.* New York: Rockefeller University Press, 1967.

Knapp, P. H. (Ed.) *Expression of the emotions in man.* New York: International Universities Press, 1963.

Mandler, G. Emotion. In R. Brown (Ed.), *New Directions in Psychology.* New York: Holt, Rinehart and Winston, 1962.

Rubin, Z. *Liking and loving: An invitation to social psychology.* New York: Holt, Rinehart and Winston, 1973.

Schachter, S. *The psychology of affiliation.* Stanford, Calif.: Stanford University Press, 1959.

Photo by Agnes M. Fromer

J

Expansion or Escape?

Unit 40
Falling Apart To Come Together

My rebellious character determined that my sole motive was not to let them break me. But that solitary — they used to call it the soul-breaker — was a four by six-and-a-half foot room. There was a steel door, no light, no wash basin, no bunk, no toilet paper. You're nude and they feed you split-pea soup once a day and they give you a carton or half a carton of water. No books, no cigarettes, no toothpaste. And they take you out every 15 days for 24 hours, the jail doctor examines you, and then they put you back in. . . . After my first experience, I was prepared for solitary when I went back in 1967. The punishment is take everything away from you that you need in order to exist. So, if you overcome that, what have you done? You've overpowered them. You can exist without those things. If you can do that, then you're not as dependent as they think.

An interview with Huey Newton, 1972.

Social Isolation

The quotation above was taken from an interview with Black Panther Huey Newton by *Los Angeles Times* book editor, Digby Diehl. Newton's experiences and efforts to overcome the negative effects of solitary confinement are virtually identical to the experiences of subjects in social isolation experiments (Altman, Taylor, and Wheeler, 1971). In an experiment designed to assess the psychiatric problems associated with the stresses experienced by small crews of men in exotic environments (e.g., submarines, spaceships, Antarctic explorations), pairs of subjects were confined to small rooms for eight days. The rooms were approximately twelve feet by twelve feet and contained no windows or plumbing — the lights remained on twenty-four hours a day and the only source of water was from supplies stored in the rooms prior to the start of the confinement period. Rations consisted of liquid diet food, canned milkshakes, and survival crackers. The only work requirement consisted of approximately four hours of experimental tasks distributed throughout each twenty-four hour period. Subjects were not allowed to take any timepieces (clocks, watches, or calendars), cigarettes, books, photographs, or recreational materials into the rooms. The rooms were partially soundproofed, thereby providing very few cues from the outside regarding the day/night cycle. Most subjects were confused about the passage of time and, as predicted by the experimenters, found the austerity of the situation quite stressful. More than half of the thirty-five pairs that participated in this experiment were unable to complete the full eight days.

Subjects who successfully completed the mission engaged in self-pacing activities and arranged their living and work schedules with a deliberate effort toward coordination:

Thus, there is an overall profile of successful completer groups being organized and forming a group, with members attuning themselves to one another in a variety of ways. . . . As days progressed, there were some dramatic behavioral changes which add to the picture of early day differences. Aborters [subjects who did not complete the mission] began to show heightened stress, anxiety, nervousness, and hyperactivity, perhaps as an overreaction to their initial lack of tension. . . . These data suggest either a belated attempt at group formation processes and/or a panic reaction which resulted in high energy expenditure and heightened social activity. . . . The completers, on the other hand, seemed to settle down to a lower level of activity and a paced and ordered existence. Their levels of stress and anxiety increased but then stabilized; their restlessness and withdrawal dropped or remained stable; their social activity declined; territorial behavior was less evident, and they gave all appearances of "settling in" to a quiet existence. They seemed to have surmounted interpersonal organization problems and made an adequate adjustment to isolation (p. 96).

Additionally, some subjects who completed the mission were noted to engage in exceptionally creative endeavors which helped them cope with the monotony of the situation. One pair constructed a chess board and a monopoly set; another kept continuous and systematic records of the time based upon their estimates and calibrations of some of the experimental instruments in the room. The experiences of Huey Newton and of these experimental subjects suggest that environmental enrichment and structure and meaning are based on strong motivational forces within the individual behaving organism. The units in this division will focus on philosophical, social, and developmental aspects of people's efforts to find meaning and purpose in their existence.

Alienation

CAUSES OF ALIENATION

Relations between human beings have changed in the broad social sphere as well as in the intimate spheres of community, neighborhood, and family from what they were thirty years ago. The most important aspect of change has been urbanization. The rapid expansion of technology has been important largely in that it has enormously accelerated the shift from an agrarian rural society to mass urbanization. A largely farming population has shifted to gigantic metropolitan centers. More importantly, however, this shift has occurred at a rate faster than any previous tempo of social change. This rapid rate of change is more critical than the fact of change itself. It is possible for human beings to adapt themselves to almost any changes when the pace of change permits gradual readjustment of habits, ideas, and values. When the pace is too rapid, however, adjustment becomes progressively more difficult. Toffler (1970) has labelled this phenomenon *future shock*. Future shock exists when our institutions, customs, mores, and ideals no longer correspond to the actual conditions of present life since they were developed under conditions of a different and simpler society.

Earlier, Kenneth Keniston (1961) addressed himself to the effects of rapid social and technical change. In his analysis, Keniston proposed that rapid, chronic social change undermines the traditions of society and makes customary models (parents, teachers, etc.) irrelevant as sources of positive identity. He further suggested that there is an undue focus on aesthetics and hedonism which has manifested itself in what has come to be called the "sensitivity" or "now" generation (see Unit 42). One of the consequences of rapid social change and the new ethic is an increase in family tensions. For men, this conflict exists between career ambitions and a desire or need for family. For women, the conflict seems to be the difficulty of combining a career and motherhood. However, this conflict is so severe for women that a national feminist movement has come into being. This has happened probably because women have a more difficult time achieving self-identity and a sense of fulfillment than do men in Western society.

The social forces contributing to alienation affect many groups: minorities, the handicapped, old people, youth, and others. In all cases the sense of alienation derives in part from social conditions that foster contradictions. The most obvious instances of these conditions occur when cherished values are not adhered to by those in leadership positions, or when paths to goals and aspirations are blocked to selected segments of society by institutional practices. For example, the contradiction between our advocacy of democratic ideals and the brutality and denial of rights experienced by minority group members has had a profound negative effect upon the life of migrant farmers and continues to exacerbate racial tensions between blacks and whites. Similarly, our ideal of fair play and equal compensation for comparable work and the actual practice of discrimination in hiring females and paying them lower salaries for the same jobs worked by men in part created the tensions that produced the feminist movement.

The number of different groups experiencing alienation suggests that society itself may be creating the problem. The many varieties and expressions of alienation are more numerous than can be dealt with in this short unit. These expressions run the gamut from innovations that have profound philosophical and spiritual implications to those reflecting bizarre pathology. Alienation, then, can contribute to both positive and destructive forces in an individual's life. The issue of drug use will be dealt with in Unit 43, but as a preview to that discussion it might be useful to consider the observations of Keniston (1969, p. 112) on student drug use:

Political and historical events do not have a direct, one-to-one relationship with drug use: The war in Vietnam does not cause students to smoke marijuana or experiment with LSD. But the political climate of the past few years has created a negative view of the possibility of meaningful involvement within the established institutions of the society, at the same time that it has convinced many students that society is in desperate need of reform. This climate of opinion in turn contributes to the assumption that if meaning, excitement, and dignity are to be found in the world, they must be found within one's own cranium. Drug use can indeed be a cop-out, not from perversity or laziness, but simply because there seems to be no other alternative. Student drug use is indeed a commentary upon American society, but it is above all an indirect criticism of our society's inability to offer the young exciting, honorable and effective ways of using their intelligence and idealism to reform our society.

It will perhaps always be difficult to separate how much of a given problem is caused by societal forces and how much is a function of the individual involved. Hence, it may be more fruitful to look at problems of alienation as an interaction between an individual's experiences and the societal forces which shape or influence them. Many authors have cited the perfect efficiency of modern society, manifested in *overorganization, overpopulation,* and *rapid expansion of technology,* as a prime source of alienation or deindividuation (i.e., feelings of estrangement or detachment from self and others). Other forms of alienation are: anxiety states (emotional tension — apprehension, fearfulness), depersonalization, rootlessness, anomie (normlessness), apathy, isolation, pessimism, and loss of beliefs and values.

Erich Fromm (1941) advanced the thesis that people have five basic needs, embedded in human nature through evolution. These are for: (1) relatedness, or a union with nature and other people; (2) rootedness, or being part of the world; (3) transcendence, which is to rise above one's biological level and be fully human; (4) personal identity; and (5) an orientation or frame of reference for perceiving and comprehending the world. Since the social arrangement according to which we live determines how these needs will develop, adjustment (or personality) is a compromise between inner and outer demands.

ALIENATION AND MORAL PROCESS

Positing that moral commitment (positive or negative) lies at the core of personal identity, M. Brewster Smith (1969) investigated the relationship between moral thinking and consequent moral behavior in the context of the Free Speech Movement at the University of California, Berkeley. The study was largely designed to uncover distinctions between the "new morality" of college students who engaged in social protest (often requiring college campuses to shut down) and their nonprotesting counterparts. The conclusions arrived at may give us insights into the coping mechanisms adopted by the alienated.

Two kinds of data were collected: respondents were asked to describe their ideal selves by a Q-sort in which 63 adjectives were to be placed into seven equal piles ranging from those felt to be most descriptive of the individual to those felt to be least descriptive. Secondly, respondents' moral judgments were arrived at by analyzing their responses to a series of ten stories, each of which posed a classic moral dilemma. This technique for assessing levels of moral development was devised by Kohlberg (1963, 1964) and will be discussed more fully in the next unit. Briefly, three levels of moral development can be identified, ranging from Premoral (Level I) to Morality of Conventional Role-Conformity (Level II) to the most sophisticated stage of development, Morality of Self-accepted Moral Principles (Level III). Each of these three stages can be subdivided into two types, giving a total of six stages: (1) obedience and punishment orientation, (2) naively egoistic orientation, (3) good-boy orientation, (4) authority and social order-maintaining orientation, (5) contractual legalistic orientation, and (6) conscience or principle orientation (see Unit 41 for a more complete explanation of these stages).

Data were collected from undergraduates at Berkeley who had been arrested during the Free Speech Movement and from a comparable cross-section of undergraduates at large. Subsequently, data were collected from students at San Francisco State College and from Peace Corps volunteers.

Activism and personality. Table 40-1 gives a summary of the values from the Q-sort that discriminated between students classified as activitists and those from a cross-section of Berkeley and San Francisco State College students (nonactivists). Separate analyses were made for men and women. Examination of these traits indicates that the nonactivists tended to describe themselves as ambitious, foresightful, planning ahead, orderly, and conventional. This cluster of traits was interpreted as reflecting the Protestant ethic. The cluster of traits that distinguished the activists was somewhat weaker in that there were fewer traits that overlapped both college populations. This may have been a function of the criteria used to define activists on the two campuses. Activists on the Berkeley campus were students who had been arrested during the Free Speech Movement and were still in college. At San Francisco State, activists were students who held membership in organizations committed to radical social change. The traits that most discriminated the activists were free, unfettered, not hung up, creative, and imaginative. These traits were characterized as being anti-Puritan and humanistic.

Activism and morality. Additional comparisons were made between the activists, other college students, and Peace Corps volunteers. Written responses to Kohlberg's moral dilemmas were scored independently by two judges and categorized into one of three levels of moral judgment: (1) Premoral, (2) Mor-

TABLE 40-1 Q-Sort Traits Discriminating Activists from Nonactivists

School	Activists		Nonactivists	
	Males	Females	Males	Females
University of California (Berkeley)	Artistic, critical, idealistic, creative, imaginative, impulsive, doubting, uncertain, rebellious, free, unfettered, not hung up, sensitive	Assertive, critical, creative, imaginative, rebellious, free, unfettered, not hung up, perceptive, aware, effective	Conventional, ambitious, competitive, likes to be the best, self-controlled, proud, practical, shrewd, foresightful, plans ahead, orderly, self-confident, masculine	Ambitious, foresightful, plans ahead, self-denying, conventional, competitive, likes to be the best, practical, shrewd, orderly, responsible
San Francisco State College	Creative, imaginative, doubting, uncertain, rebellious, empathic, feels for others, open, frank, perceptive, aware, free, unfettered, not hung up, sensitive, responsive	Artistic, sensitive, empathic, feels for others, creative, imaginative, open, frank, perceptive, aware, free, uninhibited, not hung up	Conventional, ambitious, competitive, likes to be the best, proud, orderly, foresightful, plans ahead, amusing, masculine	Ambitious, self-controlled, practical, shrewd, foresightful, plans ahead, conventional, informed, orderly, sociable, gregarious

(After Smith, 1969.)

ality of Conventional Role-Conformity, and (3) Morality of Self-accepted Moral Principles.

As can be seen in Figure 40-1, there were striking differences between the activists and nonactivists in their level of moral judgment. The largest percentage of students at the highest level of moral development, that of principled morality, was found among students who were arrested during the Free Speech Movement at Berkeley or who held membership in activist groups at San Francisco State. This outcome held for both males and females in both groups. In terms of principled morality the written responses of Peace Corps volunteers tended to resemble those of the nonactivist cross-section of Berkeley and San Francisco State students.

On the basis of responses to a biographical questionnaire, all respondents were additionally classified into one of five types of political-social orientation: (1) *Inactives* (belonged to and participated in nothing in college), (2) *Conventionalists* (membership in fraternities and sororities but little involvement in social service or protest activities), (3) *Constructivists* (high involvement in social service activities, but little involvement in protest activities), (4) *Broad-spectrum activists* (high involvement in both protest and social service activities), and (5) *Dissenters* (high involvement in protest activities only).

Figure 40-2 shows the relationship between principled morality and the five political-social action categories. As can be seen in the figure, principled morality

348 *Expansion or Escape?*

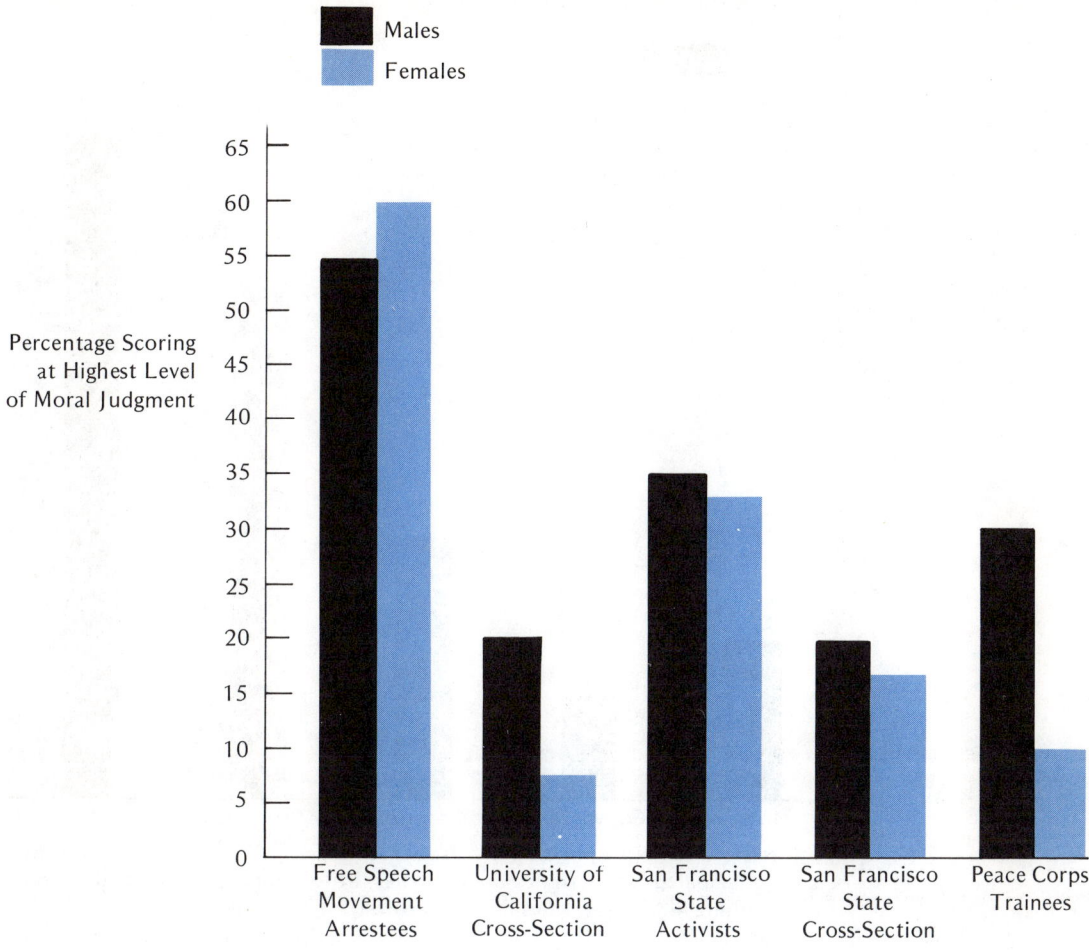

FIGURE 40-1 Level of moral judgment for selected groups

is more frequently found among the Broad-spectrum activists and the Dissenters. Again, this is true for both males and females. The fact that the Constructivists do not differ significantly from the Inactives or the Conventionalists indicates that it is the protest aspect of Broad-spectrum activists and Dissenters that is being reflected in Kohlberg's highest level of moral development. Smith interprets this pattern as clear evidence that student protest is not merely rabble rousing or thrill seeking but a reflection or manifestation of profound moral principles.

To the extent that moral and ideological commitment is important in the development of self and meaning, this research is useful in providing an understanding of the relationship between a troubled and alienated society and one popular form of response to these social conditions: student protest. Viktor Frankl's accounts of harrowing experi-

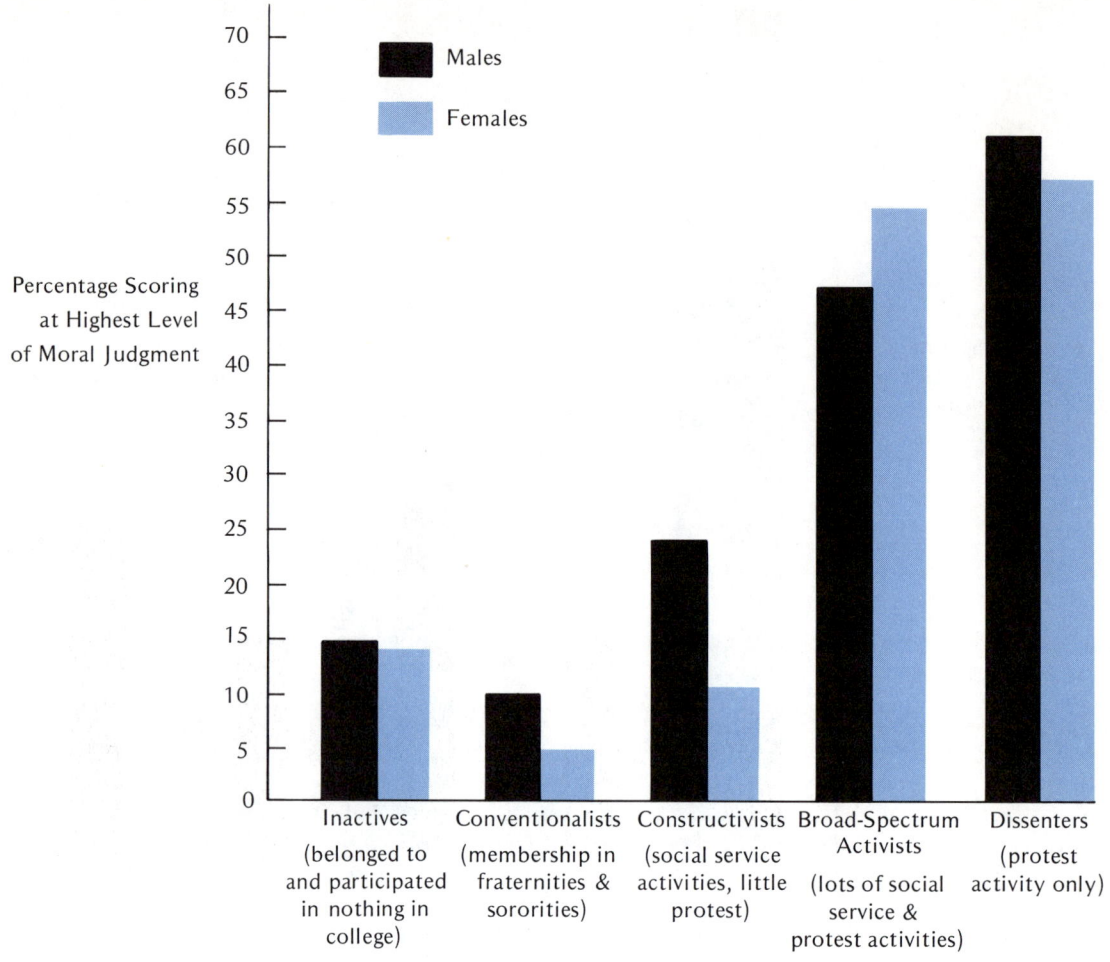

FIGURE 40-2 Political-social orientation and level of moral judgment

ences in Nazi prison camps (see Division G) and his subsequent development of a form of psychotherapy based on those hellish experiences is perhaps the most profound expression of our ability to come together and find meaning in our lives as a direct function of adversity or negative experiences. Dr. Frankl sometimes asks his patients who are tormented and suffering, "Why do you not commit suicide?" His subsequent professional treatment (logotherapy) is guided by their answers. In describing this approach, the late Gordon Allport (1963, p. ix) commented: "To weave these slender threads of a broken life into a firm pattern of meaning and responsibility is the object and challenge of *logotherapy,* which is Dr. Frankl's own version of modern *existential analysis.*"

Unit 41
Right and Wrong

There is a time when the operation of the machine becomes so odious, makes you so sick at heart, that you can't take part; you can't even tacitly take part, and you've got to put your bodies on the gears and upon the wheels, upon the levers, upon all the apparatus and you've got to make it stop. And you've got to indicate to the people who run it, to the people who own it, that unless you're free, the machines will be prevented from working at all.

Lipset and Wolin, 1965, p. 163.

Orlando, Fla.
The parents of a youth who was critically injured in an auto accident ordered doctors to let their son die so his kidneys might give life to two strangers.

Lester and Madeline Wojcik said that after talking with five surgeons and a priest Tuesday night they told doctors to remove life-sustaining breathing tubes from their 20-year old son, Paul.

Doctors said there was no hope for Paul Wojcik. The youth, an 'A' student at Florida State University, was injured Sunday when he was struck by an automobile. Police, who have withheld the name of a suspect, said the driver of the stolen car escaped on foot.

"The doctors told us from the beginning there was no hope," Mrs. Wojcik said. "His brain was damaged so severely the machines registered no activity. Five specialists told us he was not really living — the tubes simply forced his breath in and out."

Paul Wojcik died quietly shortly after the breathing apparatus was removed. Surgeons at Florida Hospital immediately removed his kidneys and prepared them for transplanting.

A hospital spokesman said, "This is the first instance we've had where a person was inevitably terminal and taken off life-sustaining facilities. The individuals involved had the right to decide and could have hung on and hoped for a miracle. . . . There was no hope from the beginning."

"I think it would help to be able to think there is someone who probably wouldn't be alive without Paul's kidneys," said the father. Mrs. Wojcik agreed, saying, "If Paul could have decided, that's what he would have wanted."

Father John Bluett, pastor of St. Margaret Mary Roman Catholic church, was consulted by the family. He said his Church holds that "extraordinary means" of preserving life need not be used.

"Paul had a lot going." Wojcik said.

"He was the most happy person," said his mother. "We're a family of worriers. We gnash our teeth. But not Paul. He made straight A's without worrying or cramming. He had a million interests."

Bridgeport Telegram, 1973.

The quotations above present two different kinds of moral dilemmas often faced in decision making. In the first instance, Mario Savio, in response to the frustrations of alienation and overcontrol by bureaucratic structures, advocates disrupting the smooth efficiency of such systems. The sentiments articulated by Savio are shared by many young people who are rejecting traditional values of material acquisition and power. The relationship between student dissent and morality was explored in the last unit. In this unit, we will deal more extensively with moral development and related behaviors.

Earlier (Unit 32) the issues of psychosurgery and other forms of behavior control were discussed. The difficult decision made by the parents of the crtically injured youth mentioned above raises still another question of "right and wrong" regarding our control over human life. As our technology has expanded, we have gained more efficiency in controlling behavior, including matters of life and death. This rapid expansion of technology seems to outpace our moral development and subsequent adjustment.

Human beings have been concerned with the issue of morality since perhaps the beginning of time. Much of the early concern emphasized the role of reason in accomplishing good ends. This line of thinking was further developed in Christian theology. The involvement of reason in the development of morality was seriously challenged in the writings of Sigmund Freud. For Freud, moral development was a function of the interaction of the three systems in personality — id, ego, and superego. While many theorists, notably the neo-Freudians, disagree with this emphasis, Freud's ideas have led to the postulation of theories that emphasize developmental aspects of morality. However, none of these later theories focus on the sexuality theme so characteristic of Freud's theory of personality and moral development.

Piaget's Theory of Moral Development

COGNITIVE DEVELOPMENT

An early departure from the thinking of Freud approached morality on a cognitive (or mental) developmental basis. This approach was initially associated with the Swiss psychologist Jean Piaget (1965) who formulated hypotheses regarding cognitive development as a result of watching growing children interact with their environments. Through observation of and interaction with children (Piaget often played marbles with kids), Piaget observed that children of different ages solved problems differently; further, he saw that there was a systematic and hierarchical sequence in their approach to understanding and problem solving. Cognitive development, then, is characterized by the child's growing older and becoming able to perform more complex mental tasks and functions at abstract intellectual levels. In other words, the child grows from having the cognitive ability to deal only with concrete and immediate sensations to having the ability to deal with a wide range of abstract concepts and their interrelationships. Moral development for Piaget was an outgrowth of this progression to higher stages of mental development.

MORAL DEVELOPMENT

To investigate moral development, Piaget presented children with stories, each of which contained a moral dilemma. In the example in Figure 41-1, the stories compare two kinds of clumsiness. In story A, John, who is going to the dining room for dinner, accidently knocks over a tray and breaks fifteen cups (considerable damage). In story B, Henry was engaged in a disobedient act which led to the breakage of a single cup (negligible damage). Analysis of children's responses to stories like those in Figure 41-1 revealed two kinds of moral judgement: *moral realism* and *moral relativism*. The judgments of younger children (up to age eight) tend to reflect moral realism: acts leading to considerable damage are judged the naughtiest whether or not they were intended. Rules come from authority or some other source. The judgments of older children (age eight and above) take intentions and circumstances into account and reflect moral relativism, in which rules are often modified to fit the needs of a particular situation.

Moral realism. Moral realism is characterized by a very rule-oriented approach to right and wrong. This kind of absolutism results in acts being evaluated as good or bad without taking circumstances or intentions into account. When Piaget looked at the kinds of punishment children advocated for rule breaking, he discovered that judgments characterized as

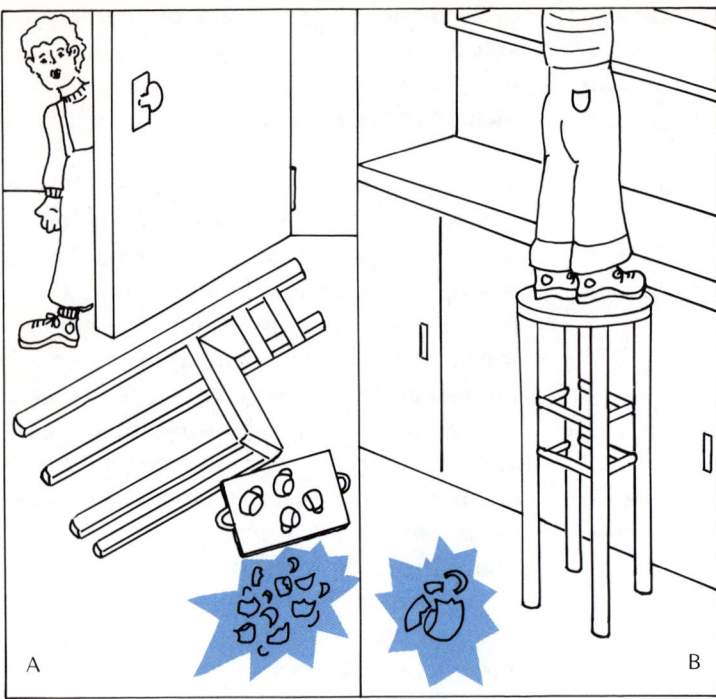

FIGURE 41-1 Stories of moral decision from Piaget

(A) A little boy who is called John is in his room. He is called to dinner. He goes into the dining room. But behind the door there was a chair, and on the chair there was a tray with fifteen cups on it. John couldn't have known that there was all this behind the door. He goes in; the door knocks against the tray, bang go the fifteen cups, and they all get broken!

(B) Once there was a little boy whose name was Henry. One day when his mother was out he tried to get some jam out of the cupboard. He climbed onto a chair and stretched out his arm. But the jam was too high up, and he couldn't reach it and have any. While he was trying to get it, he knocked over a cup. The cup fell down and broke.

moral realism were accompanied by recommendations for an equally absolute and severe punishment. Piaget called this approach to punishment *expiative justice,* which is justice based on strict rules in which the consequences of an act are punishment for the wrongdoer.

Moral relativism. Moral relativism is a more flexible morality based on general and abstract conceptions of right and wrong. The act alone does not determine the degree of wrongness. Rather, the judgment is based on circumstances, intentions, and amount of harm done. From this description, it should be easy for the reader to understand why Piaget regarded this as a relativistic approach to morality. Punishment at this stage of moral development is based on *restitutive justice,* which involves concern with restitution or redress of harm done by wrongdoers rather than punishment. If a little boy breaks another's toy, expiative justice would imply that he should be spanked. In restitutive justice, he should give one of his own toys in repayment. In moral realism, severity of punishment determines in part the "wrongness" of the act.

Kohlberg's Theory of Moral Development

Kohlberg's (1963, 1969) theory of moral development is an extension of Piaget's theory. He has devised a series of dilemmas, although more complex than Piaget's for presentation to both children and adults, and he has outlined six stages within three major levels of moral development (see Box 41-1).

MORAL-JUDGMENT STORIES

The moral-judgment stories that Kohlberg presented to his subjects usually conflicted a legal rule or social norm with a human need (Brown, 1965). The complexity of the dilemma in such instances is probably similar to the decision situation presented to the parents of the Floria State University student mentioned at the beginning of this unit. A typical example of Kohlberg's hypothetical dilemmas or conflict situations is:

In Europe, a woman was near death from a special kind of cancer. There was one drug that the doctors thought might save her. It was a form of radium that a druggist in the same town recently discovered. The drug was expensive to make, but the druggist was charging ten times what the drug cost him to make. He paid $200 for the radium and charged $2,000 for a small dose of the drug. The sick woman's husband, Heinz, went to everyone he knew to borrow money, but he could only get together about $1,000, which is half of what it cost. He told the druggist that his wife was dying, and asked him to sell it cheaper or let him pay later. But the druggist said, "No, I discovered the drug and I'm going to make money from it." So Heinz got desperate and broke into the man's store to steal the drug for his wife.

Should Heinz have done that? Was it actually wrong or right? Why?

Is it a husband's duty to steal the drug for his wife, if he can get it no other way? Would a good husband do it?

Did the druggist have the right to charge that much when there was no law actually setting a limit to the price? Why?

If the husband does not feel very close or affectionate to his wife, should he still steal the drug?

Suppose it wasn't Heinz's wife who was dying of cancer, but it was Heinz's best friend. His friend didn't have any money, and there was no one in his family willing to steal the drug. Should Heinz steal the drug for his friend in that case? Why?

Suppose it was a person whom he knew that was dying but who was not a good friend. There was no one else who could get him the drug. Would it be right to steal it for him? Why?

What is there to be said on the side of the law in this case?

Would you steal the drug to save your wife's life? Why?

If you were dying of cancer but were strong enough, would you steal the drug to save your own life?

> **BOX 41-1 KOHLBERG'S MORAL DEVELOPMENT STAGES** (Kohlberg, 1969.)
>
> | Level | Basis of moral judgment | Stages of development |
> |---|---|---|
> | I | Moral value resides in external, quasi-physical happenings, in bad acts, or in quasi-physical needs rather than in persons and standards. | Stage 1: Obedience and punishment orientation. Egocentric deference to superior power or prestige, or a trouble-avoiding set. Objective responsibility.

Stage 2: Naively egoistic orientation. Right action is that instrumentally satisfying the self's needs and perspective. Naive egalitarianism and orientation to exchange and reciprocity. |
> | II | Moral value resides in performing good or right roles, in maintaining the conventional order and the expectancies of others. | Stage 3: Good-boy orientation. Orientation to approval and to pleasing and helping others. Conformity to stereotypical images of majority or natural role behavior, and judgment by intentions.

Stage 4: Authority and social order–maintaining orientation. Orientation to "doing duty" and to showing respect for authority and maintaining the given social order for its own sake. Regard for earned expectations of others. |
> | III | Moral value resides in conformity by the self to shared or sharable standards, rights, or duties. | Stage 5: Contractual legalistic orientation. Recognition of an arbitrary element or starting point in rules or expectations for the sake of agreement. Duty defined in terms of contract, general avoidance of violation of the will or rights of others, and majority will and welfare.

Stage 6: Conscience or principle orientation. Orientation not only to actually ordained social rules but to principles of choice involving appeal to logical universality and consistency. Orientation to conscience as a directing agent and to mutual respect and trust. |

Heinz broke in the store and stole the drug and gave it to his wife. He was caught and brought before the judge. Should the judge send Heinz to jail for stealing, or should he let him go free? Why? (Kohlberg, 1969)

Another example of the type of conflict situations Kohlberg used is the following:

Joe is a fourteen-year-old boy who wanted to go to camp very much. His father promised him he could go if he saved up the money for it himself. So Joe worked hard at his paper route and saved up the $40.00 it cost to go to camp and a little more besides. But just before camp was going to start, his father changed his mind. Some of his father's friends decided to go on a special fishing trip, and Joe's father was short of the money it would cost. So he told Joe to give him the money he had saved from the paper route. Joe didn't want to give up going to camp, so he thought of refusing to give his father the money. Should Joe refuse to give his father the money? (Tracy and Cross, 1973)

LEVELS OF MORAL JUDGMENT

The basis of moral judgment at the preconventional level is cultural rules and prescriptions for good and bad. Judgments are motivated by fear of punishment from those who establish the rules. Conventional morality, the second level, rests in performing proper roles. Loyalty and conformity in the service of fulfilling the expectations of others is the basic orientation at this level. Individuals operating at this level also engage in active support and justification of the social order (e.g., "my country, right or wrong"). At the third level of moral judgment, postconventional morality, judgment resides in rational principles independent of society or authority. The individual's behavior at this level is oriented away from convention or stereotypes. Each of these three levels is subdivided into two stages, as indicated in Box 41-1, resulting in six stages in all.

An example of stage 1 morality is seen in Table 41-1, in which Kohlberg's system is applied to statements attributed to Nazi officer Lt. Col. Adolf Eichmann. As can be seen, most of Eichmann's statements represent stages 1 and 2 (preconventional level), in which an individual's judgments are characterized by a responsiveness to cultural rules. On the other hand, Martin Luther King's letter from a Birmingham jail provides an example of stage 6, the highest level of moral development (see Box 41-2). A perusal of Eichmann's statements clearly reveals a deference to power and an orientation toward obedience and punishment, whereas King's letter reflects a respect for justice that can promote the seemingly contradictory outcomes of obedience to law and disobedience to law. Kohlberg's stages, then, represent a progression similar to that reflected in Piaget's theory — movement from concrete inflexible thinking to an abstract and relativistic approach to problem solving and judgment.

Value Clarification

Instead of giving young people the impression that their task is to stand a dreary watch over the ancient values, we should be telling them the grim but bracing truth that it is their task to re-create those values continuously in their own behavior, facing the dilemmas and catastrophes of their own time. . . . a society is being continuously recreated, for good or ill, by its members. This will strike some as a burdensome responsibility, but it will summon others to greatness. (John Gardner, 1964, pp. 126–127.)

Adults struggle in their search for ways to transfer personal and cultural values to the young and the newest members of a family group or society. In an effort to offer the next generation guidelines for what they consider to be happy and useful lives, adults commonly try such persuasion strategies as:

1. *Moralizing:* "My set of values will be right for you." So speak parents, the church group, the peer group, teachers, political groups — and many more. As a result, the values offered are often inconsistent or in direct conflict with one another.

TABLE 41-1 Scoring of Moral Judgments of Adolf Eichmann for Developmental Stage

Moral Judgments	Stage
In actual fact, I was merely a little cog in the machinery that carried out the directives of the German Reich.	1
I am neither a murderer nor a mass-murderer. I am a man of average character, with good qualities and many faults.	3
Yet what is there to "admit"? I carried out my order. It would be as pointless to blame me for the whole final solution of the Jewish problem as to blame the official in charge of the railroads over which the Jewish transports traveled.	1
Where would we have been if everyone had thought things out in those days? You can do that today in the "new" German army. But with us an order was an order.	1
If I had sabotaged the order of the one-time Fuhrer of the German Reich, Adolf Hitler, I would have been not only a scoundrel but a despicable pig like those who broke their military path to join the ranks of the anti-Hitler criminals in the conspiracy of July 20, 1944.	1
I would like to stress again, however, that my department never gave a single annihilation order. We were responsible only for deportation.	2
My interest was only in the number of transport trains I had to provide. Whether they were bank directors or mental cases, the people who were loaded on these trains meant nothing to me.	2
It was really none of my business.	2
But to sum it all up, I must say that I regret nothing. Adolf Hitler may have been wrong all down the line, but one thing is beyond dispute: the man was able to work his way up from lance corporal in the German army to Fuhrer of a people of almost eighty million.	1
I never met him personally, but his success alone proves to me that I should subordinate myself to this man. He was somehow so supremely capable that the people recognized him. And so with that justification I recognized him joyfully, and I still defend him.	1
I must say truthfully, that if we had killed all the ten million Jews that Himmler's statisticians originally listed in 1933, I would say, "Good, we have destroyed an enemy."	2
But here I do not mean wiping them out entirely. That would not be proper — and we carried on a proper war.	1

(Kohlberg, 1967, p. 177.)

> **BOX 41-2 LETTER FROM A BIRMINGHAM JAIL**
>
> There is a type of constructive non-violent tension which is necessary for growth. Just as Socrates felt it was necessary to create a tension in the mind so that individuals could rise from the bondage of half-truths . . . so must we see the need for non-violent gadflies to create the kind of tension in society that will help men rise from the dark depths of prejudice and racism. . . .
>
> One may well ask, "How can you advocate breaking some laws and obeying others?" The answer lies in the fact that there are two types of laws, just and unjust. . . . One has not only a legal but a moral responsibility to obey just laws. Conversely, one has a moral responsibility to disobey unjust laws.
>
> . . . An unjust law is a human law that is not rooted in eternal law and natural law. Any law that uplifts human personality is just, any law that degrades human personality is unjust.
>
> An unjust law is a code that a numerical or power majority group compels a minority group to obey but does not make binding on itself. This is difference made legal.
>
> In no sense do I advocate evading or defying the law as would the rabid segregationist. That would lead to anarchy. One who breaks an unjust law must do so openly, lovingly, and with a willingness to accept the penalty. . . . an individual who breaks a law that conscience tells him is unjust, and who willingly accepts the penalty of imprisonment in order to arouse the conscience of the community over its injustice, is in reality expressing the highest respect for law (King, 1963).

2. *Modeling:* "If I impress others by my behavior, they will want to adopt my set of values." Current historical models present so many models to emulate that an individual can find it difficult to develop a personal and useful set of values.
3. *Limiting Choices:* "When a person is offered a choice between something I value and an absurd or unappealing alternative, my value will be chosen."
4. *Setting Rules:* "There are acceptable standards for behavior to which a person must conform without thinking or questioning."

An alternative to the above approaches is proposed by Raths, Harmin, and Simon (1966) in their *value theory,* which is based on the concept of human potential, emphasizing people's capacity for intelligent, self-directed behavior. The theory deals with the relationships between an individual and the environment, concentrating on what the person does with his or her existence.

Several hypotheses emerge from the assumption that persons of average emotional health can have a large degree of control over their existences:

1. Society does not always provide situations or experiences that help persons develop this control.

2. Persons without this control usually relate to their surroundings with behavior patterns of overconformity, flightiness, apathy, phoniness, or role acting.
3. Given the opportunity to clarify their relationship to their surroundings, persons will develop rational control over their lives.

Following these principles, then, value clarification is essentially a way of encouraging individuals to recognize the patterns that exist in their lives and then examine those patterns in a rational way. Hence, any strategy involved in clarifying values comes from the experiences of the individuals involved. A given individual may help others become aware of beliefs and behaviors they prize through three processes of valuing. These are *choosing*, *prizing*, and *acting*. In *choosing*, individuals can be encouraged to make choices freely without coercion but with support for discovering and examining alternatives. Once a choice has been made, value clarification strategy would call for efforts to encourage individuals to cherish or *prize* their choice through opportunities for public affirmation. *Acting* in ways consistent with one's choice provides experiences useful in examining the consistency of developing values.

This approach is intended to be nonjudgmental and to allow others to arrive at their own ideas and behaviors. Its authors argue that it can be successful in an accepting, nonpunitive environment. Value clarification offers an interesting analysis of moral development, and focuses on development at levels comparable to the advanced stages of Piaget's and Kohlberg's schemata.

Although these theories have not been extensively studied, the theories of Piaget and Kohlberg have achieved some validation and support in the research literature. Kohlberg is presently formulating modifications of his stages in response to research findings. The value theory of Rath and co-workers has not been subjected to the type of rigorous study typical of research on the theories of Piaget and Kohlberg. No doubt it will be studied more closely, since its application would have much to offer as we attempt to understand problem solving and interpersonal development in group and organizational settings.

Kohlberg's theory seems to be the best validated at this point. Additional research will undoubtedly strengthen its ability to provide an understanding of the development of morality.

Unit 42
Encounter! The Elusive Search

At the end of the 1960's, organizationally as well as ideologically, sensitivity training reached the end of an era. The ideas of sensitivity training are no longer new. A movement committed to change and novelty cannot subsist even on its own innovations. The glamour has faded. Clients have seen intensive group techniques introduced and abandoned; social scientists are waiting for hard research results; even the popular media are abandoning the wide-eyed picture of the breakthrough in human relations and the equally exaggerated picture of the sinister group leader manipulating the group for his nefarious ends. Nevertheless, the groups still attract many participants who need, if only for a short time, a feeling of purpose and meaning in the universe which they have not found in their secular middle-class life.

Back, 1973, p. 235.

The quotation above, from *Beyond Words,* is the summary of Kurt Back's analysis of the apparent failures and threats to the establishment of the sensitivity movement. A part of this analysis suggests that the sensitivity movement paralleled or was perhaps a reflection of the radical mood of the 1960s, in which change was advocated and charted in the absence of clearly defined goals. Needless to say, this point of view is not shared by all members of the behavioral science community.

Sensitivity training has been characterized as an effort to regenerate individuals in the pursuit of new values and solutions to pressing social problems. One serious difficulty with this claim, however, is couched in the skepticism of the scientific community. Approximately twenty years of research on various kinds of group experience has produced very little positive evidence for the effectiveness of sensitivity training. Before pursuing this point further, it might be useful to examine the various kinds of group experiences that have characterized the sensitivity movement.

Intensive Group Experiences

Encounter group. The most popular format in the group movement today is the encounter group. The basic goal of this group is to provide an intensive interpersonal experience in a small group, focusing on the interactions and feelings that emerge within the group setting itself. An effort is made to create an atmosphere that encourages openness, honesty, emotional sensitivity, and freedom of expression. Participants are encouraged to give prompt and honest feedback. Encounter groups provide an opportunity for intimacy with others as well as an opportunity for social comparison of oneself with others. This approach focuses primarily on intense discussion and group exercises.

Sensitivity group. A sensitivity group is a collection of individuals whose common goal is the achievement of greater awareness in the interpersonal process. The activities of such groups often include heavy doses of such nonverbal behaviors as touching, body movement, dance, and massage. When properly used, these activities can be quite useful in increasing self-awareness and greater sensitivity to body emotions in interpersonal events.

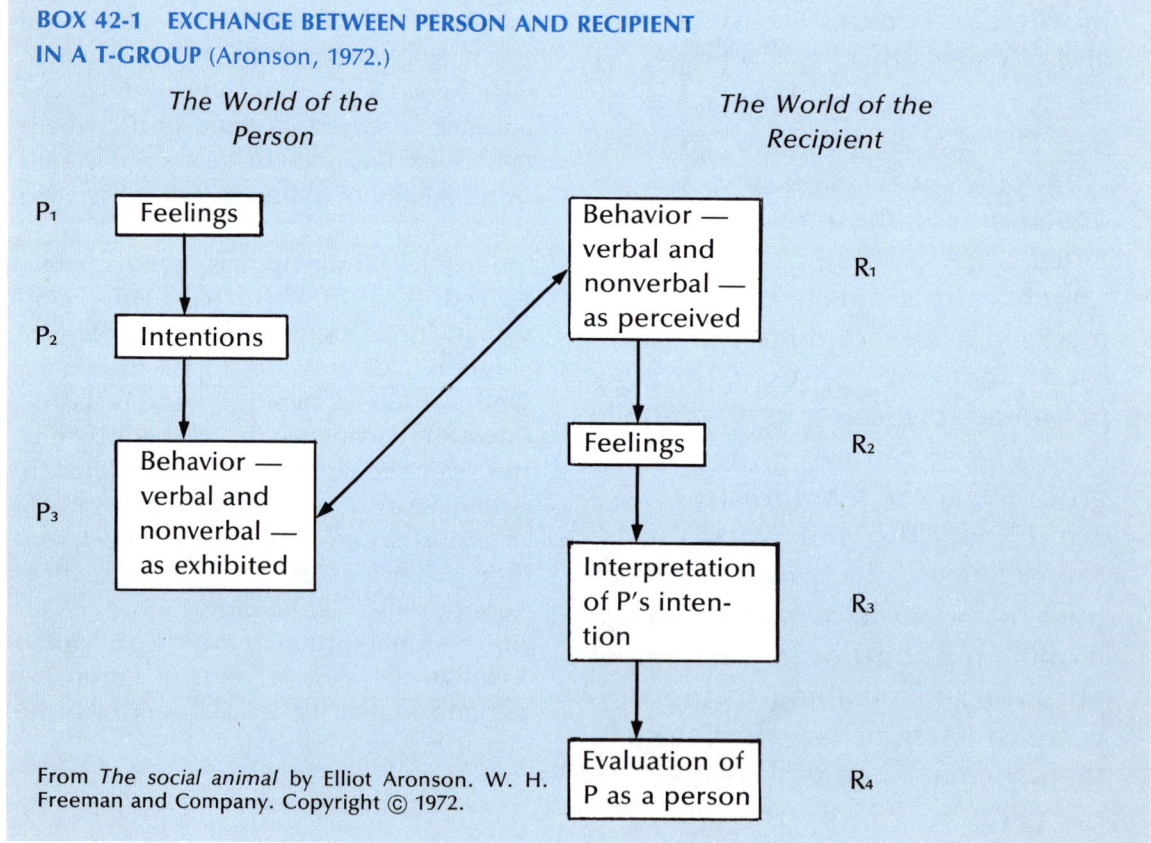

BOX 42-1 EXCHANGE BETWEEN PERSON AND RECIPIENT IN A T-GROUP (Aronson, 1972.)

From *The social animal* by Elliot Aronson. W. H. Freeman and Company. Copyright © 1972.

When abused, these techniques can be a waste of effort and time or responsible for severe damages that can be long-lasting.

T-group. Broadly speaking, the term *T-group* refers to the more conservative, more traditional group, in which the primary emphasis is on verbal behavior and the group discussions are almost exclusively confined to the here-and-now. In recent years, T-groups have incorporated some nonverbal procedures; however, verbal interaction continues to be the primary source of contact. In a T-group, people learn through doing and experiencing (see Box 42-1). Participants in these groups learn by trying things out, by "getting in touch" with their feelings, and by expressing those feelings to others, either verbally or nonverbally.

As can be seen in the above examples, there is a good deal of overlap between the various experiential groups. They have in common a framework and techniques conducive to learning experiences that facilitate interpersonal growth. Additionally, they attempt to facilitate the development of self-expression and personal and social change. In all cases, the general thrust of the group process involves a combination of group techniques

---

We can explain the dynamics of Aronson's schema as follows:

The Person (P) has some feelings about the Recipient (R). He intends to communicate a particular feeling. This manifests itself in some kind of behavior — words, gesture, smile, etc. This behavior is perceived by the Recipient (R) in the context of his own feelings, needs, and prior knowledge of P. This perception evokes feelings in R (warmth, anger, love, fear, etc.) which get translated into interpretations of P's intention. Evaluations of what kind of a person P is flow directly from R's interpretation.

Error can occur at any point in this sequence of events. We often attribute motives or personality predispositions to individuals based on our observations of their behavior. Careful examination of this process can produce a great deal of potential learning about interpersonal relations. Rarely does the opportunity for critical examination of interpersonal events occur in on-going interactions. The T-group, however, was designed to provide such opportunities for examining interpersonal processes. The T-group provides an atmosphere in which feelings can be expressed and worked through. This is accomplished by encouraging participants to share their feelings and avoid skipping or mislabeling behaviors along the chain of events. For example, it is critically important to explore the intervening events between a person's feelings (P_1) and an evaluation of those feelings by a recipient (R_4). To gloss over these intervening events can contribute to distortion, inaccuracy, and confusion.

designed to provoke stronger expressions from individuals as well as efforts to subordinate individual feelings and expressions in the interest of "groupness" or togetherness (see Box 42-2). In summary, the movement focuses on the search for new values of relatedness through a regeneration of the individual and a changing society.

Group Compatibility and Development

Schutz (1958) has developed a theory called *Fundamental Interpersonal Relations Orientation (FIRO)* which summarizes several interpersonal behavior statements relevant to encounter-group experiences. The theme on which this theory is based is that individuals interact primarily on the basis of three interpersonal needs: (1) *inclusion:* the desire to be part of a group, combined with the ability to function alone; (2) *control:* the need to control others or be controlled by them; and (3) *affection:* the need to receive warmth and give it to others. Compatibility in groups is thought to be directly related to the harmony and satisfaction of these needs between group members. More importantly, Schutz's theory describes group development processes. Individuals in groups go through successive cycles or phases of inclusion, control, and affection, moving from one phase to the other only after they have successfully resolved the phase they are in. Schutz also distinguishes between short-term and long-term relationships in making assessments of compatibility. A temporary relationship (e.g., hitchhiker) will be affected only by considerations of inclusion, whereas college roommates will be motivated by compatibility of needs in the control and affection areas of exchange.

Rapid advances in technology and accompanying problems of interpersonal adjustment have negatively affected group development experiences. Toffler (1970) has called this difficulty in adjustment "future shock," the symptoms of which include "erratic swings in interest and life style, followed by an effort to 'crawl into . . . shells' through social, intellectual and emotional withdrawal" (p. 290). Some have suggested that the emergence of sensitivity groups is a part of the shifting life-styles characteristic of future shock, or represents an exaggerated attempt to develop techniques and skills useful in promoting greater interpersonal openness and competence.

In *Joy,* Schutz has applied his theory of FIRO to sensitivity groups, offering an organizational structure to be followed in the attainment of more effective interpersonal relationships. Schutz suggests that joy (interpersonal pleasure) is found through greater awareness of or sensitivity to one's bodily states in relationship to others. Presumably, through greater awareness we can enter more fully and meaningfully into interpersonal relations. *Joy* is a kind of manual in which methods and techniques based on assumptions from humanistic psychology are utilized to create new learning and eliminate bad learning. Considerable value is placed on honesty, awareness of feelings and emotions, subjectively experienced freedom from internal and external constraints and inhibitions, and a belief that people are

BOX 42-2 SAMPLE INTERACTION OF A T-GROUP MEETING

At the fifth meeting the group's feelings about its own progress became the initial focus of discussion. The "talkers" participated as usual, conversation shifting rapidly from one point to another. Dissatisfaction was mounting, expressed through loud, snide remarks by some and through apathy by others.

George Franklin appeared particularly disturbed. Finally pounding the table, he exclaimed, "I don't know what is going on here! I should be paid for listening to this drivel! I'm getting just a bit sick of wasting my time here. If the profs don't put out — I quit!" George was pleased; he was angry, and he had said so. As he sat back in his chair, he felt he had the group behind him. He felt he had the guts to say what most of the others were thinking! Some members of the group applauded loudly, but others showed obvious disapproval. They wondered why George was excited over so insignificant an issue, why he hadn't done something constructive rather than just sounding off as usual. Why, they wondered, did he say their comments were "drivel"?

George Franklin became the focus of discussion. "What do you mean, George, by saying this is nonsense?" "What do you expect, a neat set of rules to meet all your problems?" George was getting uncomfortable. These were questions difficult for him to answer. Gradually he began to realize that a large part of the group disagreed with him; he began to wonder why. He was learning something about people he hadn't known before. "How does it feel, George, to have people disagree with you when you thought you had them behind you?..."

Bob White was first annoyed with George and now with the discussion. He was getting tense, a bit shaky perhaps. Bob didn't like anybody to get a raw deal, and he felt that George was getting it. At first Bob tried to minimize George's outburst, and then he suggested that the group get on to the real issues; but the group continued to focus on George. Finally Bob said, "Why don't you leave George alone and stop picking on him? We're not getting anywhere this way."

With the help of the leaders, the group focused on Bob. "What do you mean, 'picking' on him?" "Why, Bob, have you tried to change the discussion?" "Why are you so protective of George?" Bob began to realize that the group wanted to focus on George; he also saw that George didn't think he was being picked on, but felt he was learning something about himself and how others reacted to him. "Why do I always get upset," Bob began to wonder, "when people start to look at each other? Why do I feel sort of sick when people get angry at each other?" ... Now Bob was learning something about how people saw him, while gaining some insight into his own behavior (Tannenbaum, Weschler, and Massarik, 1961, p. 123).

basically good — or at least not inherently bad. Hence, a general goal of the encounter approach is the elimination of emotional barriers impeding individual development and restricting the capacity for fulfillment in all facets of life.

Evaluation

There has not been an overwhelming effort at evaluating the outcome of encounter group experiences. Opinions regarding the outcome of these experiences range from disappointment with what is considered to be inadequate assessment approaches to the frank conclusion that the aesthetic experience derived from participation in encounter groups does not produce change. Despite this wide range of opinion, efforts at evaluation continue to be important.

One application of encounter techniques that has undergone extensive evaluation is in managerial training and development. In a review of these research studies, Campbell and Dunnette (1968) concluded that "while T-group training seems to produce observable changes in behavior, the utility of these changes for the performance of individuals in their organizational roles remains to be demonstrated" (p. 73). This conclusion is virtually identical to that reached by Back (1973) in a more extensive review of evaluation studies between 1945 and 1970: "Research and evaluation studies tend to show that something happens as a consequence of sensitivity training, but that the effect is not reproducible and that intended benefits are as likely as not to result" (p. 193).

It is possible that no more conclusive findings have been derived on the outcome of sensitivity experiences because of poor measurement techniques or simply asking the wrong questions.

In probably the best-designed evaluative study to date, Lieberman, Yalom, and Miles (1971) offer a little more encouragement. These authors randomly assigned students to encounter groups using different training techniques, with two groups using each technique. All participants evaluated themselves and each other; additionally, group members were evaluated by observers and a sample of their friends. From the massive data analyses it was determined that a large majority of participants had positive feelings and enhanced self-esteem resulting from the group experience, and a small

TABLE 42-1   Changes in Encounter-Group Members

| Time | Group | NEGATIVE (%) | | NEUTRAL (%) | POSITIVE (%) | | Total |
		Casualty	Negative Change	Dropouts	Unchanged	Moderate Change	High Change	
Immediately after groups	Participants	8	8	13	38	20	14	206
	Control group	...	23	...	60	13	4	69
Six to eight months after groups	Participants	10	8	17	33	23	9	160*
	Control group	...	15	...	68	11	6	47*

* Data not available on total sample.
(After Lieberman, Yalom, and Miles, 1973.)

TABLE 42-2 Dimensions of Outcome

	Level	
State	Headshrinking (− to 0)	Mind-expanding (0 to +)
	Discomfort	*Pleasure*
Affective	Distress	Joy
	Dissatisfaction	Love
	Dysphoria	Verve
	Ineffective	*Creative*
Effective	Inept	Energetic
	Incompetent	Powerful
	Inefficient	Persuasive

(Parloff, 1970.)

percentage experienced difficulties serious enough to warrant psychiatric treatment (see Table 42-1).

Parloff (1970) has provided a useful model for examining some of the problems of inconsistency in findings regarding group outcomes. Many of the studies reported do not take baseline assessments prior to the group experience. Parloff's distinction between "headshrinking" and "mind-expanding" experiences makes the issue of baseline level an important one (see Table 42-2). Parloff's model consists of two basic outcome dimensions: (1) Patient State: affective (subjective experiences and feeling tone) and effective (objective, observable behaviors) and (2) Level of each state: headshrinking (experiences from negative to neutral) and mind-expanding (experiences from neutral to positive). Persons falling into the negative or suffering category have typically been viewed as candidates for psychotherapy. Mind-expanding experiences, however, are the appropriate domain of the various group approaches. It becomes critically important therefore to know the pregroup state of each individual in order to examine and relate process with outcome variables. Future research efforts to evaluate the outcome of encounter group experiences should be facilitated by this innovative model. In the meantime, we must agree with Parloff in his general conclusion regarding the demonstrated effectiveness of encounter group experiences (1970, p. 279):

. . . Participants in encounter group report favorable reactions and are frequently described by others as showing improved interpersonal skills. The evidence is meager that such participants undergo significant attitude change or personality change, and evidence that group training improves organizational efficiency is not compelling. What is clearest is that these groups provide an intensive affective experience for many participants. In this sense, the groups may be described as potent. As is the case with all potent agents, they may be helpful when properly administered inert in "subclinical" dosages, and noxious when excessive or inappropriate.

Unit 43
The Trip to Nowhere?

Marijuana

The cartoon portrays what many believe to be the basic dilemma in the approach of society to the use of marijuana. Unlike heroin, the power and danger of which are acknowledged by user and nonuser alike, marijuana is attacked primarily by the nonuser. What are the facts about marijuana? Is it a danger both to the user and to society? Or is it a relatively harmless substance which has somehow gotten a very bad reputation?

EFFECTS

The history of marijuana use is a long one which covers all parts of the world and all levels of society. The effect that it has on the individual has been the source of much controversy. It has at various times been credited with causing almost every type of negative behavior imaginable. In one particular work (Rowell and Rowell, 1939), marijuana was held responsible for destruction of will power and of the ability to distinguish between right and wrong, making one's actions a result of one's own "warped desires" or the "base suggestion" of others (p. 33). These authors in addition attributed crime, immorality, accidents, insanity, and career ruin to the use of marijuana. The belief in the "evil power" of marijuana persists even today. Yet as early as 1944, New York Mayor LaGuardia's committee on marijuana dispelled most of the myths regarding the evils of the drug (Mayor LaGuardia's committee, 1966). The study is probably the most extensive and careful one to date. Yet it took almost twenty more years, much additional research, and many vocal spokespersons before attitudes toward marijuana softened.

Most recent studies find that the effects of marijuana, when the drug is used in moderation, are for the most part quite mild. It tends to produce a state of euphoria, followed by relaxation, minor changes in blood pressure and pulse rate, alteration of blood sugar level leading to increase in hunger, decrease in physical coordination, some distortion of time and space perception, reduction of inhibitions, and impairment of judgment and memory (Ausubel, 1964; Bloomquist, 1968; Lindesmith, 1965).

Occasional more serious effects have been reported, including panic reactions, gross confusion, depression, paranoia,

Copyright © 1973 by Robert Allen Salazar

"Too bad you didn't kill somebody — they could'a rehabilitated you for that!"

hallucinations, and psychotic reactions (Keeler, 1967). There is even a case report in which a subject lost the use of his eye muscles for about six weeks (Mohan and Sood, 1964). Such reactions are relatively rare (Louria, 1968) and are probably not caused directly by the marijuana. Rather, the drug "may precipitate such [psychopathologies] in individuals who are so predisposed" (Keeler, 1967, p. 677).

It is generally conceded that marijuana is not physiologically addicting. In other words, the use of marijuana is not characterized by an increased tolerance nor by withdrawal symptoms. The drug can, however, create a psychological dependency. Psychological dependency, however, is a function of the individual rather than the drug. Such dependency can be developed to any substance. One can develop psychological dependency on chewing gum or one's mother, as well as marijuana.

Claims have been made that marijuana serves as an aphrodisiac, increasing sexual activity and enjoyment. This is unlikely, as pointed out by Louria (1968), for although the drug may decrease inhibitions, it also increases passivity. Another positive effect of marijuana which has been posited is that it increases creativity. As yet there is little objective support for this claim.

USERS

What about marijuana users? What kind of people are they? In the 1940s reports characterized marijuana users as emotionally immature and abnormal (Gaskill, 1945). They were found to come from the lower socioeconomic classes, from broken homes, to have records of other criminal activity, and to have abnormal sex drives and anxiety (Charen and Perelman, 1946). Such a view of users may have been relatively accurate at that time, when only those on the fringes of society used the drug. Today, however, the use of marijuana is more widespread, with surveys showing between 10 and 20 percent of the population as having used it. Therefore, no single characterization can describe marijuana users.

Bloomquist (1968) uses a threefold classification system to describe users. His system is as follows:

1. The antisocial misfits are the same type of individuals who used the drug in the 1940s. Their marijuana use is usually only one of many antisocial behaviors. This is the group which is most likely to go on to hard drugs, such as heroin.
2. Individuals who are interested in self-exploration and mind expansion make up the second group. These users include the hippies, the intellectuals and pseudointellectuals, and the religious and pseudoreligious. They are looking for new experiences and represent the people who are not likely to go on to more powerful hallucinogens such as LSD.
3. The last group is the largest and is composed of the average, curious, relatively uninhibited individual. Few of these users will go on to the use of hard drugs or more powerful hallucinogens.

Given such a widely divergent group of marijuana users, it is clear that no broad, general statement can be made about the personality characteristics of the users.

LEGALIZATION

At the current time the most heated controversy deals with whether or not marijuana should be legalized. As early as 1938, one year after the passage of the original legislation to control marijuana, Williams (1967) argued for legalization on the grounds that the law would lead to the development of rackets to smuggle and distribute marijuana. His warning has come true. Murtagh has also argued for legalization, stating that the current drug laws are "immoral in principle and ineffectual in operation" (1967, p. 220).

Several arguments are commonly used in the debate over legalization. The opponents of legalization argue that marijuana use produces criminal behavior. Such a belief is supported by police reports. Most objective information, however, indicates that marijuana does not cause criminal behavior, although such behavior can be stimulated by marijuana use. The relation of marijuana and crime is probably an associative one rather than a causal one. As the LaGuardia report pointed out, marijuana may reduce inhibitions and release latent thoughts, but does not produce responses totally alien to the undrugged state (Mayor LaGuardia's Committee, 1966).

The proponents of legalization argue that marijuana is no more serious or dangerous than alcohol or tobacco. Although this is probably true, this is essentially a negative argument. Bloomquist (1968) notes the massive social problems resulting from the use of alcohol and argues that marijuana, although no worse than alcohol, would merely add another large problem. The existence of one legal evil, in Bloomquist's view, does not justify the creation of another.

The comparison of marijuana and tobacco is a weak one, for although tobacco is probably far more dangerous physically, its negative action is primarily operative on the individual and does not extend outward to society. The negative effects of marijuana, although admittedly rare, often involve acts against other individuals. In addition, use of marijuana does impair coordination and can lead to serious dangers in the operation of automobiles.

Another frequently used argument by the opponents of marijuana legalization is that most individuals who go on to the more serious drugs such as heroin and LSD start with marijuana. This is quite true, but seems to be a backward statement of the problem. It is similar to saying that all alcoholics at one time took a first drink and that all hardened criminals committed a first crime. A more accurate view of these statistics is to ask how many marijuana users go on to harder drugs. As pointed out above, the largest category of marijuana users are the normal, curious individuals, and they rarely go on to more serious drugs. Marijuana functions as a preliminary step to hard drugs primarily in those who already have psychological or sociological adjustment problems. The vast majority of marijuana users do not go on to hard drugs or powerful hallucinogens (Bloomquist, 1968; Lindesmith, 1965; Louria, 1968).

Perhaps one of the strongest arguments in favor of legalization is the purely practical one put forth by Kaplan (1970). In his book he argues that the cost of enforcing the marijuana laws far exceeds the benefits. He advises that the sale of the drug should be put under strict regulation with high taxes. The tax money could then be put to use in other ways more productive than apprehending and prosecuting individuals in possession of one marijuana cigarette. Although legalization may, as Louria (1968) points out, increase the use of marijuana, Kaplan notes that it may also reduce the use of more dangerous drugs by providing a convenient and legal alternative.

Marijuana is a relatively harmless substance and is far less powerful and dangerous than its opponents have claimed. At the same time, it is far less valuable than its proponents have stated. In seeking a solution to the legal question, one must carefully weigh all the personal, social, and financial rewards and costs. It does, however, seem clear that it is necessary for at least some revamping of a law which can impose a thirty-year sentence and a $30,000 fine for the possession of less than half an ounce of marijuana, as was done in the case of Timothy Leary. In addition, correction of the logical inconsistencies involved in equating marijuana with heroin, while prescribing far less severe penalties for LSD use, would be valuable.

LSD

The injustice of the marijuana law becomes apparent when it is compared with the laws that govern lysergic acid diethylamide (LSD). Although LSD is far more powerful, and hence potentially more dangerous, than marijuana, in many cases the laws governing the possession and use of LSD are far milder than those for marijuana. LSD has been said to be the "most potent mind-altering drug in common use" (Louria, 1968, p. 11). It apparently can have long-term effects, both positive and negative. The use of LSD in medical settings is widespread. Although its effects are still not fully understood, much research has shed light on the functioning of the drug.

Psychological effects. The reaction of individuals to LSD varies greatly from person to person, but certain common responses have been found. Subjects taking LSD may have changes in body image, mood changes, difficulty in thinking and concentrating, auditory and visual hallucinations, anxiety, euphoria, paranoid thinking, hostility, underactivity, and blurred vision. The visual and auditory hallucinations which occur during the LSD experience, may recur days, weeks, or months later (Frosch, Robbins, and Stern, 1965).

In tests of specific behavior, it has been found that LSD alters size constancy and space and color perception and raises the threshold of light perception. All of these perceptual changes contribute to the unusual and sometimes beautiful experience of an LSD trip.

The findings on intellectual functioning are conflicting. Some investigators find that LSD reduces intellectual functioning, while others fail to find any effect. It is probable that intellectual functioning is reduced at least to the extent that the individual has lessened powers of concentration. The person simply doesn't care to perform intellectual tasks during the LSD experience.

It should be remembered that the effect LSD has on the individual varies with a number of factors. Hoffer and Osmond (1967) list 12 factors that can affect the reaction to the drug, including the subject's personality, education, reasons for taking the drug, and previous experience with hallucinogens.

The setting in which the drug is taken will also affect the response. Such things as lighting and music can alter the LSD experience, as can an appropriate "guide" for the trip. The presence of other people also appears to have a strong effect. Slater, Morimoto, and Hyder (1967) found subjects taking LSD as a group showed less anxiety, depression, inappropriate behavior, illusions, hallucinations, and thinking and speech disorders than did individuals taking the drug alone. The group subjects also tended to show more elation than did individual subjects.

Therapeutic effects. Great claims have been made for the therapeutic value of LSD since its first use as a therapeutic tool in 1947. The drug has been found to have beneficial effects on a number of problem behaviors, including homosexuality, drug addiction, alcoholism, neurosis, psychosis, character disorders, and some types of childhood schizophrenia. Kurland, Savage, Shaffer, and Unger (1967) point out that the drug does not have "any inherent beneficial effects" (p. 34) but serves to activate the patient and allows the bringing out of material which would otherwise be difficult or impossible to recover. Other investigators have expressed doubts as to the value of LSD therapy, while still others have pointed to the need for more rigor and control in the study of the therapeutic effects of LSD before any conclusion can be reached.

Nonmedical use. This discussion of LSD so far has concerned itself with the medical uses. But what about the nonmedical or private use of the drug? The most noted advocate of LSD, Timothy Leary, has made great claims for its positive effects. He argues that the legal banning of the drug is not due to any physical or psychological dangers, but has been done for political reasons by the politicians who fear the social changes that the LSD insight will produce. In one statement, he claims that within "20 years, every social institution will have been transformed by the new insight, provided by consciousness-expanding drugs" (Leary and Alpert, 1967). However, close perusal of the scientific literature demonstrates little corroboration for such claims and much evidence of physical and psychological damage from nonmedical use.

There is also little if any evidence for the claims that LSD heightens creativity or improves one's sexual activity. Rather, it has been found to produce psychotic reactions, violent behavior, panic reactions, and suicide. The exact incidence of these negative effects is not clear, but it is apparent that they occur at a higher frequency in private use than in medical studies (Louria, 1967). Louria (1967, 1968), for example, points out that one-sixth of the patients referred to Bellevue Hospital for LSD psychosis had prolonged reactions which required care in other institutions. One-half of these subjects had previous histories of psychiatric abnormalities. The others probably had underlying personality problems also. It is unlikely that well-adjusted individuals would have long-term psychotic reactions. But the evaluation of adjustment is probably more reliably done by a physician or psychiatrist than by an individual or his or her friends.

As pointed out above, even those investigators who have stated strong beliefs in the positive value of the drug stress the need for careful control both during and after the LSD experience. Such controls are not instituted in private use, which probably accounts for the higher percentage of negative after-effects found by those working with individuals who have taken the drug outside of the medical setting (Louria, 1967, 1968).

Chromosomal damage. Perhaps the most serious danger of all in the use of LSD, whether in private or medical situations, is the reported chromosomal damage resulting from the drug. Studies have been conducted on both human and animal subjects, and the results are not entirely consistent. In a brief review of the literature in this area, Louria (1968) notes that some investigators report chromosomal breaks and rearrangement, or both, in up to 80 percent of LSD users. The more frequent the use and the greater the dose, the more likely such damage will occur. This chromosomal damage may be passed on to the children if LSD is taken during pregnancy. It is still unclear whether damage can be passed on by the mother to her children when she has taken LSD prior to pregnancy, whether LSD produces chromosomal abnormalities in the reproductive tissue, and whether the father can transmit the abnormalities. As yet there have been no reports of infant abnormalities attributed to LSD. But full evaluation of the effects of LSD in this area may take up to two generations to accomplish (Louria, 1968).

The problem of chromosomal abnormalities need not be an argument against all LSD use. In some cases, the damage would be secondary to the improvement of certain psychological disturbances. But chromosomal damage does seem to be a strong argument against the use of the drug for private, mind-expanding experiments by those of childbearing age.

LSD is a powerful hallucinogen which may prove useful for the treatment of certain psychological disorders. Its use is well justified in medical settings. As far as private use is concerned, Leary presents a philosophical argument for such use when he states that ". . . man's natural state is ecstatic wonder, ecstatic intuition, ecstatic accurate movement. Don't settle for less" (Leary and Alpert, 1967, p. 210). The contrasting scientific evidence pointing to serious and long-term complications and negative side effects, however, appear valid enough to make the use of LSD for a private "trip" a highly risky venture.

SUMMARY

The needs for environmental enrichment, structure, and meaning are strong motivational forces within the individual behaving organism. This has been suggested by the responses of individuals in prison solitary confinement and in social isolation experiments. In one experiment, pairs of subjects were confined for eight days in small rooms which provided few external cues. The pairs that completed the full eight days engaged in self-pacing activities and coordination of living and work schedules.

Relations between human beings have changed from what they were thirty years ago. The rapid shift from an agrarian rural society to mass urbanization has made adjustment to the changes more difficult, thus creating what has been labelled *future shock*. *Alienation* derives in part from social conditions that foster contradictions. The most obvious instances of these conditions occur when cherished values are not adhered to by those in leadership positions, or when paths to goals and aspirations are blocked to selected segments of society by institutional practices. Because of the difficulty in separating how much of a given problem is caused by societal forces and how much is a function of the individual, it may be fruitful to look at the problems of alienation as a joint interaction of an individual's experiences and the societal forces which shape or influence them. Many authors have cited the perfect efficiency of modern society as being primarily responsible for alienation. Erich Fromm has advanced the thesis that the failure of society to fill people's five basic needs may be a causal factor in alienation.

Advancing the belief that moral commitment lies at the core of personal identity, M. Brewster Smith investigated the relationship between moral thinking and consequent moral behavior in the context of the Free Speech Movement. This effort was largely designed to uncover distinctions between the "new morality" of college students engaged in social protest and the morality of their nonprotesting counterparts. The data indicate that the nonactivists tended to describe themselves as ambitious, foresightful, orderly, and conventional. The traits that most discriminated the activists were free, unfettered, not hung up, creative, and imaginative. Additional comparisons regarding moral process revealed that the largest percentage of students at the highest level of moral development were found among the activists. The combined results were interpreted as demonstrating that student protest is not merely rabble rousing or thrill seeking, but a reflection of profound moral principles.

In another approach to morality, theories have been postulated that emphasize its developmental aspects. Jean Piaget's cognitive developmental approach postulates that a child grows from having the cognitive ability to deal only with concrete and immediate sensations to the ability to deal with a wide range of abstract concepts and their interrelationships. Moral development, for Piaget, is an outgrowth of this progression. Piaget sees two basic kinds of moral judgment: moral realism and moral relativism. Moral realism is an absolute, rule-oriented approach to right and wrong. Acts are evaluated as good or bad without taking circumstances or intentions into account. Moral relativism is based on a more general and abstract concept of right and wrong.

Kohlberg's theory of moral development is an extension of Piaget's theory. He has outlined six stages within three major levels of development: preconventional, conventional, and postconventional. The basis of moral judgment for the preconventional level rests in cultural rules and prescriptions for good and bad. Judgments are motivated by fear of punishment. Conventional morality rests in performing proper behaviors in an attempt to fulfill the expectations of others. In postconventional morality, judgment resides in rational principles independent of society or authority, with an orientation away from convention. Kohlberg's stages, then, represent a progression similar to Piaget's theory — movement from concrete, inflexible thinking to an abstract relativistic approach to moral judgment.

An alternative to the above approaches is the *value clarification theory,* which is based on the notion of human potential, emphasizing the capacity of human beings for intelligent self-directed behavior. Value clarification is essentially a way of encouraging individuals to look at patterns that exist in their lives and examine them in a rational way to make choices freely on the basis of their own experiences. This approach is intended to be nonjudgmental, allowing others to arrive at their own ideas and behaviors.

Intensive group experiences have been developed in an effort to regenerate individuals in the pursuit of new values and solutions to social problems. The various experiential groups *(encounter, sensitivity, and T-groups)* have in common a framework and techniques conducive to learning experiences that facilitate interpersonal growth as well as the development of self-expression. Schutz has developed a theory called *Fundamental Interpersonal Relations Orientation (FIRO)* which summarizes several factors relevant to group experiences. The theory proposes that compatibility in groups is related to the harmony and satisfaction of three interpersonal needs: inclusion, control, and affection.

There has not been an overwhelming effort to evaluate the outcome of encounter group experiences, and findings from such evaluations are inconclusive. Some positive effects have been found, but the extent and utility of these effects are not clear.

Parloff has provided a useful model for examining some of the problems in results on group experiences. This model stresses the critical importance of knowing the pregroup state of each individual. Future research efforts to evaluate the outcome of encounter group experiences should be facilitated by Parloff's analysis.

The history of marijuana use is a long one which covers all parts of the world and all levels of society. It's effects have been the source of much controversy. It has been credited with causing almost every type of negative behavior imaginable. Most recent studies, however, find that the effects of moderate marijuana use are for the most part quite mild. Reports of more serious effects are relatively rare, and these reactions are probably not caused directly by the marijuana. It is generally conceded that marijuana is not physiologically addicting: i.e., that its use is not characterized by an increased tolerance nor by withdrawal symptoms. The drug can create a psychological dependency, but this is a function of the individual rather than the drug and can be developed to any substance. In an attempt to describe marijuana users, Bloomquist uses a threefold classification system: 1) antisocial misfits, 2) individuals who are interested in self-exploration and mind expansion, and 3) average, curious, relatively uninhibited individuals. Given such a widely divergent group of marijuana users, it is clear that no broad general statement can be made about the personality characteristics of the users.

At the current time, the most heated controversy deals with whether or not marijuana should be legalized. Several arguments are commonly used in the debate about legalization. The opponents of legalization argue that marijuana use produces criminal behavior. Most objective information, however, indicates that marijuana does not cause criminal behavior. Opponents also argue that most marijuana users go on to more serious drugs, such as heroin and LSD. However, the vast majority of marijuana users do not go on to hard drugs or powerful hallucinogens; marijuana functions as a preliminary step to hard drugs primarily in those who already have psychological or sociological adjustment problems.

The proponents of legalization argue that marijuana is no more serious or dangerous than alcohol or tobacco. Although this is probably true, it is essentially a negative argument. Perhaps one of the strongest arguments in favor of legalization is that the cost of enforcing the marijuana laws far exceeds the benefits.

Marijuana is a relatively harmless substance, being far less powerful and dangerous than its opponents have claimed and far less valuable than its proponents have stated.

The marijuana laws do seem logically inconsistent when compared with the laws that govern LSD. Although LSD is far more powerful and dangerus than marijuana, in many cases the laws governing its possession and use are far milder than those for marijuana. Although its effects are still not fully understood, research has shed much light on the functioning of the drug. Certain common responses to LSD have been found, but the reaction of individuals to the drug varies greatly from person to person with a number of factors. Although great claims have been made for the therapeutic value of LSD, a more rigorous and controlled study of the therapeutic effects of the drug is needed before any conclusion can be reached.

Perhaps the most serious danger of all in the use of LSD, in private or medical situations, is the reported chromosomal damage resulting from the drug. In some cases, this damage would be considered secondary to the concomitant improvement of certain psychological disturbances; thus, its use is well justified in medical settings. The scientific evidence pointing to possible serious and long-term complications and negative side effects, however, presents a strong argument against the use of LSD for private mind-expanding experiments.

GLOSSARY

Affection: according to Schutz, the need to receive or give warmth to others

Alienation: a generalized sense of meaninglessness, helplessness, and social isolation which derives in part from social conditions that foster contradictions; constitutes a reduction of personal controls against engaging in deviance

Anomie: the social state in which norms are persistently and successfully disregarded in human behavior; implies a lessened social control against deviance

Anxiety: a generalized, diffuse apprehension about the future

Baseline level: defined pregroup state of each individual in an encounter group; necessary in order to examine and relate process with outcome variables in an evaluation of the effectiveness of encounter group experiences

Compatibility: according to Schutz, the harmony and satisfaction of the three interpersonal needs (inclusion, control, and affection) between group members

Control: according to Schutz, one of our three interpersonal needs

Conventional: according to Kohlberg, the middle level of moral development, in which moral value resides in performing good or right roles and in maintaining the conventional order and the expectancies of others

Deindividuation: a state of relative anonymity, in which a group member does not feel singled out or identifiable

Expiative justice: the belief, which according to Piaget, is held by younger children, that a wrongdoer should suffer a punishment that is painful in proportion to the seriousness of the offense but not necessarily related to the nature of the offense

Feminist movement: recent movement consisting mostly of urban, white, college-educated, middle-class women in an attempt to be recognized first as human beings and only secondarily as females

Fundamental Interpersonal Relations Orientation (FIRO): theory developed by Schutz based on the theme that individuals interact with each other primarily on the basis of three interpersonal needs: inclusion, control, and affection

Future shock: Alvin Toffler's term for the disorientation resulting from the superimposition of a new culture upon an old one; a product of the greatly accelerated rate of change in society

Group psychotherapy: methods of treatment in which patients meet together to discuss and interpret their problems in a framework conducive to learning experiences facilitating interpersonal growth and to the development of self-expression and personal and social change

Inclusion: according to Shutz, the desire to be part of a group, coupled with the ability to function alone — one of three interpersonal needs

Logotherapy: a form of psychotherapy, developed by Viktor E. Frankl as a result of his experiences in Nazi prison camps, which has as its goal helping individuals to achieve the distinctively human capacity of rising above their outward fate. Logotherapy focuses on the future, on the assignments and meanings to be fulfilled by the patient, in an attempt to reorient the patient toward the meaning of his or her life.

Lysergic acid diethylamide (LSD): a powerful hallucinogen which has proven useful in medical settings for the treatment of certain psychological disorders but which may have serious and long-term complications and negative side effects producing physical and psychological damage in nonmedical usage

Moral judgment: as studied by Piaget, Kohlberg, and others, a subject's beliefs regarding good and bad behavior in certain situations

Moral realism: according to Piaget, the belief held by young children that good behavior is obedient behavior and that acts should be judged in terms of the consequences, not on the basis of the motive behind the act

Moral relativism: according to Piaget, the belief held by older children that an act alone does not determine the degree of wrongness; rather, the judgment is based on circumstances, intention, and amount of harm done

Physiological addiction: a physiological dependency on a drug; there is increased tolerance for the drug with increased usage and, when usage is stopped, there are physiological withdrawal symptoms

Postconventional: according to Kohlberg, the highest level of moral development, in which moral value resides in conformity by the self to shared or sharable standards, rights, or duties

Preconventional: according to Kohlberg, the lowest level of moral development, in which moral value resides in external, quasi-physical happenings, in bad acts, or in quasi-physical needs rather than in persons and standards

Psychological addiction: dependency on an agent or a substance as the result of emotional rather than physiological factors; therefore, not characterized by an increased tolerance or by physiological withdrawal symptoms

Psychotherapy: the application of psychological techniques to the treatment of mental disorders

Q-sort: technique used in personality assessment in which respondents describe their ideal selves by placing adjectives into equal piles ranging from those felt to be most descriptive of the individual to those least descriptive

Restitutive justice (reciprocity): the belief, which according to Piaget is held by older children, that punishment should be logically related to the offense so that the rule-breaker will understand the implications of his misconduct

Self-expression: the release and utilization of one's own feelings, ideas, and motives

Sensitivity training: an effort to regenerate individuals in the pursuit of new values and solutions to their pressing social problems

REFERENCES

Allport, G. W. Preface to *Man's search for meaning* by Viktor E. Frankl. New York: Washington Square Press, 1963.

Altman, I., Taylor, D. A., and Wheeler, L. Ecological aspects of group behavior in social isolation. *Journal of Applied Social Psychology,* 1971, *1,* 76–100.

Aronson, E. *The social animal.* San Francisco: W. H. Freeman and Company, 1972.

Ausubel, D. P. *Drug addiction: Physiological, psychological and sociological aspects.* New York: Random House, 1964.

Back, K. W. *Beyond words.* Baltimore: Penguin Books, 1973.

Bloomquist, E. R. *Marijuana.* Beverly Hills: Glencoe Press, 1968.

Bridgeport (Conn.) *Telegram,* August 31, 1973, p. 31.

Brown, R. *Social psychology.* New York: Free Press, 1965.

Campbell, J., and Dunnette, M. Effectiveness of T-group experiences in managerial training and development. *Psychological Bulletin,* 1968, *70*(2), 73–104.

Charen, S., and Perelman, L. Personality studies of marijuana addicts. *American Journal of Psychiatry,* 1946, *102,* 674–682.

Frankl, Viktor. *Man's search for meaning.* New York: Washington Square Press, 1963.

Fromm, Erich. *Escape from freedom.* New York: Holt, Rinehart and Winston, 1941.

Frosch, W. A., Robbins, E. S., and Stern, M. Untoward reactions to lysergic acid diethylamide (LSD) resulting in hospitalization. *New England Journal of Medicine,* 1965, *273,* 1235.

Gardner, John. *Self renewal: The individual and the innovative society.* New York: Harper & Row, 1964.

Gaskill, H. S. Marijuana, an intoxicant. *American Journal of Psychiatry,* 1945, *102,* 202.

Hoffer, A., and Osmond, H. *The hallucinogens.* New York: Academic Press, 1967.

An interview with Huey Newton. *The Washington Post,* August 16, 1972.

Kaplan, J. *Marijuana: The new prohibition.* New York: World, 1970.

Keeler, M. H. Adverse reaction to marijuana. *American Journal of Psychiatry,* 1967, *124,* 674–677.

Keniston, K. Social change and youth in America. In E. H. Erikson (Ed.), *Youth: Change and challenge.* New York: American Academy of Arts and Sciences, 1961.

Keniston, K. Heads and seekers. *American Scholar,* 1969, *38,* 97–112.

King, M. L., Jr. *Why we can't wait.* New York: Harper & Row, 1963, pp. 81–86.

Kohlberg, L. The development of children's orientations toward a moral order: I. Sequence in the development of moral thought. *Vita Humana,* 1963, *6,* 11–33.

Kohlberg, L. Development of moral character and moral ideology. In M. L. Hoffman and L. W. Hoffman (Eds.), *Review of child development research.* Vol. 1. New York: Russell Sage Foundation, 1964.

Kohlberg, L. The cognitive-developmental approach to socialization. In D. A. Goslin (Ed.), *Handbook of socialization theory and research.* Chicago: Rand McNally, 1969.

Kurland, A. A., Savage, C., Shaffer, J. W., and Unger, S. The therapeutic potential of LSD in medicine. In R. C. DeBold and R. C. Leaf (Eds.), *LSD, man, and society.* Middletown, Conn.: Wesleyan University Press, 1967.

Leary, T., and Alpert, R. The politics of consciousness expansion. In G. Andrews and S. Vinkenoog (Eds.), *The book of grass.* New York: Grove Press, 1967.

Lieberman, M., Yalom, I. D., and Miles, M. B. The group experience project: A comparison of ten encounter technologies. In L. Blank, G. Gottsegen, and M. Gottsegen (Eds.), *Encounter: Confrontations in self and interpersonal awareness.* New York: Macmillan, 1971.

Lieberman, M., Yalom, I. D., and Miles, M. B. Encounter: The leader makes the difference. *Psychology Today,* March, 1973, 69–76.

Lindesmith, A. R. *The addict and the law.* Bloomington, Ind.: Indiana University Press, 1965.

Lipset, S. M., and Wolin, S. S. (Eds.), *The Berkeley student revolt: Facts and interpretations.* Garden City, N.Y.: Doubleday, 1965.

Louria, D. B. The abuse of LSD. In R. C. DeBold and R. C. Leaf (Eds.), *LSD, man and society.* Middletown, Conn.: Wesleyan University Press, 1967.

Louria, D. B. *The drug scene.* New York: McGraw-Hill, 1968.

Mayor LaGuardia's Committee on Marihuana. The marihuana problem in the city of New York. In D. Solomon (Ed.), *The marihuana papers.* Indianapolis: Bobbs-Merrill, 1966.

Mohan, H., and Sood, G. C. Conjugate deviation of the eyes following cannabis india intoxication. *British Journal of Ophthalmology,* 1964, *48,* 160–161.

Murtagh, J. M. Two statements. In G. Andrews and S. Vinkenoog (Eds.), *The book of grass.* New York: Grove Press, 1967.

Newcomb, T. M. The prediction of interpersonal attraction. *American Psychologist,* 1956, *11,* 575–586.

Parloff, M. B. Assessing the effects of headshrinking and mind-expanding. *International Journal of Group Psychotherapy,* 1970, *20*(1), 14–24.

Parloff, M. B. Group therapy and the small-group field: An encounter. *International Journal of Group Psychotherapy,* 1970, *20*(3), 267–304.

Piaget, J. *The moral judgment of the child.* New York: Macmillan, 1965.

Raths, L. E., Harmin, M., and Simon, S. B. *Values and teaching.* Columbus, Ohio: Charles E. Merrill, 1966.

Rowell, E. A., and Rowell, R. *On the trail of marihuana, the weed of madness.* Mountain View, Calif.: Pacific Press Publishing Association, 1939.

Schutz, W. C. *FIRO: A three-dimensional theory of interpersonal behavior.* New York: Rinehart & Company, 1958.

Schutz, W. C. *Joy.* New York: Grove Press, 1968.

Slater, P. E., Morimoto, K., and Hyder, R. W. The effect of group administration on symptom formation under LSD. *Journal of Nervous and Mental Disorders,* 1957, *25,* 312–315.

Smith, M. Brewster. Morality and student protest. From *Social Psychology and human values* by M. Brewster Smith. Chicago: Aldine Publishing Company, 1969.

Tannenbaum, R., Weschler, I. R., and Massarik, F. *Leadership and organization: A behavioral science approach.* New York: McGraw-Hill, 1961.

Toffler, A. *Future shock.* New York: Random House, 1970.

Tracy, J. J., and Cross, H. J. Antecedents of shift in moral judgment. *Journal of Personality and Social Psychology,* 1973, *26*(2), 238–244.

Williams, H. S. Abuse of American law. In G. Andrews and S. Vinkenoog (Eds.), *The book of grass.* New York: Grove Press, 1967.

SUGGESTED READINGS

Erikson, E. H. (Ed.), *Youth: Change and challenge.* New York: American Academy of Arts and Sciences, 1961.

Frankl, V. *Man's search for meaning.* New York: Washington Square Press, 1963.

Sawrey, J. M., and Telford, C. W. *Psychology of adjustment.* (3rd ed.). Boston: Allyn & Bacon, 1971.

Schutz, W. C. *Joy.* New York: Grove Press, 1968.

Smith, M. B. *Social psychology and human values.* Chicago: Aldine Publishing Company, 1969.

Yalom, I. D. *The theory and practice of group psychotherapy.* New York: Basic Books, 1970.

Acknowledgments

Figure Acknowledgments

Division B. Fig. 4-1, p. 28: Adapted from Chapanis, A., Garner, W. R., and Morgan, C. T., *Experimental psychology*. New York: John Wiley & Sons, 1949, by permission of the publisher. Fig. 4-4, p. 31: Adapted from *Psychology — Brief edition* by Robert E. Silverman. Copyright © 1971, 1972; Meredith Corporation. Reproduced by permission of Appleton-Century-Crofts, Educational Division, Meredith Corporation. Fig. 4-7, p. 35: *View in Venice,* Canaletto. National Gallery of Art, Washington. Widener Collection. Fig. 4-8, p. 36: *Waterfall,* original lithograph by M. C. Escher. Reproduction courtesy of the Vorpal Galleries, San Francisco and Chicago. Figs. 4-10, 4-11, p. 38: Adapted from Held, R., and Hein, A. Movement-produced stimulation in the development of visually guided behavior. *Journal of Comparative and Physiological Psychology,* 1963, *56*, 872–876. Copyright 1963 by the American Psychological Association. Reprinted by permission. Fig. 6-1, p. 49: Adapted from Morgan, C. T., and King, R. A. *Introduction to psychology,* 4th ed. New York: McGraw-Hill Book Company, 1971. Reprinted by permission of the publisher. Originally appeared in Hernandez-Peon, R., Scherrer, H., and Jouvet, M. Modification of electric activity in cochlear nucleus during "attention" in unanesthetized cats. *Science,* February 1956, *123*, 331–332. Fig. 6-10, p. 56: From Carmichael, L., Hogan, H. P., and Walter, A. A. An experimental study of the effect of language on the reproduction of visually perceived form. *Journal of Experimental Psychology,* 1932, *15*, 73–86. Copyright 1932 by the American Psychological Association. Reprinted by permission. Fig. 7-4, p. 61: From Amoore, J. E., Johnston, J. W., Jr., and Rubin, M. The stereochemical theory of odor. *Scientific American,* 1964, *210*(2), 42–49. Copyright © 1964 by Scientific American, Inc. Reproduced with permission.

Division C. Fig. 8-1, p. 78: From Heron, W. Cognitive and physiological effects of perceptual isolation. In P. Solomon et al. (Eds.), *Sensory deprivation*. Copyright © 1961 by the President and Fellows of Harvard College. Reproduced by permission of the publisher, Harvard University Press. Fig. 10-1, p. 87: Adapted from Fig. 2-4 in *Psychology: An introduction,* 2d ed., by J. Kagan and E. Havemann. © 1968, 1972 by Harcourt Brace Jovanovich, Inc., and reproduced with their permission. Original version in Watson, J. B., and Raynor, R. Conditioned emotional reactions. *Journal of Experimental Psychology,* 1920, *3*, 1–14. Copyright 1920 by the American Psychological Association. Reprinted by permission. Fig. 10-3, p. 90: Adapted from *Psychology: An introduction* by Charles G. Morris. Copyright © 1973 Meredith Corporation. Reproduced by permission of Appleton-Century-Crofts, Educational Division, Meredith Corporation. Fig. 12-1, p. 98: From *Pygmalion in the classroom: Teacher expectation and pupil's intellectual development* by Robert Rosenthal and Leonore Jacobson. Copyright © 1968 by Holt, Rinehart and Winston, Inc. Reprinted by permission of Holt, Rinehart and Winston, Inc.

Division D. Fig. 15-1, p. 126: From *Introduction to psychology,* 3rd ed., p. 423, by Norman L. Munn, L. Dodge Fernald, and Peter S. Fernald. Copyright © 1974 by Houghton Mifflin Company. Used by permission. [Photo by Sheila A. Farr.] Fig. 15-2, p. 131: From *Children's drawings as a measure of intellectual maturity* by Dale B. Harris, © 1963, by Harcourt Brace Jovanovich, Inc., and reproduced with their permission.

Division E. Fig. 18-1, p. 154: From *Negro family: The case for national action* by D. P. Moynihan. Published by the U.S. Department of Labor, Office of Policy Planning and Research, 1965. Fig. 18-2, p. 157:

From *General psychology* by D. C. Edwards. Copyright © 1972 by The Macmillan Co., Inc. Reproduced by permission. Fig. 18-3, p. 158: From Hollingshead, A. B., and Redlich, F. C., *Social class and mental illness*. New York: John Wiley & Sons, 1958, by permission of the publisher. Fig. 19-1, p. 162: From *Psychology: An introduction* by Charles G. Morris. Copyright © 1973 Meredith Corporation. Reproduced by permission of Appleton-Century-Crofts, Educational Division, Meredith Corporation. Fig. 19-2, p. 163: Adapted from Hollingshead, A. B., and Redlich, F. C., *Social class and mental illness*. New York: John Wiley & Sons, 1958, by permission of the publisher. Figs. 20-1, p. 167, and 20-2, p. 169: From data furnished by the National Institute of Mental Health, 1969. Fig. 20-3, p. 173: From Howard H. Kendler, *Basic psychology*, 2d ed., copyright 1968, W. A. Benjamin, Inc., Menlo Park, California. Fig. 21-1, p. 176: U.S. Army photograph. Medical Audio-Visual Dept. Walter Reed Army Institute of Research, Washington, D.C. Property of U.S. Government.

Division F. Fig. 23-1, p. 200: From Dahlstrom, W. Grant, Welsh, George Schlager, and Dahlstrom, Leona E., *An MMPI handbook: Volume I, clinical interpretation*, rev. ed. University of Minnesota Press, Minneapolis. © 1960, 1972 by the University of Minnesota. Fig. 23-2, p. 201: From *Personality measurement* by B. Kleinmuntz. Homewood, Ill.: Dorsey Press, 1967 ©. Reproduced by permission of the publisher.

Division G. Fig. 27-1, p. 238: From Asch, S. E. Studies of independence and submission to group pressures: 1. A minority of one against a unanimous majority. *Psychological Monographs*, 1956, *70*, No. 9 (Whole No. 416). Copyright 1956 by the American Psychological Association. Reprinted by permission. Fig. 29-2, p. 249: Adapted from Jones, J. M., *Prejudice and racism*. Reading, Mass.: Addison-Wesley, 1972, by permission of the publisher. Fig. 29-3, p. 251: Adapted from *Racially separate or together* by T. F. Pettigrew. Copyright © 1971 by McGraw-Hill, Inc. Used with permission of McGraw-Hill Book Co. Fig. 30-1, p. 256: From *Aggression: A social learning analysis* by Albert Bandura, 1973. Reproduced with permission of the publisher, Prentice-Hall, Inc.

Division H. Fig. 31-1, p. 274: From Calhoun, J. B., Population density and social pathology. *Scientific American*, 1962, *206*(2), 139–150. Copyright © 1962 by Scientific American, Inc. Fig. 33-1, p. 285: Redrawn from Morgan, C. T., and King, R. A., *Introduction to psychology*, 3rd ed. © 1966 by McGraw-Hill, Inc. Used with permission of McGraw-Hill Book Co.

Division I. Fig. 37-1, p. 322: From Hebb, D. O. Drives and the C.N.S. (conceptual nervous system). *Psychological Review*, 1955, *62*, 243–254. Copyright 1955 by the American Psychological Association. Reprinted by permission.

Division J. Figs. 40-1, p. 349, and 40-2, p. 350: Adapted from Smith, M. Brewster, Morality and student protest. In *Social psychology and human values* by M. Brewster Smith. Chicago: Aldine Publishing Co., 1969, by permission of the publisher. Fig. 41-1, p. 354: Adapted from J. Piaget, *The moral judgment of the child*. Copyright 1935 by Routledge & Kegan Paul, Ltd. Copyright 1965 by The Macmillan Company. Reproduced by permission.

Text, Table, and Box Acknowledgments

Division C. Table 13-1, pp. 104–6: From "Teaching Sign Language to a Chimpanzee" by R. A. Gardner and B. T. Gardner. Copyright 1969 by the American Association for the Advancement of Science.

Division D. Box 15-1, p. 129: From *The measurement and appraisal of adult intelligence*, 3rd ed., by D. Wechsler. Copyright © 1944 The Williams & Wilkins Co., Baltimore.

Division E. Excerpt, p. 151: From "One Sick Assassin," TIME, August 14, 1972. Reprinted by permission from TIME, The Weekly Newsmagazine; Copyright Time Inc. Excerpt, pp. 168–9: From *Textbook of abnormal psychology* by N. H. Pronko. Copyright © 1963 The Williams & Wilkins Co., Baltimore. Excerpts, pp. 170 and 171, and Box 20-3, p. 172: From *Fundamentals of behavior pathology* by R. M. Suinn. Copyright © 1970 by John Wiley & Sons, Inc. Reprinted by permission of John Wiley & Sons, Inc.

Division F. Box 23-1, pp. 198–9: Reproduced with permission from Kleinmuntz, *Personality measurement* (Homewood, Ill.): The Dorsey Press, 1967 © p. 220. Excerpt, p. 211: From *Beyond freedom and dignity* by B. F. Skinner. Copyright © 1971 by B. F. Skinner. Reprinted by permission of Alfred A. Knopf, Inc.

Division G. Excerpt, pp. 229–30: From Frankl, Viktor E., *Man's search for meaning: An introduction to logotherapy*. Copyright © 1959, 1962 by Viktor

Frankl. Reprinted by permission of Beacon Press. Excerpt, p. 241: From *Beyond freedom and dignity* by B. F. Skinner. Copyright © 1971 by B. F. Skinner. Reprinted by permission of Alfred A. Knopf, Inc. Excerpt, p. 251: From *Teahouse of the August Moon: A play,* by John Patrick and Vern Sneider. G. P. Putnam's Sons, 1954.

Division H. Excerpt, pp. 271–2: From Freedman, J. L., Klevansky, S., and Ehrlich, P. R. The effect of crowding on human task performance. *Journal of Applied Social Psychology,* 1971, *1*(1), 7–25. Reprinted by permission of V. H. Winston & Sons, Inc. Excerpt, p. 284: from *The terminal man* by Michael Crichton. Copyright © 1972 by Michael Crichton. Reprinted by permission of Alfred A. Knopf, Inc.

Division I. Table 36-1, p. 317: Adapted from Schachter, S., The interaction of cognitive and physiological determinants of emotional state. In Berkowitz, L., *Advances in experimental social psychology.* New York: Academic Press, 1964. Reprinted by permission of the publisher. Boxes 39-1, p. 332, and 39-2, p. 333: From *Liking and loving: An invitation to social psychology* by Zick Rubin. Copyright © 1973 by Holt, Rinehart and Winston, Inc. Reprinted by permission of Holt, Rinehart and Winston, Inc.

Division J. Excerpt, p. 351: From *The Berkeley student revolt* by Seymour Martin Lipset and Sheldon S. Wolin. Copyright © 1965 by Seymour Martin Lipset and Sheldon S. Wolin. Used by permission of Doubleday & Company Inc. Box 41-1, p. 356, and Table 41-1, p. 358: From *Religion and public education* by Theodore R. Sizer (Ed.). Copyright © 1967 by Houghton Mifflin Company. Reprinted by permission. Box 41-2, p. 359: Abridged and adapted from pp. 81–86 "Letter from a Birmingham Jail — April 16, 1963" in *Why we can't wait* by Martin Luther King, Jr. Copyright © 1963 by Martin Luther King, Jr. By permission of Harper & Row, Publishers, Inc. Excerpt, p. 361: From *Beyond words* by K. W. Back, New York: Russell Sage Foundation, 1972. © 1972 by Russell Sage Foundation. Table 42-1, p. 366: From Lieberman, M. L., Miles, M. B., and Yalom, I. D. *Encounter group: First facts.* New York: Basic Books, Inc., 1973, by permission of the publisher.

Name Index

Adorno, T.W., 198, 231
Allport, G.W., 251–252, 262, 329, 331, 338, 350, 379
Alpert, R., 373, 374, 379
Altman, I., 330, 338, 339, 343, 379
Amoore, J.E., 61, 72
Anastasi, A., 197, 223
Anderson, J., 289
Ardrey, R., 275, 292, 306
Aristotle, 16
Aronson, E., 363, 379
Asch, S.E., 238–239, 240, 261, 265
Asher, J., 145
Atkinson, J.W., 55, 72, 116
Ausubel, D.P., 368, 379

Back, K.W., 361, 366, 379
Backman, C.W., 240, 267
Bales, R.F., 185, 191
Bandura, A., 292, 306
Bard, P., 315, 316, 335, 337
Barlow, J.D., 30, 72
Barron, F.K., 240, 265
Baumrind, D., 8, 23
Benedict, R., 153, 191
Berkowitz, L., 258, 265, 291, 306
Bernard, C., 282
Berscheid, E., 331, 338
Bexton, W.H., 322, 338
Biesanz, J., 247, 265
Billingsley, A., 248, 265
Binet, A., 122, 125, 126, 145
Birney, R.C., 117
Blake, R.R., 258, 266
Bloomquist, E.R., 368, 369, 370, 371, 379
Bodmer, W.F., 147
Boltwood, C.E., 254, 265
Bovard, E.W., Jr., 321, 338
Brady, J., 175, 191

Brandon, A.C., 236, 267
Bremer, Arthur, 151–152, 156, 202
Broen, W.E., 193
Brown, D., 230
Brown, N., 141, 145
Brown, R., 355, 379
Bryan, J.H., 258, 265
Burdick, H., 117
Burgess, A., 285, 306
Burks, B.S., 137, 145
Buss, A.H., 193, 308
Butcher, H.J., 147
Byrne, W.L., 288, 306

Caggiula, A.R., 256, 267
Calhoun, J.B., 271, 273, 274, 302, 306, 307
Calley, William, 235, 260
Campbell, J., 366, 379
Campbell, J.D., 184, 192
Cannon, W.B., 280, 307, 315, 316, 335, 337, 338
Carmichael, L., 55, 72
Carmichael, S., 248, 268
Cavalli-Sforza, L.L., 147
Chandler, P.G., 258, 266
Chapanis, A., 72
Charen, S., 369, 379
Charles, D.C., 137, 145
Clark, K., 250, 265, 293, 307
Clark, M., 250, 265
Cleckley, H.M., 162, 193
Coleman, J.C., 154–155, 158, 191, 193
Collins, M.E., 252, 265
Condon, R., 307
Cooper, M.R., 254, 265
Copernicus, 16, 173
Cory, D.W., 184, 191
Crichton, M., 284, 286, 307
Crutchfield, R.S., 239, 261, 265

Dahlstrom, L.C., 223
Dahlstrom, W.G., 223
Daniels, L.R., 258, 265
Darley, J.M., 259
Darwin, C., 314
Davis, C.M., 301, 307
Davis, K., 321, 338
Delgado, J., 286, 307
Dember, W.N., 67, 72
de Nike, L.D., 159, 162, 192
Dennis, W., 130, 145
Descartes, 16, 22
Deutsch, M., 141, 145, 252, 265
Diem, Ngo Dinh, 253
Doll, E.A., 135, 136, 145
Dollard, J., 291, 307
Doob, L.W., 291, 307
Drew, C., 250
Duc, Thic Quang, 253
Dunnette, M., 366, 379

Eckert, J.F., 299, 308
Edwards, D.C., 67, 72, 192
Ehrlich, P.P., 271, 307
Eichmann, Adolf, 244, 357, 358
Elms, A.C., 324, 338
Emerson, R., 236, 266
Emerson, Ralph Waldo, 237
Erikson, E.H., 381
Ertl, J., 125, 132, 140, 145
Evers, Medgar, 254
Eysenck, H.J., 218, 223

Fader, D.N., 77, 116
Fawcett, J.T., 308
Fein, V.E., 254, 265
Feshbach, N., 326, 338
Feshbach, S., 326, 338
Festinger, L., 237, 242–243, 246, 261, 266
Fleming, J.D., 107, 116
Flourens, Pierre, 65
Forgus, R.H., 73
Forrester, B.J., 142, 145
Frankl, V., 230, 266, 349, 350, 378, 379, 381
Freed, A.M., 258, 266
Freedman, D.X., 193
Freedman, J.L., 271–272, 307
Freedman, M.J., 183, 192
French, J.R.P., Jr., 241, 261, 266
Freud, A., 224
Freud, S., 183, 203, 207, 208, 209, 211, 212, 213, 219, 220, 224, 324, 353, 354
Fritsch, G., 278, 307
Fromm, E., 346, 379

Frosch, W.A., 372, 379
Fuller, J.L., 308

Gagnon, J.H., 184, 192
Galileo, 16, 173
Galton, F., 137, 145, 293, 307
Gardner, B.T., 103, 106, 116
Gardner, J., 357, 379
Gardner, R.A., 103, 106, 116
Garner, W.R., 72
Garrett, H.E., 139, 145
Gaskill, H.S., 369, 379
Gebhard, P.H., 192
Genovese, Kitty, 258–259
Gibbons, D.C., 184, 192
Gibby, R.G., 161, 192
Gilbert, G.M., 179, 192
Giovannoni, J.M., 248, 265
Glaser, R., 117
Glass, D.C., 339
Goddard, H.H., 121, 145–146
Goering, Hermann, 179
Goldberg, P., 18
Goldberg, P.A., 250, 266
Goldstein, M.J., 159, 161, 192
Goodenough, F.L., 130, 146
Goodman, N.E., 142, 146
Graham, C.H., 73
Greenspan, H.G., 184, 192
Gruenberg, E.M., 158, 192
Guilford, J.P., 147

Hall, C.S., 204, 224, 294, 307
Hamilton, C.V., 248, 268
Hansel, C.E.M., 73
Harlow, H.F., 329, 330, 336, 338
Harmin, M., 359, 381
Harris, D.B., 130, 146
Havemann, E., 116
Hebb, D.O., 323, 338
Heber, R., 134, 135, 146
Hein, A., 37, 38, 72
Held, R., 37, 38, 72
Heller, J.R., 231
Hernandez-Peon, R., 48, 72
Heron, W., 116, 322, 338
Hersher, L., 214, 224
Hilts, P.J., 216, 224
Hitzig, E., 278, 307
Hoffer, A., 372, 379
Hoffman, M.L., 240, 266
Hogan, H.P., 55, 72
Hollingshead, A.B., 158, 192
Hollingsworth, L.S., 138, 146

Hooker, E., 18, 23
Horwitz, W.A., 136, 146
Howard, R., 236, 265
Hutt, M.L., 161, 192
Hyder, R., 372, 381
Hynek, R.M., 176, 192

Jacobson, A., 287, 288, 307
Jacobson, L., 97, 99, 116
James, W., 17, 315, 316, 334, 337, 338
Janis, I.L., 240, 266
Janisse, M.P., 30, 72
Jarvik, L., 136, 146
Jenkins, J.J., 67, 72
Jensen, A.R., 124, 139, 140
Jensen, D.W., 137, 145
Jenson, D.D., 288, 307
Johnston, J.W., Jr., 61, 72
Jones, E., 203, 224
Jones, J.M., 248, 262, 266
Jouvet, M., 48, 72

Kagan, J., 116, 147
Kales, A., 288, 307
Kaplan, J., 371, 380
Kardiner, A., 142, 146
Karon, B.P., 142, 146
Keeler, M.H., 369, 380
Kelman, H.C., 235, 247, 266
Keniston, K., 345, 380
Kennedy, John F., 237, 254
Kennedy, Robert, 254
Kepler, J., 16
Kestenbaum, C., 136, 146
Kety, S.S., 193
Kiesler, S.B., 250, 266
Kimble, D.P., 287, 307
Kimbrell, D., 258, 266
King, Martin Luther, Jr., 30, 254, 357, 359, 380
King, R.A., 73
Kinsey, A.C., 183, 188, 192
Kirk, S.A., 137, 146
Kisker, G.W., 158, 166, 167, 168, 181, 182, 192
Klaus, R.A., 142, 145
Klein, S.J., 294, 307
Kleinmuntz, B., 198–199, 224
Klevansky, S., 271, 307
Klineberg, O., 139, 141, 142, 146
Knapp, P.H., 339
Knight, R.P., 218, 224
Koestler, A., 293, 307
Kohlberg, L., 347, 348, 349, 355, 356, 357, 358, 360, 375, 377, 378, 380
Krasner, L.A., 193

Kreuger, W.C.F., 110, 116
Kubrick, S., 285
Kurland, A.A., 380
Kutner, B., 245, 266

LaGuardia, F., 368, 370, 380
Landaver, T.K., 308
Lange, C., 315, 316, 334, 337
LaPiere, R.T., 245, 266
Latané, B., 259, 266
Lawrence, L.H., 235, 266
Lazarus, A.A., 224
Leary, T., 373, 374, 380
Lee, E.S., 141, 146
Lehmann, D., 288, 307
Levine, L., 258, 267
Liberman, A.M., 55, 72
Lieberman, M., 366, 380
Lindesmith, A.R., 368, 371, 380
Lindzey, G., 204, 224
Lipset, S.M., 351, 380
Logan, F.A., 117
London, I.D., 57, 72
Lorenz, K., 275, 307
Louria, D.B., 369, 371, 373, 374, 380
Luria, A.R., 110, 111, 116

Maddi, S.R., 204, 224
Mai, Nhat Chi, 253, 267
Malcolm X, 254
Mandler, G., 339
Martin, C.E., 192
Massarik, F., 365, 381
McClelland, D.C., 55, 72
McConnell, J.V., 287, 307
McCurdy, H.G., 138, 146
McGrath, S.E., 240, 266
McGuire, R.M., 183, 192
McIntosh, M., 183, 192
Melzack, R., 63, 72, 73
Merton, R.K., 142–143, 145, 146
Miles, M., 366, 380
Milgram, S., 8, 233, 250, 260, 266, 267
Miller, G.A., 109, 116
Miller, N.E., 291, 307, 327, 335, 338
Milner, P., 279, 284, 286, 307
Mischel, W., 224
Mohan, H., 369, 380
Morgan, C.T., 72, 73
Morimoto, K., 372, 381
Moros, N., 185, 192
Morrison, Norman, 253
Mouton, J.S., 258, 266
Mowrer, O.H., 291, 307

Moynihan, D.P., 153, 192
Mueller, C.G., 73
Murray, H.A., 326, 338
Murtagh, J.M., 370, 380

Neisser, U., 73
Neumann, Teresa, 176
Newcomb, T.M., 240, 267, 331, 339, 380
Newton, Huey, 343, 380
Nisbett, R.E., 313, 317, 339

Oden, M.H., 137, 146
Olds, J., 279, 284, 286, 307
Osmond, H., 372, 379
Oswald, Lee Harvey, 254
Ovesey, L., 142, 146

Palmer, J.C., 159, 161, 192
Parloff, M.B., 367, 376, 380, 381
Patrick, John, 251, 267
Pavlov, I.P., 88, 116, 117
Perelman, L., 369, 379
Person, E., 136, 146
Pervin, L.A., 204, 205, 224
Pettigrew, T.F., 247, 267
Pheterson, G.I., 250, 266
Piaget, J., 353, 355, 357, 360, 375, 377, 378, 379, 381
Piliavin, I.M., 260, 267
Piliavin, J.A., 260, 267
Pomeroy, W.B., 192
Postman, N., 80, 99, 116
Premack, D., 103, 116
Pronko, W.H., 168, 192

Rabin, A.I., 224
Rand, Ayn, 237, 267
Raths, L.E., 359, 381
Raven, B.H., 241, 261, 266
Ray, James Earl, 254
Raynor, R., 86, 116
Redlich, F.C., 193
Redlich, F.G., 158, 192
Richter, C., 299, 301, 308
Robbins, E.S., 372, 379
Rodin, J., 259, 260, 267
Rogers, C.R., 203, 209, 210, 211, 213, 220, 224
Rooney, E.A., 184, 192
Rosenhan, D., 258, 267
Rosenhan, D.L., 155, 192
Rosenkranz, P., 250, 267
Rosenthal, D., 193
Rosenthal, R., 97, 99, 116
Rosenzweig, S.A., 218, 224
Ross, D., 292, 306

Ross, S., 292, 306
Rowell, E.A., 368, 381
Rowell, R., 368, 381
Rubin, M., 61, 72
Rubin, Z., 331, 332, 333, 334, 336, 337, 339
Russell, B., 319, 339

Sagarin, E., 183, 192
Sampson, E.E., 236, 267
Sarnoff, I., 326, 335, 339
Savage, L., 372, 380
Savio, Mario, 352
Sawrey, J.M., 381
Schachter, S., 236, 237, 267, 316, 317, 320, 324, 325, 326, 327, 335, 338, 339
Scherrer, H., 48, 72
Schrank, H., 99, 116
Schutz, W.C., 362, 375, 377, 378, 381
Scott, T., 322, 338
Scott, T.H., 63, 72
Sears, R.R., 291, 307
Secord, P.F., 240, 267
Selye, H., 320, 335, 337, 339
Semmelweis, I.P., 237
Shaevitz, M.H., 77, 116
Shaffer, J.W., 372, 380
Shaffer, L.F., 314, 339
Sheer, D., 308
Sherif, M., 18, 237–238, 239, 240, 252, 261, 267
Shuey, A.M., 139, 140, 146
Simon, S.B., 359, 381
Simon, T., 122, 125, 145
Simon, W., 184, 192
Singer, J.E., 237, 267, 316, 317, 339
Sinnett, E.R., 187, 192
Sirhan, Sirhan, 156, 254
Skinner, B.F., 117, 203, 210, 211, 224, 241, 267, 295, 308
Slater, P.E., 372, 381
Smith, L.M., 247, 265
Smith, M.B., 346, 347, 349, 374, 381
Snow, C.P., 232, 267
Sood, G.C., 369, 380
Speck, Richard, 254
Spitz, R.A., 322, 339
Spuhler, J.N., 147
Stern, M., 372, 379
Stevens, S.S., 73
Suinn, R.M., 170, 171, 172, 193
Sumner, W.G., 244, 251, 267

Tannenbaum, R., 365, 381
Taylor, D.A., 330, 338, 339, 343, 379
Teevan, R.G., 117

Telford, C.W., 381
Terman, L.M., 126, 137, 138, 144, 145, 146
Test, M.A., 258, 265
Thigpen, C.H., 162, 193
Thompson, W.R., 308
Tiber, N., 159, 162, 192
Toffler, A., 295, 308, 345, 364, 378, 381
Treisman, M., 174, 193
Tryon, R.C., 294, 308
Turnbull, C.M., 57, 73

Ullmann, L.P., 193
Unger, G., 288
Unger, S., 372, 380

Valins, S., 313, 317, 318, 337, 339
Vernon, P.E., 147

Waelder, R., 224
Wagner, C., 258, 267
Wall, P.D., 63, 73
Wallace, George, 31, 151, 202, 254
Walster, E.H., 331, 338
Walter, A.A., 55, 72

Warshofsky, F., 73
Washburn, P.W., 254, 265
Watson, J.B., 86, 116
Wechsler, D., 122, 129, 146
Wegrocki, H.J., 154, 193
Weingartner, C., 80, 99, 116
Welsh, G.S., 223
Weschler, I.R., 365, 381
Wheeler, L., 256, 258, 262, 267, 343, 379
White, G.M., 258, 267
Wilkins, C., 245, 266
Wilkins, L., 301, 308
Williams, H.S., 370, 381
Winch, R.F., 331, 336, 339
Wolin, S.S., 351, 380
Wolpe, J., 215, 224
Wrightsman, L.S., Jr., 142–143, 146

Yalom, I.D., 366, 380, 381
Yarrow, R.R., 245, 266

Zimbardo, P., 326, 335, 339
Zweizig, J.R., 288, 307

Subject Index

Terms and page numbers in blue indicate glossary entries.

Abortion, 288
Absolute threshold, 39, 68, 70
  in audition, 68
  in vision, 39
Acrophobia, 160
Actualizing tendency, 209, 210, 220, 221
Acupuncture, 63
Adaptation, 47–48, 68, 70
Adrenal glands, 273, 282, 304
Adrenalin, 282, 319
Affective psychosis, 166, 169, 171–173, 187–188, 189
Afferent code, 67, 70
  audition, 43
    loudness, 44
    pitch, 44
    timbre, 44
  vision, 31–32
    brightness, 32
    hue, 31–32
    saturation, 32
Affiliation, 80, 325, 329, 335, 337
Aftereffect, 49, 68, 70
Aggression, 181, 182, 203, 256, 275, 277, 291, 292, 293, 302, 304
  catharsis, 303
  frustration-aggression hypothesis, 291, 305
  and television, 291
Agoraphobia, 160
Aichmophobia, 160
Alcohol, 370
Alcoholism, 167, 180, 184–185, 189
Alcohol psychosis, 177–178, 188
Alienation, 344–345, 346, 374, 377
All-or-none principle, 278, 304
American Psychological Association, 7
Amnesia, 160, 162, 187, 189, 211

Amplitude, of sound wave, 42, 43, 45, 46, 68
Ampulla, 65, 70
Amygdala, 277, 279, 304
Anal stage, 206–207, 219, 221
Antisocial personality disorder, 179, 180, 182, 188, 189, 206
Anvil, 43, 44, 68, 70
Anxiety, 159, 180, 187, 206, 207, 210, 212, 215, 324–325, 335
Anxiety reaction, 159, 160, 187, 189
Aphasia, 101
Aphrodisiac, 369
A priori, 15, 21
Arousal, 316–317, 319, 320, 323, 335, 337
Artificial insemination, 288
Assassination, 254
Asthma, 177, 188
Attention, 48–49, 68
Attitude, 244–245, 251–252, 263
  affective component, 245, 261
  behavioral component, 246, 261
  cognitive component, 245, 261
Attractiveness, and pupil size, 30
Attribution, 317, 318, 337
Auditory canal, 43, 44, 68
Authoritarian personality, 231, 239, 263
Autokinetic effect, 237, 261, 263
Autonomic nervous system, 175, 280, 303, 304
Avoidance learning, 94, 113, 114

Behavioral contagion, 255–258, 262
Behavioral model (of abnormality), 157–158, 186–187
Behavioral sink, 271, 273, 304
Behavior therapy, 215–216, 220, 221
Berkeley study, 232
Binocular cues, 32–33, 68
Biofeedback, 286, 303, 304
Blind spot, 30, 70

Blood pressure, 281
Brain, 278–279, 304
  forebrain, 278
  frontal lobes, 217
  hindbrain, 278
  left hemisphere, 278
  midbrain, 278
  right hemisphere, 278
  temporal lobes, 278
Brain disorders, 156, 167, 169, 174–175, 177–178, 188, 189
Brain stem, 304
Brain tumor, 175, 177, 188
Brightness, 28, 29, 39, 40, 67
  afferent code for, 32
  constancy, 50–51
Bystander intervention, 258–259

Caffeine, 300
Causal explanation of relationships, 10, 12
Central nervous system (CNS), 175, 276, 278, 304. *See also* Brain
Cerebellum, 304
Cerebral cortex, 31. *See also* Cerebrum
Cerebral palsy, 134, 144
Cerebrum, 278, 279, 305, 316
Chemotherapy, 217, 221
Chunking, 109, 114
Ciliary muscles, 29, 30, 70
Cingulate gyrus, 279
Clairvoyance, 66, 70
Classical conditioning, 86–90, 112–113, 114, 286
  higher-order, 88, 115
Claustrophobia, 160
Client-centered therapy, 213–215, 220
Closure, 52, 69
Cochlea, 43, 44, 65, 68, 70
Cochlear nucleus, 48–49
Cognitive development, 353, 375
Cognitive dissonance, 246, 261, 263
Cognitive labeling, 316–317, 327, 337
Cold, 58, 62, 64, 69
Color, 28, 29, 30, 31, 32, 67
Complexity
  of light, 27, 28, 29, 67
  of sound, 42–43, 44, 45, 68
Compliance, 247–248
Compulsion, 161, 189
Concept, 107–108, 114, 115
Conditioned emotional response (CER), 88–89, 112–113, 160, 328, 337
Conditioned response (CR), 87, 88, 89, 112, 113, 115

Conditioned stimulus (CS), 86, 87, 88, 89, 112, 113, 115
Conditions of worth, 210, 220, 221
Cones, 30, 31, 32, 67, 70
Conflict, 275
Conformity, 239–240, 247, 255, 260, 263
Congruence, 210, 220, 221
Constancy, 49–51, 69, 70
  brightness, 50–51
  shape, 51
  size, 50
Convergence, 33, 68, 70
Conversion reaction, 160, 161, 163, 175, 187, 188, 189
Cornea, 29, 30, 67, 70
Corpus callosum, 278, 305
Correlation, 123
Correlational research, 13
Counterconditioning, 215, 221
Curiosity, 79, 80, 112

DDT, 297
Decay theory, 109, 114, 115
De facto, 249
Defense mechanism, 166, 187, 207–208, 220, 221. *See also specific mechanisms*
Delirium tremens, 177
Delusion, 167–168, 170, 171, 187, 189
Denial, 208, 210, 221
Density, 271, 273
Dependent variable, 13–14, 21, 22
Depressive reaction, 160, 162–163, 187, 189
Depth perception, 32–37, 68
Densensitization, 215, 221–222
Deviation, 236, 263
Diabetes, 283
Diencephalon, 278
Difference threshold, 39, 68, 70
  in audition, 45–46, 68
  in vision, 39
Discrimination learning, 94, 113, 115
Dissociative reaction, 160, 162, 187, 189
Down's syndrome, 134, 144–145
Dream
  analysis of, 212–213, 220
  latent content, 213, 222
  manifest content, 213, 222
Drug addiction, 167, 180, 185–186, 189
Drug use, 346
Dyssocial personality disorder, 180, 182, 188, 189

Ear, 41
  structure of, 43
Eardrum, 43, 44, 68, 70

394 *Subject Index*

Ego, 205, 206, 207, 212, 213, 219, 220, 222
Ego ideal, 206, 222
Electrical stimulation of the brain (ESB), 279, 286, 303
Electromagnetic spectrum, 27, 28, 39, 67
Electrophysiology, 17
Emotion, 313–314, 334, 337
   theories of, 315–316, 334–335
Encounter group, 362, 367, 375, 376
Endocrine glands, 279, 281–283, 305
Epilepsy, 279
Epinephrine, 282, 316–317, 319, 337
Equal-status contact hypothesis, 251, 252, 262
Escape learning, 95, 113, 115
Ethical code, 7–8, 22
Ethnocentrism, 232, 247, 248, 263
Euphoria, 368
Exhibitionism, 180, 183, 188, 189–190
Existential analysis, 350
Expectancy, 97, 99
   and perception, 55
Experimental manipulation, 10–12, 22
Expiative justice, 354, 377
Extinction, 115
   in classical conditioning, 87–88, 112
   in operant conditioning, 92, 93, 94, 96, 103, 113, 215
Extrasensory perception (ESP), 66–67, 70
Eye, 27, 28, 29, 30, 41, 67
   structure of, 30–31

Fascism, 231
Fear, 314, 321, 324, 326, 335, 337
   as acquired drive, 327, 335
   arousal and perception, 326, 335
Feedback, 273, 305
Figure-ground perception, 52, 53, 69
Fixation, 206, 219, 222
Folie à deux, 171
Forgetting, 109, 207
Fovea, 29, 30, 70
Free association, 212, 220, 222
Free Speech Movement, 348, 374
Frequency, of sound wave, 42, 45, 46, 68
F scale, 231–232
Fugue reaction, 162, 187, 190
Functional model (of abnormality), 157–158, 186–187, 190
Fundamental Interpersonal Relations Orientation (FIRO), 362–364, 375, 377
Future shock, 345, 364, 374, 378

Galvanic skin response (GSR), 281, 305
Gastrointestinal tract, 280

Gate control theory of pain, 63
"Gating mechanism," 48, 68, 70–71
Gay liberation, 18
Gay Liberation Front, 184
General Adaptation Syndrome (GAS), 320, 335, 337
Generally Regarded As Safe (GRAS) List, 299
Gene therapy, 288
Genetic engineering, 285, 288, 305
Genetic screening, 288
Genital stage, 207, 220, 222
Gestalt psychology, 51, 69, 71
Ghetto, 274
Gonads, 283, 305
Goodenough-Harris Drawing Test, 130–131, 143
Grammar, 102–103, 107, 114, 115

Hair cell
   in ear, 43, 44, 68
   in tongue, 59, 69
Hallucination, 168, 169, 170, 171, 172, 187, 190, 369
Hallucinogens, 371, 374
Hammer, 43, 44, 68, 71
Hedonism, 16, 22
Heroin, 185, 376
Hijacking, 254–256
Homeostasis, 301, 304, 305, 320, 335
Homosexuality, 155, 180, 183–184, 188–189, 190, 285
Hue, 28, 67
   afferent code for, 31–32
Human ecology, 274
Humanism, 209
Hypochondriacal reaction, 160, 161, 190
Hypothalamus, 279, 302, 305, 316
Hysterical reaction, 160, 161, 163, 187, 190, 197, 198

Id, 205, 206, 212, 219, 222
Identification
   as defense mechanism, 207, 222
   type of conformity, 247, 248
"Idiot savant," 136
Illusions, 52, 54, 69
Imitation, 103, 114, 256
Incus, 43, 71. See also Anvil
Independent variable, 13–14, 21, 22
Insulin, 283
Intellectual deficiency, 133, 144. See also Mental retardation
Intellectual superiority, 133, 137–138, 145
Intelligence, 97, 121, 132, 143
   definition, 121–122, 143
   hereditary and environmental effects, 122–124, 143
   racial differences, 139–143, 144

Intelligence tests, 122, 125, 132, 143. *See also* Goodenough-Harris Drawing Test; Neural efficiency analyzer; Stanford-Binet Intelligence Test; Wechsler Adult Intelligence Scale
  cultural bias in, 127, 128–130, 140, 142, 143
Intelligence quotient (IQ), 98, 121, 123, 124, 127, 128, 132, 134, 135, 137, 138, 141, 143, 144
Intensity, light, 27, 28, 29, 32, 50, 67
Interference theory, 109, 114, 115
Internalization, 248
Interpersonal attraction theory, 331, 336
Interposition, 33–34, 68, 71
Involutional melancholia, 166, 173, 188, 190
Iris, 29, 30, 67, 71
Isolation, 321

Jukes family, 293
Just noticeable difference (j.n.d.), 39, 68, 70, 71

Kallikak family, 121, 122, 293
Kinesthesis, 64–65, 69
Korsakoff's syndrome, 177, 190

La belle indifference, 161, 190
Language, 102, 114, 141, 142
  learning of, 103
  nonhuman, 103–107
  structure, 102–103
Latency stage, 207, 220, 222
Law of Prägnanz, 51, 69, 71
Learning, 115. *See also* Classical conditioning; Operant conditioning
Learning theory, and personality, 210, 220
Lens, 29, 30, 31, 67, 71
Lie detector, 281
Light, 27, 28, 29, 30, 67
Limbic system, 279, 286, 303, 305
Lobotomy, 217, 221, 222, 277, 286
Logotherapy, 350, 378
Loudness, 42, 46, 68
  afferent code for, 44
Love, 329–336
  mother, 329, 336
  romantic, 331, 334, 336, 337
Love scales, 331–333
Lysergic acid diethylamide (LSD), 184, 346, 371, 373, 377, 378

Malleus, 43, 71. *See also* Hammer
Manic-depressive reaction, 166, 171–173, 188, 190
Marijuana, 20, 184, 346, 368–369, 376
  addiction, 376
  legalization of, 370, 376

psychotic reactions, 369
  users of, 369–370, 376
Mass killings, 254
Mattachine Society, 183
Meaningfulness, 108, 114
Medical model (of abnormality), 157, 186–187, 190
Memory, 108
  long-term, 108–109, 114
  short-term, 108–109, 114
Mental age, 126, 127, 143, 145
Mental retardation, 133, 143, 145, 167. *See also* Intellectual deficiency
  classification system, 134–135, 144
  familial, 133–134, 144, 145
  physiologically defective, 134, 144, 145
Mexican-American Political Association, 249
Mind-body formulation, 16, 22
Minnesota Multiphasic Personality Inventory (MMPI), 197–200, 202, 219
M'Naghten's rule, 235
Mnemonic devices, 110–111, 114, 115
Model, 256, 257, 260, 262
Mongolism, 145. *See also* Down's syndrome
Monocular cues, 33–36
Moral behavior, 374
Moral development, 375
  Freudian theory, 205–206, 207
  Kohlberg's theory, 347, 348, 349, 355–356, 358
    conventional level, 348, 349, 357, 375, 378
    postconventional level, 357, 375, 378
    preconventional level, 357, 375, 378
  Piaget's theory, 352–353
Moral judgment, 355–356, 378
Moral principles, 357, 375
Moral process, 346–348, 375
Moral realism, 353, 375, 378
Moral relativism, 353, 375, 378
Morpheme, 102, 103, 114, 115
Motivation, 77–81, 82, 85, 101, 111, 112, 115, 141, 142
  and perception, 55
Movement
  as depth cue, 36, 68
  and depth perception, 37
  perception of, 65–66
Multiple personality, 160, 162, 187, 190
My Lai massacre, 235

NAACP, 249, 254
National Organization for Women, 249
Needs, 77
  inborn, 77–79, 111
  learned, 79–80, 111, 112
  stimulus, 78–79, 111–112

Neural efficiency analyzer, 131–132, 140, 143
Neural energy
　in audition, 41, 43, 68
　in vision, 27, 29, 30, 31, 32, 67
Neurons, 278, 305
Neurosis, 156, 159–164, 165, 167, 169, 179, 183, 187, 190, 212, 218
　and social class, 158, 163–164
Nonconformity, 236–237, 239
Noradrenalin, 282
Norepinephrine, 282
Normality, approaches to definition
　cultural, 153–154, 186, 189
　normative, 154, 186, 190
　statistical, 152, 153, 186, 191
　subjective, 152, 186, 191
Norms, 237–238, 240, 247, 250, 260–261, 264
　on MMPI, 197, 200, 219
　on Rorschach, 202
Nose, structure of, 59–60

Obedience, 232–233, 250, 260
Observational learning theory, 103, 114
Obsession, 161, 190
Obsessive-compulsive personality disorder, 180, 181, 188, 190
Obsessive-compulsive reaction, 160, 161, 163, 187, 190–191
Odor, 58, 60. *See also* Smell
Oedipus complex, 207, 220, 222
Olfactory epithelium, 60, 61, 69, 71
Olfactory sense. *See* Smell
Operant conditioning, 91–96, 113, 115
　in language learning, 103, 114
　as therapy, 96, 215–216, 221
Operational definition, 10–11, 22, 121
Optic chiasma, 30, 31, 71
Optic nerve, 29, 30, 67
Oral stage, 206, 219, 222
Organic Merchants, 298
Organism, 209, 210, 220
Otoliths, 66, 71
Oval window, 43, 44, 68, 71
Ovaries, 283
Overcrowdedness, 272, 273, 275
Overlearning, 110, 114
Overtones, 43

Pain, 58, 62–64, 69, 77, 205, 210
Pancreatic gland, 283, 305
Papillae, 59, 71
Paradoxical cold, 64, 71
Paradoxical heat, 64, 71
Paranoid reaction, 166, 171, 187, 191

Parasympathetic nervous system, 280, 281, 315
Parathyroid glands, 282, 305
Passive-aggressive personality disorder, 180, 181–182, 188, 191
Pedophilia, 180, 182, 188, 191
Perception, 17–18, 22, 97, 99, 101, 113
Perceptual organization, 51–52, 69
Peripheral nervous system
　somatic component, 279, 303, 305–306
　visceral component, 280, 306
Personality disorder, 156, 167, 179–186, 188–189, 191
Perspective, 34, 68
　linear, 35
Phallic stage, 207, 219–220, 222
Phenylketonuria (PKU), 134, 145
Phobic reaction, 159–160, 187, 191
Phoneme, 102, 103, 114, 115
Phrenology, 17, 22
Pitch, 42, 46, 68
　afferent code for, 44
Pituitary gland, 274, 279, 282, 302, 306
Pleasure principle, 205, 219, 222–223
Population theories, 272, 302
Power
　coercive, 241, 242, 260
　expert, 241, 243, 260
　legitimate, 241, 242, 260
　referent, 241, 242, 260
　reward, 241–242, 260
　social, 241, 248, 260
Precognition, 66, 70, 71
Prejudice, 208, 244, 247, 250, 252, 264
Pressure, 58, 62, 69
Projection, 208, 223
Projective techniques, 200, 201, 219, 223
Prosocial behavior, 258
Protestant ethic, 348
Proximity, 51, 52, 69
Psyche, 3
Psychiatrist, 4–6, 22
Psychoactive drugs, 277
Psychoanalysis, 211–213, 218, 220
Psychoanalytic theory, 204–209, 219
Psychologist, 22
　types of, 7–8
Psychophysics, 39, 68, 71
　in audition, 45–46
　in vision, 38–40
Psychophysiological disorders, 156, 174–177, 188, 191
Psychosexual development, 206–207, 219–220
Psychosis, 156, 165–173, 179, 187–188, 191
　and social class, 158

Psychosomatic disorders, 320. *See also* Psychophysiological disorders
Psychosurgery, 217, 221, 277, 279, 283, 286, 306
Punishment, 84, 90, 103, 107, 112, 115, 207
Pupil, 29, 30, 31, 67, 71
Purity, of wavelength, 28, 67

Q-sort, 347, 379

Racism, 244, 247, 248, 250, 251, 252, 261, 264
   cultural, 248, 249, 262
   individual, 248, 262
   institutional, 248, 262
Rationalization, 208, 223
Reaction formation, 208, 223
Reality principle, 205, 219, 223
Regression, 208, 223
Reinforcement, 82–85, 87, 92, 94, 101, 103, 112, 115, 215, 221
   negative, 83–84, 85, 94, 95, 112, 115. *See also* Punishment
   positive, 83, 84, 85, 94, 96, 112, 115. *See also* Reward
   schedules of, 92–94, 113
      continuous, 92–93, 94, 113, 115
      partial, 93–94, 113, 115
Reliability, 22, 127–128, 145
Repression, 207, 223
Repression theory of forgetting, 109, 114, 116
Response, 9, 17, 22
Response patterns, 10
Restitutive justice, 355, 379
Retina, 29, 30, 31, 32, 67, 68, 71
Retinal disparity, 33, 68, 71–72
Retrieval theory, 109, 114
Reversible figure, 52, 54
Reward, 79, 83, 91, 92, 95, 96, 103, 107, 112. *See also* Reinforcement, positive
Ribonucleic acid (RNA), 287, 303, 306
Rods, 30, 31, 32, 67, 72
Rorschach Inkblot Test, 200–202, 219

Sacculus, 65, 66, 72
Saturation
   of light, 28, 29, 67
   afferent code for, 32
Schizoid personality disorder, 156, 157, 158, 180, 181, 188, 191
Schizophrenia, 156, 157, 158, 166, 169–171, 187, 191
   catatonic, 166, 170, 187, 189
   hebephrenic, 166, 170, 187, 190
   paranoid, 166, 170–171, 187, 191
   simple, 166, 169–170, 187, 191
Scotophobin, 288

Selective breeding, 294
Self, 209, 210, 211, 213, 220, 223
Self-actualizing tendency, 209, 210, 223
Self-concept, 209, 213
Self-fulfilling prophecy, 18, 143, 145
Self-immolation, 253
Self-report inventory, 197, 219
Self theory, 209–210, 220
Semicircular canals, 65
Senile psychosis, 177, 188, 191
Sense receptors, 9, 279
Sensitivity group, 362, 375
Sensitivity movement, 361
Sensory deprivation, 77, 322, 335, 337
Separation, 328–329
Septal area, 279, 285, 306
Set, 55. *See also* Expectancy
Sex, as inborn need, 77
Sexism, 184
Sexual behavior, 205, 206, 207, 209, 212
Sexual deviations, 180, 182–184, 188–189
Shaping, 91–92, 113, 116
Shock therapy, 216–217
   electroshock, 216, 221
   insulin, 216, 221
Similarity, 51, 69
Simultaneous contrast, 40
Skin senses, 62–64. *See also* Cold; Pain; Pressure; Warmth
Smell, 41, 59–61, 69
Social class, and mental illness, 158, 163–164
Social comparison theory, 242, 264
Social exchange theory, 330, 336
Social facilitation, 256
Social isolation, 343–344, 374
Social penetration theory, 330, 335–336, 337
Social reality, 238, 265
Sound, 41
   localization of, 44–45
Sound wave, 41–42, 45, 46, 68
Spinal cord, 278
Spontaneous recovery, 88, 116
   in classical conditioning, 88, 112
   in operant conditioning, 94
Stanford-Binet Intelligence Test, 125–128, 130, 134, 143
Stapes, 43, 72. *See also* Stirrup
Stereochemical theory, 60–61, 69, 72
Stereotypes, 133, 137, 138, 143, 144, 208, 245, 250, 251, 252, 265
Stigmatization, 176–177
Stimulants, 217
Stimulus, 9, 17, 22
   distal, 49–50, 70
   proximal, 49–50, 71

Stimulus generalization, 116
  in classical conditioning, 89, 90, 112, 113
  in operant conditioning, 94, 113
Stimulus situations, 9
Stirrup, 43, 44, 68, 72
Stress, 338
  alarm, 320
  exhaustion, 320, 335
  resistance, 320
Successive approximations, method of, 91, 112
Superego, 205–206, 207, 212, 219, 223
Surrogate mother, 330, 338
Sympathetic nervous system, 280, 303, 306, 315

Taste, 58–59, 69
Taste bud, 59, 69
Telepathy, 66, 70, 72
Terracide, 304, 306
Territorial imperative, 275
Testes, 283
Texture gradient, 35
T-group, 362, 366, 375
Thalamus, 217, 278, 279, 306, 316
Theory, 22
  definition of, 204, 219
Therapy
  directive, 212, 222
  nondirective, 212, 220, 222
Thyroid gland, 282, 306
Thyroxin, 282
Timbre, 43, 68
  afferent code for, 44
Token economy, 215, 221, 223
Tones
  fundamental, 43
  pure, 43, 71

Touch, 58, 62
Tranquilizers, 217, 221, 277
Transference, 220, 223
  negative, 213
  positive, 213
Type A cells, 32
Type B cells, 32

Ulcer, 174, 175–176, 188
Unconditioned response (UR), 86, 87, 88, 89, 112, 113, 116
Unconditioned stimulus (US), 86, 87, 88, 89, 112, 113, 116
Unconscious, 207, 209, 212, 220
Utriculus, 65, 66, 72

Validity, 23, 127, 128, 145
Value clarification theory, 357, 359, 360
Values, 357–359
Valuing process, 210, 220, 223
Vestibular sense, 65–66, 69
Vineland Social Maturity Scale, 135–136, 144, 145
Visual cliff, 37, 38
Visual projection area, 31
Vitamins, 297, 299
Voyeurism, 180, 182–183, 188, 191

Warmth, 58, 62, 64, 69
Wavelength, 27, 28, 29, 32, 38, 67
Wechsler Adult Intelligence Scale (WAIS), 128–130, 143
Women's liberation movement, 18